THE HIDDEN HALF OF THE FAMILY

A Sourcebook for Women's Genealogy

CHRISTINA KASSABIAN SCHAEFER

GENEALOGICAL · PUBLISHING Co., Inc

Published by Genealogical Publishing Co., Inc.
1001 N. Calvert St., Baltimore, Md. 21202
Second printing 1999
Library of Congress Catalogue Card Number 98-73684
International Standard Book Number 0-8063-1582-2
Made in the United States of America

To my daughter, Alice,

my mother, Lareine,

my grandmothers, Frances and Leonora,

and my great-grandmothers, Alice, Almas, Anna, and Honora

Table of Contents

Illustrations

Preface

I always seem to write books that begin out of my own need to use a single-source reference tool for a particular aspect of research. This book is no exception. Women in colonial America and the U.S. has been the subject of a vast amount of recent scholarship which focuses on their legal and social status and on gender-related issues. It is not always easy or practical to use these works as finding aids; as a matter of fact, it takes a finding aid on the study of women's history to keep up with the growing body of work in this field.

What I have attempted to do is to identify then demonstrate how the legal status of women can be applied to genealogical research. The time period I have covered is from the 1600s to the outbreak of World War II. By doing this, I believe researchers can learn to look for their female progenitors by becoming aware of important changes in written law and common custom. Women's history should not reflect only an isolated tale of victims, but should give a full context of the events which women helped to shape.

It is not my intention to evaluate records of an ecclesiastical nature: parish and church records are a subject unto themselves and are noted here only when they provide a source of information that significantly predates civil records. I have contacted every state archive, historical society, or library that is an official repository of state records, and the response has been very positive, with the exception of three states that did not respond at all. To attempt to list every law in each state would be beyond the scope or the purpose of this work. What I have tried to highlight are those laws that indicate when a married woman could own real estate in her own name, sign a deed, devise a will, enter into contracts, etc. The federal and state laws regarding women and land ownership are included. I have also addressed the subjects of marriage and divorce law, immigration, citizenship, passports, military records, suffrage, welfare, slave manumission, miscellaneous federal records, and census records. Full explanations of the content of the federal schedules are provided; colonial, territorial, and state censuses have been identified as to their dates and availability. Bibliographical items include background references for women's social and cultural history, including extensive citations on the history of textiles.

Material is included for both African American and Native American women; research about Asian American women, specifically those of Chinese and Japanese heritage, is also addressed. I have included patterns of European immigration in the latter nineteenth and early twentieth centuries, and how to find ethnic surnames and maiden names in different types of records.

Looking for women requires a readjustment in how we view traditional record sources. Since a woman's identity was usually under that of her husband, a *feme covert* (literally meaning "covered woman") must be sought by the ways in which she was permitted to interact with the various jurisdictions of government. The following categories are examples of alternate ways of examining traditional sources:

- **Land records**. Look for dower releases when property was being sold, and marital agreements regarding a woman's land from a previous marriage; in federal land records, look for a widow providing proof of marriage to continue a land claim of her late husband.
- **Guardianship records**. Look for male relatives being appointed as guardians for minor children, posting a bond, or acting as surety.

- **Probate and will records**. Look in wills of husbands, fathers, and brothers for information on marital status, number of living children, estates or heirs of deceased children, explanations of family and marital relationships, bequests to servants, manumissions of slaves, etc.
- **Affidavits of witnesses, all types of records**. Look in federal land applications, local land conveyances, affidavits for naturalization petitions, pension applications, criminal court cases, witnesses to testaments and estate inventories, etc.
- **Public welfare records**. Look for pensions and annuities, applications for aid for minor children, hospital ledgers, public burial records, county and town farm records, almshouse and poorhouse records, aid to the elderly, the indigent, and widows, etc.
- **License applications**. Look in applications for peddlers and vendors and for operating businesses, e.g. grocers, tavern keepers, bakers, etc. Look also for registrations of farms, both locally and in the non-population schedules of the federal censuses.
- **Sheriff's records**. Look at summonses, writs, appearances, bonds, testimonies, and pleas.

Breaking new ground is always a learning process. The more we understand about the lives of our female ancestors, the easier it will become to put ourselves in their place. As I attempted to do this with my own family, I drew a mental picture of what my life *now* might be like under similar conditions:

> *I cannot put gas in my car without a note from my husband. The car, the house, and everything else I think that I own is in his name. When I die, I cannot decide who will receive my personal effects. If he dies first, I may be allowed to stay in my home, or may be given a certain number of days to vacate the premises. Any real estate I inherit from my husband is not mine to sell or devise in a will. All the money I earn belongs to my husband. I cannot operate or engage in business in my own name. If my ancestor is enslaved, I cannot marry, may not be allowed to raise my own children, join a church, travel freely, own property, or testify against those who harm me.*

I would like to especially thank the following individuals and agencies for their help and support: Tim Backer, Oregon State Archives, Salem; Sheila Bearor, Maine State Law Library, Augusta; Matthew Benz, Archives Library, Ohio Historical Society, Columbus; Rose Byrne, Arizona Historical Society, Tucson; Leslie Cade, Kansas State Historical Society, Topeka; Mary Ellen Chijioke, Friends Historical Library, Swarthmore College, Swarthmore, Pennsylvania; Judith Clarke, Oklahoma Department of Libraries, Oklahoma City; Tom Davis, North Carolina Supreme Court Library, Raleigh; Art Dostie, Maine State Archives, Augusta; Lathel Duffield, Bureau of Indian Affairs, Washington, DC; Kim Efird, Illinois State Archives, Springfield; Steve Grimes, Rhode Island Judicial Records Center, Pawtucket; Barbara Haase, Special Collections, Fenwick Library, George Mason University, Fairfax, Virginia; Dave Henry, Bureau of Land Management-Eastern States, Springfield, Virginia; Sheridan Harrey, Library of Congress, Washington, DC; Catherine Lemann, Law Library of Louisiana, New Orleans; James Muhn, Bureau of Land Management, Denver, Colorado; Grace-Ellen McCrann, North Carolina State Archives, Raleigh; Mark Miller, Maryland State Law Library, Annapolis; Allen Moye, George Mason University Law Library, Arlington, Virginia; Marian L. Smith, Immigration and Naturalization Service, Washington, DC; Eleanor Thompson, Winterthur Library, Wilmington, Delaware; Genevieve Troka, California State Archives, Sacramento; and Irene Wainwright, New Orleans Public Library.

Most of all, I would like to thank my editor, Eileen Perkins, for her continued support in this project, and my husband and children for their encouragement and assistance.

How to Use This Book

INTRODUCTION

This section contains a time line of events and sections on searching federal records, non-government sources, and state records.

STATE INFORMATION

The introductory material on general research in the U.S. is followed by a section for each state and the District of Columbia. The categories are organized as follows:

- **IMPORTANT DATES IN HISTORY**: basic information about settlement, events, etc., in chronological order. For a chronology of events in colonial America, see Schaefer, Christina K. *Genealogical Encyclopedia of the Colonial Americas: A Complete Digest of the Records of All the Countries in the Western Hemisphere* (Baltimore: Genealogical Publishing Co., 1998).
- **MARRIAGE AND DIVORCE**: information regarding record keeping, marriage and divorce laws, and where to find marriage and divorce records. *Note*: not all state registration is open to the public.
- **PROPERTY AND INHERITANCE**: women's legal status in a state as reflected in statute law, code, other legislative acts, and decisions of the court.
- **SUFFRAGE**: information as to when any voting rights were granted to women prior to the passage of the 19th Amendment in 1920.
- **CITIZENSHIP**: dates when residents of an area became U.S. citizens, except for Native Americans whose tribes were considered a separate nation until 1924.
- **CENSUS INFORMATION**: includes special notes on searching federal census records; and state and territorial enumerations, if applicable.
- **OTHER**: information on welfare, pensions, important record sources not cited above, other laws affecting women, and selected events and accomplishments of women.
- **BIBLIOGRAPHY**: general genealogical references, books, and articles relating to women in the state, historical and biographical sources, and publications regarding legal history and jurisprudence.
- **SELECTED RESOURCES FOR WOMEN'S HISTORY**: addresses of state archives, historical societies, and libraries, women's studies programs, women's history programs, and some URLs relating to women's history in the state. Unless otherwise specified, all URLs begin with **http://**. For additional bibliographic information, see the regional sections of the bibliography at the end of this book. All URLs in this book are current as of May 1998.

❧ All film numbers cited are either from the Family History Library of the Church of Jesus Christ of Latter-day Saints in Salt Lake City, Utah or the National Archives and Records Administration.

- Microform numbers with seven digits, such as **film 1687776**, or **fiche 6634000**, are from the Family History Library Catalog. The abbreviation "ff." following the number indicates that this is the first film or fiche in a series.
- Microform numbers beginning with the letter A, M, or T are from the National Archives, such as **M804** or **T288**.

GLOSSARY

BIBLIOGRAPHY

The bibliography is divided into general genealogy reference; general U.S. law reference; general U.S.

history reference; women's studies, general; women's studies, references for ethnic research; women's studies and general reference, New England; women's studies and general reference, the South; women's studies and general reference, the Midwest; women's studies and general reference, the West.

Abbreviations Commonly Cited

BIA. Bureau of Indian Affairs
BLM. Bureau of Land Management
BLM-EOS. Bureau of Land Management-Eastern States
FHL. Family History Library (Salt Lake City, Utah)
GLO. General Land Office
ILL. Inter-library loan
INS. Immigration and Naturalization Service
LDS. The Church of Jesus Christ of Latter-day Saints
NARA. National Archives and Records Administration
RG. Record Group
WPA. Work Projects Administration or Works Progress Administration

---

❧ *Women "covered" in surviving documents were quite visible in ordinary life . . . in the small communities of seventeenth- and eighteenth- century America, women were everywhere, in gardens and fields, kitchens and taverns, on horseback and in canoes, in stagecoaches and at ferry crossings, in church pews and at the front lines of armies.*

Laurel Thatcher Ulrich, "Of Pens and Needles: Sources in Early American Women's History." *The Journal of American History* (June 1990): 201.

INTRODUCTION

IMPORTANT DATES AND EVENTS SINCE THE AMERICAN REVOLUTION

1780 Congress authorizes half-pay to widows and orphans of officers in the Continental Army killed during the War.

1783 The American Revolution ends. The Mississippi territory is ceded from Great Britain to Spain; the Ohio Valley is ceded from Great Britain to the U.S.

1787 The Northwest Territory is organized and includes future states of Ohio, Indiana, Michigan, Wisconsin, and part of Illinois.

1790 The Southwest Territory is organized and includes the future states of Kentucky and Tennessee.

1795 Act provides derivative citizenship for minor children (1 Stat. 414 § 1). Wives are also included but not written in the law.

1796 The Mississippi territory (see 1783) passes from Spanish to U.S. possession.

1803 The Louisiana Purchase includes the future states of Arkansas, Iowa, Louisiana, Missouri, Nebraska, North Dakota, Oklahoma, South Dakota, the major parts of Colorado, Idaho, Kansas, Minnesota, Montana, and Wyoming, and parts of New Mexico and Texas.

1804 The Louisiana Purchase is divided into the Orleans Territory and the District of Louisiana. A widow and children of an alien who dies before filing his final papers are eligible for U.S. citizenship.

1812 The War of 1812 begins.

1813 The Muskogee Indian War in Alabama, Georgia, Mississippi, and Tennessee begins.

1814 The War of 1812 ends; the Muskogee Indian War ends.

1818 The area of the future Oregon Territory is jointly occupied by the U.S. and Great Britain. Congress enacts the Revolutionary War Pension Act.

1819 Spanish Florida is ceded to the U.S. by Spain.

1820 The Missouri Compromise bans slavery in northern states above latitude 36° 30′.

1832 Widows and orphans of Revolutionary veterans may claim unpaid pensions.

1836 Act provides pensions to widows (for five years) of Revolutionary War veterans who married the veteran while he was in service.

1838 Widows who married Revolutionary War veterans after their service, but before 1 January 1794, may apply for pensions.

1841 Amendment to Preemption Act of 1818 allows widows to apply for land preemptions.

1846 The independent Republic of Texas becomes a U.S. state. The boundary between British North America and the U.S. is fixed at the 49th Parallel.

1848 The Treaty of Guadalupe-Hildago with Mexico cedes the territory of the future states of Arizona, California, Nevada, New Mexico, and Utah. The switch from civil law to common law changes the status of many married women in the Southwest; they lose property rights, cannot enter into contracts, sue in court, or operate their own businesses. The first women's rights convention is held in Seneca Falls, New York. Widows who married Revolutionary War veterans after their service, and before 1 January 1800, may apply for pensions.

1850 Oregon Donation Land Act provides that half of a land grant be in the name of the wife.

1853 By the Gadsen Purchase, the U.S. acquires the territory on the U.S.-Mexico border south of the Gila River. Widows who married Revolutionary War veterans after their service, and after 1 January 1800 may apply for pensions.

1855 An alien female who marries a U.S. citizen is automatically naturalized (10 Stat. 604 § 2). This is repealed in 1922.

1858 All widows who married Revolutionary War veterans after their service may apply for pensions.

1860 The first Southern state (South Carolina) secedes from the U.S. in December.

1861 The Confederate States of America is formed by Alabama, Arkansas, Florida, Georgia, Louisiana, Mississippi, North Carolina, South Carolina, Tennessee, Texas, and Virginia. The War of the Rebellion (Civil War) begins. Married Women's Property acts have been adopted in twenty-five states and one territory. Union widows (and mothers who have been dependents) of Civil War veterans deceased since 4 March 1861 may apply for pensions.

1862 The Homestead Act allows single women over twenty-one, widows, and wives who have been deserted by their husbands to apply for federal land. Congress makes bigamy a crime in U.S. territories.

1863 Massachusetts becomes the first state to create a state welfare system.

1864 Congress amends the pension bill, providing that "widows and children to colored soldiers. . . shall be entitled to receive the pensions now provided by law, without other proof of marriage than that the parties had habitually recognized each other as man and wife . . ."

1865 The Civil War ends. The federal government establishes the Bureau of Refugees, Freedmen, and Abandoned Lands, under the War Department to assume welfare for emancipated slaves who cannot care for themselves because of old age or illness, provide employment, settle abandoned property, maintain courts, found schools, distribute food, etc.

1867 The U.S. annexes Alaska from Russia by treaty, and all residents of Alaska become U.S. citizens, except for Native Americans, whose tribes are considered a separate nation until 1924.

1868 African Americans become citizens of the U.S. by passage of the 14th Amendment.

1872 The first federal military records for women are military nursing payments for services during the Civil War (H. Ex. Doc. 270, 42nd Cong., 2nd Sess., 1872). The Freedman's Bureau is liquidated.

1873 Comstock Act prohibits any material regarding abortion to be carried by the U.S. mail.

1874 Women's Christian Temperance Union is formed.

1878 Married Women's Property acts exist in thirty-seven states, six territories, and the District of Columbia.

1879 Congress passes a law permitting women to practice law in all federal courts. The first woman attorney argues a case before the U.S. Supreme Court.

1881 The New England Divorce Reform League is organized to work for the curtailment of "liberal" divorce laws.

1882 Chinese are excluded from becoming U.S. citizens (22 Stat. 58). This is repealed in 1943 (57 Stat. 600). The Chinese population of the U.S. drops from over 105,000 in 1880 to 71,000 in 1910.[1]

1885 The National Divorce Reform League is organized to work for the curtailment of "liberal" divorce laws.

1886 All but seven states permit divorce on grounds of cruelty.

1888 All Native American women who are members of a tribe and married to U.S. citizens are declared to be citizens (25 Stat. 392).

1890 Congress passes a law to provide pensions for U.S. Army nurses in the Civil War (S. Rept. 326, 51st Cong., 1st Sess., 1890. Serial 2704). The Dawes Act (passed in 1887), designed to break up Native American reservations, is amended to grant land allotments to women as well as men; Native Americans lose their tribal citizenship and automatically become U.S. citizens. The General Federation of Women's Clubs is formed.

---

[1] Corinne K. Hoexter, *From Canton to California: The Epic of Chinese Immigration* (New York: Four Winds Press, 1976), 125, 239.

1891 The Office of Immigration is established. Polygamists and those convicted of certain crimes or who carry certain diseases are excluded from U.S. citizenship (26 Stat. 1084).

1892 Ellis Island receiving station opens in New York for processing, detaining, and deporting alien arrivals.

1895 Of forty-six states: in fourteen states a wife's wages still belong to her husband; in thirty-seven states a married woman has no legal right over her children; and only four states or territories allow a woman to vote in general state and federal elections.

1896 U.S. Army nurses who served in the Civil War may be buried at Arlington National Cemetery (H. Rept. 2127, 54th Cong., 1st Sess., 1896). Congress establishes a one-year residency period for filing divorces in U.S. territories.

1898 Hawaii is annexed by the U.S.

1904 Angel Island (California) receiving station is opened for processing, detaining, and deporting alien arrivals, mostly Chinese.

1906 The Bureau of Immigration and Naturalization is established. Alien registration is required. Derivative citizenship is still practiced (34 Stat. 596 § 3). All U.S. states, except New York and South Carolina, require marriage licenses.

1907 The Expatriation Act states that a female U.S. citizen who marries an alien loses her U.S. citizenship and takes on the nationality of her husband (34 Stat. 1228 § 3). This is repealed in 1922, but citizenship is not restored until 1936.

1910 Most states require the inclusion of the names of the parents of the bride and groom in vital records.

1911 Missouri becomes the first state to pass a widows' pension law.

1912 Volunteer civilian nurses who served in the Civil War are also granted pensions (H. Rept. 1006, 62nd Cong., 2nd Sess., 1912. Serial 6133).

1914 The Homestead Act is amended so that an entrywoman who marries an alien may retain title to her entry if her husband is eligible for citizenship (S. Rept. 679, 63rd Cong., 2nd Sess., 1914. Serial 6553).

1916 Divorced wives and widows of U.S. citizens who are living abroad must register with a U.S. consulate within one year to retain their citizenship.

1918 Widows of Civil War veterans may apply for pensions on the basis of service. Women married to German citizens have their property confiscated.

1919 Thirty-nine states have a widows' pension law.

1920 The 19th Amendment to the Constitution is ratified, giving women in the U.S. the right to vote. Women married to German citizens who have had their property confiscated may reclaim their property, under certain conditions (this is also the case in 1948, after World War II, for women married to Bulgarian, German, Hungarian, Japanese, and Romanian citizens).

1921 The first Immigration Act to establish quotas of immigrants based on national origin is enacted. The American Association of University Women is formed.

1922 The Cable Act establishes independent citizenship for women twenty-one years of age and over (42 Stat. 1022 § 4). Derivative citizenship is discontinued.

1924 The Citizen Act provides that "all non-citizen Indians born within the territorial limits of the United States be, and they are hereby declared to be citizens of the United States," including Indians living on tribal reservations. The National Association of College Women is formed by African American women.

1932 The National Recovery Act (NRA) limits the number of federal workers in a family to one; many women lose their jobs.

1934 The Dawes Act is suspended (see 1890). Congress passes the Indian Reorganization Act, providing for tribal self-government.

1935 Federal Social Security Act is passed. All states except Georgia and South Carolina have widows' pension laws.

1938 A survey in *Ladies' Home Journal* finds that seventeen percent of American women favor birth control.[2]

1940 The Alien Registration Act requires immigrants to present themselves for registration and fingerprinting at a local post office within thirty days of arrival (54 Stat. 1137 § 301).

1941 Almost seven million women enter the workforce as a result of the labor shortage caused by World War II.

FINDING WOMEN IN FEDERAL RECORDS

IMMIGRATION, CITIZENSHIP, AND PASSPORT RECORDS

When searching for women, it is a good idea to understand the ethnic immigration patterns (forced or voluntary) associated with the different nationalities. Here are some examples:

- In colonial times, many English women were transported in bondage or as indentured servants, particularly from the port of Bristol.
- After 1808, the official traffic in the African slave trade had ended, but some slaves were still transported to the U.S. illegally.
- Beginning in the 1890s, Armenian women emigrated from Turkey as refugees from the Turkish massacres. Family units were often broken up, and many women and children came alone as refugees.
- Chinese women were completely banned from entry for a period of time, especially if they had a husband who was a laborer in the U.S.
- From the time before the Great Famine until the late nineteenth century, single Irish women without marriage prospects in Ireland immigrated to the U.S. and were often employed as domestics.
- In the late nineteenth century, Italian women and children would immigrate after their husbands had made a home for them in the U.S.
- Women from the Russian Empire, especially Jewish women, came in large numbers with their families beginning in the late nineteenth century.

Who Came When

A study of immigration to the U.S. from 1820 to 1950 estimated the following years to be the peaks of arrival from the following countries and regions:

1824 West Indies
1851 France, Ireland
1882 China, Denmark, Germany, The Netherlands, Norway, Sweden
1883 Switzerland
1888 Great Britain
1907 Austria-Hungary, Greece, Italy, Japan
1913 Belgium, Russia, Turkey (mostly Armenian refugees)
1921 Czechoslovakia, Poland, Portugal, Romania, Spain
1924 Canada and Newfoundland, Mexico, South America

From Oscar Handlin, *The Immigration Factor in American History* (Englewood Cliffs, NJ: Prentice-Hall, Inc., 1959), 16.

[2] Henry Pringle, "What Do the Women of America Think about Birth Control?" *Ladies Home Journal* (March 1938): 14.

In 1917, the Federal Immigration Act put restrictions on women entering the U.S. Unmarried mothers and their children could be excluded from entry on the grounds of moral turpitude, fearing they might become a burden on the welfare system. Single women could enter the U.S. only if they had a sponsor in this country, usually a male relative, and written proof of sponsorship. She (and her children, if she had any) would be detained (usually at Ellis Island) until she was claimed by the sponsor. If no one claimed her, she was usually deported. Women who were meeting future husbands often had the marriage ceremony performed at Ellis Island to prove that they were not being brought into the U.S. as part of a prostitution ring.

PASSENGER ARRIVAL RECORDS

Passenger lists since the nineteenth century are basically categorized as follows:

- 1798 and 1800, Customs Lists of Aliens (small area of Massachusetts only).
- 1800–19, Cargo Manifests (locations in New Jersey, Pennsylvania, and Virginia).
- 1820–91, Customs Passenger Lists (the first official immigration records), include the following passenger information: names of vessel and master, port of embarkation, date and port of arrival; name, age, and sex; country of residence; country of intended residence; death information, if died en route.
- 1891–1954 (1883 in Philadelphia), Immigration Passenger Lists (records of thirty-six ports at the National Archives), include the following passenger information: names of vessel and master, port of embarkation, date and port of arrival; name, age, sex, and marital status; occupation and nationality; last residence and final destination; name, address, and relationship of person passenger is joining. After 1907 there is also a personal description, place of birth, and the name and address of the nearest relative in the country from which the passenger is emigrating.

Passenger lists for ship ports of entry from 1892 to the 1950s have been transferred from the Immigration and Naturalization Service (INS) to the National Archives. Land ports of entry from Mexico, 1908 to the 1950s, and Canada, 1895 to the 1950s, are also at the National Archives. Some of the Canadian entries are filmed; the Mexican entries are not on film for public access. Records of air ports of entry have been kept since the early 1930s. These are in INS custody.

Passenger lists for New York from 1847 to 1896 are not indexed on microfilm. The Balch Institute for Immigration Research at Temple University in Philadelphia has the original manifests and has indexed them in a database. Some indexes have been published by ethnic group, such as Irish, German, Italian, and Russian. For more information, see the bibliography on passenger lists, Meyerink, Kory L. "Recent Books of Passenger and Immigration Lists." *Utah Genealogical Society Quarterly* (Spring 1998): 24–36.

For a description on how to use federal passenger lists, see Schaefer, Christina K. *The Center: A Guide to Genealogical Research in the National Capital Area* (Baltimore: Genealogical Publishing Co., 1996), 29–35. For an in-depth discussion of these records, see Tepper, Michael. *American Passenger Arrival Records: A Guide to the Records of Immigrants Arriving at American Ports by Sail and Steam.* Updated and enlarged (Baltimore: Genealogical Publishing Co., 1993).

NATURALIZATION

The procedure by which an alien by birth is granted citizenship in a new country is known as naturalization. In the U.S., these records can be found in a variety of courts. The process of naturalization could be initiated in one state, often the port of entry, and completed in a different state. Records are sometimes kept in separate journals; often they are intermixed in the court dockets with other court proceedings. Citizenship was not mandatory, but many immigrants obtained it as part of establishing their national identity in a new country.

The first federal naturalization legislation was passed in 1790. In 1804 the law distinguished derivative citizenship (based on that of the husband) for minor children and a wife, from a single woman. This was written into law in 1855. In 1922 this law was repealed, and women were required to apply for individual citizenship. In 1929 certificates of derivative naturalization could also be obtained by women who fell into the earlier time period. There are, however, exceptions as laws were not uniformly enforced.[3]

Women Born in the U.S. Who Lost Their Citizenship

In 1907 a female U.S. citizen who married an alien lost her U.S. citizenship and took on the nationality of her husband (34 Stat. 1228 § 3). This law was repealed in 1922, but citizenship was not restored until 1936, when Congress passed an act providing that a woman who had lost her citizenship due to her marital status could apply for repatriation after the death of or divorce from her alien husband. These petitions were filed from 1936 until the late 1960s. The form was entitled "Application to Take Oath of Allegiance to the United States under the Act of June 25, 1936, as Amended, and Form of Such Oath." Supporting documentation could include a certificate of birth in the U.S., a marriage license, a copy of a divorce decree, a husband's death certificate, etc. The maiden name of the woman was not required on the form itself but was sometimes added (see Illustration 2).

Duplicate copies of court records for naturalization of individuals from 1906 to 1956 are at the INS headquarters. Records since 1960 have been computerized and can be accessed by district and regional INS offices. Activity in a file that predates 1960, such as a request for replacement papers, would also be in the database.

The INS headquarters has a Soundexed index for naturalization stubs beginning with 27 September 1906, but this is not open to the public. If there is no other way to determine when a person was naturalized, the most effective way to make use of this index is to request the information to locate the original court and to obtain the copies from the court rather than the INS. Requests must be made in writing, either by a letter or by using Form G-639. If writing a letter, state that this is an FOIA/PA request. The following information must be included: the full name of the immigrant, including all variant spellings, the country or place of birth, and the date of birth.

Chinese American Women

The Chinese Exclusion Act of 1882 (22 Stat. 58), the first law that ethnically restricted immigration, was enacted amid the height of the anti-Chinese movement in America. For a period of time, Chinese women were denied entry into the U.S. In 1930, Chinese wives were allowed entry if they had married a U.S. citizen before 1924. The War Brides Act of 1945 (60 Stat. 339) permitted the wives and children of Chinese American citizens to petition for citizenship. Angel Island was a detention center established in San Francisco in 1910 for processing Chinese immigrants, although it eventually handled other nationalities as well. Angel Island was closed in 1940, but immigrants continued to be detained at the Appraiser's Building in San Francisco until 1952. Most Chinese were processed at Angel Island; however, other ports of entry were Port Townsend, Washington, Ellis Island, New York, San Pedro, California, Honolulu, Hawaii, and Galveston, Texas. Some of the records created include:

---

[3] See Marian L. Smith, " Women and Naturalization, ca. 1802–1940." *Prologue* 30 2 (Summer 1998): 146–53.

- Chinese Certificates of Identity, 1908–43, and an index binder to Certificates of Identity cards from San Francisco and Hawaii, at the NARA Pacific Region in San Francisco.
- Records of immigration of Chinese women at San Francisco, 1896–7 (**M802**), at the NARA Pacific Region in San Francisco.
- A database, *Chinese Immigration Records*, at the NARA Northeast Region in New York City, indexes the case files, 1882 to 1952, that were part of the Chinese Exclusion Files. The database can be searched by name, town of origin, or miscellaneous other fields.

Japanese American Women

Japanese immigrants were known as *Issei*. Between 1910 and 1919 about half of the married women who came to the U.S. from Japan were *shashin kekkom*, or "picture brides." By arrangement between families, these women would marry in Japan, although the groom was residing in the U.S. The new husband was required to register the marriage in the *koseki*, a family register, at the nearest Japanese consulate.

Before 1915 male laborers did not qualify to bring wives to the U.S. After 1915 this restriction was lifted if the man had at least $800 in savings. Before 1917 the U.S. did not recognize picture-bride marriages, and a second ceremony had to be performed after the bride's arrival. She was required to have with her a Japanese passport, a copy of the family registry, and a certificate of health. She could not be more than thirteen years younger than her husband and had to be claimed by him upon arrival.

❧ *Household registers, or* koseki, *are civil registrations of vital records, citizenship, and other information. The Japanese continued to use these registers in the U.S. until 1952 because they were ineligible for U.S. citizenship. The registers were kept at Japanese consulates and in local government offices in Japan. Withdrawn registers, or* joseki, *are those that are older than eighty years.*

By the end of 1919, the Japanese government stopped issuing passports to picture brides and only provided them to women who emigrated from Japan with their spouses. The first American-born generation of Japanese were called *Nisei*. Japanese law stated that *Nisei* were considered dual citizens of Japan and the U.S. *Nisei* women lost their U.S. citizenship if they married an *Issei* man before 1924.

During World War II, the West Coast was declared a military area, which gave the War Department the "legal" authority to "evacuate" Japanese Americans, despite citizenship status. These people were moved to internment camps administered by the War Relocation Authority (WRA). From 1942 to 1946, the WRA detained 120,000 Japanese Americans in ten camps located in isolated areas of the U.S. Some sixty percent of the internees were U.S. citizens.[4]

PASSPORT APPLICATIONS

The U.S. Passport Office considers a passport to be a "travel document attesting to the citizenship of the bearer." Some 2.6 million passports were issued by this office between 1795 and 1929. Although passports were not required of U.S. citizens traveling abroad before World War I, except for a short time during the Civil War, they were frequently obtained because of the added protection they afforded. Passports show where the person planned to travel abroad, perhaps to his or her homeland (see

[4] For information on the internment of Japanese Americans and other nationalities during World War II, see Christina K. Schaefer, *Guide to Naturalization Records of the United States* (Baltimore: Genealogical Publishing Co., 1997), 6–9.

Illustration 1). Unless traveling alone, a married woman was usually listed on her husband's passport. Passport applications usually contain the following information:

- Name, age, signature
- Place of residence
- Personal description
- Names or number of persons in family intending to travel
- Date
- Date and court of naturalization
- Date and place of birth of applicant, spouse, minor children
- Date, ship, and port of entry in U.S.

Passports from 1791 to 1925 are in National Archives Record Group 59 (film 1463566 ff./**M1371–2, M1490**). The original records are at the National Archives, Washington, DC.

CENSUS AND MORTALITY SCHEDULES (RG 29)

Federal census records begin in 1790. Only heads of households were enumerated until 1850, which left only single women and widows who were heads of households being recorded under their own names. Federal censuses from 1850 have listed every member of a household, including mothers, wives, and daughters. Sometimes a woman can also be found on a census schedule as a sister, sister-in-law, niece, stepdaughter, stepmother, etc. within the household of a male relation. The 1880, 1900, 1910 (1910 not for all states), and 1920 censuses are Soundexed by state.

Soundex Code

The Soundex coding guide requires a surname to be coded:

1. Retain the first letter of the surname
2. Discard the next letters if they are A, E, I, O, U, W, Y, H
3. The number 1 represents the letters B, P, F, V
4. The number 2 represents the letters C, S, K, G, J, Q, X, Z
5. The number 3 represents the letters D, T
6. The number 4 represents the letter L
7. The number 5 represents the letters M, N
8. The number 6 represents the letter R

❧ *Special note on the Soundex when searching for women: if searching for a woman with a religious title, such as "Sister," and the person used no surname, she might be Soundexed under S-236, for Sister.*

Searching Soundex Card Abbreviations for Women

The following abbreviations and terms are some of the abbreviations used on Soundex cards, particularly in reference to females:

A	aunt	FM	foster mother	HGi	hired girl
AdD	adopted daughter	GA	great aunt	Hk	housekeeper
AdM	adopted mother	GD	granddaughter	Hmaid	housemaid
Al	aunt-in-law	GGGM	gr. gr. grandmother	Hsi	half sister
Bgirl	bound girl	GGM	gr. grandmother	Hsil	half sister-in-law
Cha	chamber maid	GM	grandmother	HW	houseworker
D	daughter	Gml	grandmother-in-law	Lau	launderer
Dl	daughter-in-law	Gni	grand or great niece	M	mother
DOM	domestic	Go	governess	Maid	maid

Mat	matron	Sd	stepdaughter	Sml	step mother-in-law
ML	mother-in-law	Sdl	step daughter-in-law	Ssi	stepsister
Ni	niece	Se	servant	Ssil	step sister-in-law
Nil	niece-in-law	SeCl	servant's child	Vi	visitor
Nu	nurse	Sgd	step granddaughter	W	wife
R	roomer	Si	sister	Wai	waitress
Sal	saleslady	Sm	stepmother	Ward	ward

Searching the Soundex for Ethnic Names

- Names with prefixes (D', De, Di, Le, van, etc.) may be filed under the prefix or the surname.
- Double letters, as in the name *Lloyd*, should be treated as one letter.
- Native American names without identifiable surnames are often coded by the first word in a name. Single term names are coded as surnames.
- Asian names where the surname could not be identified are often coded as one name; sometimes Chinese names are anglicized under the preface *Ah* instead of the surname, e.g. the name Wong Ah So might be Soundexed under *Ah*.

Personal information given (this list does not include real estate-related information):

1940 and 1930 censuses: have not been published; however, records can be obtained by a blood relative of a deceased person shown in the census through the Freedom of Information Act (FOIA).[5] The 1930 schedules will be published in 2002.

1920 census (T625): gives the name of each person and age, name of street and number of house, relationship to head of family, month of birth (if born within the year), sex, color, birthplace, occupation (detailed information), year of immigration, whether naturalized or an alien, year of naturalization, year of immigration to the U.S.; marital status; whether able to speak English, whether able to read or write, and if attended school within the year; birthplaces of father and mother, mother tongue and that of parents. This census is Soundexed **(M1548–605)**.

1910 census (T624): gives the name of each person and age, name of street and number of house, relationship to head of family, sex, color, birthplace, occupation, whether naturalized or if naturalization papers had been taken out, number of years in the U.S.; marital status, number of years in present marriage; time unemployed during the census year, whether deaf, dumb, blind, or insane; whether able to speak English; whether able to read, write, and if attended school within the year; birthplaces of father and mother, whether parents were of foreign birth; number of living children, if a mother; whether soldier, sailor, or marine during the Civil War, or widow of such person; number of children born; mother tongue. This census is Soundexed or indexed (Miracode) for the following states **(T1259–79)**: Alabama, Arkansas, California, Florida, Georgia, Illinois, Kansas, Kentucky, Louisiana, Michigan, Mississippi, Missouri, North Carolina, Ohio, Oklahoma, Pennsylvania, South Carolina, Tennessee, Texas, Virginia, and West Virginia.

1900 census (T623): gives the name of each person and age, name of street and number of house, relationship to head of family, month of birth (if born within the year), sex, color, birthplace, occupation, whether naturalized or naturalization papers had been taken out, number of years in the U.S., marital status; time unemployed during the census year, whether able to speak English; whether able to read, write, and if attended school within the year; birthplaces of father and mother, whether

---

[5] Information for this census must be obtained through the Bureau of the Census by filing a Freedom of Information Privacy Act form (BC-600). Proof of death must be submitted, or permission of the living person. Contact Bureau of the Census, PO Box 1545, Jeffersonville, IN 47131.

parents were of foreign birth; number of living children, if a mother; whether soldier, sailor, or marine during the Civil War, or widow of such person; number of years in present marriage, number of children born. This census is Soundexed **(T1030–83)**.

1890 census (M407): gives the name of each person and age, name of street and number of house, relationship to head of family, sex, color, birthplace, occupation, whether naturalized or naturalization papers had been taken out, number of years in the U.S.; marital status, whether married within the year; whether crippled, maimed, or deformed, whether suffering from a chronic disease, time unemployed during the census year, whether deaf, dumb, blind, or insane; whether a pauper, prisoner, homeless child, or convict; whether able to speak English; whether able to read, write, and if attended school within the year; birthplaces of father and mother, whether parents were of foreign birth; number of living children, if a mother; whether soldier, sailor, or marine during the Civil War, or widow of such person. Although much of this census was destroyed by fire in 1921, it is worth checking to see if the area being researched has survived. There are surviving portions for Alabama, the District of Columbia, Georgia, Illinois, Minnesota, New Jersey, New York, North Carolina, Ohio, South Dakota, and Texas, that have been indexed in Nelson, Ken. *1890 U.S. Census Index to Surviving Population Schedules and Register of Film Numbers to the Special Census of Union Veterans* (Salt Lake City: Genealogical Library, the Church of Jesus Christ of Latter-day Saints, 1991, film 1421673). This index covers the few 1890 census schedules not destroyed by fire and contains 6,160 names. The index gives the name of individual, geographical location, and census schedule page number, and is transcribed from the index to the eleventh census of the U.S., 1890 (film 0543341 ff./**M496**). The special schedule enumerating Union veterans and widows **(M123)** exists for all or parts of the District of Columbia (all), Kentucky, Louisiana, Maine, Maryland, Massachusetts, Michigan, Minnesota, Mississippi (all), Missouri, Montana (all), Nebraska, Nevada (all), New Hampshire (all), New Jersey, New Mexico (all), New York, North Carolina (all), North Dakota (all), Ohio, Oklahoma (all), Oregon (all), Pennsylvania, Rhode Island (all), South Carolina (all), South Dakota (all), Texas, Utah (all), Vermont (all), Virginia, Washington (all), West Virginia, Wisconsin, and Wyoming (all). The following states are under miscellaneous (bundle 198, roll 118): California (Alcatraz), Connecticut (Fort Trumbull, Hartford County Hospital, and U.S. Naval Station), Delaware (Delaware State Hospital for the Insane), Florida (Fort Barrancas and Saint Francis Barracks), Idaho (Boise Barracks and For Sherman), Illinois (Cook County and Henderson County), Indiana (Warrick County and White County), and Kansas (Barton County). In the early 1890s, the Census Bureau also transcribed some of the widows' and veterans' information onto 304,607 cards, some of which may have been placed in individual service files. For other 1890 censuses, see also the report on Indians taxed and Indians not taxed in the U.S., except Alaska (film 0599813) and the territorial census for Oklahoma **(M1811)**.

1885 special census in Colorado (M158), Florida (M845), Nebraska (M352), the Dakota Territory, and New Mexico Territory, including Arizona (M846): gives the name of each person and age, name of street and number of house, relationship to head of family, month of birth (if born within the year), sex, color, birthplace, occupation, marital status, whether married within the year; whether temporarily or permanently disabled, crippled, maimed, or deformed, time unemployed during the census year, whether deaf, dumb, blind, or insane; whether able to read, write, and if attended school within the year; birthplaces of father and mother, whether parents were of foreign birth. The mortality schedule gives the name, age, sex, state of birth, month of death,and cause of death, place of birth of parents, and how long the deceased was a citizen or resident of the area. The schedules for North and South Dakota are at the National Archives on film only **(GR27)**.

1880 census (T9): gives the name of each person and age, name of street and number of house, relationship to head of family, month of birth (if born within the year), sex, color, birthplace, occupation, marital status, whether married within the year; whether temporarily or permanently disabled, crippled, maimed, or deformed, time unemployed during the census year, whether deaf, dumb, blind, or insane; whether able to read, write, and if attended school within the year; birthplaces of father and mother, whether parents were of foreign birth. The mortality schedule gives the name, age, sex, state of birth, month of death and cause of death, place of birth of parents, and how long the deceased was a citizen or resident of the area. This census is Soundexed (**T734–80**).

1870 census (M593, T132): gives the name of each person and age, sex, color, birthplace, occupation, month of birth (if born within the year), if married within the year and the month; whether deaf, dumb, blind, or insane; whether able to read, write, and if attended school within the year; whether parents were of foreign birth. The mortality schedule gives the name, age, sex, state of birth, month of death, and cause of death.

1860 census (M653): gives the name of each person and age, sex, color, birthplace, occupation, if married within the year; whether deaf, dumb, blind, or insane, whether a pauper or convict; whether able to read, write, and if attended school within the year. The mortality schedule gives the name, age, sex, state of birth, month of death, and cause of death. See this schedule especially for slaves, who were not enumerated by name on the slave schedules.

1850 census (M432): first federal census to list every member of a household; gives name, age, sex, color, birthplace, occupation, if married within the year; whether deaf, dumb, blind, or insane; whether a pauper or convict; whether able to read, write, and if attended school within the year. The mortality schedule gives the name, age, sex, state of birth, month of death, and cause of death. See this especially for slaves, who were not enumerated by name on the slave schedules.

1840 census (M704): women enumerated by name as heads of household only; gives name and age of each person receiving a federal military pension; gives number of free white females within specified age groups in each household. The pensioners, including widows, have been indexed in *A General Index to Census of Pensioners for Revolutionary or Military Service, 1840* (1965. Reprint. Baltimore: Genealogical Publishing Co., 1992, fiche 6046771).

1830 census (M19): women enumerated by name as heads of household only; gives the number of foreigners not naturalized in each household; gives number of free white females within specified age groups in each household.

1820 census (M33): women enumerated by name as heads of household only; gives the number of foreigners not naturalized in each household; gives number of free white females within specified age groups in each household.

1810 census (M252): women enumerated by name as heads of household only; gives number of free white females within specified age groups in each household.

1800 census (M32): women enumerated by name as heads of household only; gives number of free white females within specified age groups in each household.

1790 census (M637, T498): women enumerated by name as heads of household only; schedules for Delaware, Georgia, Kentucky, New Jersey, Tennessee, and Virginia are missing. Virginia schedules are reconstructed from state enumerations.

State and territorial census records vary greatly as to the frequency in which they were taken and the content of the records. For more information on these records, see the sections for individual states.

For a state-by-state description of federal censuses, see Greenwood, Val D. *Researcher's Guide to American Genealogy*. 2nd ed. (Baltimore: Genealogical Publishing Co., 1990). "Chart 3" lists important census data but is missing some pre-territorial information. "Chart 4" lists the availability of census mortality schedules, 1850 to 1880.

Women and Maiden Names

There are some exceptions to note when searching for women, not only in census records, but other legal documents:

- French women frequently used their maiden names on legal documents.
- Married women from countries using patronymics, who traditionally retained their maiden name after marriage, should be checked under both their maiden name and their husbands' surname (Scandinavian countries).
- In colonial times, traditional Dutch *usus* marriage contracts allowed women to retain their maiden name and their separate legal status.[6] After 1690, Dutch colonists began to adopt the English usage of the husband's surname.
- In many localities in Europe, German and Polish Catholic women were recorded in death registers only by their maiden names.[7]
- Hispanic surnames are often dual surnames, the first being the paternal name, the second the maternal name. Married women always used their maiden names, *apellidos de la mujer*, in legal records.[8] In indexes, they should be searched by their maiden name and by their husbands' surnames, with or without the prefix *de* (short for *esposa de* [wife of] or *viuda de* [widow of]).
- Italian women used their maiden names on official records.[9]
- Jewish family names ending with *-s* or *-es* are derived from the name of a mother or a wife.[10]
- Quaker women frequently used their maiden name as a middle name after marriage, partly because there were so many people with similar names in small communities.
- In Scotland, widows reverted to their maiden names after the death of their husbands.[11]
- In some parts of Wales, women traditionally retained their maiden names, even into the twentieth century.[12]

FEDERAL LAND RECORDS (RG 49)

In 1785 the Continental Congress enacted a land disposal ordinance that established a Public Land Survey System, based on a rectangular grid, and authorized the Treasury Board to sell public lands for revenue. The General Land Office (GLO) was created in 1812 to oversee all survey and land title records. This agency became the Bureau of Land Management (BLM) in 1949. Public land has been sold or granted in all states, except the original Thirteen Colonies, the District of Columbia, Hawaii, Kentucky, Maine, Tennessee, Texas, and West Virginia.

Very few lands that were sold through private land companies and public land offices were purchased by widows and female heads of families between 1811 and 1830. The 1811 and 1820 Congressional

---

[6] Carol Berkin, *First Generations: Women in Colonial America* (New York: Hill & Wang, 1996), 79–81.

[7] Shirley J. Riemer, *The German Research Companion* (Sacramento, CA: Lorelei Press, 1997), 97.

[8] George R. Ryskamp, *Finding Your Hispanic Roots* (Baltimore: Genealogical Publishing Co, 1997), 4.

[9] Sharon DeBartolo Carmack, *Italian-American Family History: A Guide to Researching and Writing About Your Heritage* (Baltimore: Genealogical Publishing Co., 1997), 34.

[10] Dan Rottenberg, *Finding Our Fathers: A Guidebook to Jewish Genealogy* (Baltimore: Genealogical Publishing Co., 1995), 53.

[11] Kathleen B. Cory, *Tracing Your Scottish Ancestry* (Baltimore: Genealogical Publishing Co., 1993), 26.

[12] John Rowlands and Sheila Rowlands, *The Surnames of Wales* (Baltimore: Genealogical Publishing Co., 1996), 12–13.

reports on land sales listed at least eight women (out of 407 and 953 entries, respectively), the 1830 Congressional report included five sales purchased by one woman (out of 73 entries).[13]

Land Acts

Under the land act of 1841, widows could apply for federal land, but a married woman could not apply for land in her own name. The 1862, 1873, and 1877 acts were expanded to include women who were single and over twenty-one or heads of household. A wife who had been deserted by her husband could also apply for land.

The Preemption Act of 1841 allowed those who were already homesteading on public land to purchase adjoining land when it became available for sale. Among the documents found in a case file are the application, the preemption proof, and the final certificate.

The Oregon Donation Land Act of 1850 required acreage granted to married couples to be registered equally in the names of the husband and wife: half in her name, half in his name. The requirements to receive land were to be a citizen, or to have filed a declaration of intention prior to 1 December 1850, and to reside on a specific acreage in the Oregon Territory for four consecutive years. A case file contains the notification on the settlement and the donation certificate.

Under the terms of the Homestead Act of 1862, a citizen, or an alien who had filed his declaration of intention, twenty-one years of age or older, was eligible to claim 160 acres of unoccupied land on the public domain, providing he or she fulfilled certain requirements. The provisions of the act required that the homesteader build a home on the land, cultivate the land, and reside there for five years. Among the documents found in a case file are: the application, the homestead proof, a final certificate, a copy of naturalization proceedings (if applicable), and, after 1872, a copy of a Union veteran's discharge (if applicable). If a husband died after filing a claim, a widow would have to provide a supplement proof of their marriage and his death but could inherit the land entirely and absolutely, whether or not she remarried.

❧ *When searching records involving the inheritance of public domain land, always note if land is an original homestead grant, which a widow inherited entirely and absolutely. State or territorial law would not apply in this case, under which she might receive only one-third or one-half of the real estate, sometimes for life use only.*

The New Mexico donation lands were granted from 1853 to 1858 and required that the land was surveyed and then resided upon and cultivated for four years. Those who had previously claimed Spanish or Mexican grants were ineligible, as were those who had preemption claims. A recipient of a New Mexico donation land could not file for a homestead claim. The original records are at the BLM in Santa Fe and the University of New Mexico in Albuquerque.

The Timber Culture Act of 1873 granted lands to settlers who planted and cared for trees on the plains. Case files are similar to those of homestead claims. The Desert Land Act of 1877 granted lands that, upon proof of reclamation by irrigation, had been arid. Case files are similar to those of homestead claims.

[13] Richard H. Chused, "The Oregon Donation Act of 1850 and Nineteenth-Century Federal Married Women's Property Law," *Law and History Review* 2 (Spring 1984): 47–8.

The 1890 amendment to the Dawes Act of 1887, designed to break up Indian reservations, was amended to grant tribal allotments to women as well as men. A woman receiving a land allotment lost her tribal membership and became a U.S. citizen.

In 1900 the Homestead by Married Women Act protected an unmarried woman's rights to apply for a homestead entry after marriage.

The pre-1908 general land entry case files for Alabama, Alaska, Arizona, Florida, Louisiana, Nevada, and Utah are indexed in the "Seven State Index (RG 49)" at Archives I. The index gives the entryman's name, state of land location, land office where the entry was made, type of entry, and final certificate or file number. This includes both patented entries and those that were relinquished or canceled.

The *General Land Office Automated Records* CD-ROM series allows federal land records to be searched by the owner's name, the acreage, the legal description, and the document signature date. The Pre-1908 homestead and cash entry patents are available on CD-ROM for the Eastern states of Alabama, Arkansas, Florida, Indiana, Louisiana, Michigan, Minnesota, Mississippi, Missouri, Ohio, and Wisconsin, and are being completed for Illinois and Iowa. This information is also available online at **<www.glorecords.blm.gov>**, including electronic images of original documents. The index covers only patented entries and does not include canceled or relinquished claims.

Examples of other land entry case file information for Western states available on microfilm are:

- Federal land records for Phoenix GLO, 1873–1942 (film 1639026 ff./**M1628**), Prescott, 1871–1908 (film 1639158 ff./**M1629**), and records of the Surveyor General of Arizona, 1891–1905 (film 1639163 ff./**M1627**).
- Indexes to private land grant cases, U.S. District Court, Northern District of California (film 0940851/**T1214**), Southern District of California (film 0940513/**T1215**), and Northern and Southern Districts (film 0940512/**T1216**); records of the Los Angeles District GLO, 1859–1936 (film 1639328 ff./**M1630**).
- Federal land records for Idaho, 1860–1934 (film 1617970 ff./**M1620**).
- Correspondence received by the Surveyors General of New Mexico, 1854–1907 (film 1017567 ff./**M1288**).
- Oregon and Washington Donation Land files, 1851–1903 (film 1028543 ff./**M815**), abstracts of Oregon claims (film 0847554 ff./**M145**), and abstracts of Washington claims (film 1024457 ff./**M203**).
- Federal land records for Oregon, 1854–1908 (film 1630932 ff./**M1621**).
- Federal land records for Washington, 1860–1908 (film 1637768 ff./**M1622**).

Bounty-Land Warrants

Bounty-land warrants for Revolutionary War service under acts from 1850 to 1855 extended the eligibility to receive warrants to widows and other survivors. The most comprehensive name index to these warrants is the bounty and land warrant application files held by NARA, most of which have been filmed (film 0970001 ff./**M804**). For a published index, see White, Virgil. *Genealogical Abstracts of Revolutionary War Pension Files*. 4 Vols. (Waynesboro, TN: National Historical Publishing Co., 1990–2). The warrants granted under the act of 1855 are partially indexed on microfilm. For other warrant applications, an *Order for Copies of Veterans Records* (NATF form 80) requesting the land warrant application should be used.[14] This will give the warrant number, the acreage granted, and the year of the act granting the warrant. This information can then be used to request a surrendered bounty-land warrant file.

War of 1812, military bounty-land warrants, 1815–58 (film 0983163 ff./**M848**), were issued between 1815 and 1858 to veterans of the War of 1812. The first series of warrants resulted from acts passed in 1811 and 1812, and provided that noncommissioned officers and soldiers serving for five years (unless discharged sooner), or their heirs, would be entitled to 160 acres of land from the public domain in the Territories of Michigan, Illinois, and Louisiana (present-day Arkansas) in partial compensation for military service. The second series resulted from an act in 1814, by which Congress doubled the acreage offered to soldiers enlisting after that date. Warrants issued under this act were called double bounty warrants.

Private Land Claims

These claims were made by individuals, or their descendants, who were granted lands by foreign governments or who claimed land that had come into the U.S. public domain. States with private claims are Illinois, Indiana, Michigan, and Wisconsin (Northwest Ordinance); Arkansas, Iowa, Louisiana, and Missouri (Louisiana Purchase); Florida (Florida Cession); and Arizona, California, Colorado, and New Mexico (Treaty of Guadalupe-Hildago). Information on women in these records will vary greatly: in most cases it will be necessary to trace females through a male relative. Two finding aids for these records are:

- *American State Papers, Public Lands [1790–1837]*. 38 Vols. (Washington, DC: Gates and Seaton, 1832–61, film 0944496 ff.).
- McMullin, Philip. *Grassroots of America* (Salt Lake City: Universal Printing, 1972, fiche 6051323), an index to the *State Papers*.

Where to Find Federal Land Records

Records are found in multiple locations. The most important land records and their repositories are:

National Archives (Archives I), Washington, DC: bounty-land warrant applications, surrendered bounty-land warrants, credit, cash, homestead, donation, timber, desert, and preemption case files; private land claim case files; Western states tract books; and Eastern states notes and plats for Illinois, Indiana, Iowa, Missouri, and Ohio.

National Archives (Archives II) at College Park, Maryland: Eastern closed states and Kansas notes and plats; GLO maps; BIA maps; and other maps.

Bureau of Land Management, Eastern States (BLM-EOS), Springfield, Virginia: Eastern states patents and bounty-land warrant patents; Eastern states tract books; Eastern states plats and notes for Alabama, Arkansas, Florida, Louisiana, Michigan, Minnesota, Mississippi, and Wisconsin; duplicate Western states notes and plats; and Indian allotment patents. The original notes and plates for the eleven Western states, except for Kansas, are filed with the individual Western states offices.

Other repositories: federal land records are also held at National Archives' regional record services facilities, state BLM offices, and state repositories.[15]

---

[14] Forms and costs may be obtained from the National Archives and Records Administration, 8th and Pennsylvania Avenue NW, Washington, DC 20408.

[15] For a state-by-state summary of land records, see Loretto Dennis Szucs and Sandra H. Luebking, "Research in Land and Tax Records," in *The Source: A Guidebook of American Genealogy*. Rev. ed. (Salt Lake City: Ancestry, Inc., 1997), 267–85. For a table of the opening dates of district land offices in various states, see Vernon Carstensen, *The Public Lands: Studies in the History of the Public Domain* (Madison: University of Wisconsin Press, 1962), 499–504.

MILITARY RECORDS

In the seventeenth, eighteenth, and early nineteenth centuries, women's main contact with the military, besides as wives of personnel, was when they sought pensions based on the service of male relatives or for their work as cooks, laundresses, hospital matrons, and in similar occupations. Notable exceptions in the Revolutionary War were Deborah Sampson (serving under the name Robert Shurtleff), and Margaret Corbin and Mary Ludwig (alias Molly Pitcher), both of whom replaced their husbands in the line after they were killed. These women received federal pensions.

During the Revolution, the British Army had an allotted number of wives who could receive rations permitted in each regiment. Those who exceeded this number and traveled with the regiment were known as camp followers. In 1777 the number of women (on the ration) in the company of British troops in North America was 2,776, including 381 German women from Hesse and Waldeck. By 1781 the total had risen to 3,615 women, 679 of whom were German.[16] Unfortunately, the Continental Army did not establish fixed quotas for women on the ration, but from time to time there were incidental head-counts in various regiments. There were also far fewer women with the Continental Army because camp wives were discouraged.

Women's Military Service

In 1890 nurses who served with the U.S. Army in the Civil War became the first women eligible to receive federal pensions based on their own service, except for the few women who had disguised themselves as men and managed to successfully apply for a pension (there were also women's military pensions granted by the states). They became eligible for burial in Arlington Cemetery in 1896. Eventually, the volunteer nurses who served in the Civil War were also eligible for pensions. The first female nurses to officially serve with the military were in the Spanish-American War.

The Army Nurse Corps was officially established in 1901, and the Navy Nurse Corps was established in 1908. The first enlisted military service by women was in World War I. The U.S. Navy gave them the rank of yeoman(f). The Marine Corps Women's Reserve was also created during World War I.

At the outbreak of World War II, women were again needed to step into roles normally filled by men. The following organizations were formed:

- Women's Auxiliary Army Corps (WAAC), succeeded by the Women's Army Corps (WAC)
- Women Accepted for Volunteer Emergency Service (WAVES), established by the U.S. Navy
- Women's Auxiliary Ferrying Service (WAFS)
- Women's Coast Guard Reserve (SPAR)
- Women Airforce Service Pilots (WASP)

In 1948, the Women's Armed Services Integration Act made military service by women a permanent part of the U.S. military establishment.

Records of the Veterans Administration (RG 15)

Case files of pension and bounty warrant applications based on Revolutionary War service, 1808–1900 (film 0970001 ff./M804). An excellent finding aid is the published index: White, Virgil. *Genealogical Abstracts of Revolutionary War Pension Files*. 4 Vols. (Waynesboro, TN: National Historical Publishing Co., 1990–2). Some of the noteworthy records in widows' pension application files include testimonies to

[16] Walter H. Blumenthal, *Women Camp Followers of the American Revolution* (New York: Arno Press, 1952), 93–5.

establish a date of marriage, often provided by other women and family members who attended the ceremony.

Case files of claims for half-pay and pensions based on Revolutionary War service, 1800–59 (film 1024434 ff./**M910**). After 1832, widows and orphans of a veteran who died while receiving a pension could claim the final payment. This also included Virginia's half-pay-for-life claims.

Case files of pension applications based on death or disability incurred in service between 1783 and 1861 (except the War of 1812 and the Mexican War), 1800–1930 (film 0821603 ff./**T316**), include pensions for women and children of men who died in service.

Case files of pension and bounty-land warrant applications based on service in the War of 1812, 1812–1900 (index on film 0840431 ff./**M313**), include some pensions filed under the names of widows (most are under the names of veterans). See also White, Virgil. *Index to the War of 1812 Pension Files*. 3 Vols. (Waynesboro, TN: National Historical Publishing Co., 1989).

Ledgers of payments, 1818–72, to pensioners, under acts of 1818 through 1858 (film 1319381 ff./**T718**). Each entry shows the name of the pensioner, the name of the veteran (if different), the name of the pension agency through which payment was made, and the quarter and year of the last payment to the pensioner. When an heir or a legal representative claimed an unpaid balance due the pensioner at the time of death, the date of death of the pensioner is given and the date of the final payment made to the family or heirs.

Letters received by the Secretary of War, unregistered series, 1789–1860 (film 1579139 ff./**M222**). Some letters relate to the granting of pensions.

Pension files, service records, land warrants, 1775–1913 (film 0833170 ff.). Includes miscellaneous bounty-land and pension files from the Revolutionary War and War of 1812, Civil War service record pension files, and Oregon donation land claims.

Index to pension application files of remarried widows, based on service in the Civil War and later wars, and in the Regular Army after the Civil War (**M1785**), and index to pension application files of remarried widows, based on service in the War of 1812, Indian War, Mexican War, and Regular Army before 1861 (**M1784**), are filed according to the latest surname.

Index to general correspondence of the Record and Pension Office, 1889–1904 (film 1527667 ff./**M686**).

Selected pension application files for members of the Mormon Battalion, Mexican War, 1846–48 (film 0480130 ff./**T1196**). The original records date from 1887 to 1917 and include applications of widows and dependents. These records are indexed in Mexican War index to pension files, 1887–1926.

List of application and certificate numbers assigned to pension case files, based on service between 1774 and 1865. Wars and types of applications are grouped together. There is a numerical index, 1812–1930 (**A1158**), and alphabetical name indexes:

- White, Virgil D. *Index to Mexican War Pension Files* (Waynesboro, TN: National Historical Publishing Co., 1989). Transcribed from the Mexican War series (film 0537000 ff./**T317**).
- White Virgil D. *Index to Indian War Pension Files, 1882–1926*. 2 Vols. (Waynesboro, TN: National Historical Publishing Co., 1989). Transcribed from the Indian War series (film 0821610 ff./**T318**).

- White, Virgil D. *Index to Old Wars Pension Files, 1815–1926*. Rev. ed. (Waynesboro, TN: National Historical Publishing, 1993). Transcribed from Old War index to pension files, 1815–1926 (film 0821603 ff./**T316**), a card index to the Old Wars series of pension files, relating chiefly to claims based on death or disability incurred in service in the U.S. Army, the U.S. Navy, and the U.S. Marine Corps between the end of the Revolutionary War in 1783 and the outbreak of the Civil War in 1861. Some of the claims are for service during the War of 1812, the Indian Wars, the Mexican War and Civil War service, while other claims are based on death or disability incurred by accident or illness and not due to any hostile action. Each card shows the name of a veteran and contains all or part of the following: name of veteran and any aliases used, name of widow and surname if remarried and, in some cases, the name of second husband, names of minors, numbers for certificates, applications and files, state or country from which claim was made, date claim was filed, war and or dates served. In many of the U.S. Navy claims, the name of the ship or ships served on are listed. Some of the claims have the date and place of death of the soldier or sailor, and a few list the widow's death date.
- Case Index to pension files, 1861–1934 (film 0540757 ff./**T288**), covers case files of approved pension applications of widows and other dependents of veterans of the U.S. Army and U.S. Navy; disapproved applications; and approved applications of veterans (including female nurses, scouts, guides, etc.). The organization index to pension files of veterans who served between 1861 and 1900 (film 1725491 ff./**T289**) and of pension applications of veterans who served in the U.S. Army between 1861 and 1917 is virtually the same as that in the Case Index to pension files (**T288**), except this index is arranged according to the units in which they served. The majority of the records pertain to Civil War veterans, but they also include veterans of the Spanish-American War, the Philippine Insurrection, the Indian Wars, and World War I.

Veteran's Administration pension payment cards, 1907–33 (film 1634036 ff./**M850**). These are pension payment cards for recording payments made from 1907 to 1933 to members of the regular military, arranged in alphabetical order by surname of the U.S. Army or U.S. Navy invalid or widow, except that cards with Indian names have been filmed alphabetically at the beginning of the respective letter of the alphabet. On the Army Widow and Navy Widow cards, the widow's name replaces the veteran's, and the veteran's name replaces the information about the disability for which pensioned.

U.S. Navy veterans for whom there are Navy Widow and other dependent pension files (Navy Widow originals), 1861–1910. There are two series:

- Case files of disapproved pension applications of widows and other dependents of Civil War and later U.S. Navy veterans (Navy Widow Originals) (fiche 6333626 ff./**M1274**), indexed by lists of disapproved pension applications (fiche 6333805 ff./**M1391**).
- Case files of approved pension applications of widows and other dependents of U.S. Navy veterans (**M1279**). The records are arranged numerically by application or file number.

A typical Navy Widow or dependent pension application file includes:

- ➢ an application
- ➢ names, ages, residences, and dates and places of birth, marriage, and death of family members, documented by pages from Bibles and other books submitted by pension applicants; copies of marriage records prepared by town clerks, clergymen, and justices of the peace; and birth and death certificates
- ➢ brief of the case prepared by the Bureau of Pensions
- ➢ statement of service supplied by the Navy Department and/or certified copies of the veteran's service record provided by state officials

- documentary evidence of service, such as commissions or discharge certificates; information about naval commands where the veteran served, details of battles and campaigns; and correspondence with offices of the Department of the Treasury concerning verification of service, dates of discharge or death, and pay
- affidavits or written declarations made by the widow, dependents, physicians, other veterans, and persons having knowledge of the facts made before a probate judge or clerk of the court testifying to the service and physical condition of the veteran
- depositions made by individuals in support of the claim
- property schedules, often giving names and ages of a veteran's wife and children
- papers giving powers of attorney
- papers relating to guardianship
- letters from attorneys, Members of Congress, pensioners, and other interested persons relating to the progress of the claim
- papers relating to burial expense claims

Letter from the Secretary of the Navy Transmitting the Annual Report in Relation to the Navy Pension Fund, March 14, 1828 (1828. Reprint. Signal Mountain, TN: Mountain Press, 1994). Includes list of naval pensioners and list of widow and orphan pensioners in Connecticut, District of Columbia, Georgia, Kentucky, Maine, Maryland, Massachusetts, New Hampshire, New York, North Carolina, Pennsylvania, South Carolina, and Virginia.

Letter from the Secretary of War: Transmitting a Report of the Names, Rank, and Line of Every Person, Placed on the Pension List, in Pursuance of the Act of the 18th of March, 1818 & January 20, 1820, Read, and Ordered to Lie on the Table (1820. Reprint. Apollo, PA: Closson Press, 1987).

The Pension Roll of 1835. 4 Vols. (1835. Reprint. Baltimore: Genealogical Publishing Co., 1992, fiche 6046995). A new index has been added.

Witt, Mary Emily Smith. *An Alphabetical List of Navy, Marine, and Privateer Personnel and Widows from Pension Rolls, Casualty Lists, Retirement, and Dismission Rolls of the United States Navy Dated 1847* (Dallas: MEW Publishing, 1986).

Please note: Confederate pensions were issued only by individual Southern states. For more information, see the state sections in this book, and also Allen, Desmond Walls. *Where to Write for Confederate Pension Records* (Bryant, AR: Research Associates, 1991). Some Union states also issued pensions to veterans and widows.

Records of the Army Air Forces (RG 18)

Look in: general correspondence, including societies and associations, welfare worker reports, civilian employees; Reduction in Force files, 1901–38, including the women who lost their jobs in the Economy Act of 1933; women pilots, 1939–42, etc.

Records of the Bureau of Ships (RG 19)

Look in: the name index to correspondence for names of women employees and yeomen(f).

Records of the Bureau of Personnel (BUPERS) (RG 24)

Look in: correspondence registers, including women overseas volunteers in World War I; Navy nurses in

World War I; assignments of U.S. Navy nurses and doctors, 1925–45; and women yeomen(f) in World War I, including dates of release from duty and home addresses of each woman.

Records of the Quartermaster General (RG 29)
Look in: General correspondence for nurses buried in military cemeteries; women civilian employees; Southern Claims Commission letters for loyalist Confederate women during the Civil War; register of Gold Star Mothers and Widows (of World War I), 1930, etc.

Naval Records Collection of the Office of Naval Records and Library (RG 45)
Look in: subject file of the Confederate States Navy, including women who served as nurses or provided other services.

Records of the Bureau of Medicine and Surgery (RG 52)
Look in: letters sent for widows seeking information regarding pension applications; history of the Nurse Corps, including nurses who were POWs in World War II, etc.

Records of the Adjutant General's Office (RG 94)
Look in: subject index to Precedent Files; medical records of births and marriages of civilian employees; volunteer nurses' aides; contract civilian employees; burials of wives of officers and enlisted men; medical histories of posts, including vital records of civilian women and children, etc.

Records of the Bureau of Refugees, Freedmen, and Abandoned Lands (RG 105)
Look in: selected series of records, 1865–72 (**M742**), and 1865–71 (film 1695186 ff./**M803**), including name and subject indexes, marriage certificates, marriage registers, labor contracts, claims of widows of black soldiers, etc. See also records by state: Alabama (film 1695841 ff./**M810**), Arkansas (film 1695811 ff./**M980**), Georgia (film 1685269 ff./**M799**), Louisiana (film 1695273 ff./**M1026**), Tennessee (film 1685219 ff./**M1000**), Texas (film 1695168 ff./**M822**), Virginia (film 1549578 ff./**M1053**), and the District of Columbia (film 1605536 ff./**M1056**). The records for the District of Columbia also include Delaware, Maryland, Virginia, and West Virginia. There are additional series filmed for some states.

Records of the Office of the Secretary of War (RG 107)
Look in: appointment registers; applications for employment; relief of U.S. women in Europe at the outbreak of World War I; employees missing in the Philippine Islands at the outbreak of World War II.

War Department Collection of Confederate Records (RG 109)
Look in: payrolls, including female clerks; passports issued (several volumes labeled "ladies"); hospital muster rolls for patients and employees, slave payrolls, etc. Some of the hospitals included are *Alabama*: Fort Morgan, Ross General (Mobile), and Shelby Springs; *Arkansas*: Rock Hotel (Little Rock); *Georgia*: Walker General, General (Savannah), and various hospitals in Dalton, Macon, etc.; *Kentucky*: Bowling Green; *Louisiana*: Shreveport General; *Mississippi*: Lauderdale Springs, Way and Yandell (Meridian), and Saint Mary's (West Point); *New Mexico*: Fort Filmore and Don Anna; *North Carolina*: General (Raleigh), Military Prison (Salisbury), General (Wilmington), and various hospitals at Charlotte, Fort Fisher, Goldsboro, Greensboro, and Wilson; *Tennessee*: Overton General (Memphis); *Texas*: Franklin General, El Paso General, Galveston General, and Houston General; *Virginia*: General Nos. 1–27 (Richmond), Chimbaza Nos. 1–5 (Richmond), Howard's Grove (Richmond), Jackson (Richmond), Camp Winder (Richmond), Danville, Orange and Farmville, Petersburg, and Williamsburg. See the filmed series (film 1549425 ff./**M935**) of the War Department, and other series (film 16664681 ff./**M346**), also of the War Department.

Records of the Office of the Surgeon General (RG 112)
Look in: personnel records; historical files of the Army Nurse Corps; station books of nurses; war service of nurses; personal data cards of nurses, contract nurses in the general correspondence under "c," etc.

Records of the American Expeditionary Force (RG 120)
Look in: correspondence of the civilian personnel division; returns of Army Nurse Corps at evacuation hospitals; base hospital records, etc.

Records of the United States Marine Corps (RG 127)
Look in: women's reserve enrollment; correspondence relating to dependents, etc.

Records of the Office of the Judge Advocate General (RG 153)
Look in: courts-martial case files; statements of POWs in World War II, including women civilians, nurses, nuns, missionaries, etc.

Records of the U.S. Army Continental Commands (RG 393)
Look in: correspondence of civil affairs, including letters from widows and deserted wives; questionnaires of servicemen applying for marriage licenses, etc.

Records of U.S. Army Overseas Operations and Commands (RG 394)
Look in: Army Nurse Corps personnel in Tientsin, China, 1911–39; vital records, etc.

Records of the Adjutant General's Office (RG 407)
Look in: list of U.S. Army nurses who died in the line of duty, 1941–6.

Blanton, DeAnne. "Women Soldiers of the Civil War." *Prologue* (Spring 1993): 27–33.

Christides, Michelle A. "Women Veterans of the Great War: Oral Histories." *Minerva: Quarterly Report on Women and the Military* 3 (Summer 1985): 103–27.

Friedl, Vicki L. *Women in the United States Military, 1901–1995: A Research Guide and Annotated Bibliography* (Westport, CT: Greenwood Press, 1996).

Hall, Richard. *Patriots in Disguise: Women Warriors in the Civil War* (New York: Paragon House, 1993).

National Society of the Daughters of the American Revolution. "Roster of Women Nurses Enlisted for the Spanish-American War and the Philippine Insurrection, 1898–1901," in *Third Annual Report of the National Society of the Daughters of the American Revolution* (Washington, DC: The Society, 1898–1901), 277–83.

Poulous, Paula Nassen. *A Woman's War Too: U.S. Women in the Military in World War II* (Washington, DC: National Archives and Records Administration, 1996).

Samuelson, Nancy B. "Employment of Female Spies in the American Civil War." *Minerva: Quarterly Report on Women and the Military* 7 (Fall/Winter 1989): 57–66.

Schulz, Constance B. "Daughters of Liberty: The History of Women in the Revolutionary War Pension Records." *Prologue* 16 (Fall 1984): 139–53.

Schneider, Dorothy and Carl J. Schneider. *Into the Breach: American Women Overseas in World War I* (New York: Viking, 1991).

Seeley, Charlotte Palmer. *American Women and the U.S. Armed Forces: A Guide to the Records of Military Agencies in the National Archives Relating to American Women* (Washington, DC: National Archives and Records Administration, 1992).

Sherrow, Victoria. *Women and the Military: An Encyclopedia* (Santa Barbara: CLIO, 1996).

Stewart, Miller J. "Army Laundresses: Ladies of the Soap Suds Row." *Nebraska History* 61 4 (1980): 421–36.

RECORDS OF THE BUREAU OF INDIAN AFFAIRS (RG 75)

The first removals of Native Americans from their ancestral tribal lands began in 1803. From 1830 to 1934 the U.S. Government dismantled many reservations, which were held as common land, by allotting tracts of land to individual tribal members and selling off the rest. Once an Indian accepted the allotment, he or she was no longer a tribal member and became a U.S. citizen. Native Americans living on reservations were considered a separate nation until 1924.

Indian society, such as that of the Cherokee, Crow, Iroquois, Keres, Navajo, and Pueblo people, was not only matrilineal (tracing the ancestors through the female line), it was also matrilocal. For instance, in the Cherokee Nation, a husband and wife lived in a house on land owned by the wife's family. The children and their property belonged to the wife. Cherokee women also sat on tribal councils. The original Indian deeds that were conveyed to the Proprietors of the Carolinas in the seventeenth century were signed by women.[17]

❧ *The length and bond of marriage between Native Americans varied among the different tribes. Both serial monogamy and polygamy were practiced. In a matrilineal society, membership is to a clan rather than a nuclear family. Clan membership is determined through the mother.*

In 1803, the Cherokee Nation began to adopt a patriarchal society when the National Council met without any women members to record the first written laws. Between 1817 and 1819, the first Cherokee lands were ceded to the U.S. in Alabama, Georgia, and Tennessee. If women were removed from their hereditary tribal lands, they lost their real property. If they transitioned into white society, they came under common law and were no longer able to hold land in their own names. In 1825, Cherokee law extended citizenship to white women who married Cherokee men. The following year, voting rights in the Cherokee Nation were limited to men only. The first removal rolls of 1835 show only one-third of women were recorded as heads of households.[18]

From 1884 to 1940, Indian censuses of reservations were required. All censuses give each name in Indian and English (if provided), age, sex, tribal enrollment number, and relationship to the head of household.

---

[17] Theda Perdue, "Cherokee Women and the Trail of Tears," in Vicki L. Ruiz and Ellen Carol DuBois, *Unequal Sisters: A Multi-Cultural Reader in U.S. Women's History*. 2nd ed. (London: Routledge, 1994), and Theda Perdue, "Southern Indians and the Cult of True Womanhood," in Catherine Clinton, *Half Sisters of History: The Southern Woman and the American Past* (Durham, NC: Duke University Press, 1994).

[18] The removal rolls of 1835 are in National Archives Record Group 75.

Censuses can also include information such as whether an individual is a husband or wife of an intermarried citizen (a person who married into a tribe). Enumerations after 1913 also include the date of birth; enumerations taken after 1929 also include marital status and degree of blood. The censuses are available through the FHL and the National Archives (**M595**).

Tribal enrollment records give birth names and married names, the names of both parents, census cards, testimony taken in the enrollment process, vital records and evidence filed with the application, and the enrollment.

In addition to censuses, enrollments, land allotments, removal rolls, depredations, and other well-known BIA records, women may be found in other types of records. The following are *examples* of the depth of the documentation of Native American existence on the reservations (see also chapters on individual states):

- Alaska Division: records of reindeer herding, 1877-1940
- Juneau, Alaska Area District Office: Tlingit-Haida births, marriages, and deaths, 1890-1972; welfare cases, 1931-63; native store records, 1939-64; village rolls, 1913, 1934-66
- Alaska Reindeer Service: apprenticeship contracts, 1921-32; reindeer herd case files, 1901-74; village subsistence case files, 1935-72
- Phoenix, Arizona Area District Office: apprenticeship application files; individual pay cards
- Apache Indian Agency, Arizona: field matron quarterly reports, 1903-6; rationing records, 1943-5; Indian court records, 1903-12
- Papago Indian Agency, Arizona: birth and death registers, 1913-36; marriage records, 1902-48
- Southern Superintendency: Fort Smith, Arkansas post office records, 1858-62; Sebastian County, Arkansas sheriff's records, 1857-62
- Fort Bidwell School and Indian Agency, California: Fort Bidwell Hospital records, 1906-40; field matron annual family reports, 1922-5
- Round Valley Indian Agency, California: registers of Liberty Bond purchases, 1918-19; court records, 1874-86; birth and death registers and certificates, 1901-24
- Leech Lake Indian Agency, Minnesota: field matron quarterly reports, 1911-15; marriage licenses and certificates, 1901-6; trader's licenses, 1899-1909
- Consolidated Chippewa/Minnesota Indian Agency: voter rolls, 1926-36; social service case files, 1927-43; birth and death correspondence, 1922-52
- Crow Indian Agency, Montana: Indian court records, 1919-31; Indian wills, 1911-39; family registers, 1902-17; register of births, marriages, and deaths, 1890-1921
- Fort Belknap Indian Agency, Montana: trader's licenses, 1878-1915; family history cards, 1909; U.S. Army discharges of Indian scouts, 1883-94; ration records, 1904-46
- Fort Peck Agency, Montana: trader's and other licenses, 1895-1914; birth, marriage, death, adoption, and divorce records, 1882-1920
- Fort Totten Agency, North Dakota: court journals, 1881-1919; ration journals, 1934-9; birth and death certificates, 1919-45; birth and death registers, 1924-33; burial and removal permits, 1934-40
- Standing Rock Indian Agency, North Dakota: pony payment roll, 1893; ration issue records, 1879-1907; Indian fair records, 1915-31
- Five Civilized Tribes Agency, Oklahoma: Oklahoma Presbyterian College for Girls; Saint Agnes Academy; Tuskahoma Female Academy
- Portland, Oregon, Area District Office: individual probate case files, 1914; trader's licenses; social worker files
- Cheyenne River Indian Agency, South Dakota: family registers, 1879-1937; hospital reports, 1925-33; tribal court records, 1914-15, 1935-6; pony claim records, 1890

- Crow Creek Agency, South Dakota: matron, farmer, and stockman reports, 1910–15; steamboat and ferry records, 1869–72; vital statistics, 1881–1921
- Unitah and Ouray Indian Agency, Utah: family registers, 1904–5; birth and death registers, 1922–7
- Colville Indian Agency, Washington: farming and grazing permits, 1900–73; Indian court records, 1904–79

In 1871 Congress enacted that no Indian nation or tribe would be recognized "as an independent power with whom the United States may contract by treaty." Native Americans who committed what were considered major crimes were tried under the jurisdiction of the U.S. federal courts. In 1924, U.S. citizenship was granted to all Indians born in the U.S. The Indian Reorganization Act of 1934 allowed tribes to organize tribal governments, adopt constitutions, and manage their own internal affairs. In 1953, Congress subjected Native Americans in California, Minnesota, Nebraska, Oregon (excluding the Warm Springs reservation), and Wisconsin (excluding the Lake Chippewa and Menominee reservations) to the criminal and civil jurisdiction of the state courts. Some rights were retroceded to tribes during the 1980s.

There is not sufficient space in this book to give full consideration to the complexities of tribal government. Civil and criminal jurisdiction may be exclusive or concurrent (shared) between tribal and state or federal courts. Marriages may follow tribal tradition or state law, and both are recognized as valid. Approximately 140 tribes have their own court systems. Seventy percent of the cases heard in tribal courts are criminal misdemeanors; the other thirty percent are civil cases, such as divorce, probate, adoption, child custody, property disputes, etc.[19] In areas of the U.S. where tribal courts still exist, these courts follow the codes of the state and generally have jurisdiction over the following:

- ➢ inheritance of lands on the reservation
- ➢ divorces where both parties are tribal members
- ➢ concurrent jurisdiction with state courts for divorces between tribal members and non-member spouses residing on the reservation

There are now federally recognized tribes in the following states: Alaska, Arizona, California, Colorado, Connecticut, Florida, Idaho, Iowa, Kansas, Louisiana, Maine, Michigan, Minnesota, Mississippi, Missouri, Montana, Nebraska, Nevada, New Mexico, New York, North Carolina, North Dakota, Oklahoma, Oregon, Rhode Island, South Carolina, South Dakota, Texas, Washington, Wisconsin, and Wyoming. For a directory of these tribes, see the URL **<www.indians.org/tribes/>**. There are also some state-recognized tribes, not federally recognized, but having lands and rights acknowledged by a state government.

The Cherokee Indian Nation maintained its own government for many years. See the Indian Archives Division records at the Oklahoma Historical Society in Oklahoma City, such as:

- Cherokee Nation records (film 1666294 ff.), including the following district marriages: Canadian (1879–98), Delaware (1867–98), Flint (1893), Illinois (1859–98), Saline (1866–98), Sequoyah (1870–98), and Tahlequah (1839–1910). There are also divorce records in this series.

The Choctaw-Chickasaw Citizenship Court was established by Congress from 1902 to 1904. In 1905 all records were transferred to the Dawes Commission. The citizenship court heard 256 cases and admitted 161 persons, while denying the applications of 2,792 others. The original records are at the NARA

---

[19] Sharon O'Brien, *American Indian Tribal Court Governments* (Norman: University of Oklahoma Press, 1989), 293–4.

Southwest Region in Fort Worth, Texas. For more information, see:

- Choctaw-Chickasaw Citizenship Court records of lists of claimants, 1902, indexes to dockets, 1903, appearance dockets, 1902–4 (film 1730868 ff./**M1301, M1650**).
- The case file enrollment records of the Five Civilized Tribes are now available from the National Archives online at **<www.nara.gov/nara/nail.html>**.
- Oklahoma Historical Society, Indian Archives Division, U.S. court records of Indians (film 1671169 ff.), at the Oklahoma Historical Society in Oklahoma City, including court records, vital records, probate records, etc.
- Barr, Charles B. *Records of the Choctaw-Chickasaw Citizenship Court Relative to Records of the Enrollment of the Five Civilized Tribes, 1898–1907* (Independence, MO: The Author, 1990, film 1697437).

MISCELLANEOUS FEDERAL RECORDS

If any ancestor, male or female, came in contact with the federal government, some type of record was usually created. By evaluating the occupation of an individual and the historical context, it is possible to search some rather unusual records. A few such *examples* follow:

One record group that is usually only considered for the records and reports it generated is the Work Projects Administration (**RG 69**), 1922–44, and its predecessor and successor organizations. Known for the Soundex program of federal censuses and passenger records, published slave narratives, and the *American Guide* series, the Administration was established to provide relief for unemployed persons through public works projects, grant applications, "white collar" projects, etc. Between World War I and World War II it employed thousands of Americans in the course of carrying out these programs. Other activities included the administration of relief funds; historic site restoration; programs of the motion picture, photographic, and radio sections; engineering and construction projects, a women's and professional projects division; the Federal Writers' Program; the Historical Records Survey; the Federal Archives Survey, etc.

The Records of the U.S. Department of Labor, Women's Bureau (**RG 86**), 1918–65, involves the coordination of integrating female labor into the workforce in wartime. These records contain a large body of information about women in industry, clerical, and other jobs, especially during World War II (some of these records are available on microform through the University Publications of America in Bethesda, Maryland).

The Records of the Office of Alien Property (**RG 131**), 1878–1965, seized, controlled, and disposed of enemy-owned property, particularly during World War I and II. Women who were either classified as enemy aliens or married to non-U.S. citizens who held such a classification could have had their property confiscated. In 1920 and 1948 many women filed claims to have their property restored. Most of them were Bulgarian, German, Hungarian, Japanese, and Romanian, or married to aliens of those nationalities. There are also indexes to property holdings in Honolulu (Hawaii), 1942–5, and records of the Philippines Branch, 1917–20.

The Farmers Home Administration (**RG 96**), 1918–75, provided assistance to small farmers to construct or repair existing farm buildings and dwellings, aid in resettlement, oversee migratory labor camps, make feed loans, and other functions. Many rural women had dealings with this administration. The records are divided regionally among the National Archives regional record services facilities:

- *Atlanta:* Alabama, Florida, Georgia, Kentucky, North Carolina, South Carolina, Tennessee, Virginia, West Virginia

- *Boston*: Connecticut, Delaware, Maine, Maryland, Massachusetts, New Hampshire, New Jersey, New York, Pennsylvania, Rhode Island, Vermont
- *Chicago*: Illinois, Indiana, Iowa, Michigan, Minnesota, Missouri, Ohio, Wisconsin
- *Denver*: Colorado (part), Montana, Wyoming
- *Fort Worth*: Arkansas, Colorado (part), Kansas (part), Louisiana, Mississippi, New Mexico, Oklahoma, Texas
- *Kansas City*: Kansas (part), Nebraska, North Dakota, South Dakota
- *San Francisco*: Arizona, California, Nevada, Utah
- *Seattle*: Alaska, Idaho, Oregon, Washington

There are also some separate records of paid rural rehabilitation loans which are organized separately.

CONSULAR RECORDS

Consular records are an untapped source of genealogical information. Correspondence involving naturalization cases can be found in both the records of foreign service posts of the U.S. Department of State (**RG 84**) and those of foreign governments. Two series of other nations that contain a wealth of information are:

The registers and indexes of correspondence of the British Foreign Office to the U.S. for 1793 to 1919 (Alexandria, VA: Chadwyck-Healey, 1990, fiche 6069741 ff.) contain information about British subjects, including vital statistics, applications for citizenship, and deportations.

The records of the Russian Consulate offices in the U.S., 1862 to 1928 (film 1497998 ff./**M1486**), are primarily in Russian, although other languages are used. During the time these records were created, the U.S. had Russian Consulate Offices in Chicago, Honolulu, New York, Philadelphia, Portland, San Francisco, and Seattle. These records contain data on subjects of the Russian Empire (Armenians, Finns, Jews, Lithuanians, Poles, Ukrainians, and others) who came to the U.S. in the late nineteenth and early twentieth centuries. They include passports and passport applications, visas, nationality certificates, certificates of origin, inheritance information, contracts, and correspondence. They contain information including name, date of birth, exact place of birth, details on family relationships, relatives living in the U.S. and Russia, physical description, photographs, details of military service, reasons for immigration, date and place of immigration, religion, and other information. The original records are at the National Archives, Washington, DC. For an index to these records, see Sack, Sallyann. *The Russian Consular Index and Catalog* (New York: Garland Publishing, 1987, film 1605681). For availability of records from other countries, see the Family History Library Catalog under the locality to be searched.

SEARCHING NON-GOVERNMENT SOURCES

NEWSPAPERS

Newspapers contain a wealth of genealogical information, including birth notices, announcements of betrothal, marriage notices, anniversary announcements, divorce notices, obituaries and death notices, notices of probate proceedings, port arrivals, and more.

Obituary notices often contain biographical information on parentage, surviving heirs, place of birth or country of origin, and year of immigration to the U.S. Maiden names are frequently included in obituaries, and sometimes a woman's parents' names. The location of a burial is often given, possibly leading to cemetery inscriptions for other family members buried in the same plot. Many newspapers have been abstracted and published. Some papers have been indexed, such as *The New York Times Obituaries Index, 1858–1978* (New York: The New York Times, 1970–80), and many smaller papers have also been indexed by individuals and genealogical societies. Death notices, or paid obituaries, appear at the bottom of the obituary pages and include similar information but are not usually indexed. For more information, see Jarboe, Betty. *Obituaries: A Guide to Sources* (Boston: G.K. Hall, 1989). See also bibliographies of ethnic newspapers, such as:

- Henritze, Barbara K. *Bibliographic Checklist of African American Newspapers* (Baltimore: Genealogical Publishing Co., 1995).
- Lo, Karl and Him Make Lia. *Chinese Newspapers Published in North America, 1854–1975* (Washington, DC: Center for Chinese Research Materials, 1977).

CEMETERY RECORDS

Cemeteries are literally monuments to the past. Inscriptions vary greatly in what they contain, sometimes depending on the ethnic or religious background. Commonly found are names, family relationships, and age at death. Sometimes there is a birth date or year and a place of birth, particularly if the deceased is from another state, country, etc. Some of the information that can be determined from gravestone inscriptions is:

- an approximate marriage date, based on births and deaths of deceased children.
- information as to causes of multiple deaths over a short period of time (epidemics, floods, etc.).
- ethnic origins, based on inscriptions in foreign languages, see Meyer, Richard E. "The Literature of Necroethnicity in America: An Annotated Bibliography," in *Ethnicity and the American Cemetery* (Bowling Green, OH: Bowling Green State University Popular Press, 1993), 222–37.
- family relationships and maiden names, based on families in adjoining plots.
- migration patterns, based on places of birth of members from multiple families in the same cemetery.
- denominations, occupations, and society and organization memberships, based on symbols carved on headstones.
- marital status, see Rotundo, Barbara. "Gender Reading from Grave Markers." AGS (Winter 1994): 11–13.

For an up-to-date directory of cemeteries, see Burek, Deborah. *Cemeteries of the U.S.* (Detroit: Gale Research, 1994).

CITY DIRECTORIES

City directories can help to locate families in census schedules that have no indexes and to determine when a family moved between census years. When compared for a series of consecutive years, they can also show when a family began residency in an area. Directories can be searched by surname, and then the street address of a family can be used to narrow down the search on a census film. Some city directories also give background information on communities, including time periods when different ethnic groups settled in the area and when churches were established.

CHURCH RECORDS

In some instances, church institutions provided the government and laws in colonial America. Church records as a subject are not addressed in this book, except in specific cases where parish records pre-date civil records.

SEARCHING STATE COURT RECORDS

WOMEN IN CIVIL LAW AND IN COMMON LAW

Civil law, the older of the two legal traditions, has its roots in the XII Tables of Rome, published in 450 BC; this was later codified by the publication of the *Corpus Juris Civilis* of Justinian, published in Constantinople in AD 533. The Custom of Paris, written in AD 1510 (the customary law of provincial Paris) was established as law in French Canada in 1663 and was the basis for the French Civil Code of 1804, the *Code Napolèon*. Family law was first recorded in Spain in the Laws of El Toro in 1369. It was codified by the *Nueva Recopilacion* of 1567, which was the basis for the Spanish Civil Code of 1805. These laws were the foundation of law in the Spanish American colonies. Civil law recognizes only statutes, regulations, and custom as sources of law, in descending order of authority.

Common law dates from the Norman conquest of England at Hastings in AD 1066 and from Chapter 39 of the Magna Charta, written in 1215, the source of modern due process. Sources of law are found in constitutions, statutes, decided cases, principles, customs, and rules established by usage and judicial decision.[20]

Common law is based on the doctrine of *stare decisis*, literally meaning the decision stands, or the power to base decisions on prior decisions, or the law of the case. Decision and opinion become what is known as precedent. While judges in common law are endowed with expansive interpretive powers, a civil-law judge is essentially a bureaucrat or a master clerk. The French *Code Napolèon* is an example of the belief "that it was possible to draft a systematic legislation that would have those characteristics [separating legislative from judicial power] to such a degree that the function of the judge would be limited to selecting the applicable provision of the code and giving its obvious significance in the context of the case."[21] In common law, a judge can rule existing law to be unconstitutional, effectively making new law upon which future decisions may be based.

Civil law has separate codes for criminal and civil procedure. While civil cases under common law are basically one event, civil cases under civil law are conducted in three parts: the preliminary stage, or pleading, the evidence taking and creating of a written summary record, and the decision making. There are no trial and no civil jury.

- ➢ Elements in civil cases under *common law* not usually found in civil law are: the importance placed on discovery (advance information on opponent's witnesses and evidence), the pretrial, exclusionary rules regarding the admissibility of evidence and hearsay, and contempt of court.
- ➢ Elements in civil cases under *civil law* not usually found in common law are: the evidence is heard immediately by the judge and jury; questions are put to witnesses by the judge at the request of counsel, rather than by counsels, and appeals in civil law can introduce new evidence.
- ➢ Procedures in criminal cases under *common law* not usually found in civil law are: public trial by jury, plea bargaining, and the cross-examination of witnesses by counsels.
- ➢ Procedures in criminal cases under *civil law* not usually found in common law are: a separate investigative phase; an instructional phase whereby a judge examines the evidence, decides if a crime

---

[20] W.S. McClanahan, *Community Property Law in the United States* (Rochester, NY: The Lawyers Cooperative Publishing Co., 1982), 21.

[21] John Henry Merryman, *The Civil Law Tradition*. 2nd ed. (Stanford: Stanford University Press, 1985), 29.

has been committed, and prepares a written report; a private trial where a judge is free to seek evidence, a prosecutor may suggest questions for the judge to put to the defendant, and penalties are established by statute.

The concept of dower is a tenet of common law. The English Statute of Distributions of 1670 provided for a widow to inherit her husband's personal estate in intestacy of one-third under common law. Common law found a husband and wife to be one person in law. In 1765, the British jurist William Blackstone defined the legal status of married women in the following way:

"The husband and wife are one person in law: that is, the very being or legal existence of the woman is suspended during the marriage, or at least incorporated and consolidated into that of the husband . . . and therefore is called in our law-french a *femme covert* . . . or under the protection and influence of her husband, her baron, or lord; and her condition during her marriage is called coverture."[22]

Under common law, a wife's separate property was managed by her husband, and he could take the profits and rents of the land for his own enjoyment by a principle called tenancy in the entirety and such property became hers only by rights of survivorship. A husband also owned his wife's personal property. A wife could not enter into contracts by herself, as her husband held authority over her.

Civil law did not have the concept of dower, as the husband and wife were considered co-owners of community property, the management of which was vested in the husband. A married woman could manage and control her own separate property.

❧ *In colonial times, when a husband died, a widow usually did not have enough inheritance to live without supplemental income. Her options included any of the following:*

- *She could live with relatives, especially if her husband's will required her children to support her.*
- *She could remarry.*
- *She could attempt to continue her husband's business, farm, etc., on her own.*
- *She could hire herself out as a domestic in someone else's home.*
- *She could turn her home into a business, such as a tavern for overnight travelers and public meetings.*
- *If she could read and write, she could open a day school or boarding school for children.*
- *She could prepare and sell food from her home, either in her own shop or to other merchants.*
- *She could become a nurse or a midwife.*
- *She could work as a seamstress or in other textile crafts.*
- *She could work in the "cottage industry," doing piecework for merchants, coloring pages for magazine publishers, etc.*

Widows who entered the business world took out advertisements in newspapers, applied for licenses, had their names on tax lists, and had their names entered in other public records. They were still not on an equal status with men, could neither vote nor hold office, and frequently could not represent themselves in court.

Marriage under French and Spanish civil law was considered a civil contract, separate from the ecclesiastical convention of matrimony. To dissolve a marriage, however, required the action of the Roman Catholic Church. English law required marriages to be dissolved in ecclesiastical courts. These courts were not available in the British American colonies.

---

[22] *Commentaries on the Laws of England* (Oxford, 1765).

For this reason absolute divorce existed only in Puritan New England, where marriage was considered a civil contract and not a sacrament. The legal tradition in all of English North America, however, was still common law. Southern and middle colonies also employed the English concepts of primogeniture and jointure. Chancery courts (courts of equity) administered trust estates which allowed wives to own property separate from their husbands, although the property was still vested in the husband. When a wife remarried, the property could remain in her name and be passed to her children. A wife could also serve as executrix for her husband's estate and act as guardian for her minor children.

Spanish civil law specifically provided dower as a married woman's separate property. The dower could contain money, possessions, slaves, and, sometimes, real estate. The husband could manage his wife's dower but had to restore it in his will or upon dissolution of the marriage. Gifts of money from the groom to the bride, *arras*, were often bestowed by older men marrying younger women, or on suitable women from good, but impoverished, families.

As the needs of colonial society demanded, the common and civil law were adapted and sometimes blended to accommodate the expanding roles that both men and women were to play in the New World. The law of primogeniture was gradually replaced by the practice of partible inheritance.[23]

❧ *Some places to find a marriage record or proof of a marriage:*

- *official vital records, including birth and death records of children*
- *church records and parish registers*
- *Bible records*
- *probate records*
- *dower releases in land records*
- *applications for federal land, naturalization, passports, etc.*
- *census records*
- *newspapers, including obituaries*
- *divorce decrees or orders of legal separation*
- *civil lawsuits regarding paternity, bastardy, bigamy, child support, alimony, etc.*
- *military pension applications*
- *other entitlement applications, for such as welfare, civil pensions, insurance claims, etc.*
- *any types of claims based on marital status or residency*

THE NINETEENTH CENTURY

The community property system of marital law presently exists in the states of Arizona, California, Idaho, Louisiana, Nevada, New Mexico, Texas, Washington, and the Commonwealth of Puerto Rico. At the time of statehood, this system was a continuation of existing civil law in all but Idaho, Nevada, and Washington, the first three states which were not previously under Mexican or Spanish sovereignty. Louisiana is the only state to retain a civil-law system; the others adopted common law.

Women's suffrage progressed faster in the Western states and territories where they served on juries, obtained full or partial suffrage, and were elected to political office, sometimes decades before women in the East. Wyoming was the first territory to grant women complete suffrage in 1869, followed by the Utah Territory in 1870, Colorado in 1893, and Idaho in 1896.

Married Women's Property Acts were adopted in the U.S. states and territories in the mid-nineteenth century, changing the common law, and varying in intent from securing a wife's property from her

[23] Carol Shammas, et al., *Inheritance in America: From Colonial Times to the Present* (1987. Reprint. Galveston, TX: Frontier Press, 1997), 7.

husband's creditors to making her the legal owner and giving her full capacity to deal with her separate property as if unmarried. Some *general* descriptions of provisions that may be contained in a Married Women's Property Act are:

1. All property owned by the wife before marriage, or received after marriage and held as her separate property, can be sold and transferred without the consent of her husband.
2. If a husband fails to make proper provision for the support of his wife, the law will compel him to furnish her proper support if he has sufficient property.
3. The wife must support her husband out of her separate property when he has no separate property and is without help or means of support.
4. The earnings of the wife are not liable for the debts of the husband.
5. The separate property of the wife is not liable for the debts of her husband.
6. The property owned by the husband before marriage, or acquired after marriage by gift or inheritance, is his separate property; his wife, however, has a dower interest in his real estate where dower rights are recognized.
7. The wife who deserts her husband cannot hold him for her support, unless she was justified in leaving or offers to return.
8. The earnings of the wife and her minor children after living separate from her husband are the property of the wife.
9. If the husband or the wife transfers real estate of any kind, both must sign the deed, mortgage, or contract.

By the end of the nineteenth century, a widow's rights in intestacy (where there are children of the marriage) still limited her to life use only of one-third of her husband's real estate in twenty-nine of the forty-two common-law states and territories. In intestacy, in the eight community property states and territories, a widow inherited half of the community property, and one quarter to one-third of her husband's separate property, except for Louisiana, where she received none. In situations where there were no children, parents, or other heirs (based on the laws of descent), a widow's share usually increased under both common law and the

---

Living Conditions

In a survey by the General Federation of Women's Clubs, called "What Women Want in Their Homes," 1.4 million women in forty-one states responded. The Federation gathered the following information:

Cities reporting:

Largest city with 100% electrification: Salt Lake City (Utah)

90% of homes equipped with electric washing machines: Park Ridge (Illinois); American Fork, Garland, and Murray (Utah)

Every home in town with a gas cooking range: Redondo Beach, El Segundo, and Mar Vista (California); Durango (Colorado); Daytona (Florida); Park Ridge (Illinois); Melrose, Newburyport, and Harvard (Massachusetts); Agricultural and Mechanical College (Mississippi); Wyoming (Ohio); Oregon City (Oregon); Bala-Cynwyd (Pennsylvania); Harrogate (Tennessee); Park Place (Texas); Piedmont and Gassaway (West Virginia)

Every home in town with a stationary laundry tub: Park Ridge (Illinois)

Every home in town with flush toilets: Redondo Beach, San Fernando, Watsonville, El Segundo, and Mar Vista (California); Durango (Colorado); Daytona (Florida); Park Ridge (Illinois); Hingham (Massachusetts); Agricultural and Mechanical College (Mississippi); Wyoming (Ohio); Oregon City (Oregon); Bala-Cynwyd (Pennsylvania); Harrogate (Tennessee); Park Place (Texas); Piedmont and Gassaway (West Virginia)

From Mary Sherman, "The Home Equipment Survey," *Women's Home Companion* (March 1926), 34–5.

---

community property system of marital law.[24]

THE EARLY TWENTIETH CENTURY

In 1924 the League of Women Voters conducted a survey on the legal status of women in each state. Here are some of their findings:

Number of states in which . . .

- married women have an absolute right of contract: 16
- married women have the right to convey real estate if the husband joins the deed: 4
- community property states: 8
- married women are denied the right to become a surety: 8
- married women are denied the right to become a surety and have no right of general contract: 9
- women are under common law: 2
- dower and curtesy are practiced: 8
- wives share equally with their husbands in their children's earnings: 17
- equal guardianship laws exist: 37
- women may serve on juries: 2
- a father may will a child (born or unborn) away from the mother: 1
- common-law marriage has been abolished: 14
- health certificates are required for marriage: 5
- a woman's age of consent to marry is twenty-one: 9
- a woman's age of consent to marry is eighteen: 31
- a woman's age of consent to marry is sixteen: 3
- a woman's age of consent to marry is fifteen: 1
- a woman's minimum age to marry, with parental consent, is twelve: 6
- a woman's minimum age to marry, with parental consent, is fourteen: 7
- a woman's minimum age to marry, with parental consent, is fifteen: 5
- a woman's minimum age to marry, with parental consent, is sixteen: 10

RECOGNITION OF COMMON-LAW MARRIAGE TO THE PRESENT DAY

Alabama: recognized
Alaska: recognized until 1917
Arizona: recognized until 1913
Arkansas: not recognized by law
California: recognized until 1895
Colorado: recognized
Connecticut: not recognized by law
Delaware: not recognized by law
District of Columbia: recognized
Florida: recognized until 1968
Georgia: recognized
Hawaii: not recognized by law
Idaho: recognized
Illinois: recognized until 1905
Indiana: recognized
Iowa: recognized
Kansas: recognized
Kentucky: recognized until 1866
Louisiana: not recognized by law
Maine: not recognized by law
Maryland: not recognized by law
Massachusetts: not recognized by law
Michigan: recognized until 1957
Minnesota: recognized until 1941
Mississippi: recognized until 1956
Missouri: recognized until 1921
Montana: recognized until 1978
Nebraska: recognized until 1923

---

[24] For a detailed survey of inheritance laws in 1890, see "Appendix B" in Carole Shammas, Marylynn Salmon, and Michael Dahlin, *Inheritance in America: From Colonial Times to the Present* (1987. Reprint. Galveston, TX: Frontier Press, 1997).

Nevada: recognized until 1943
New Hampshire: not recognized by law
New Jersey: recognized until 1939
New Mexico: recognized until 1912
New York: recognized until 1902 and 1908–33
North Carolina: not recognized by law
North Dakota: recognized
Ohio: recognized until 1890
Oklahoma: recognized
Oregon: recognized until 1877
Pennsylvania: recognized
Rhode Island: recognized
South Carolina: recognized
South Dakota: recognized until 1959
Tennessee: not recognized by law
Texas: recognized
Utah: recognized until 1898
Vermont: not recognized by law
Virginia: not recognized by law
Washington: recognized until about 1883
West Virginia: not recognized by law
Wisconsin: recognized until 1917
Wyoming: not recognized by law

THE LAWS OF DIVORCE

A general description of information that may be found in a divorce record is:

1. names of plaintiff and defendants
2. date and place of marriage
3. names and ages of minor children
4. name of wife's father
5. property owned jointly and separately
6. criminal charges and court of record
7. occupation of husband
8. current and previous residences of both parties
9. if an alien, length of time in the U.S.; citizenship status
10. testimonies and affidavits of neighbors, family members, and other witnesses

SUMMARY OF GROUNDS FOR DIVORCE IN 1895

Adultery: all *except* South Carolina, which has no divorce laws

Impotency: all *except* Arizona, California, Connecticut, Idaho, Iowa, Louisiana, New Mexico, New York, North Dakota, South Carolina, South Dakota, Texas, and Vermont

Willful abandonment or desertion: all *except* New York, North Carolina, and South Carolina (time period of desertion varies)

Habitual drunkenness, or intemperance: all *except* Maryland, New Jersey, New York, North Carolina, Pennsylvania, South Carolina, Texas, Vermont, Virginia, and West Virginia

Cruelty, inhuman treatment, etc: all *except* Maryland, New Jersey, New York, North Carolina, South Carolina, Virginia, and West Virginia; in Alabama, Kentucky, and Tennessee these are grounds for the wife only

Conviction of felony or infamous crime, sentence to imprisonment, imprisonment: all *except* the District of Columbia, Florida, Maine, New Jersey, New Mexico, New York, North Carolina, and South Carolina

Failure or neglect of husband to provide for wife: Arizona, California, Colorado, Delaware, Idaho, Indiana, Maine, Massachusetts, Michigan, Nebraska, Nevada, New Hampshire, New Mexico, North Dakota, Rhode Island, South Dakota, Tennessee, Utah, Vermont, Washington, Wisconsin, and Wyoming (time period varies)

Disappearance, absence without being heard from: Connecticut, New Hampshire, Rhode Island, and Vermont

Voluntary separation: Kentucky and Wisconsin

Having former wife or husband living: Arkansas, Colorado, District of Columbia, Florida, Illinois, Kansas, Mississippi, Missouri, Montana, New Jersey, Ohio, Pennsylvania, and Tennessee

Joining a religious sect that believes marriage to be unlawful: Kentucky, Massachusetts, and New Hampshire

Indicted for felony and a fugitive from justice: Louisiana and Virginia

Husband indicted for felony and flees the state: North Carolina

Refusal of wife to remove with husband to this state: Tennessee

Indignities rendering condition intolerable or life-burdensome: Arkansas, Missouri, Oregon, Pennsylvania, Tennessee, Washington, and Wyoming

Conduct rendering it unsafe for wife to live with husband: Tennessee

Turning wife out of doors: Tennessee

Habitually violent and unforgivable temper: Florida

Attempt by either party upon life of another: Illinois, Louisiana, and Tennessee

Gross neglect of duty: Kansas and Ohio

Wife given to intoxication: Wisconsin

Husband a vagrant under the statutes: Missouri and Wyoming

Insanity or mental incapacity at time of marriage: District of Columbia, Georgia, and Mississippi

Insanity, permanent and incurable, occurring subsequent to marriage: Arkansas

Incurable chronic mania or dementia, having existed ten years or more: Washington

Any cause rendering marriage originally void: Maryland and Rhode Island

Marriage with prohibited degrees: Florida, Georgia, Mississippi, New Jersey, and Pennsylvania

Marriage by force, duress, or fraud: Connecticut, Georgia, Kansas, Kentucky, Ohio, Pennsylvania, and Washington

Marriage solemnized while either party was under the age of consent: Delaware

When one of the parties has obtained a divorce in another state: Florida, Michigan, and Ohio

Public defamation: Louisiana

Any other cause deemed by the court sufficient and when the court shall be satisfied that the parties can no longer live together: Washington

RESIDENCY REQUIREMENTS TO OBTAIN A DIVORCE IN 1895 (SHORTER OR LONGER PERIODS IN SOME CIRCUMSTANCES):

Five years: Massachusetts

Three years: Connecticut and New Jersey

Two years: Delaware, District of Columbia, Florida, Indiana, Maryland, Michigan, New Jersey, North Carolina, Tennessee, and Vermont

One year: Alabama, Arkansas, Colorado, Georgia, Illinois, Iowa, Kansas, Kentucky, Maine, Minnesota, Mississippi, Missouri, Montana, New Hampshire, Ohio, Oregon, Pennsylvania, Rhode Island, Utah, Virginia, Washington, West Virginia, and Wisconsin

Six months: Arizona, California, Idaho, Nebraska, Nevada, New Mexico, Texas, and Wyoming

Ninety days: North and South Dakota, and Oklahoma

None: New York

Marriages solemnized in the state, and action may be brought by the wife, regardless of the residence of the husband: Louisiana

RESTRICTIONS ON REMARRIAGE OF DIVORCED PERSONS IN 1895

No restrictions: Arizona, Connecticut, the District of Columbia, Florida, Illinois, Minnesota, Missouri, New Mexico, North Carolina, North Dakota, Ohio, South Dakota, Texas, Utah, and Wyoming

Five-year waiting period: Arkansas and Georgia

Two-year waiting period and permission of the court: Massachusetts
Two-year waiting period: Indiana, Iowa, Montana, New Hampshire, and Vermont
One-year waiting period: California, Colorado, New Jersey, and Wisconsin
Six-month waiting period: Idaho, Kansas, Nebraska, Nevada, Oklahoma, Oregon, Rhode Island, and Washington
Decree of the court restraining remarriage: Virginia
Permission of the court required to remarry: Maine and Michigan
Defendant in divorce prohibited from remarrying during plaintiff's lifetime: Alabama, Delaware, Kentucky, Maryland, New York (unless five years have elapsed and the plaintiff has remarried), Pennsylvania, and Tennessee
Defendant in divorce prohibited from remarrying at any time: Louisiana (plaintiff may remarry in ten months), Mississippi, and West Virginia

Courts of every state guarded their jurisdiction very carefully. They generally refused to recognize as a valid divorce against one of their citizens of the state by the court of another state, unless both parties to the suit were subject at the time to the jurisdiction of the court granting the divorce. For example, Kansas courts could grant divorces if the applicant's husband or wife had obtained a divorce in another state and the applicant had been forbidden to remarry.

If a wife in New York obtained a divorce from her husband and he was forbidden to remarry, he could go to Kansas and obtain a divorce on those grounds. If his wife contested the case, or if she could be served with the papers in Kansas so that she was brought under the jurisdiction of the Kansas court, the courts of New York would have to recognize the divorce as valid and could not prohibit the husband from remarrying in New York.

APPROXIMATE DATES FOR EARLIEST STATE AND COUNTY MARRIAGE AND DIVORCE REGISTRATION

	State	County
Alabama		
marriage	1936	1818
divorce	1950	1864
Alaska		
marriage	1913	—
divorce	1950	—
Arizona		
marriage	—	1864
divorce	—	1864
Arkansas		
marriage	1917	1848
divorce	1923	1848
California		
marriage	1905	1851
divorce	1962	1851
Colorado		
marriage	1900	1860
divorce	1900	1860
(state has index only)		
Connecticut		
marriage	1897	—
divorce	1897	1711
(see town records for vital records beginning in 1635)		
Delaware		
marriage	1847	1832
divorce	1703	1900
District of Columbia		
marriage	1811	—
divorce	1803	—

Florida

marriage	1927	1825
divorce	1927	1825

Georgia

marriage	1952	1800
divorce	1952	1835

Hawaii

marriage	1842	1905
divorce	1849	1905

Idaho

marriage	1947	1865
divorce	1947	1865

Illinois

marriage	1962	1813
divorce	1962	1813

(marriage licenses required after 1877)

Indiana

marriage	—	1811
divorce	—	1853

Iowa

marriage	1880	1836
divorce	1906	1838

Kansas

marriage	1913	1832
divorce	1951	1832

Kentucky

marriage	1958	1797
divorce	1958	1809

Louisiana

marriage	1948	1808
divorce	—	1818

Maine

marriage	1923	—
divorce	1892	1738

(see towns for vital records beginning ca. 1653)

Maryland

marriage	1951	1640
divorce	1961	1829

(licenses required after 1777; ministers' returns filed after 1865)

Massachusetts

marriage	1841	1636
divorce	1952	1738

(see also towns for vital records beginning in 1620)

Michigan

marriage	1867	1805
divorce	1897	1857

Minnesota

marriage	1958	1842
divorce	1970	1842

(state has indexes only)

Mississippi

marriage	1926	1836
divorce	1920	1859

Missouri

marriage	—	1816
divorce	1948	1808

Montana

marriage	1943	1883
divorce	—	1883

(state has indexes only)

Nebraska

marriage	1909	1855
divorce	1909	1855

Nevada

marriage	1968	1861
divorce	1968	1861

New Hampshire

marriage	1883	—
divorce	—	1774

(see town vital records beginning in 1639)

New Jersey

marriage	1848	1699, most 1795
divorce	1850	1743

(see also town records beginning in 1666)

New Mexico

marriage	—	1850
divorce	—	1850

New York

marriage	1847-65	1848
	1881	1908 (most)
divorce	1963	1787

(state records do not include New York City boroughs, or Albany, Yonkers, or Buffalo before 1914; see also town and city records from the 1640s)

North Carolina

marriage	1962	1669
divorce	1958	1814

North Dakota

marriage	1925	1872
divorce	—	1872

Ohio

marriage	1949	1789
divorce	1949	1852

(copies of state records are not available)

Oklahoma

marriage	—	1890
divorce	—	1907

Oregon

marriage	1906	1847
divorce	1925	1853

Pennsylvania

marriage	—	1852, most 1885
divorce	1946	1804

Rhode Island

marriage	1894	—
divorce	1644	1749 (or earlier)

(see town records for vital records beginning in 1636)

South Carolina

marriage	1950	1836
divorce	1962	1949

(divorce illegal until 1949)

South Dakota

marriage	1905	1873
divorce	1905	1873

Tennessee

marriage	1945	1786
divorce	—	1797

Texas

marriage	1966	1837
divorce	1968	1841

(copies of state records not available by mail)

Utah

marriage	1978	1887
divorce	1978	1851

(copies of state records are not available)

Vermont

marriage	1857	—
divorce	1860	—

(see town records for vital records beginning in 1760)

Virginia

marriage	1853	1646
divorce	1853	1848

(see also vestry records)

Washington

marriage	1968	1852
divorce	1968	1889

West Virginia

marriage	1921	1754
divorce	—	1848

Wisconsin

marriage	1907	1823
divorce	—	1823

Wyoming

marriage	1941	1864
divorce	1941	1864

DATES OF EARLIEST PUBLISHED STATE COURT REPORTS BEFORE 1900

State court reports contain decisions of cases of the courts of the fifty states and are published both officially and unofficially. The courts published are usually only the higher level and appellate courts (or court of last resort), but some of the more populous areas include decisions of lower courts. Some states that include lower court trial court decisions are New York, Pennsylvania, and Ohio. West's National Reporter System, begun in 1879, is one of the best unofficial publications. The online databases, WEST LAW and LEXIS, contain decisions from the mid-1930s, but some cases dating back to the nineteenth century are being added. The databases can be searched by name, jurisdiction, topic, issue, etc. Also important are the series of *Shepard's Citations* for each state.

The best way to access lower court records is still by searching the original records, either on microfilm or on-site. States marked with an asterisk (*) have additional publications and manuscripts of records prior to the American Revolution, which are sometimes called public records. If a female ancestor came in contact with the colonial or provincial government (particularly legislative divorce, annulments, manumissions, and petitions for *feme sole* status), there would be a record; in most instances, however, it is necessary to trace a family through the husband.

EARLIEST PUBLISHED COURT REPORTS

Alabama	
Supreme Court	1820
Alaska	
District Court	1869
Arizona	
Supreme Court	1866
Arkansas	
Supreme Court	1837
Other courts	1820
California*	
Supreme Court	1850
District Court	1857
Colorado	
Supreme Court	1864
Court of Appeals	1891
Connecticut*	
Supreme Court of Errors	1785
Delaware*	
Supreme Court	1832
Court of Chancery	1814
Miscellaneous	1792
District of Columbia	
U.S. Court of Appeals for the DC Circuit Court (and predecessors)	1801
Florida*	
Supreme Court	1846
Georgia*	
Supreme Court	1846
Miscellaneous	1805
Hawaii	
Supreme Court	1847
Idaho	
Supreme Court	1866
Illinois*	
Supreme Court	1819
Appellate Court	1877
Court of Claims	1889
Circuit Court	1866
Indiana	
Supreme Court	1817
Appellate Court	1890
Iowa	
Supreme Court	1838

Kansas
Supreme Court 1838
Court of Appeals 1895

Kentucky
Supreme Court 1785

Louisiana*
Supreme Court 1809
Court of Appeals 1881

Maine*
Supreme Judicial Court 1820

Maryland*
Court of Appeals 1826
General Court 1658
High Court of Chancery 1811
Baltimore City Reports 1888

Massachusetts*
Supreme Judicial Court 1804
Superior Court 1761

Michigan
Supreme Court 1805
Miscellaneous 1805

Minnesota
Supreme Court 1851

Mississippi*
Supreme Court 1818
Chancery Court 1839
Miscellaneous 1818

Missouri*
Supreme Court 1821
Court of Appeals 1876

Montana
Supreme Court 1868

Nebraska
Supreme Court 1860

Nevada
Supreme Court 1865

New Hampshire*
Supreme Court 1796

New Jersey*
Court of Errors and Appeals 1789
Superior Court 1790
Manumission cases 1775

New Mexico*
Supreme Court 1852

New York*
Court of Appeals 1847
Supreme Court, Appellate Division 1869
Court for the Correction of Errors and Supreme Court of Judicature 1791
Mayor's Court 1674
Vice-Admiralty Reports 1715
City Hall Recorder 1816
Common Pleas 1850
Criminal Court 1791
New York City Court 1874

North Carolina*
Supreme Court 1778

North Dakota
Supreme Court 1890
Supreme Court of the Dakota Territory 1867

Ohio
Supreme Court 1821
Miscellaneous 1807
Common Pleas 1816
Annals of Cleveland 1837
Cincinnati Superior Court 1854
Dayton (miscellaneous) 1865
Circuit Court 1885

Oklahoma
Supreme Court 1890
Court of Appeals of the Indian Territory 1896

Oregon

Supreme Court	1853

Pennsylvania*

Supreme Court	1754
Superior Court	1895
Lower Courts:	
Pittsburgh Legal Journal	1853
Chester County Reports	1879
Schuylkill Legal Record	1879
Delaware County Reports	1880
York Legal Record	1880
Luzerne Legal Register	1882
Lancaster Law Review	1883
Montgomery Law Reporter	1885
Northampton County Reports	1887
Lackawanna Jurist	1888
Dauphin County Reports	1895
Miscellaneous	1779

Rhode Island*

Supreme Court	1828

South Carolina*

Supreme Court	1868
South Carolina Law Reports	1783
South Carolina Equity Reports	1784

South Dakota

Supreme Court	1890
Supreme Court of the Dakota Territory	1867

Tennessee

Supreme Court	1791
Chancery Court	1878

Texas*

Supreme Court	1840
Court of Criminal Appeals	1892
Court of Civil Appeals	1892
Miscellaneous	1876

Utah

Supreme Court	1855

Vermont*

Supreme Court	1789

Virginia*

Supreme Court of Appeals	1789
Virginia Colonial Decisions	1728
General Court	1730
Chancery Court	1788

Washington

Supreme Court	1854

West Virginia

Supreme Court	1864

Wisconsin

Supreme Court	1839

Wyoming

Supreme Court	1870

APPROXIMATE DATES RECORDS BEGIN IN COUNTIES

Alabama
1809

Alaska
1897 land offices and district courts; no counties

Arizona
1850

Arkansas
1803

California
1850

Colorado
1853

Connecticut
1666; see town records for land and vital records beginning in 1635; check probate districts for probate records beginning in 1698

Delaware
1680

District of Columbia
1801; no counties

Florida
1821

Georgia
1756

Hawaii
1905

Idaho
1863

Illinois
1724

Indiana
1790

Iowa
1830

Kansas
1855

Kentucky
1779

Louisiana
1735; records are in parishes, not counties

Maine
1636; see town records for vital records

Maryland
1634

Massachusetts
1632; see also town records from 1620

Michigan
1808

Minnesota
1847

Mississippi
1798

Missouri
1814; see also City of Saint Louis, beginning in 1764

Montana
1864

Nebraska
1854

Nevada
1855

New Hampshire
1769; see also town records from 1623

New Jersey
1667 (East Jersey), 1690 (West Jersey); see also town records from 1666

New Mexico
1800

New York
1652; see also town records from 1640

North Carolina
1696

North Dakota
1872

Ohio
1789

Oklahoma
1886

Oregon
1833

Pennsylvania
1681

Rhode Island
1703; see town records for vital, land, and probate from ca. 1636

South Carolina
1700; prior to 1868 counties were called districts

South Dakota
1862

Tennessee
1779

Texas
1836; see also Spanish records in the Bexar County Archives from 1718

Utah
1852

Vermont
1760; for probate records see probate districts; see also town records

Virginia
1632

Washington
1850

West Virginia
1754

Wisconsin
1772

Wyoming
1864

STATES ALSO HAVING LEGISLATIVE DIVORCES AND MANUMISSIONS

Divorces, legal separations, and petitions for *feme sole* status were passed as private acts or statutes in some states. In some cases lower courts held coterminous jurisdiction with a general assembly, territorial legislature, or other legislative body, making it necessary to check several sets of records to find where the decree was granted. The last state to abolish legislative divorce was Delaware, in 1897. For more information, see the chapters on individual states. Manumissions of slaves granted by legislative acts are also noted here.

Alabama

1818–64 See *Acts of Alabama*, or compiled records by the Alabama Department of Archives and History (film 1653551), for divorces occurring from 1818 to 1864. Legislative manumissions were also allowed from 1805 to 1834.

Arizona

1864–82 Recorded as statutes in the records of the Arizona Territorial Legislature, filed under the Howell Code.

Connecticut

1655–77 See Vols. 1 and 2 of Trumbull, J. Hammond. *The Public Records of the Colony of Connecticut*. 3 Vols. (Hartford: Case, Lockwood, 1850–9, fiche 6051120). There were also some divorces recorded in the acts of the Connecticut State Legislature in the nineteenth century.

Dakota Territory

1862–6 Recorded as private acts of the Dakota Territorial Legislature.

Delaware

1703–1897 Recorded in the titles to private acts of the Delaware State Legislature; indexed in a card file at the Hall of Records in Dover; some have been published for the years 1789 to 1849 in the *Delaware Genealogical Society Journal* (7:46).

Georgia

1798–1835 Granted by the Georgia State Legislature, indexed by the Name File Index at the Georgia Department of Archives and History in Atlanta. Legislative manumissions were also allowed from 1801 to 1865.

Illinois

1809–37 Recorded as acts in the territorial and state legislatures. See "Divorce Documents in the Illinois General Assembly Files and Journals." *Illinois State Genealogical Society Quarterly* 17 (Winter–Fall 1985).

Indiana

1817–51 See Newhard, Malenda E.E. *Divorces and Name Changes Granted by the Indiana Assembly Prior to 1852* (Harlan, IN: The Author, 1981). These were legal separations, not absolute divorces.

Iowa

1838–46 See *Acts and Resolutions Passed at the Several Sessions of the Territorial Legislature of Iowa, 1840–1846* (Des Moines: Secretary of State, 1912).

Kentucky
1792–1849 See *Acts of the General Assembly of the Commonwealth of Kentucky.*

Louisiana
1805-46 See the *Legislative Calendar and Official Journal.*

Maryland
1634–1854 See Meyer, Mary K. *Divorces and Names Changed in Maryland: By Act of the Legislature, 1634–1867* (Mount Airy, MD: Pipe Creek Publications, 1991). Material was taken from the published laws of Maryland. These were not absolute divorces, but legal separations, known as *mensa et thoro.*

Massachusetts
1650–1889 Recorded in the records of the Governor and Council and published in the records of the General Court and the Court of Assistants (see the chapter on Massachusetts).

Michigan
1805–12 Recorded in the acts of the Michigan Territorial Legislature, see *Laws of the Territory of Michigan* (Lansing: W.S. George, 1871).

Mississippi
1817-59 See Pearce, Charles. *Index to the Laws of the Mississippi Territory* (Jackson: Mississippi Department of Archives and History, 1985), and Humphreys, Rena and Mamie Owen. *Index of Mississippi Session Acts, 1817–1865* (Jackson: Tucker Printing House, 1937). Legislative manumissions were also allowed from 1801 to 1865.

Missouri
1833–53 See Blattner, Theresa. *Divorces, Separations, and Annulments in Missouri, 1769–1850* (Bowie, MD: Heritage Books, 1992), and Stanley, Lois. *Divorces and Separations in Missouri, 1808–1853* (Greenville, SC: Southern Historical Press, 1990).

Montana
1863–5 Recorded as private laws in the acts of the Montana Territorial Legislature.

New Hampshire
1680–1774 See *The New Hampshire Provincial and State Papers*. 40 Vols. (Concord: George E. Jenks, 1867–1943, film 1033734 ff.).

New Jersey
1743–1850 See McCracken, George E. "New Jersey Legislative Divorces, 1778–1844." *The American Genealogist* 34 (1958): 107–12, and Hood, John. *Index of Colonial and State Laws of New Jersey, Between the Years 1663–1903 Inclusive* (Camden: Sinnickson & Sons, 1905).

New York
1670–2 See Lincoln, Charles Z. *The Colonial Laws of New York from the Year 1664 to the Revolution*. 5 Vols. (New York: AMS Press, 1894–6), and "Divorce in Colonial New York." *New-York Historical Society Quarterly* 3 (October 1955): 422.

North Carolina

1790–1835 — See McBride, B. Ronan. "Divorces and Separations Granted by Act of the North Carolina Assembly from 1790 to 1818." *North Carolina Genealogical Society Journal* 3 (February (1977): 43–7. For other records, see the "Legislative Papers" at the North Carolina State Archives in Raleigh and the printed session laws of the North Carolina General Assembly. Between 1783 and 1827, at least 265 petitions seeking private acts granting divorce and 238 petitions from women asking to be granted the status of *feme sole* can be found in the Assembly's Committee of Divorce and Alimony.[25] Legislative manumissions were also allowed from 1715 to 1741 and from 1777 to 1831.

Ohio

1803–52 — Granted by the State Supreme Court and requiring an act of legislation. See Null, David G. "Ohio Divorces, 1803-1852." *National Genealogical Society Quarterly* 69 (March 1981): 109–14.

Oregon

1848–53 — Recorded in the acts of the Oregon Territorial Legislature. There is an electronic index at the Oregon State Archives in Salem that indexes all 326 divorce entries.

Pennsylvania

1682–1847 — See Livengood, Candy Crocker. *Genealogical Abstracts of Pennsylvania and the Statutes at Large* (Westminster, MD: Family Line Publications, 1990).

Rhode Island

1644–1851 — Recorded in the records of the Governor and Council and as private acts of the legislature. Most divorces took place before 1749.

South Carolina

none — Divorce was illegal in South Carolina until 1949. Legislative manumissions were also allowed from 1722 to 1800.

Tennessee

1797–1858 — See Bamman, Gale Williams and Debbie W. Spero. *Tennessee Divorces, 1797–1858: Taken from 750 Legislative Petitions and Acts* (Thorndike, MA: Van Volumes Unlimited, 1990).

Texas

1837–41 — Recorded in the acts of the Texas Congress.

Virginia (and West Virginia before 1863)

1803–48 — See Casey, Joseph J. *Personal Names in Hening's Statutes at Large of Virginia, and Sheperd's Continuation* (1896. Reprint. Baltimore: Genealogical Publishing Co., 1967, fiche 6051115); for cases to 1848, see *Acts of the General Assembly of Virginia* (Richmond, 1807–48). Legislative manumissions were also allowed from 1732 to 1782.

---

[25] Helen F.M. Leary and Maurice R. Stirewalt, *North Carolina Genealogical Research: Genealogy and Local History* (Raleigh: North Carolina Genealogical Society, 1980), 290.

Washington

1853–89 Recorded in the territorial district courts and are in the Washington Territory records at the Washington State Library in Olympia. See Washington Division of Archives and Record Management. *Frontier Justice: Abstracts and Indexes to the Records of the Territorial District Courts, 1853–1889* (Olympia: The Secretary of State, 1987).

MANUMISSION RECORDS

Ironically, one of the few legal inheritances that passed from a mother to a child was that of enslavement. Virginia passed a law in 1662 which declared that "all children borne in this country shall be held bond or free according to the condition of their mother." Other colonies passed similar laws, guaranteeing slavery for the children of black mothers.

By 1804, most northern states had either abolished slavery or instituted gradual emancipation acts. The Northwest Ordinance of 1787 prohibited slavery within the Northwest Territory. The states and territories that allowed slavery are as follows:

- The Missouri Compromise of 1820 excluded slavery in states and territories above latitude 36° 30′, except for Missouri. The slave states and territories at that time were: Alabama, Arkansas, Delaware, Florida, Georgia, Kentucky, Louisiana, Maryland, Missouri, North Carolina, South Carolina, Tennessee, and Virginia.
- Texas became a slave state in 1845.
- The Compromise of 1850 added the following territories to those where slavery was legal: New Mexico and Utah.

The Kansas-Nebraska Act of 1854 allowed Kansas and Nebraska to decide as territories on the issue of slavery (both became free states). The 1857 Dred Scott decision by the U.S. Supreme Court made slavery legal in all territories, a decision highly condemned by the population in the free states and territories.

The following table outlines the dates and conditions by which a slave was able to obtain freedom by manumission.

State	Manumissions banned	Act requiring the slave to leave the state	Legislative manumissions allowed	Manumission by certificate allowed	Security required for manumission	Slavery abolished
Alabama	1860	1834-	1805-34	–	1805-34	–
Arkansas	1859	–	–	1804-59	–	–
Connecticut	–	–	–	1777-1848	–	1848 (1784 for children, with service to age 25)
Delaware	–	–	–	1740-67	1740-1852	–
District of Columbia	–	–	–	1796-1862	–	–
Florida	–	1829-	–	–	1829-	–
Georgia	–	–	1801-65	–	–	–
Kentucky	–	1851-	–	–	1794-1851	–
Louisiana	1857	1830-	–	1804-7	1830-55	–
Maine (part of Massachusetts until 1820)	–	–	–	–	see Massachusetts	–
Maryland	1860	1832-	–	1752-1860	1832-	–
Massachusetts (and Maine)	–	–	–	–	1703-80	1780
Mississippi	1857	–	1805-65	–	–	–
Missouri	–	–	–	1804-20	–	–

State	Manumissions banned	Act requiring the slave to leave the state	Legislative manumissions allowed	Manumission by certificate allowed	Security required for manumission	Slavery abolished
New Jersey	–	–	–	1786-	1713-	1846; 1804 for children with service until age 25 (males) and 21 (females)
New Hampshire	–	–	–	–	–	1784
New York	–	–	–	1785-1827	1712-1801	1827; 1799 for children, with service to age 28 (males) and 25 (females)
North Carolina	–	1715-77 1831-	1715-41 1777-1831	–	1801-	–
Pennsylvania	–	–	–	1780-	1726-80	1780; children to serve until age 28
Rhode Island	–	–	–	1784-1842	1728-98	1843 (1784 for children, from birth)
South Carolina	–	1722-1800	1820-65	1800-20	–	–
Tennessee	–	1831-	–	–	1801-51	–
Texas	–	1832-	–	–	1832-	–
Vermont	–	–	–	–	–	1777
Virginia	–	1691-1732 1806-	1723-82	1782-		–

Port Clarence, Alaska
Eskimo woman,
Unger-Kee-Kluk, age 22
(Bureau of American
Ethnology, 1894)

ALABAMA

IMPORTANT DATES IN STATE HISTORY

1702 Mobile founded by French colonists.
1763 Ceded from France to Great Britain.
1783 West Florida portion of Alabama (including Mobile) is ceded from Great Britain to Spain; the rest of Alabama is claimed by Georgia.
1795 The Pinckney Treaty with Spain gives the U.S. all of West Florida above the 31st parallel (does not include Biloxi, Mississippi and Mobile, Alabama).
1796 The U.S. takes possession of the area claimed by Georgia.
1798 Part of the Mississippi Territory.
1802 Georgia cedes its claims to the area.
1812 U.S. forces capture Mobile; West Florida portion of Alabama ceded from Spain to U.S. and called the District of Mobile.
1813 Creek Massacre at Fort Minns.
1817 Organized as a separate U.S. territory.
1819 Statehood.
1821 First laws written; patterned after Mississippi statutes.
1836-7 Federal troops drive Indians from their lands.
1861 11 January secedes from the Union.
1864 Battle of Mobile Bay.
1868 11 June readmitted to the Union.

MARRIAGE AND DIVORCE

1852 marriage settlements must be recorded.
1868 "freedmen and women . . . living together as man and wife, shall be regarded as lawful man and wife (Ord. 23)."
1886 marriages of women under eighteen require a $200.00 bond to be posted with the county judge of probate. The judges are also required to issue marriage licenses.

Where to Find Marriage and Divorce Records

The early county marriage records were usually recorded in the courts of probate. Statewide marriage registration began in 1836 and is indexed from 1936 (film 1907711 ff.) at the Department of Health in Montgomery. Divorces required an act of legislature from 1818 to 1864. After this time they were filed in county chancery courts. After 1917, county circuit courts were given jurisdiction for divorce cases. Lists of county vital records on film, including marriage and divorce, are available online at **<www.ase.edu/archives/reference/vital.html>**. Also given is information on which counties have burned records and the locations of original records. Many county records have been filmed, such as:

- Autauga County Judge of Probate marriage records, 1839-1950 (film 1289186 ff.), at the Autauga County Courthouse in Prattville.
- Etowah County Judge of Probate marriage records, 1867-1928 (film 1035364 ff.), at the Etowah County Courthouse in Gadsden.

For divorce records, see:

- Alabama Chancery Court, First District Southern Division divorce cases, 1816-47 (film 1940655), at the University of South Alabama Archives in Mobile.
- Alabama Bureau of Vital Statistics county divorce reports, 1818-1929; index, 1908-37 (film

1653550 ff.), at the Alabama Department of Archives and History in Montgomery. This includes the early legislative divorces granted between 1818 and 1864.

- Thirteenth Judicial Circuit Court of Alabama, Chancery Court divorce cases, 1816–1917; Circuit Court in Equity divorce cases, 1917–18; and Law and Equity Court in Equity divorce cases, 1907–16 (film 1940898 ff.), at the University of South Alabama Archives.
- *Index to Divorce Cases of the Thirteenth Judicial Court of Alabama, 1916–1918* (Mobile: University of South Alabama Archives, 1994).
- Divorce records and index from 1935 (film 1908984 ff.), at the Department of Health in Montgomery.

There are also published compilations of marriages, such as:

- Gandrud, Pauline Myra Jones. *Marriage, Death and Legal Notices from Early Alabama Newspapers, 1819–1893* (Easley, SC: Southern Historical Press, 1981).
- Vidrine, Jacqueline O. *Love's Legacy: The Mobile Marriages Recorded in French, Transcribed with Annotated Abstracts in English, 1724–1786* (Lafayette, LA: Center for Louisiana Studies, University of Southwestern Louisiana, 1985).

PROPERTY AND INHERITANCE

1853 "all property held before, or acquired after marriage is secured to the married woman's use (§ 1982)," the proceeds of a sale of her property are her separate estate, which the husband may use as he deems most beneficial to her (§ 1985). The husband may receive property coming to her. Her estate is liable for the "necessaries" of the family (§ 1986–9). A "married woman may be entitled to a legacy, or to a distributive share, of the estate of a deceased person (§ 1)." Married women "have a right to dispose of any such property, real or personal, by will, and in case of her death, without having made such disposition, the same shall be divided and distributed as in other cases of intestacy (§ 3)."

1861 Supreme Court rules that in a divorce granted in favor of the wife she will receive the residence and lot in which they reside and the furnishings.

SUFFRAGE

1920 Alabama women receive complete suffrage by passage of the 19th Amendment to the Constitution.

CITIZENSHIP

1796 all residents of Alabama become U.S. citizens by treaty, except for Native Americans, whose tribes are considered a separate nation until 1924.

CENSUS INFORMATION

1855, 1866 state censuses, at the Alabama Department of Archives and History.

OTHER

1886 Alabama begins granting pensions to Confederate widows.

1907, 1921, 1927 censuses of Confederate soldiers in Alabama (film 1533727 ff.), at the Alabama Department of Archives and History. All series give information about wives; the 1927 series gives the birth and marriage of each Confederate widow pensioner.

See also county records, such as cotton mill records, Volunteers Aid Fund (1860s), dower records, etc. For a list of records by county (except for vital records), see **<www.asc.edu/archives/reference/procount.html>**, available online.

BIBLIOGRAPHY

Amos, Harriet E. "City Belles: Images and Realities of the Lives of White Women in Antebellum Mobile." *Alabama Review* 34 (January 1981): 3-19.

Barefield, Marilyn Davis. *Researching in Alabama: A Genealogical Guide* (Easley, SC: Southern Historical Press, 1987).

Boucher, Ann. *Alabama Women: Roles and Rebels* (Troy, AL: Troy State University Press, 1978).

Cott, Nancy F., et al. "Conditions of Women in Rural Alabama [in 1904]," in *Roots of Bitterness: Documents of the Social History of American Women.* 2nd ed. (Boston: Northeastern University Press, 1996), 367-71.

Foley, Helen S. *Marriage and Death Notices from Alabama Newspapers and Family Records, 1819–1890* (Easley, SC: Southern Historical Press, 1981).

Hague, Parthenia A. *A Blockaded Family: Life in Southern Alabama During the Civil War* (Lincoln: University of Nebraska Press, 1991).

Higganbotham, Jay. "Preparation for the Voyage of the Pelican to Louisiana, 1703-1704." *Alabama Historical Society Quarterly* 37 3 (1975): 165-75. Female immigrants from Paris to Mobile.

League of Women Voters of Alabama. *A Collection of Biographies of Women Who Made a Difference in Alabama* (Birmingham: The League, 1995).

Primary Source Material on Women and Alabama Held in the William Stanley Hoole Special Collection Library, The University of Alabama (Montgomery: The Library, 1990).

Saunders, James R. and Elizabeth Stubbs. *Early Settlers of Alabama with Notes and Genealogies* (1899. Reprint. Baltimore: Genealogical Publishing Co., 1969, fiche 6051449).

Sterkx, H.E. *Partners in Rebellion: Alabama Women in the Civil War* (Rutherford, NJ: Fairleigh Dickinson University Press, 1970).

Thomas, Mary Martha. *Riveting and Rationing in Dixie: Alabama Women and the Second World War* (Tuscaloosa: University of Alabama Press, 1987).

—. *Stepping Out of the Shadows: Alabama Women, 1819–1990* (Montgomery: University of Alabama Press, 1995).

Treschel, Gail Andrews. *Alabama Quilts* (Birmingham: Birmingham Museum of Art, 1982).

Wiener, Jonathan M. "Female Planters and Planters' Wives in Civil War and Reconstruction Alabama, 1850-1870." *Alabama Review* 30 2 (1977): 135-49.

SELECTED RESOURCES FOR WOMEN'S HISTORY

Alabama Department of Archives and History
624 Washington Avenue
Montgomery, AL 36130-3601

Women's Army Corps Museum
Building 1077
Fort McClellan, AL 36205-5000

W.S. Hoole Special Collections Library
University of Alabama
PO Box S
Tuscaloosa, AL 35487

Women at War, available online at **<www.redstone.army.mil/history/women/welcome.html>**

Women's History Research Sources at the Alabama Department of Archives and History, available online at **<www.asc.edu/archives/women/cover.cover.html>**

ALASKA

IMPORTANT DATES IN STATE HISTORY

1784 First permanent Russian settlement at Three Saints Bay, Kodiak Island.
1799 Sitka established as a Russian trading post.
1804 Sitka becomes the capital of the Russian settlement.
1834 Russian fort established at Nulato.
1847 Fort Yukon established by the Hudson's Bay Company.
1849 Gold discovered on Kenai Peninsula.
1867 U.S. purchases Alaska from Russia for 7.2 million dollars.
1869 *Sitka Times*, the first newspaper, begins publication.
1872 Gold discovered at Sitka.
1880 Gold discovered at Juneau.
1884 Organic Act establishes federal courts and a governor.
1898 Gold discovered at Nome; homesteading is legalized in Alaska.
1912 Becomes an official territory.
1914 Construction of the Alaska Railroads begins (completed in 1923).
1942 Japanese forces bomb Dutch Harbor and occupy Attu and Kiska Islands. Construction begins on the Alaska-Canada (Alcan) Highway.
1943 U.S. forces retake Japanese-occupied territory.
1956 Constitution adopted.
1959 Statehood.

MARRIAGE AND DIVORCE

1884 federal courts begin issuing marriage licenses.

Where to Find Marriage and Divorce Records

The earliest recorded marriages are in the registers of the Russian Orthodox Church. The original records are at the Library of Congress in Washington, DC, and on microfilm at the NARA Pacific Alaska Region in Anchorage and the University of Alaska in Fairbanks. For more information, see:

- *Index to Baptisms, Marriages, and Deaths in the Archives of the Russian Orthodox Church in Alaska, 1816–1866*. 3 Vols. (Washington, DC: Library of Congress, 1970, film 0944197).
- Kalnins, Zuzanne D. *Indexes to Baptisms, Marriages, and Deaths in the Archives of the Russian Orthodox Greek Catholic Church in Alaska, 1867–1899*. 2 Vols. (Washington, DC: Library of Congress, 1965, film 1445902).
- Dorosh, Elizabeth and John Dorosh. *Index to Baptisms, Marriages, and Deaths in the Archives of the Russian Orthodox Greek Catholic Church in Alaska, 1900–1936* (Washington, DC: Library of Congress, 1964, film 0944197).

A federal district court was created in 1884 and given complete civil and criminal jurisdiction, including issuing marriage licenses and granting divorces. The administration was divided into three districts in 1903 and four districts in 1909. The seats of the district courts are as follows:

- Sitka, 1884–1903
- Eagle City, Juneau, and Saint Michaels, 1903–9
- Fairbanks, Juneau, Nome, and Valdez, 1909–43
- Anchorage, Fairbanks, Juneau, and Nome, 1943–59

The records for Anchorage, Juneau, and some records of the other courts are at the NARA Pacific Alaska Region in Anchorage. Other records remain in the custody of the original courts or their successors. Superior courts in the four judicial districts hold current jurisdiction for divorce, issuing marriage licenses, and probate. There are fifteen boroughs (three unified home-rule municipalities that are combination borough-city and twelve boroughs), and twelve home-rule cities, and the judicial districts cross borough boundaries. For a list of all villages in Alaska that have been given tribal status, see **<www.narf.org/resource/guide/states/ak/htm>**. Territorial marriage registration began in 1913 and is kept at the Bureau of Vital Statistics in Juneau. State divorce registration began in 1950. Alaska's regional geographical divisions are districts, boroughs, and reservations, not counties. See also:

- Bradbury, Connie, David A. Hales, and Nancy Lesh. *Index to Births, Deaths, Marriages, and Divorces in Fairbanks Newspapers, 1903 to 1930* (Anchorage: Anchorage Historical Commission, 1986).
- Miller, Betty J. *Vital Records from Alaska Daily Empire, Juneau, Alaska [1916–1925]*. 2 Vols. (Juneau: The Author, 1994).
- —. *1898–1922 Vital Records of Alaska and the Yukon as Reported in the Weekly Douglas Island Newspaper, Douglas, Alaska* (Juneau: The Author, 1991).

PROPERTY AND INHERITANCE

1884 federal district courts hold jurisdiction over all civil and criminal cases.

1898 homesteading begins in Alaska.

1959 a superior court, a supreme court, and magistrate courts are created. Superior district courts have jurisdiction for probate records; the District Recorder maintains land records.

SUFFRAGE

1913 the territorial legislature gives Alaska women (non-native) complete suffrage.

CITIZENSHIP

1867 all residents of Alaska become U.S. citizens by treaty, except for Native Americans, whose tribes are considered a separate nation until 1924.

CENSUS INFORMATION

The first federal census for Alaska was in 1900.

There have been miscellaneous censuses of posts, villages, and islands. The following have been filmed (film 0982947):

- Census of Eskimos at the Cape Smythe Village for 1885
- Censuses of Saint Paul Island for 1870, 1904, and 1906
- Censuses of Sitka for 1870, 1880, and 1881
- Annual censuses of the Pribilof Islands for 1890–5

OTHER

1877 the first woman missionary in Alaska arrives at Fort Wrangell.

1913 the first Alaska Pioneers' Home is established at Sitka. Some records have been abstracted in Anderson, Thayne I. *Alaska Death Listing for Cemeteries, Pioneer Homes, and Hospitals* (Fairbanks: The Author, 1986).

The Alaska and Polar Regions Department, Rasmuson Library, University of Alaska, Fairbanks, has in-house databases that include the Pioneers of Alaska Index, the Alaska Newspaper Tree Database, and Alaska Oral Histories Database. For more information, see **<www.urova.fi/home/arktinen/ploarweb/polar/lbuserlu.htm>**.

BIBLIOGRAPHY

Ackerman, Maria. *Tlingit Stories* (Anchorage: Alaska Methodist University Press, 1977).

The Alaska-Yukon Gold Book: A Roster of the Progressive Men and Women Who Were the Argonauts of the Klondike Gold Stampede (Seattle: Sourdough Stampede Association, 1930, film 1598025).

Alberts, Laurie. "Petticoats and Pickaxes." *Alaska Journal* VII (1977): 146–59.

Anchorage Community College. *Alaska Women's Oral History Collection: Catalogue with Subject Index* (Anchorage: The College, 1983).

Backhouse, Frances. *Women of the Klondike* (Vancouver, BC: Whitecap Books, 1995).

Bradbury, Connie. *Genealogical Record of Point Hope, Wainwright, and Anatuvuk Pass, Alaska Eskimo Families* (Fairbanks: n.p., 1986, film 1035774).

Case, David S. *Alaska Natives and American Laws* (Fairbanks: University of Alaska Press, 1984).

Chase, William Henry. *Pioneers of Alaska: The Trail Blazers of Bygone Days* (Kansas City: Burton Publishing Co., 1951).

Chevigny, Hector. *Russian America: The Great Alaskan Adventure, 1741–1867* (New York: Viking Press, 1965).

DeArmond, Robert N. *Alaska's Book: Story of Our Northern Treasureland* (Chicago: J.G. Ferguson, 1960).

Ferrell, Ed. *Biographies of Alaska-Yukon Pioneers, 1850–1950*. 3 Vols. (Bowie, MD: Heritage Press, 1997).

Fields, Leslie Leyland. *The Entangling Net: Alaska's Commercial Fishing Women Tell Their Lives* (Urbana: University of Illinois Press, 1997).

Giffen, Naomi M. *The Roles of Men and Women in Eskimo Culture* (1930. Reprint. Washington, DC: Library of Congress, n.d., film 1009060).

Graham, Roberta L. *A Sense of History: A Reference Guide to Alaska's Women* (Anchorage: Alaska Women's Commission, 1985).

Grauman, Melody W. "Women and Culture in Russian America." *American West* 11 3 (1974): 24–31.

Hales, David A. "Genealogy Sources in Alaska." *The Sourdough* 20 (1983).

Inglis, Gordon B. "Northwest American Matriliny: The Problem of Origins." *Ethnology* 9 2 (1970): 149–59.

Jones, H. Wendy. *Women Who Braved the Far North: 200 Years of Alaskan Women* (San Diego: Grossmont Press, 1976).

Koester, Susan H. "By the Words of Thy Mouth Let Thee Be Judged: The Alaska Native Sisterhood Speaks." *Journal of the West* 27 (April 1988): 35–44.

Leahy, Marilyn. *Women of Juneau* (Juneau: Alaska Historical Commission Studies in History, n.d.).

Lake, Gretchen L. and David A. Hales. "Alaska's Native Population: Sources for Research." *National Genealogical Society Quarterly* 83 4 (December 1995): 277–92.

Leary, Lori B. *Alaska Women: Yesterday, Today & Tomorrow* (Anchorage: Alaska Viewpoint, 1990).

Mayer, Melanie J. *Klondike Women: True Tales of the 1897–1899 Gold Rush* (Columbus: Swallow Press, 1989).

Morehouse, Thomas A., et al. *Alaska's Urban and Rural Governments* (Lanham, MD: University Press of America, 1984).

Morgan, Lael. *Good Time Girls: Of the Alaska Yukon Gold Rush* (Seattle: Epicenter Press, 1998).

Murphy, Claire R. and Jane G. Haigh. *Gold Rush Women* (Anchorage: Alaska Northwest Books, 1997).

National Archives and Records Administration. *Documenting Alaskan History: Guide to Federal Archives Relating to Alaska* (Washington, DC: The Archives, 1982).

Webb, Melody. *The Last Frontier* (Albuquerque: University of New Mexico Press, 1985).

SELECTED RESOURCES FOR WOMEN'S HISTORY

Alaska Native Language Center
University of Alaska
ANLC Box 111
Fairbanks, AK 99775-0120

Archives and Manuscript Department
University of Alaska
3211 Providence Drive, K-106
Anchorage, AK 99508

Carrie McLain Memorial Museum
PO Box 1686
Nome, AK 99762

Elmer E. Rasmuson Library
University of Alaska Archives
Fairbanks, AK 99775

U.S. National Park Service
Sitka National Historical Park Library
106 Metlakatla Street
Sitka, AK 99835

Alaska Genealogy, available online at **<www.educ.state.ak.us/lam/library/is/akgene.html>**

How to Find Your Gold Rush Relative: Sources on the Klondike and Alaska Gold Rushes, 1896–1914, available online at **<www.educ.state.ak.us/lam/library/hist/parham.html>**

Pan for Gold Database: Women of the Golden North Fraternal Organization, available online at **<www.gold-rush.org/pan/gol_norb.htm>**

Women in Alaska's History, available online at **<library.advanced. org/11313/>**

ARIZONA

IMPORTANT DATES IN STATE HISTORY

1629 First missions founded by the Franciscans in northeastern Arizona.
1692 Jesuit missions founded in southeastern Arizona.
1726 Spanish settlers found Tubac.
1776 First Spanish settlement founded at Tucson.
1821 Part of the Mexican department of New Mexico.
1846 Cooke's Wagon Road opened to California by the Mormon Battalion.
1848 Acquired from Mexico in the Treaty of Guadalupe-Hildago.
1850 Becomes part of the New Mexico Territory.
1852 Under the jurisdiction of New Mexico courts.
1853 Gadsen Purchase adds territory south of the Gila River in Mexico.
1862 Confederate Congress organizes the Territory of Arizona; Texans occupy Tucson.
1863 Congress organizes Arizona into a separate U.S. territory; the territorial laws of New Mexico are continued.
1864 First territorial legislature repeals all laws of Spain, Mexico, and New Mexico, and establishes English common law.
1866 Northwestern portion of the territory ceded to Nevada.
1910 Constitution adopted.
1912 Statehood.

MARRIAGE AND DIVORCE

1864 dower is recognized (Howell Code Ch. 61 § 1).
1865 first statute on community property is enacted, and dower is repealed; pre-marital agreements are allowed, as long as they do not "alter the legal order of descent."
1887 county recorders are required to issue marriage licenses.
1889 marriage certificates replace marriage licenses.
1891 county clerks of probate begin issuing marriage licenses.
1913 common-law marriage is abrogated (§ 3844).

Where to Find Marriage and Divorce Records

The earliest marriages were recorded in the parish registers of the Catholic Church. Records for Tucson, 1793–1849, are available on microfilm at the University of Arizona in Tucson. There are also records for Tucson at the Magdalena Parish Archives in Sonora, Mexico that date from 1684.[26] Parish registers for San José de Tumacácori (near Tubac), 1768–1825, are on microfilm at the Arizona Historical Society in Tucson. Arizona civil records before 1862 are found in New Mexico territorial courts. County recorders in Arizona kept marriage records after 1864. From 1891 to 1912 the clerks of probate recorded marriages. Marriages since 1912 have been recorded by the clerk of the superior court. Inventories of Arizona county records can be found online at **<www.dlapr.lib.az.us/archives/local.htm>**. The earliest divorces were recorded as statutes in the Arizona Territorial Legislature. From 1864 to 1912, the county district courts held jurisdiction for divorce cases, and the county superior court after 1912. Many county records have been filmed, such as:

- Maricopa County Recorder marriage records, 1871–1942 (film 1955594 ff.), and Maricopa

---

[26] See Cara Richards de Dobyns, *Archivo histórico de Sonora, Museo del Estado de Sonora: indice de lo que contiene un legajo de este archivo, como ejemplo de los muchos documentos tocante del la historia del actual estado de Arizona que ya existe en él* (Sonora: The Author, 1978, film 1162420).

County Superior Court marriage affidavits, 1894–1934 (film 1926701 ff.), at the Arizona State Archives in Phoenix.

See also indexes and compiled publications, such as:

- CD-ROM: *Territorial Vital Records: Births, Divorces, Guardianships, Marriages, Naturalizations, Wills; 1800s Thru 1906 Utah Territory, Arizona, Colorado, Idaho, Nevada, Wyoming, Indian Territory; LDS Branches, Wards; Deseret News Vital Records; J.P. Marriages; Methodist Marriages* (Saint George, UT: Genealogical CD Publishing, 1994).
- Bake, Blaine. *Some Early Arizona Marriages, 1862–1912* (Rexburg, ID: Upper Snake River Family History Center, 1993).
- Whiteside, Dora M. *Arizona Territorial Marriage Records Index, 1985–1912, of Yavapai County, Prescott, Arizona* (n.p.: The Author, 1988).

PROPERTY AND INHERITANCE

1913 a married woman has the same legal rights as a man aged twenty-one years or older; no real estate held as community property may be conveyed unless both spouses join in the deed, except for mining claims; the husband holds absolute rights of personalty held as community property.

SUFFRAGE

1912 Arizona women receive complete suffrage. Voting registers, known as great registers, usually include a person's name, county of nativity, occupation, local residence, and other information.

CITIZENSHIP

1848 all residents of Arizona become U.S. citizens by legislation of Congress, except for Native Americans, whose tribes are considered a separate nation until 1924.

CENSUS INFORMATION

For pre-territorial federal censuses, see New Mexico Territory (1850 and 1860).

1766–1801 see Platt, Lyman D. *Census Records for Latin America and the Hispanic United States* (Baltimore: Genealogical Publishing Co., 1998).

1864 territorial census (film 0897437).

1866 territorial census (film 0928107).

1867 census of Mohave, Pima, and Yuma counties (not at FHL).

1869 census of Yavapai County (not at FHL).

1872, 1874, 1876, and 1882 territorial censuses (not at FHL).

Territorial census enumerations, not complete for all counties, are at the Arizona State Archives.

OTHER

The database index, *Documentary Relations of the Southwest*, at the Arizona State Museum, University of Arizona, Tucson, is a guide to archival materials relating to New Spain, 1520 to 1821. Included are family history-related materials on residents of the Southwest. States covered are Arizona, California, New Mexico, and Texas, and also Mexico. There are plans to publish this database on CD-ROM. Some of the indexes are:

- BIOFILE Master Bibliography List and Index, covering records in the Bexar Archives, University of Texas, Austin; the Spanish Archives of New Mexico, Series II, Sante Fe; the Provincias Internas, Archivo General de la Nacion, Mexico City; the Archivo de Parral, Parral, Chihuahua; and other documents in European and American archives.
- BIOFILE Relatives and Household Members Index, which links spouses and other relatives to the individual on the master list.
- BIODEX to 44,715 names of persons found in secondary works.

- Other geographic and bibliographic indexes.

1870–1880 *An Original Register of Names of Some Travelers Crossing the Arizona-Utah Border by Way of Lee's Ferry, Recorded at Houserock Spring, 1870s to 1880s* (n.p., 1989, fiche 6100896).
1944 census of Gila River Japanese concentration camp, Gila River Relocation Center (film 0496524).

BIBLIOGRAPHY

Conte, Christine. "Ladies, Livestock, Land and the Lucre: Women's Networks and Social Status on the Western Navajo Reservation." *American Indian Quarterly* 6 (1982): 105–24.

Crowe, Rosalie and Diane Tod. *Arizona Women's Hall of Fame* (Phoenix: Arizona Historical Society, 1986).

Fisher, Christiane. "A Profile of Women in Arizona Frontier Days." *Journal of the West* 16 3 (July 1977): 42–53

Frost, Helen Y. and Pam Knight Stevenson. *Grand Endeavors: Vintage Arizona Quilts and Their Makers* (Flagstaff: Northland, 1992).

Johnson, Susan. "Women's Households and Relationships in the Mining West: Central Arizona, 1863–1873." Unpublished Master's Thesis. Arizona State University, 1984.

Katz, William Loren. "Mail-Order Brides of the Southwest," in *Black Women of the Old West* (New York: Atheneum Books, 1995), 34–7.

Kelly, Rita Mae. *Women and the Arizona Political Process* (Lanham, MD: University Press of America, 1988).

McCarly, Kiernan. *Desert Documentary: The Spanish Years, 1767–1821* (Tucson: Arizona Historical Society, 1976).

Men and Women of Arizona: Past and Present (1940. Reprint. Tucson: W.C. Cox, 1974, film 0934829).

Overstreet, Daphne. *Arizona Territory Cook Book: Recipes from 1864 to 1912* (Phoenix: Golden West Publishers, 1997).

Peterson, Charles S. *Take Up Your Mission: Mormon Colonizing Along the Little Colorado River, 1870–1900* (Tucson: University of Arizona Press, 1973).

Roberts, Virginia Culin. *With Their Own Blood: A Saga of Southwestern Pioneers* (Fort Worth: Texas Christian University Press, 1992).

—. "Heroines on the Arizona Frontier: The First Anglo-American Women." *Journal of Arizona History* 23 (1982): 11–34.

Rothschild, Mary Logan and Pamela Claire Hronck. *Doing What the Day Brought: An Oral History of Arizona Women* (Tucson: University of Arizona Press, 1992).

Shaw, Anna Moore. *A Pima Past* (Tucson: University of Arizona Press, 1974).

Spiros, Joyce V. Hawley. *Genealogical Guide to Arizona and Nevada* (Gallup, NM: Verlene Publishing, 1983, fiche 6049613).

Stevens, Kathy. *Varied People, Arizona's Indians: A Sourcebook of References, Materials, and Teaching Tools on American Indian Women* (Phoenix: Arizona Department of Education, 1986).

Ward, Margery W. *Register of the Records of Mormon Settlements in Arizona* (Salt Lake City: University of Utah Libraries, 1974, fiche 6331347).

SELECTED RESOURCES FOR WOMEN'S HISTORY

Arizona Department of Library, Archives, and Public Records
1700 West Washington
Phoenix, AZ 85007

Arizona Historical Society Library
1242 North Central Avenue
Phoenix, AZ 85004

Arizona Historical Society, Manuscript Division
949 East Second Street
Tucson, AZ 85719

Cline Library, Special Collections
Northern Arizona State University
PO Box 6022
Flagstaff, AZ 86002-6002

Hayden Memorial Library
Department of Archives and Manuscripts
Arizona State University
Tempe, AZ 85287

Heard Museum of Native Cultures and Art
22 East Monte Vista Road
Phoenix, AZ 85004

Pimeria Alta Historical Society
PO Box 2281
223 Grand Avenue
Nogales, AZ 85628

Sharlott Hall Museum
415 West Gurley Street
Prescott, AZ 86301

University of Arizona Southwest Institute for Research on Women
102 Douglass Building
Tucson, AZ 85721

Woven by the Grandmothers, available online at **<www.heard.org/gallery/woven.htm>**

ARKANSAS

IMPORTANT DATES IN STATE HISTORY

1700 Area under French Civil Law and the Custom of Paris.
1763 Ceded from France to Spain.
1800 Ceded from Spain to France.
1803 Part of the Louisiana Purchase.
1804 Part of the District of Louisiana attached to the Indiana Territory.
1805 Part of the Louisiana Territory.
1812 Part of the Missouri Territory.
1819 Organized as a separate territory.
1836 Territorial constitution adopted, based on the common laws of Missouri, Tennessee, Alabama, and Mississippi.
1836 Statehood.
1861 6 May secedes from the Union.
1868 20 June readmitted to the Union.
1874 Constitution adopted.

MARRIAGE AND DIVORCE

1852 recording of marriage contracts is mandated by law.
1901 county clerks are required to issue marriage licenses.

Where to Find Marriage and Divorce Records

Marriage records have been recorded in the county clerk's office since 1820. State registration began in 1917 and is kept at the Division of Vital Records in Little Rock. County circuit and chancery courts have held jurisdiction for divorce cases since the creation of the counties. Selected county records, 1797–1950, are available on microfilm at the Arkansas History Commission in Little Rock. Many county records have been filmed, such as:

- Benton County Clerk marriage records, 1861–1952 (film 1034660 ff.), Benton County Circuit Court records, 1837–84 (film 1035157 ff.), and Benton County Chancery Court records, 1843–1952 (film 1995053 ff.), at the Benton County Courthouse in Bentonville. Divorces are not indexed separately.
- Pulaski County Clerk marriage records, 1838-51, index, 1820–1971 (film 1302792 ff.), and Pulaski County Chancery Court divorce records, 1882–1900 (film 1302850 ff.), at the Pulaski County Courthouse in Little Rock.

See also compiled publications, such as:

- Morgan, James Logan. *Arkansas Marriage Records, 1807–1835* (Conway: Arkansas Research, 1994).
- ——. *Arkansas Marriage Notices, 1819–1845* (Conway: Arkansas Research, 1992).

PROPERTY AND INHERITANCE

1846 any married woman "may become seised and possessed of any property, real or personal . . . in her own right and name . . . provided the same does not come from the husband after coverture (§ 1)." Slaves owned by her before marriage "and their natural increase shall continue to her not withstanding her coverture (§ 2)." Control and management of such slaves "shall remain to the husband agreeably to the laws heretofore in force (§ 4)." Slaves owned by a *feme covert* may be sold by joint deed of a husband and wife (§ 5). A married woman's property is defined when "she and her husband shall make out a schedule of the property derived through her, under oath, which shall be verified by the oath of some other reputable person; which shall be filed in the recorder's office of the county within which the property is, as well as which they live (§ 7)."

1852 "the property of a female, whether real or personal, and whether acquired before or after marriage, in her own right, shall not be sold to pay the debts of her husband . . . (§ 22)."

1852 a married woman cannot serve as an executrix or administratrix; a married woman cannot make a will unless empowered by a marriage settlement or by her husband.

1874 a married woman's separate property is established as that owned by her prior to or acquired during marriage.

SUFFRAGE

1917 women become eligible to vote in primary elections.

1920 Arkansas women receive complete suffrage by passage of the 19th Amendment to the Constitution.

CITIZENSHIP

1803 all residents of Arkansas become U.S. citizens by legislation, except for Native Americans, whose tribes are considered a separate nation until 1924.

CENSUS INFORMATION

1823 and 1829 sheriff's censuses (not at FHL).

1865 census for Washington County, published in Maxwell, Nancy. *Washington County, Arkansas Sheriff's Census for 1865* (Bowie, MD: Heritage Books, 1993).

1911 census of Confederate veterans, published in McLane, Bobbie Jones. *Arkansas 1911 Census of Confederate Veterans*. 3 Vols. (n.p., 1977–81, fiche 6019335). Includes family information.

These records are at the Arkansas History Commission.

OTHER

1891 Arkansas begins granting pensions to Confederate widows. Confederate pension applications (film 1722443 ff.) are at the Arkansas History Commission. See Ingmire, Frances T. *Arkansas Confederate Veterans and Widows' Pension Applications* (Saint Louis: The Author, 1985). See also Pickett, Connie. *Old Soldiers Home: Arkansas Confederate Soldiers and Widows* (Saint Louis: Francis T. Ingmire, 1985).

BIBLIOGRAPHY

Arkansas Division, United Daughters of the Confederacy. *The Garden of Memories: Stories of the Civil War as Told by the Veterans and Daughters of the Confederacy* (Camden, AR: Brown Printing, 1911).

Arkansas Quilt Guild. *Arkansas Quilts* (Paducah, KY: American Quilters Society, 1988).

Arnold, Morris S. *Arkansas Colonials: A Collection of French and Spanish Records Listing Early Europeans in the Arkansas, 1686–1804* (Gillet, AR: Grand Prairie Historical Society, 1986).

Clark, Mrs. Larry P. *Arkansas Pioneers and Allied Families* (Little Rock: The Author, fiche 6051363).

Dougan, Michael B. *Confederate Women of Arkansas in the Civil War* (1907. Reprint. Fayetteville, AR: M & M Press, 1993, film 1425569).

—. "The Arkansas Married Woman's Property Law." *Arkansas History Quarterly* 46 (Spring 1987): 3–26.

Elliot, Wendy L. *Guide to Genealogical Research in Arkansas* (Bountiful, UT: American Genealogical Lending Library, 1987, fiche 6117559).

Evins, Janie S. "Arkansas Women: Their Contribution to Society, Politics, and Business, 1865–1900." *Arkansas History Quarterly* 44 (Summer 1985): 118–33.

Jacoway, Elizabeth. *Behold: Our Works Were Good: A Handbook of Arkansas Women's History* (Little Rock: Women's History Institute, 1987).

Luster, Michael. *Stitches in Time: A Legacy of Ozark Quilts* (Rogers, WR: Rogers Historical Museum, 1986).

Patterson, Ruth Polk. *The Seed of Sally Good'n: A Black Family in Arkansas, 1833–1953* (Lexington: University of Kentucky Press, 1983).

Ragsdale, William O. *They Sought a Land: A Settlement in the Arkansas River Valley, 1840–1870* (Little Rock: University of Arkansas Press, 1997).

SELECTED RESOURCES FOR WOMEN'S HISTORY

Arkansas History Commission
Arkansas State Library
1 Capitol Mall
Little Rock, AR 72201

Arkansas State University Museum
Arkansas State University
PO Box 490
State University, AR 72467

Arkansas Women's History Institute
PO Box 77
Little Rock, AR 72217

Women's Studies Program
University of Arkansas at Little Rock
2801 South University
Little Rock, AR 72204

Manuscript Resources for Women's Studies, available online at **<cavern.uark.edu/libinfo/speccoll/specwom.html>**

Trade cards for thread and sewing machines (Author collection)

CALIFORNIA

IMPORTANT DATES IN STATE HISTORY

1768 First Spanish governor is appointed; civil law administered under Mexican jurisdiction.

1812 Russians establish a fort at the site of Fort Ross (sold to John Sutter in 1841).

1821 Created as a province of Mexico.

1835 More than three hundred Americans have settled in California.

1837 Mexican laws are adopted, recognizing the existing government of the Tribunal Superior, the Court of First Instance, *Alcades*, Prefects, Justices of the Peace, and *Ayuntamientos* (town councils).

1846 U.S. forces occupy San Francisco and San Diego.

1848 Acquired from Mexico in the Treaty of Guadalupe-Hildago; gold discovered at Sutter's Mill.

1849 U.S. Army general appointed defacto governor of California; he recognizes the existing government. A constitution is drafted. The California gold rush begins.

1850 Statehood.

1872 Modoc War (ends 1873).

1873 State legislature codifies its laws.

1906 Major earthquake strikes San Francisco.

MARRIAGE AND DIVORCE

1850 marriages may be performed by judges, justices of the peace, and all clergy; records must be sent to the county recorder. Pre-marital agreements are allowed, but may not "alter the legal orders of descent" (deleted in 1872). "Marriages of white persons with Negroes and mulattoes" are null and void.

1852 mental suffering is allowed as grounds for divorce.

1872 common-law marriage is recognized as legal.

1873 community property is divided "in such proportions as the court . . . may deem just," for divorce on grounds of extreme cruelty; a divorced woman may claim one-half of the community property.

1895 common-law marriage is abrogated (§ 55).

Where to Find Marriage and Divorce Records

The earliest marriage records are in the parish registers of the California missions. Many of the missions still in existence maintain archives that include parish registers, *padrones*, and other records. The Bancroft Library at the University of California, Berkeley, also holds originals and copies of many records. See filmed records and published indexes, such as:

- Mission San Luis Obispo de Tolosa registers, 1772–1906 (film 0913300), at the Diocesan Pastoral Office, Monterey, and at the California State Archives in Sacramento.
- Corral, Ralph Francis. *Index to Baptismal Records, Santa Clara Mission, 1777–1855* (n.p., 1979, film 1036271).

Marriage records were filed with the county recorder from 1850 to 1905. Statewide registration began in 1905 and is kept by the State Department of Health in Sacramento. Superior courts have held jurisdiction for divorce cases, and the county clerk has custody of the records. The California State Archives also has an index of inquiries regarding vital records, early nineteenth century to 1920 (film 1711369 ff.). The State Archives has original and microfilm copies of records from twenty-seven counties. Inventories of local government records at the State Archives and the at FHL are available online at **<www.ss.ca.gov/archives/ level3_county.htm>.** The following county marriage records are available at the State Archives: Alameda (1854–1955),

Amador (1905–25), Butte (1851–1933), Colusa (1907–22), El Dorado (1859–1932), Fresno (1856–1919), Imperial (1903–23), Marin (1873–1936), Napa (1893–1939), Placer (1852–1938), Santa Clara (1846–1919), Stanislaus (1854–1920), Sutter (1889–1930), Yolo (1906–20), and Yuba (1897–1923). Many county records have been filmed, such as:

- Calaveras County Recorder marriage records, 1854–1905 (film 1302999 ff.), at the Calaveras County Government Center in San Andreas.
- Los Angeles County Clerk marriage applications, 1850–1905, and marriage certificates and index, 1851–1919 (film 1033120 ff.), at the Los Angeles County Courthouse in Los Angeles.

See also compiled publications, such as:

- Bayless, Dorothy M. and M. Georgeann Mello. *Index to Early Court Records of Sacramento, California* (Sacramento: The Author, 1982). Includes a register of divorces.
- —— . *Marriage Affidavits, 1893–1897, Sacramento County, California* (Sacramento: The Authors, 1981).
- Clary, Jeanne B. *Los Angeles County Marriages, 1851–1877, With Consolidated Index* (Burbank: Southern California Genealogical Society, 1989).

PROPERTY AND INHERITANCE

1849 territorial constitution enacts first community property law, referred to as "property held in common with the husband," and "the husband shall have entire management and control of the common property . . . and the rents and profits of the separate estate of either the husband or the wife shall be deemed common property."

1850 property owned before marriage remains separate after marriage; "all property acquired after the marriage by either husband or wife except such as may be acquired by gift, bequest, devise, or descent, shall be common property (Art. XI § 14)." A married woman may become a *feme sole* trader within six months of residency, by judgment of a county court.

1872 rents, issues, and profits of separate property of either spouse shall be their separate property.

1876 a married woman may not devise her half of community property; upon the death of the wife, the husband inherits all the community property; a widow inherits only one-half of the community property.

1913 the California Alien Land Law prohibits aliens who are ineligible for citizenship to purchase farm land or to lease it for more than three years.

SUFFRAGE

1911 California women receive complete suffrage.

CITIZENSHIP

1848 all residents of California become U.S. citizens by legislation of Congress, except for Native Americans, whose tribes are considered a separate nation until 1924.

CENSUS INFORMATION

1790, 1836, and 1844 census records, *padrones*, see:

- *1790 Padron of California* (n.p., n.d., film 1036747). This is copied from "Las Familias de California" section in *Southern California Historical Society Quarterly*.
- Eldredge, Zoeth S. *Index to the Padrones* (Berkeley, CA: The Author, n.d.).

1770–1845 censuses see Platt, Lyman D. *Census Records for Latin America and the Hispanic United States* (Baltimore: Genealogical Publishing Co., 1998).

1852 state census (film 0909229 ff.).
Most of the colonial and all of the state censuses are at the California State Archives.

OTHER

1866 a black woman in San Francisco successfully sues for the right to testify against a white person.
1880 ordinance of the City of San Francisco makes it illegal to operate a laundry in the city without approval of the Board of Supervisors (board turns down all applications of Chinese aliens; law declared illegal by California Supreme Court in 1888).

BIBLIOGRAPHY

Beasley, Delilah. "California Colored Women Trail Blazers," in Brown, Hallie Q., *Homespun Heroines and Other Women of Distinction* (1926. Reprint. New York: Oxford University Press, 1988).

Dresser, Norine. "Marriage Customs in Early California." *The Californians* (November/December 1991).

Griswold, Robert. "Apart But Not Adrift: Wives, Divorce, and Independence in California, 1859–1890." *Pacific Historical Review* 49 (May 1980): 265–83.

—— . *Family and Divorce in California, 1850–1890: Victorian Illusions and Everyday Realities* (Albany: State University of New York Press, 1982).

Haskins, Charles Warren. *The Argonauts of California* (New York: Fords, Howard & Hulbert, 1890, fiche 6051188). For an index, see Spinazze, Libera M. *Index to the Argonauts of California* (New Orleans: Polyanthos, 1975, fiche 6051192).

Hirata, Lucie Cheng. "Chinese Immigrant Women in Nineteenth-Century California," in Berkin, Carol and Mary Beth Norton, *Women of America: A History* (Boston: Houghton Mifflin, 1979), 225–53.

Hoexter, Corinne K. *From Canton to California: The Epic of Chinese Immigration* (New York: Four Winds Press, 1976).

Holmes, Kenneth L. *Covered Wagon Women: Diaries and Letters from the Western Trails, 1852: The California Trail.* Vol. 4 (Lincoln: University of Nebraska Press, 1997).

Jensen, Joan and Gloria Lothrop. *California Women: A History* (Sparks, NV: Materials for Today's Learning, 1988).

Lapp, Rudolph. *Blacks in Gold Rush California* (New Haven: Yale University Press, 1977).

Laury, Jean Ray. *Ho for California! Pioneer Women and Their Quilts* (New York: E.P. Dutton /California Heritage Quilt Project, 1990).

Levy, Joann. *They Saw the Elephant: Women in the California Gold Rush* (Albuquerque: University of New Mexico Press, 1992).

Lothrop, Jensen. *California Women: A History* (New York: Heinle & Heinle Publishing, 1988).

Lortie, Francis. *San Francisco's Black Community, 1870–1890* (San Francisco: R & E Research Associates, 1976).

Myres, Sandra L. *Ho for California! Women's Overland Trail Diaries from the Huntington Library* (San Marino, CA: Huntington Library, 1980).

Northrop, Marie E. *Spanish-Mexican Families of Early California, 1769–1850.* 2 Vols. (New Orleans: Polyanthos, 1976). Organized by male heads of families, with a cross-index to every name, including wives and daughters.

Parker, J. Carlyle. *An Index to the Biographies in the 19th Century California County Histories* (Detroit: Gale Research, 1979).

Patterson, Victoria D. "Indian Life in the City: A Glimpse of the Urban Experience of Pomo Women in the 1930s." *California History* (Fall 1992): 402–31.

Sandoval, Dennis M. "The Search for the Holy Grail: The Quest to Preserve the Benefits of Community Property Ownership Under California's Transmutation Statute." *Western State University Law Review* 24 (Fall 1996): 157–92.

Sherer, Lorraine M. "The Clan System of the Fort Mojave Indians: A Contemporary." *Southern California Quarterly* 47 1 (1965) 1–72. Gathering of Mojave clan names, 1859–90.

Smith, Jean M. "The Voting Women of San Diego, 1920." *Journal of San Diego History* 26 2 (1980): 133–54.

Temple, Thomas W. *An Alphabetical Listing of the California Mission Vital Records* (Salt Lake City: Genealogical Society of Utah, fiche 6047009).

Yung, Judy. "Bowlful of Tears: Chinese Women Immigrants on Angel Island." *Frontiers* II (Summer 1977): 52–5.

SELECTED RESOURCES FOR WOMEN'S HISTORY

Bancroft Library
University of California
Berkeley, CA 94720

California Historical Society Library
2099 Pacific Avenue
San Francisco, CA 94109-2896

California State Archives
1020 "O" Street, Room 130
Sacramento, CA 95814-5719

Department of Special Collections
University of California
405 Hildegard Avenue
Los Angeles, CA 90024

Ella Strong Denison Library
Scripps College
1030 Columbia
Claremont, CA 91711

Henry E. Huntington Library
1151 Oxford Road
San Marino, CA 91108

California

Institute for Research on Women and Gender
Stanford University
Sarra House
Stanford, CA 94305-8640

National Women's History Project
7738 Bell Road
Windsor, CA 95492-8518

Pasadena Historical Society
470 West Walnut Street
Pasadena, CA 91103

Women's Heritage Museum
870 Market Street
San Francisco, CA 94102

Women's History Reclamation Project
1436 31st Street
San Diego, CA 92102

Cooking demonstration, Kassabian's Furniture & Appliance Store, Meriden, Connecticut, 1948, Levon Kassabian (Author's father) in upper right-hand corner (Author collection)

COLORADO

IMPORTANT DATES IN STATE HISTORY

1803 Most of Colorado is part of the Louisiana Purchase.
1840s Mexican land grants issued in southeastern Colorado.
1848 Remainder of Colorado acquired from Mexico in the treaty of Guadalupe Hildago.
1851 San Luis established by settlers from Rio Arriba, New Mexico.
1854 Colorado is part of the territories of Kansas, Nebraska, New Mexico, and Utah.
1858 Pike's Peak gold rush draws more than 50,000 settlers; Denver founded.
1859 Unofficially organized by local miners as the Jefferson Territory.
1861 Organized as a U.S. territory from lands in the Kansas, Nebraska, New Mexico, and Utah territories; seventeen counties established.
1863 Indian wars with the Cheyenne, Arapahoe, Kiowa, and Comanche (end 1869).
1864 Cheyenne and Arapahoe wars; massacre of 150 Cheyenne Indians (mostly women and children) at Sandy Creek.
1870 Railroad lines connect Denver to other cities.
1876 Statehood; constitution written.
1881 Western Colorado opened for white settlement.

MARRIAGE AND DIVORCE

1883 county clerks are required to issue marriage licenses.

Where to Find Marriage and Divorce Records

Marriages have been recorded by the county clerk and recorder's offices since 1861. County district courts have held jurisdiction for divorces since the creation of the counties. Very few county records have been filmed by the FHL, such as:

- Denver County Clerk marriage extracts, 1849–80 (film 0928067), at the Denver County Courthouse in Denver.
- Arapahoe County Recorder of Deeds records, 1860–1934 (film 1954194), containing some marriage certificates, at the Colorado State Archives in Denver.

There is a statewide marriage index, 1890–1939 (film 1690047 ff.), and divorce index, 1890–1939 (film 1690153 ff.), at the Colorado State Archives in Denver. There are also copies of the following county marriage registers at the State Archives (included here are only the registers that begin before 1920): Adams, Arapahoe, Baca, Bent, Boulder, Cheyenne, Clear Creek, Custer, Delta, Denver, Douglas, Elbert, El Paso, Fremont, Garfield, Gilpin, Gunnison, Hinsdale, Jefferson, Kit Carson, Lake, Larimer, Logan, Mesa, Montrose, Morgan, Otero, Ouray, Phillips, Pitkin, Saguache, Sedgwick, and Yuma. For dates of records for these counties, see the Web page of marriage records at the State Archives, available online at **<webdig01.state.co.us/gov_dir/gss/archives/marr1.html>**. See also compiled publications and indexes, such as:

- Arapahoe County Marriage Committee. *Marriages of Arapahoe County, Colorado, 1859–1901: Including Territory That Became Adams, Denver, and Other Counties* (Denver: Colorado Genealogical Society, 1986, fiche 6087871). Includes marriages as late as 1917.
- Armistead, Wanda B. *Boulder County, Colorado Marriage Records, 1860–1900* (Boulder: Boulder Genealogical Society, 1982).
- CD-ROM: *Territorial Vital Records: Births, Divorces, Guardianships, Marriages, Naturalizations, Wills; 1800s Thru 1906 Utah Territory, Arizona, Colorado, Idaho, Nevada, Wyoming, Indian Territory; LDS Branches, Wards; Deseret News Vital Records; J.P. Marriages; Methodist Marriages*

(Saint George, UT: Genealogical CD Publishing, 1994).

Most county and district courts house their records at the Colorado State Archives.

PROPERTY AND INHERITANCE

1874 a married woman may devise a will.

1876 a married woman's separate estate is property that is held prior to and after marriage (§ 1747). Her separate earnings are also her separate estate.

SUFFRAGE

1893 Colorado women receive complete suffrage by amendment to the state constitution.

CITIZENSHIP

1803 all residents of Colorado become citizens of the U.S. by legislation, except Native Americans, whose tribes are considered a separate nation until 1924.

CENSUS INFORMATION

For the 1860 federal censuses, see Kansas Territory (Arapahoe County); see Nebraska Territory (Boulder County); and see New Mexico Territory (Taos and Mora counties).

1866 partial enumeration for northeastern Colorado at the Colorado State Archives.

OTHER

Repatriations of native-born U.S. women who lost their citizenship, in the following county court records: El Paso (1938–64), Huerfano (1940–54), Las Animas (1937–67), Pueblo (1949–69), Routt (1940–57), at the Colorado State Archives. For a complete list of naturalization records at the Archives, see **<www.state.co.us/gov_dir/gss/arcives/natural.html>**, available online.

BIBLIOGRAPHY

Armitage, Susan et al. "Black Women and Their Communities in Colorado." *Frontiers* II (Summer 1977): 45–52.

Bird, Isabella. *A Lady's Life in the Rocky Mountains* (New York: Ballantine Books, 1960).

Bluemel, Elinor. *One Hundred Years of Colorado Women* (Denver: The Author, 1973).

Colorado Genealogical Society. *Colorado Families: A Territorial Heritage* (Denver: The Society, 1981).

DeGraw, Imelda. *The Denver Art Museum Quilts and Coverlets* (Denver: The Museum, 1974).

Garramore, Bonnie. "Colorado Homestead Entries Index." *Colorado Genealogist* 40 (1979) and 41 (1980).

Goodfriend, Joyce D. and Dona K. Flory. "Women in Colorado Before the First World War." *Colorado Magazine* 53 3 (1976): 201–28.

Harris, Katherine. *Long Vistas: Women and Families on Colorado Homesteads* (Niwot: University Press of Colorado, 1993).

Hinckley, Kathleen. "Colorado Research." *Colorado Genealogist* 49 (November 1988): 64–5.

—. "Genealogical Research in Colorado." *National Genealogical Society Quarterly* 77 (June 1989): 108–27.

Hoig, Stan. *The Sand Creek Massacre* (Norman: University of Oklahoma Press, 1961).

Jones-Eddy, Julia. *Homesteading Women: An Oral History of Colorado, 1890–1950* (New York: Twayne Publishers, 1992).

Katz, William Loren. "Colorado's Pioneers," in *Black Women of the Old West* (New York: Atheneum Books, 1995), 51–5.

Mattes, Merrill J. *The Great Platte River Road* (1969. Reprint. Lincoln: University of Nebraska Press, 1987).

Men and Women of Colorado: Past and Present (Phoenix: Pioneer Publishing, 1944, film 1697992).

Mulligan, Donald. *Hispanic Families of New Mexico and Southern Colorado [1538–1990]* (Albuquerque: University of New Mexico Press, 1990).

Propst, Nell Brown. *Those Strenuous Dames of the Colorado Prairie* (Boulder: Pruett, 1982).

Robertson, Janet. *The Magnificent Mountain Women: Adventures in the Colorado Rockies* (Lincoln: University of Nebraska Press, 1991).

Swagerty, William R. "Marriage and Settlement Patterns of Rocky Mountain Trappers and Traders." *Western Historical Society Quarterly* 11 (April 1980): 159–80.

Territorial Daughters of Colorado. *Pioneers of the Territory of Southern Colorado.* 4 Vols. (Mote Vista, CO: CBI Offset Printers, 1980).

Wynar, Bohdan S. *Colorado Bibliography* (Littleton, CO: Libraries Unlimited, 1980).

SELECTED RESOURCES FOR WOMEN'S HISTORY

Colorado Coalition for Women's History
PO Box 673
1200 Madison
Denver, CO 80206

Colorado Division of State Archives and Public Records
1313 Sherman Street
Floor 1B, Room 20
Denver, CO 80203

Denver Public Library
Western Historical Collection
1357 Broadway
Denver, CO 80203-2165

Stephen H. Hart Library
Colorado Historical Society
1300 Broadway
Denver, CO 80203

Western Historical Collection
University of Colorado
Boulder, CO 80309

Women of the West Museum
4001 Discovery Drive
Boulder, CO 80303-7816

Books on Women in Colorado History, available online at **<www.sni.net/bookstore/women.htm>**

Three generations of women in the Author's family: Honora Mary Heath (b. Limerick City, Ireland 26 Sep 1866, d. Waterbury, Connecticut 13 Jan 1903), Frances Honora Cosier (b. Winsted, Connecticut 3 Oct 1894, d. Meriden, Connecticut 16 Jul 1984), Lareine Alice Kinstler (living)

CONNECTICUT

IMPORTANT DATES IN STATE HISTORY

1633 Dutch trading post founded at the site of Hartford.
1634–5 First settlers from Massachusetts found Wethersfield, Windsor, and Hartford.
1637 Towns separate from Massachusetts and form the Connecticut Colony.
1638 Fundamental Orders of Connecticut written; New Haven founded.
1646 New London founded.
1662 Connecticut Colony receives a charter as a corporate colony.
1665 New Haven Colony unites with the Connecticut Colony.
1740 Most of Connecticut organized into towns.
1777 British forces raid Danbury.
1779 British forces attack New Haven and burn Norwalk and Fairfield.
1780 British forces burn New London.
1818 State constitution written.
1838 Hartford-New Haven Railroad completed.

MARRIAGE AND DIVORCE

1650 a public announcement of a marriage eight days prior to the event is required.
1655 the first divorce is granted in the General Court (General Assembly) for three years' desertion, seven years' absence without word, cruelty, fraudulent contract, and adultery. The law does not allow separations.
1656 New Haven Colony requires that "a separation or Divorce, shall, by sentence of the Court of Magistrates, be granted and published, and the innocent party shall in such cases have liberty to marry again."
1660 all married men are required by law to live with their wives.
1694 General Assembly grants clergymen the authority to perform marriages.
1796 a three-year residency requirement for divorce is established.
1811 the first legal separation is granted, based on a marriage agreement to divide the marital property.
1854 "all personal property coming to her [a wife] during his abandonment of her, or their separation from his abuse and intemperance, is hers alone; and he thereby loses control of all her property (Title 7 Ch. 1)."
1855 clergy of any denomination who are practicing in the state may perform marriage ceremonies.
1891 a five-day waiting period is established before a certificate may be issued on a marriage license application.

❧ *Connecticut was the first colony to allow absolute divorce. Couples from other colonies wishing an absolute divorce would often seek one in Connecticut, until a three-year waiting period was established in 1796. Puritans viewed marriage as a civil contract, not a sacrament, and therefore dissolvable.*

Where to Find Marriage and Divorce Records

The earliest marriages are recorded by the towns, often mixed in with the land records. Clergy were not authorized to solemnize marriages until the 1690s. The town clerks and probate clerks were required to record marriages beginning in 1849. In addition to the original town records, see the following indexes at the Connecticut State Library in Hartford:

- Barbour Index to Vital Records (film 0002887 ff.). This index is being published as an alphabetical series of towns by Genealogical Publishing Company. The series also includes Bible records at the Connecticut State Library from 1800 to 1850.

- Hale Collection of Vital Records, including marriages from newspapers (film 0003076 ff.).
- Index to vital records of Connecticut churches at the Connecticut State Library (0002806 ff.).
- For more information on the Barbour and Hale Collections, see **<www.cslnet.ctstateeu.edu/basic.htm>**.

The first divorces were recorded in the General (Particular) Court in the Connecticut Colony and in the Court of Magistrates in the New Haven Colony. After the union of the two colonies in 1665, the Court of Assistants was given primary jurisdiction, although the General Assembly continued to grant some divorces until at least 1677. The Superior Court holding sessions in the counties was given jurisdiction for divorces in 1711. Later records are held by the Clerk of the Superior Court in the county where the divorce was granted. There are also some divorce records, 1755–89 (film 0003617 ff.), indexed with land lottery records, at the Connecticut State Library. The Superior Court records containing divorce cases have been filmed for some years and are also at the State Library:

- Fairfield County, 1720-99 (film 1673219 ff.).
- Hartford County, 1725-1849 (film 1637917 ff.).
- Litchfield County, 1752-1922 (film 1664674 ff.).
- Middlesex County, 1786-97 (film 1639454 ff.).
- New Haven County, 1712-1899 (film 1672069 ff.).
- New London County, 1719-1875 (film 1638067 ff.).
- Tolland County, 1787-1910 (film 1637443 ff.).
- Windham County, 1726-1907 (film 1638582 ff.).

See also compiled publications, such as:

- Ferris, Barbara B. and Grace Louis Knox. *Connecticut Divorces: Superior Court Records for the Counties of Litchfield, 1752–1922, and Hartford, 1740–1849* (Bowie, MD: Heritage Books, 1989).
- —. *Connecticut Divorces: Superior Court Records for the Counties of New London, Tolland, and Windham, 1719–1910* (Bowie, MD: Heritage Books, 1987).
- Bailey, Frederic W. *Early Connecticut Marriages Prior to 1800* (1896. Reprint. Baltimore: Genealogical Publishing Co., 1997, film 0924061).

PROPERTY AND INHERITANCE

1656 in the New Haven Colony, a widow receives one-third of her husband's real and personal property and receives an additional third if there is only one surviving issue of the marriage.

1673 a widow "shall immediately after the death of her Husband have right and interest by way of dower in and to one third part of the real estate of her said husband that he stood of at the time of his decease." A widow does not have dower rights to personal property, which a husband may devise as he pleases.

1698 probate courts are established in districts.

1699 if "any person dyes intestate, administration of such intestates goods, and estate shall be granted to the widdowe . . . such intestate as well reall as personall . . . one-third part of the personall estate to the wife of the intestate forever, besides her dower or thirds in the housing and land during life . . ."

1714 when "the personal estate of a deceased intestate, leaving a widow, is not sufficient for the payment of the debts of the said deceased . . . the court of probates . . . shall order unto the widow of the said deceased such necessary household goods . . . for her use during life."

1723 "An Act for Preventing the Sales of the Real Estates of Heiresses, without their Consent," provides that "in the first settlement of this Colony . . . it became general custom, that the real estate of any person which either by descent or will became the estate of his daughters, whether seized of it at the time of their marriage or whether it descended or came to them during coverture, became the proper and sole estate of their husbands, and might be by him alienated or disposed of without the knowledge or consent of such wives . . . for the future, any real estate whereof any woman at the time of her marriage is seized as her estate of inheritance, or does during such coverture become so . . . shall not be alienable by her husband without her consent, testified by her hand and seal, to such deed . . . before an assistant or justice of the peace.

1736 widows and divorced women may claim their dower at law.

1750 a person dying intestate will have his estate divided "by Ancient and Immemorial Custom and common consent of the People," a wife receiving one-third personalty absolutely and also a dower in real estate for life.

1769 the heirs of an estate are liable for the support of a widow, if the dower is inadequate.

1788 the General Assembly allows a married woman to devise a will, bequeathing realty as well as personalty.

1805 wills of married women are no longer recognized.

1809 a married woman may devise a will (§ 15).

1849 "all persons at the age of twenty-one years . . . may dispose of their real estate by will; all persons of the age of seventeen years may dispose of their personal estate by will; and married women may dispose of their estate, both real and personal, by will, in the same manner as others (Title IV § 1)." The wife's personal estate is vested in the husband as a trustee for the benefit of the wife. Also, any woman who "shall earn wages by her own labor, payment of the same may be made to her (§ 8)."

1855 a married woman's property owned prior to her marriage is her sole and separate property.

SUFFRAGE

1920 Connecticut women receive complete suffrage by passage of the 19th Amendment to the Constitution.

CITIZENSHIP

One of the original Thirteen Colonies.

CENSUS INFORMATION

There are no state censuses for Connecticut; a few colonial censuses have been published, but they generally do not enumerate women.

OTHER

1673 towns are required to bear the responsibility for the local poor.

1821 anyone convicted of administering an abortion may be sentenced to life imprisonment.

1860 Connecticut becomes the first state to prohibit abortion by law.

1873 a state board of charities is established.

1879 statute forbids the use of contraceptives, also "any person who assists, abets, counsels, causes, hires, or commands another to commit any offense may be prosecuted and punished as if he were the principal offender (§ 54-196)."

BIBLIOGRAPHY

Andrews, Charles. "The Influence of Colonial Conditions as Illustrated in the Connecticut Intestacy Law," in *Essays in the History of Early American Law* (Chapel Hill: University of North Carolina Press, 1969).

Bakke, Mary Sterling. *A Sampler of Lifestyles: Womanhood and Youth in Colonial Lyme* (New Haven: Advocate Press, 1976).

Buel, Joy Day and Richard Buel, Jr. *The Way of Duty: A Woman and Her Family in Revolutionary America* (New York: W.W. Norton & Co., 1984).

Cohen, Sheldon S. "To Parts of the World Unknown: Circumstances of Divorces in Connecticut, 1750–1979." *Canadian Review of American Studies* 11 3 (Winter 1980): 275–93.

Cohn, Henry S. "Connecticut's Divorce Mechanism, 1636–1969." *American Journal of Legal History* 14 (1970): 25–54.

Dayton, Cornelia Hughes Dayton. *Women Before the Bar: Gender, Law, and Society in Connecticut, 1630–1789* (Chapel Hill: University of North Carolina Press, 1995).

Ditz, Toby L. *Property and Kinship: Inheritance in Early Connecticut, 1750–1820* (Princeton: Princeton University Press, 1986).

Edmonds, Mary Jaene. "Connecticut," in *Samplers and Samplemakers: An American Schoolgirl Art, 1700–1850* (London: Charles Letts & Co., Ltd., 1991).

Faragher, John. "Old Women and Old Men in Seventeenth-Century Wethersfield, Connecticut." *Women's Studies* 4 (1976): 11–31.

Fennelly, Catherine. *Connecticut Women in the Revolutionary Era* (Chester, CT: Pequot Press / American Revolution Bicentennial Commission of Connecticut, 1975).

Genealogies of Connecticut Families from The New England Historical and Genealogical Register. 3 Vols. (Baltimore: Genealogical Publishing Co., 1983).

Kemp, Thomas J. *Connecticut Researcher's Handbook* (Detroit: Gale Research, 1981).

Mann, Bruce H. *Neighbors and Strangers: Law and Community in Early Connecticut* (Chapel Hill: University of North Carolina Press, 1987).

Rising, Marsha Hoffman. "Researching Women in Land Conveyances: Groton, Connecticut Deeds, Volume 5, 1743-1760." *The American Genealogist* 69 (January 1994): 15–21. Abstracts every deed in Groton that includes a woman for an eighteen-year period.

Seymour, Jack H. *Ships, Sailors, and Samaritans: The Woman's Seaman's Friend Society of Connecticut, 1859–1976* (New Haven: The Society, 1976).

Sperry, Kip. *Connecticut Sources for Family Historians and Genealogists* (Logan, UT: Everton Publishers, 1980).

Stone, Robert G. *Connecticut Quilts: Bed Quilt Inventories Listed in Woodbury, Connecticut Probate Inventories, 1720–1819* (Summit, MO: The Fat Little Pudding Boy's Press, 1998).

Tomlinson, R.G. *Witchcraft Trials of Connecticut: First Comprehensive Documented History* (Hartford: The Bond Press, 1978).

SELECTED RESOURCES FOR WOMEN'S HISTORY

Beineke Library
Yale University
PO Box 5046, Yale Station
80 Wall Street
New Haven, CT 06520

Connecticut Historical Society
1 Elizabeth Street
Hartford, CT 06105

Connecticut State Library and Archives
231 Capital Avenue
Hartford, CT 06106

Godfrey Memorial Library
134 Newfield Street
Middletown, CT 06457

Institute for the Study of Women and Gender
University of Connecticut
U Box 181
417 Whitney Road
Storrs, CT 06269-1181

Litchfield Historical Society
South and East Streets
PO Box 385
Litchfield, CT 06759-0385

New Haven Colony Historical Society
114 Whitney Avenue
New Haven, CT 06510

Prudence Crandall Museum
PO Box 47
Canterbury, CT 06331

Finding Aid to Women's History Archival Resources at the Connecticut State Library, available online at **<www.cslnet.ctstateu.edu/women.htm>**

Four generations of Kiowa women, by Annette Hume. Western History Collections, University of Oklahoma Libraries

DELAWARE

IMPORTANT DATES IN STATE HISTORY

1638 Colony of New Sweden founded.
1654 Dutch colonists from New Netherland conquer New Sweden.
1664 New Netherland surrenders to English forces.
1673-4 The Dutch briefly retake New Netherland.
1682 First Quaker settlements; Delaware under the jurisdiction of Pennsylvania as the "Three Lower Counties." Counties are divided into "hundreds."
1703 Delaware establishes a separate provincial assembly.
1764 Western boundaries established with Pennsylvania.
1775 Last land ceded to Maryland.

MARRIAGE AND DIVORCE

1790 banns must be published in the bride's church for a marriage to be solemnized without a license.
1810 either the publishing of banns or the posting of a bond is required before marriage.
1901 the law requiring banns is repealed.
1903 the law requiring the posting of a bond for a marriage licenses is repealed.

Where to Find Marriage and Divorce Records

The early marriages were recorded by the county recorder of deeds beginning in 1680. County marriage records, beginning in 1832, have not been filmed by the FHL. Statewide registration began in 1847 but was not enforced until 1913. Marriage certificates prior to 1930 have been transferred to the Hall of Records in Dover. Marriage certificates issued after 1930 are on file at the Office of Vital Statistics in Dover. There are also Delaware marriages recorded in the neighboring areas of Maryland and Pennsylvania. All divorces prior 1897 were handled by the Delaware Legislative Council (which continued to grant divorces until about 1906). After 1900 the Superior Court was given jurisdiction for divorce cases, and records have been kept by the county prothonotary. See also, the following indexes and records at the Hall of Records:

- Marriage card index, 1680-1850 (film 0006416 ff.).
- Marriage records, 1865-1954 (film 2025062 ff.).
- Clerk of the peace marriage bonds, 1855-61, and licenses, 1889-94 (film 0006412 ff.).

Marriage records at the Historical Society of Delaware in Wilmington include:

- County marriage records and licenses, 1680-1850.
- Brandywine Hundred marriages, 1836-1909 (typescript).
- Wilmington marriage registers, 1856-64 (original copy).
- Miscellaneous Delaware marriage licenses, 1902- (originals).
- Marriage license applications for the Middletown area, 1926-35 (originals).

See also compiled publications, such as:

- Cope Gilbert. A *List of Marriage License Bonds, So Far as They Have Been Preserved in New Castle County, Delaware, 1744-1836* (Philadelphia: Historical Society of Pennsylvania, n.d., film 0441415).
- Richards, Mary Fallon. *Marriages from the Delaware Gazette, 1854-1859, 1861-1864* (Camden, ME: Picton Press, 1996).
- ——. *Delaware Marriages and Deaths from Newspapers, 1729–1853* (Camden, ME: Picton Press, 1997).

PROPERTY AND INHERITANCE

1683 in cases of intestacy a widow receives one-third of her husband's personal estate absolutely, and one-third of the real estate for life.

1706 act reaffirms the statute of 1683.

1742 in intestacy, a widow receives one-third of her husband's estate.

1865 any real estate, mortgages, stocks, and silver plate shall remain the property of the wife after marriage.

1871 all property acquired while living separately from and not supported by her husband shall be hers.

SUFFRAGE

1920 Delaware women receive complete suffrage by passage of the 19th Amendment to the Constitution.

CITIZENSHIP

One of the original Thirteen Colonies.

CENSUS INFORMATION

1782 state census, see Hancock, Harold B. *The Reconstructed Delaware State Census of 1782* (Wilmington: Delaware Genealogical Society, 1983). This census is incomplete.

OTHER

1742 "Act for Relief of the Poor" requires that "as one of the Poor of the Said County, shall on the Right Sleeve, or on the Back of his or her upper Garment, in an open and visible Manner, were . . . a large Roman or Capital P . . . cut in either Red or Blue Cloath . . ."

BIBLIOGRAPHY

Doherty, Thomas P. *Delaware Genealogical Research Guide.* 2nd ed. (Wilmington: Delaware Genealogical Society, 1997).

Grubb, Farley. "Servant Auction Records and Immigration into the Delaware Valley, 1745–1783: The Proportion of Females Among Servants." *Proceedings of the American Philosophical Society* 133 (June 1989): 154–69.

Jensen, Joan M. *Loosening the Bonds: Mid-Atlantic Farm Women, 1750–1850* (New Haven: Yale University Press, 1986).

A *Legacy from Delaware Women* (n.p.: Middle Atlantic Press, 1987).

Nicoll, Jessica F. *Quilted for Friends: Delaware Valley Signature Quilts, 1840–1855* (Hanover, NH: University Press of New England, 1986).

Offut, William. *Of Good Laws and Good Men: Law and Society in the Delaware Valley, 1680–1710* (Urbana: University of Illinois Press, 1995).

Reamy, Bill and Martha Reamy. *Genealogical Abstracts from the Biographical and Genealogical History of the State of Delaware* (Westminster, MD: Family Line Publications, 1998).

Samuels, Gayle B. *Women in the City of Brotherly Love, and Beyond: Tours and Detours in Delaware Valley Women's History* (Philadelphia: The Author, 1994).

Vaux, Trina. *Guide to Women's History Resources in the Delaware Valley* (Philadelphia: University of Pennsylvania Press, 1984).

Virdin, Donald O. *Maryland and Delaware Genealogies and Family Histories: A Bibliography of Maryland and Delaware Families* (Bowie, MD: Heritage Books, 1993).

—— . *Colonial Delaware Wills and Estates to 1800: An Index* (Bowie, MD: Heritage Books, 1994).

Ward, Mary Sam. *Delaware Women Remembered* (Wilmington: Modern Press, 1977).

SELECTED RESOURCES FOR WOMEN'S HISTORY

Delaware State Archives
Hall of Records
Dover, DE 19901

Historical Society of Delaware
505 Market Street
Wilmington, DE 19801

Winterthur Museum and Library
Route 52, Kenneth Pike
Winterthur, DE 19735

Women's Research Center
University of Delaware
Political Science Department
Newark, DE 19716

Are You Well?
Have You a Good Figure?

You can surprise your husband and friends by giving 15 minutes a day, in your room, to special directions which I give you to strengthen vital organs and nerves, so you are relieved of chronic ailments. Your body can be rounded and you can have as good a figure, as gracefully carried as any woman of your acquaintance.

A pupil who was thin writes me:

"I just can't tell you how happy I am! I wore low neck and short sleeves the other night and I was so proud of my neck and arms! My busts are rounded out and I have gained 28 pounds; it has come just where I wanted it and I carry myself like another woman. My old dresses look stylish on me now. You remember I have not been constipated since my second lesson and I had taken something for years. I guess my stomach must be stronger too, for I sleep like a baby and my nerves are so rested. I feel as if I had missed so much enjoyment in life, for I never did have such good times before. I feel so well all the time."

I have built up thousands of women—why not you? Write me, and if I cannot help your particular case I will tell you so.

I give each pupil the individual, confidential treatment which her case demands.

SUSANNA COCROFT

Department 101 246 Michigan Avenue, CHICAGO

Note: Miss Cocroft's name stands for progress in the scientific care of the health and figure of woman.

I Can Reduce Your Flesh

Would you like to reduce it by natural means and in a scientific, dignified manner?

I have reduced 25,000 women in the past seven years by a few simple directions followed in the privacy of their own rooms.

I can reduce you and at the same time strengthen stomach and heart and relieve you of such chronic ailments as *rheumatism, indigestion, constipation, weak nerves, torpid liver* and such difficulties as depend upon good circulation, strong nerves, strong muscles, good blood, correct breathing. You can be as good a figure as any woman of your acquaintance. Why not?

One pupil writes:

"Miss Cocroft, I have reduced 78 pounds and I look 15 years younger. I have reduced those hips and I feel so well I want to shout! I was rheumatic and constipated, my heart was weak and my head dull, my liver all clogged up and oh, dear, I am ashamed when I think how I used to look"

Send 10 cents for instructive booklet showing how to stand and walk correctly.

SUSANNA COCROFT

Department 101 246 Michigan Avenue, CHICAGO

Author of "Character as Expressed in the Body," Etc.

Burr McIntosh Monthly, November 1909

DISTRICT OF COLUMBIA

IMPORTANT DATES IN HISTORY

1788 Lands ceded from Maryland and Virginia to the federal government.
1800 Federal government moves to Washington.
1802 City of Washington incorporated.
1812 Most of the public buildings burned by the British during the War of 1812.
1846 Territory (including the city of Alexandria) is retroceded to Virginia.
1871 Washington becomes a federal territory.
1895 Washington and Georgetown merge and become the District of Columbia.

MARRIAGE AND DIVORCE

1804 Congress endows the District of Columbia District Court with the power to grant divorces.

1896 a copy of a marriage certificate must be kept by the clerk of the supreme court.

1901 Congress amends the District of Columbia divorce law to grant a divorce only on grounds of adultery.

Where to Find Marriage and Divorce Records

Marriage registers date from 1811 to 1990 and are kept at the District of Columbia Archives. Divorces prior to 1956 were filed with the U.S. District Court and are part of National Archives Record Group 21, along with some marriage licenses, 1837 to 1862. There is an index to the divorce cases at the office of the U.S. District Court for the District of Columbia.

- Transcripts of marriages, 1811-58 (film 0845767 ff.), at the Library of the National Society of the Daughters of the American Revolution in the District of Columbia.
- Pippenger, Wesley E. *District of Columbia Marriage Licenses: Register 1, 1811-1858* (Westminster, MD: Family Line Publications, 1994).
- —. *District of Columbia Marriage Licenses, 1858-1870* (Lovetsville, VA: Willow Bend Books, 1997).
- Sluby, Paul Edward, Sr. *Blacks in the Marriage Records of the District of Columbia, December 23, 1811-June 16, 1870*. 2 Vols. (Washington, DC: Columbian Harmony Society, 1988, film 1597787).
- Wright, F. Edward. *Marriage Licenses of Washington, DC, 1811-1830* (Westminster, MD: Family Line Publications, 1988).
- U.S. Circuit Court for the District of Columbia, minutes, 1801-63 (film 0940130 ff./ M1021), at the National Archives.

PROPERTY AND INHERITANCE

1896 Congress amends the law to allow a married woman to control her own income and to serve as guardian to her minor children (S. Rept. 836, 54th Cong., 1st Sess., 1896. Serial 4904).

1906 act on dower amends the code to allow a widow the title to land held by her deceased husband (S. Rept. 474, 59th Cong., 1st Sess., 1906. Serial 4904).

1926 Congress amends the District code to allow married women the power to make contracts.

SUFFRAGE

1919 Congress allows women to vote in parish meetings of the Protestant Episcopal Church in the District of Columbia, governed by an at of the Legislative Assembly of the District of Columbia.

1920 District of Columbia women receive complete suffrage by passage of the 19th Amendment to the Constitution.

CITIZENSHIP

Within the jurisdiction of the original Thirteen Colonies.

CENSUS INFORMATION

For the 1790 federal census, see Maryland (Montgomery and Prince George's counties).
1885–1925 police censuses, in National Archives Record Group 351, at the National Archives.

OTHER

1801–74 indentures of apprenticeship records (RG 21), at the National Archives.
1844 Congress establishes the Orphan Asylum and Free Female School of Alexandria.
1880 Congress establishes an industrial school for homeless and orphan girls in the District (H. Rept. 1010, 46th Cong., 2nd Sess., 1880. Serial 1937).
1887 Congress incorporates a reform school for girls in the District (H. Rept. 4030, 49th Cong., 2nd Sess., 1887. Serial 2501).
1906 Congress establishes the Edes Home for aged and indigent widows in the District (S. Rept. 998, 59th Cong., 1st Sess., 1906. Serial 4904).
1909 The National Training School for Women and Girls is the first boarding school in the north for black girls.
1926 Congress allows women in the District to serve on juries.
1930 Congress authorizes payment to certain widows whose husbands have been killed in the line of duty in the District of Columbia police and fire departments (H. Rept. 1635, 71st Cong., 2nd Sess., 1930. Serial 9196).

BIBLIOGRAPHY

Bergheim, Laura. *The Look-It-Up Guide to Washington Libraries & Archives* (Osprey, FL: Beacham Publishing, 1995).

Borchert, James. *Alley Life in Washington: Family, Community, Religion, and Folklife in the City, 1850–1970* (Urbana: University of Illinois Press, 1982).

Cary, Francine Curro. *Urban Odyssey: A Multicultural History of Washington, DC* (Washington, DC: Smithsonian Institution Press, 1996).

Clark-Lewis, Elizabeth. *Living In, Living Out: African American Domestics in Washington, DC, 1910–1940* (Washington, DC: Smithsonian Institution Press, 1994).

Deutsch, Davida T. and Betty Ring. "Homage to Washington in Needlework and Prints." *Antiques* 119 2 (February 1981): 402–19.

Dixon, Joan M. *National Intelligencer and Washington Advertiser Newspaper Abstracts [1808–1820]*. 6 Vols. (Bowie, MD: Heritage Books, 1996–8).

Duncan, Jacci and Lynn Page Whittaker. *The Women's History Guide to Washington* (Alexandria, VA: Charles River Press, 1998).

Pippenger, Wesley E. *District of Columbia Ancestors: A Guide to the Records of the District of Columbia* (Westminster, MD: Family Line Publications, 1997).

Provine, Dorothy S. *District of Columbia Free Negro Registers, 1821–1861.* 2 Vols. (Bowie, MD: Heritage Books, 1996).

—. *Index to District of Columbia Wills [1801–1920]* (Baltimore: Genealogical Publishing Co., 1992).

Schaefer, Christina K. *The Center: A Guide to Genealogical Research in the National Capital Area* (Baltimore: Genealogical Publishing Co., 1996).

Smith, Kathryn Schneider. *Washington at Home: An Illustrated History of Neighborhoods in the Nation's Capital* (Northridge, CA: Windsor Publications, 1988).

Weller, Charles Frederick. *Washington, Neglected Neighborhoods: Stories of Life in the Alleys, Tenements, and Shanties of the National Capital* (Philadelphia: John C. Winston, 1909).

SELECTED RESOURCES FOR WOMEN'S HISTORY

American Historical Association
Committee on Women Historians
400 A Street SE
Washington, DC 20003

Historical Society of Washington, DC
(formerly the Columbia Historical Society)
1397 New Hampshire Avenue NW
Washington, DC 20036-1507

General Federation of Women's Clubs
Women's History and Resource Center
1734 N Street NW
Washington, DC 20036-2990

Library of Congress
Washington, DC 20540

Marguerite Rawalt Resource Center
Business and Professional Women's Foundation
2012 Massachusetts Avenue NW
Washington, DC 20036

Martin Luther King Memorial Library
901 G Street NW
Washington, DC 20001-4599

National Archives
Pennsylvania Avenue and 8th Street NW
Washington, DC 20408

National Archives for Black Women's History
Mary McLeod Bethune Council House National Historic Site
1318 Vermont Avenue NW
Washington, DC 20005

National Museum of American History Library
Smithsonian Institution
Constitution Avenue NW
Washington, DC 20560

National Museum of Women in the Arts
Library and Research Center
1250 New York Avenue NW
Washington, DC 20005-3920

National Society of the Daughters of the American Revolution
1776 D Street NW
Washington, DC 20006

U.S. Holocaust Memorial Museum
1000 Raoul Wallenberg Place SW
Washington, DC 20024-2150

Women in Military Service to America Memorial
Arlington National Cemetery
Arlington, VA 22211

Trade cards, 1880s
(Author collection)

FLORIDA

IMPORTANT DATES IN STATE HISTORY

1565 Spain founds the first permanent European settlement in North America at Saint Augustine.
1763 Ceded from France to Great Britain; Florida divided into East and West Florida.
1783 British East Florida ceded to Spain.
1795 The Pinckney Treaty with Spain gives the U.S. all of West Florida above the 31st parallel.
1814 U.S. forces capture Spanish Pensacola.
1817 First Seminole War (ends 1818).
1819 Spanish Florida ceded to the U.S.; separate governments established for East and West Florida.
1822 Organized as a U.S. territory.
1829 Territorial Council adopts common law and jurisprudence practices of the U.S., replacing Spanish law.
1835 Second Seminole War (ends 1842).
1838 Constitution drafted.
1845 Statehood.
1855 Third Seminole War (ends 1858).
1861 11 January secedes from the Union.
1868 11 June readmitted to the Union.

MARRIAGE AND DIVORCE

1829 rights and privileges of husbands and wives that were established in Florida under the jurisdiction of Spanish law are excepted from common law.
1887 county judges are required to issue and record marriage licenses.

Where to Find Marriage and Divorce Records

Marriages and divorces have been handled by the county circuit court from the creation of the county (earliest in 1822) until 1927. Statewide registration began in 1927. See the marriage index, 1927–69 (fiche 6081726 ff.), and a divorce and annulment index, 1927–69 (fiche 6081683 ff.), at the Florida Department of Health in Jacksonville. Many county records have been filmed, also available at the Florida State Archives in Tallahassee, such as:

- Dade County Clerk marriages, 1840–71 (film 1010085), Dade County Judge marriage license applications, 1887–92, index, 1889–1911 (film 1870454 ff.), and marriage records, 1905–11 (film 1010085), at the Dade County Records Center in Miami.
- Escambia County Clerk of the Circuit Court marriage records, 1822–1927 (film 0941001 ff.), at the Escambia County Courthouse and at the Special Collections of the University of West Florida, both in Pensacola.

See also transcriptions of original records, such as:

- McFadden, Ann Josberger. *Dade County, Florida Marriage Records, 1840–1911.* 2 Vols. (Miami: Genealogical Society of Miami, 1991).

PROPERTY AND INHERITANCE

1828 any person over twenty-one years of age has the right to dispose of real or personal property by will.
1868 a married woman's separate property (Art. 4 § 6) law is established as an amendment to the state constitution.
1881 a married woman may devise her separate estate, free from the debts of her husband.

SUFFRAGE

1920 Florida women receive complete suffrage by passage of the 19th Amendment to the Constitution.

CITIZENSHIP

1819 all residents of Florida become U.S. citizens by treaty, except Native Americans, whose tribes are considered a separate nation until 1924.

CENSUS INFORMATION

The first federal census for Florida is 1830.

1784–1820 see Coker, William S. and Douglas Ingles. *The Spanish Censuses of Pensacola, 1784–1820: Genealogical Guide to Spanish Pensacola* (Pensacola: Perdido Bay Press, 1980).

pre-1821 censuses, see Mills, Donna Rachal. *Florida's First Families: Translated Abstracts of Pre-1821 Spanish Censuses* (Tuscaloosa, FL: Mills Historical Press, 1992).

1783–1812 censuses, see Platt, Lyman D. *Census Records for Latin America and the Hispanic United States* (Baltimore: Genealogical Publishing Co., 1998).

1825, 1855, 1867, 1868, 1875, decennial thereafter (not at FHL).

1875 state census, Alachua County (film 0006962).

1885 state census (film 0888962 ff./M845).

Most of the existing state censuses, including complete enumerations of 1885, 1935, and 1945, are at the Florida State Archives.

OTHER

1928–55 registration of certified midwives (mss. S1481), at the Florida State Archives in Tallahassee. See also Susie, Debra Anne. *In the Way of Our Grandmothers: A Cultural View of Twentieth-Century Midwifery in Florida* (Athens: University of Georgia Press, 1988).

Florida Confederate Pension Application Files from 1885 include widows' names and maiden names and are in a searchable database available online at **<www.dos.state.fl.us/barm/PensionIntroduction. htm>.** Widows began receiving pensions in 1889. See also White, Virgil. *Register of Florida Confederate CSA Pension Applications* (Waynesboro, TN: National Historical Publishing Co., 1989).

BIBLIOGRAPHY

Babb, Ellen and Milly St. Julien. "Public and Private Lives: Women in Saint Petersburg at the Turn of the Century." *Tampa Bay History* 8 (Summer 1986): 4–27.

Blackman, Lucy W. *Women of Florida.* 2 Vols. (Jacksonville: Southern Historical Publishing, 1940).

Bodziony, Gill T. *Genealogy and Local History: A Bibliography* (Tallahassee: State Library of Florida, 1978).

Carson, James Milton. "Historical Background of Florida Law." *Miami Law Quarterly* 3 (1949): 254–63.

Carver, Joan S. "Women in Florida." *Journal of Politics* 41 3 (1979): 941–55.

Cozens, Eloise. *Florida Women of Distinction* (Daytona Beach: College Publishing Co., 1956).

Cutler, Harry Gardner. *History of Florida, Past and Present, Historical and Biographical.* 3 Vols. (Chicago: Lewis Publishing Co., 1923, film 1321188 ff.).

Davis, Karen. *Public Faces, Private Lives: Women in South Florida, 1870s–1910s* (Miami: Pickering Press, 1990).

Feldman, Lawrence H. *Anglo-Americans in Spanish Archives: Lists of Anglo-American Settlers in the Spanish Colonies of America; A Finding Aid* (Baltimore: Genealogical Publishing Co., 1991).

Meyer, Jessie Hamm. *Leading the Way, A Century of Service: The Florida Federation of Women's Clubs, 1895–1995* (Lakeland, FL: The GFWC Florida Federation of Women's Clubs, 1994).

Michaels, Brian E. "Genealogical Research in Florida." *National Genealogical Society Quarterly* 76 2 (June 1988): 89–100.

Monroe, Mary Barr. "The Seminole Women of Florida." *Tequesta* 41 (1981): 23-32.

Mormino, Gary R. and George E. Pozzetta. "Immigrant Women in Tampa: The Italian Experience, 1890–1930." *Florida History Quarterly* (January 1983): 296–312.

Reinersten, G.G. and R.L. Brown. *Guide to Florida Legal Research.* 2nd ed. (Tallahassee: Florida Bar, Continuing Legal Education, 1986).

Taylor, Anne Wood. *Florida Pioneers and Their Descendants* (Tallahassee: Florida State Genealogical Society, 1992).

Williams, Charlotte Allen. *Florida Quilts* (Gainesville: University Press of Florida, 1992).

Wolfe, William A. and Janet B. Wolfe. *Names and Abstracts from the Acts of the Legislative Council of the Territory of Florida, 1822–1845* (Tallahassee: Florida State Genealogical Society, 1991).

SELECTED RESOURCES FOR WOMEN'S HISTORY

Broward County Women's History Coalition
1350 East Sunrise Boulevard
Suite 114
Fort Lauderdale, FL 33304

Community Coalition for Women's History
351 NW 5th Street
Miami, FL 33128-1615

Florida State Archives
R.S. Gray Building
Mail Station A
500 South Bronough Street
Tallahassee, FL 32399-0250

The Florida State Archives: Collections Pertaining to Women's History and Women's Issues, available online at **<www.dos.state.fl.us/dlis/barm/fsa/ women'sguide.htm>**

SHE WILL RESTORE THE BALANCE.

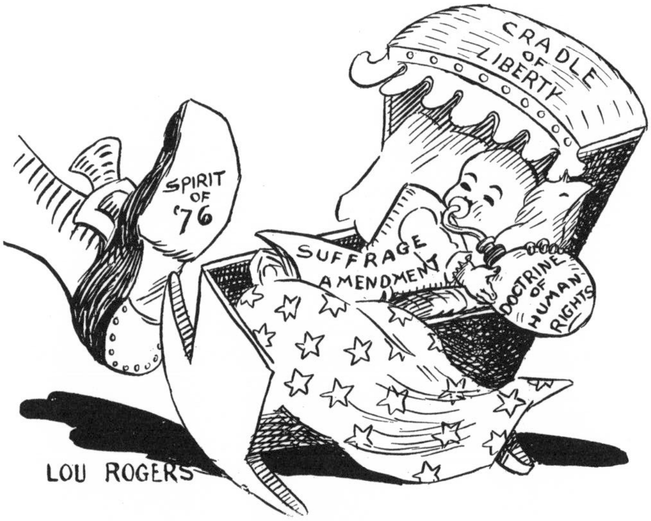

ROCKED IN THE SAME OLD CRADLE BY THE SAME OLD FOOT.

Women's world, women's choices, 1900–16

GEORGIA

IMPORTANT DATES IN STATE HISTORY

1733 First English settlers found Savannah; slavery is made illegal.
1734 Effingham County area settled by German Protestant refugees from Salzburg.
1742 Battle of Bloody Marsh.
1749 Slavery legalized.
1752 Becomes a Royal colony.
1758 Georgia divided into twelve parishes.
1777 Parishes formed into seven counties.
1778 British forces occupy Savannah (evacuated in 1782).
1838 Federal troops remove the Cherokee Indians from Georgia to Indian territory.
1861 19 January secedes from the Union.
1864 The Union Army captures Atlanta and Savannah.
1870 20 April readmitted to the Union.

MARRIAGE AND DIVORCE

1799 marriage licenses are required, as an alternate to banns.

1804 the Ordinary (an ecclesiastical judge) of the county is required to keep a written record of licenses issued.

1851 marriage settlements are invalid if not recorded within a specified time.

1861 requirements for a marriage contract are: the male at least seventeen years of age, the female at least fourteen years of age, have parental consent if the female is under eighteen years, be unmarried, and have no close blood relationships with each other. Either a license or the publishing of banns for three Sundays prior to marriage is required. If married by license, it shall be recorded by the Ordinary in the county of the bride's residence. If married by bann, the minister shall also record the marriage contract in the license book.

1895 county recorders are required to issue marriage licenses.

Where to Find Marriage and Divorce Records

Counties began recording marriages in 1785, and records have been kept by the clerk of the county court or the clerk of the county Ordinary court. From 1798 to 1835, divorces were handled by the Georgia State Legislature (291 divorces are granted during this period). After that time, jurisdiction was given to the county superior courts. For the dates of the creation of Georgia's counties, see the URL **<www.sos.state.ga.us/archives.creation.htm>**. Many county records have been filmed, such as:

- Baker County Court of Ordinary marriage records, 1874–1935 (film 0522798 ff.).
- Baker County Superior Court minutes, 1879–1914 (film 0522793 ff.), at the Baker County Courthouse in Newton.
- Effingham County Court of Ordinary marriages and miscellaneous records, 1791–1943 (film 0180394 ff.), and marriage index, 1790–1935 (film 0180393).
- Effingham County Superior Court minutes, 1821–1901 (film 0180383 ff.), at the Effingham County Courthouse in Springfield.

See also published compilations, such as:

- Maddox, Joseph T. 37,000 *Early Georgia Marriages* (Irwinton, GA: The Author, 1975, fiche 6046751).
- ——. 40,000 *Early Georgia Marriages* (Irwinton, GA: The Author, 1976, fiche 6051217).
- ——. *Early Georgia Marriage Roundup* (Irwinton, GA: The Author, 1980, fiche 6049619).

- —— . *Early Georgia Marriages* (Irwinton, GA: The Author, 1981, film 1033953).
- Hageness, Marilee Beatty. *Georgia Divorces, 1793–1833* (Anniston, AL: The Author, 1993, fiche 6125982).

PROPERTY AND INHERITANCE

1754 a woman's property before her marriage shall remain separate.

1760 a *feme covert* must "willingly consent to part with her right by becoming a party with her husband and . . . shall sign and seal the same before the chief justice or assistant judges, or one of His Majesty's justices of the peace for the parish where such contracts shall be made . . ."

1773–4 a husband and wife are no longer one person in law, so far as property is concerned. All married property is vested with the husband as head of the family, but other property is owned by two distinct and separate persons, with distinct and separate rights.

1785 in marriage, since 22 February 1785, "the wife's real estate vests in the husband, like personalty."

SUFFRAGE

1920 Georgia women receive complete suffrage by passage of the 19th Amendment to the Constitution.

CITIZENSHIP

One of the original Thirteen Colonies.

CENSUS INFORMATION

The federal census for 1790 is reconstructed; the 1800 census exists for Oglethorpe County only; all of the 1810 census is missing.

1827–90 state censuses, see Townsend, Brigid S. *Indexes to Seven State Census Reports for Counties in Georgia, 1838–1845* (Atlanta: R.J. Taylor, Jr., Foundation, 1975).

OTHER

1862–4 lists of families supplied with salt (State Archives Record Group 22-8, also on film at the State Archives)

1891–1953 Confederate pension payments to veterans (film 10359873 ff.), granted to widows from 1896. Pension applications are also being digitized, available online at **<docuweb.gsu.edu/htbin/collection/colid=15/77>.**

The above records are at the Georgia Department of Archives and History in Atlanta.

BIBLIOGRAPHY

Alexander, Adele Logan. *Ambiguous Lives, Free Women of Color in Rural Georgia, 1789–1879* (Little Rock: University of Arkansas Press, 1991).

Atlanta Historical Society. *Southern Comfort: Quilts from the Atlanta Historical Society* (Atlanta: The Society, 1978).

Austin, Jeanette Holland. *The Georgians: Genealogies of Pioneer Settlers* (Baltimore: Genealogical Publishing Co., 1984).

Azar, Robert. "The Liberation of Georgia Women for Jury Service." *Atlanta History Journal* (Fall 1980): 21–6.

Boatwright, Eleanor Miwot. *Status of Women in Georgia, 1783–1860* (New York: Carlson Publishing, 1994).

Chanin, Leah F. *Reference Guide to Georgia Legal History and Legal Research* (Norcross, GA: Harrison Co., 1990).

Coulter, E. Merton and Albert B. Saye. *A List of the Early Settlers of Georgia* (1953. Reprint. Baltimore: Clearfield Co., 1998).

Emory University General Libraries. *Manuscript Sources for Women's History: A Descriptive List of Holdings in the Special Collections Department* (Atlanta: The Libraries, 1987).

Hehir, Donald M. *Georgia Families: A Bibliographic Listing of Books About Georgia Families* (Bowie, MD: Heritage Books, 1993).

Hotchkiss, William A. *Codifications of Statute Law of Georgia and Collections of State Papers of English, American, and State Origin* (New York: John F. Trow & Co., 1845).

Rapport, Sara. "The Freedman's Bureau as a Legal Agent for Black Men and Women in Georgia: 1865–1868." *Georgia Historical Quarterly* 73 (Winter 1989): 26–53.

Roth, Darlene R. and Virginia Shadron. *Women's Records: A Preliminary Guide* (Atlanta: Georgia Department of Archives and History, 1978).

Swan, Lee Ann Caldwell. "Landgrants to Georgia Women, 1755–1775." *Georgia Historical Quarterly* 61 1 (1977): 23–4.

Wadsworth, Anna. *Missing Pieces: Georgia Folk Art, 1770–1976* (Atlanta: Georgia Council for the Arts, 1976).

SELECTED RESOURCES FOR WOMEN'S HISTORY

Georgia Department of Archives and History
330 Capitol Avenue SE
Atlanta, GA 30344

Juliet Gordon Low Girl Scout National Center
142 Bull Street
Savannah, GA 31405

Robert W. Woodruff Library
Emory University
1380 South Oxford Road NE
Atlanta, GA 30322

Southern Association of Women Historians
Department of History
Agnes Scott College
Decatur, GA 33030-3797

William Russell Pullen Library
Georgia State University
University Plaza
Atlanta, GA 30303

Georgia Women's Collection Project, available online at **<www.lib.gsu.edu/ spcoll/woman/wom.htm>**

Manuscript Sources for Women's History [Emory University], available online at **<www.emory.edu/lib/ wompre.htm>**

Women's History Resources at the Georgia Archives, available online at **<www.sos.state.ga.us/archives/ women/html>**

Jemima Lougheed McCarthy, Rochester, New York, 1908
(Courtesy of Dorothy Driscoll Armstrong, cousin of the Author)

HAWAII

IMPORTANT DATES IN STATE HISTORY

1778 Captain James Cook makes first recorded European visit; the *alii* (hereditary ruling class) have ruled the Hawaiian Islands for more than 1,000 years.
1819 The *kapu* (taboo) forbidding men and women to eat together is abandoned.
1820 First missionaries (including women) and whaling ships from New England arrive at Honolulu.
1822 Missionaries produce first written primer in Hawaiian.
1826 Influenza epidemic kills large numbers of Hawaiians.
1842 Court system organized.
1848 Measles epidemic further decimates the Hawaiian people.
1852 Sugar plantations begin to import labor from China.
1853 Smallpox epidemic kills entire families of Hawaiians; the population is 75% less than that of 1778.
1865 A Bureau of Immigration is established.
1875 Hawaii grants to the U.S. the exclusive use of Pearl Harbor.
1876 Reciprocity treaty with the U.S. gives raw sugar duty-free entry into U.S. ports.
1884 Japanese immigration begins; "picture brides" are imported by professional matchmakers.
1893 Liluokalani, Queen of Hawaii, abdicates, and the government changes from a kingdom to a republic.
1895 First public school opened in Honolulu.
1898 Cedes itself to the U.S.
1900 Becomes a U.S. territory.
1905 Counties organized: Hawaii and Oahu are separate counties; Lanai, Maui, and Molokai are part of Maui County; Kauai and Niihau are part of Kauai County.
1941 Japanese forces launch an air attack on Pearl Harbor.
1959 Statehood.

MARRIAGE AND DIVORCE

1863 law requires a bride to take the name of her husband.

Where to Find Marriage and Divorce Records

The earliest marriage records date from the early 1800s. Kingdom marriage and divorce records began in 1853. Beginning in 1884, lists of marriages were normally submitted on a quarterly basis and were used to compile two indexed volumes of marriage records covering the entire kingdom. Most records before 1896 are at the Archives of Hawaii in Honolulu; those after 1896 are at the Department of Health in Honolulu.

- Marriage records, 1826–1929 (film 1031145).
- Marriage records, 1909–20, and index, 1909–46 (film 1851162 ff.).
- Index to the Archives of Hawaii collection of marriage records, 1826–1910 (film 1031145), at the Bernice P. Bishop Museum in Honolulu. Index includes island of Hawaii, 1832–1910, island of Maui, 1842–1910,

❧ *Prior to 1820, before written records, Hawaiian genealogies were only recorded for those of the ruling class, the* alii. *Some of these records have been recorded, notably, Kamakau, Kelou.* Fournander Collection of Hawaiian Antiquities and Folklore *(Honolulu: Bernice B. Bishop Museum, 1919–20), and Kamakau, Samuel.* Ka Po'e Kahiko: The People of Old *(Honolulu: Bishop Museum Press, 1964).*

island of Kauai, 1826–1910, and island of Molokai, 1850–1910.

- Kingdom of Hawaii marriage records for districts on the islands of Hawaii, Maui, Molokai, Oahu, and Kauai, 1884–96 (film 1205810 ff.).
- Territory of Hawaii marriage records, Hawaii, Oahu, Kauai, and Maui, 1904–9 (film 1955531 ff.), at the Hawaii Department of Health in Honolulu.
- Miscellaneous marriage records, 1800–50 (index on film 1031144), at the Daughters of the American Revolution Memorial Library in Honolulu.
- Early Congregational Church records from 1820, at the Hawaiian Mission Children's Society Library in Honolulu.
- Index to marriages in Hawaiian newspapers prior to 1950 (film 1002822).
- Marriage notices extracts from the newspaper, *Ka Nupepa kuokoa*, 1862–1909 (film 1675269 ff.), prepared by the Genealogical Service Center in Honolulu.

See also the records of individual islands for the Kingdom of Hawaii:

- Island of Hawaii reports of marriages, 1851–96 (film 1014410 ff.), and marriage certificates and licenses, 1846–1900 (film 1014411 ff.).
- Islands of Maui, Lanai, and Molokai reports of marriages, 1842–96 (film 1014413 ff.), and marriage certificates, licenses, and applications, 1842–1900 (film 1014413 ff.).
- Island of Molokai reports of marriages, 1859–79 (film 1014411 ff.), and Molokai marriages in Honolulu registers, 1863–8 (film 0295831).
- Island of Oahu reports of marriages, 1837–96 (film 1014410 ff.), marriage certificates and licenses, 1847–95 (film 1205811 ff.), registers of marriages, except Honolulu, 1847–96 (film 1205690 ff.), marriage license requests and approvals for remarriage, 1852–3 (film 1014414), and marriage licenses of foreigners, 1852–79 (film 1014414).
- Islands of Kauai and Niihau reports of marriages, 1846–96 (film 1014412 ff.), Kauai marriages, 1865–96 (film 1205809 ff.), and Kauai marriage certificates, 1845–94 (film 1014412 ff.).

There are also records for the Territory of Hawaii:

- Island of Oahu marriage registers, 1896–1903, and indexes, 1896–1909 (film 1205810 ff.).
- Islands of Maui, Molokai, and Lanai marriage registers, 1896–1903, indexes, 1896–1909 (film 1205809 ff.), and Maui marriage records, 1896–1900 (film 1955532).

❧ *In 1853, of the 577 foreign men who married within the Kingdom of Hawaii, 419 (72.6%) married Hawaiian women.*

Romanzo Adams. *Interracial Marriage in Hawaii* (New York: Macmillan & Co., 1937), 76.

❧ *Social status in pre-conquest Hawaii was earned by raising or lowering the status of one's birthright. Within the hierarchy of chiefs, commoners could tie into the* kaukauali'i *rank (lesser chief) by marriage. Parentage was often claimed by more than one father, by* po'olua, *literally meaning "two heads." In addition to biological links, a* maka'ainana *woman was given a name to recognize her child in relation to the* mana *(status) of a chief. Chief genealogies can also be traced through the unions of siblings, where a brother married a sister to continue a matrilineal descent. These lines transmitted the female* kapu *(authority, power) to a daughter.*

Jocelyn Linnekin, *Sacred Queens and Women of Consequence: Rank, Gender, and Colonization in the Hawaiian Islands* (Ann Arbor: University of Michigan Press, 1990), 94–7.

- Islands of Kauai and Niihau marriage registers, 1896–1903 (film 0295833 ff.).

Divorce records have been under the jurisdiction of the circuit courts and are at the Archives of Hawaii, and some have been filmed, 1849–1915 (film 1015620 ff.).

PROPERTY AND INHERITANCE

1846 King Kamehameha III appoints a commission to study the Hawaiian land system.

1848 the first written division of lands is recorded in the *Mahele Book* (film 0986199 ff.).

1849 the feudal land system is abolished; a land commission is given authority to award titles in fee simple on claims of tenants; 30,000 acres are owned by commoners, landlord chiefs own 1.5 million acres; the Crown lands are about a million acres.

SUFFRAGE

1917 Congress provides the territorial legislature with the power to grant female suffrage (S. Rept. 108, 65th Cong., 1st Sess., 1917. Serial 7249).

CITIZENSHIP

1898 all persons who are citizens of the Republic of Hawaii are granted U.S. citizenship by an act of Congress.

CENSUS INFORMATION

The first federal census for Hawaii is 1900.

1840–66 censuses (film 1009896).

1896 census for the city of Honolulu (not at FHL).

These censuses are at the Archives of Hawaii.

❧ *In Hawaiian genealogy, there is no distinction between male and female lines. The following terms for sibling and half-sibling are applicable to both sexes:*

- kaikunane (*female speaker*): *brother*
- kaikuahine (*male speaker*): *sister*
- kaikua'ana *older siblings, same sex*
- kaikaina *younger siblings, same sex*

OTHER

1922 Congress amends Hawaii's Organic Act to qualify women to serve in the territorial legislature and to serve as delegates to the House of Representatives (H. Rept. 1082, 67th Cong., 2nd Sess., 1992. Serial 17957).

1927 Congress allows women in Hawaii to serve on juries.

1893–8 entry permits for Chinese women, at the Archives of Hawaii, along with general records including photograph books, certificates of identification, etc.

BIBLIOGRAPHY

Akana, Elizabeth. *Hawaiian Quilting: A Fine Art* (Honolulu: Hawaiian Mission Children's Society, 1981).

Chai, Alice Yun. "Freed from the Elders but Locked in Labor: Korean Immigrant Women in Hawaii." *Women's Studies* 13 3 (1987): 223–34.

——. "Picture Brides: Feminist Analysis of Life Histories of Hawaii's Early Immigrant Women from Japan, Okinawa, and Korea," in Gabaccia, Donna, *Seeking Common Ground: Multi-Disciplinary Studies of Immigrant Women in the United States* (Westport, CT: Greenwood Press, 1992), 128–38.

Chapin, Helen G. "From Sparta to Spencer Street: Greek Women in Hawaii." *Hawaii Journal of History* 13 (1979): 136–56.

Cheng, C.K. and Douglas S. Yamamura. "Interracial Marriage and Divorce in Hawaii." *Social Forces* 36 1 (October 1957): 77–84.

Conrad, Agnes C. *Genealogical Sources in Hawaii* (Honolulu: Honolulu Library Association, 1987).

Gething, Judith. "Christianity and Coverture: Impact on the Legal Status of Women in Hawaii, 1820–1920." *Hawaiian Journal of History* 11 (1977): 188–220.

Grimshaw, Patricia. *Paths of Duty: American Missionary Wives in Nineteenth-Century Hawaii* (Honolulu: University Press, 1989).

Historians Committee, Foundation for Hawaii Women's History. *The Written Record of Hawaii's Women: An Annotated Guide to Sources of Information in Hawaii* (Honolulu: Honolulu County Committee on the Status of Women, 1984).

Kahle, R.F. *How to Research Constitutional, Legislative, and Statutory History in Hawaii* (Honolulu: Hawaii Legislative Reference Bureau, 1986).

Lebra, Joyce Chapman. *Women's Voices in Hawaii* (Niwot: University Press of Colorado, 1991).

Linnekin, Jocelyn. *Sacred Queens and Women of Consequence: Rank, Gender, and Colonialism in the Hawaiian Islands* (Ann Arbor: University of Michigan Press, 1990).

McKinzie, Edith Kawelohea. *Hawaiian Genealogies Extracted from Hawaiian Language Newspapers* (Honolulu: University of Hawaii Press, 1986).

Parker, Linda S. *Native American Estate: The Struggle Over Indian and Hawaiian Lands* (Honolulu: University of Hawaii Press, 1989).

Peterson, Barbara B. *Notable Women of Hawaii* (Honolulu: University of Hawaii Press, 1984).

Russ, William Adam. *The Hawaiian Republic and Its Struggle to Win Annexation* (Selinsgrove, PA: Susquehanna University Press, 1992).

Saki, Patsy S. *Japanese Women in Hawaii: The First 100 Years* (Honolulu: Kisaku, 1985).

Shaw, Robert. *Hawaiian Quilt Masterpieces* (New York: Hugh Lauter Levon Associates, 1996).

Spurrier, Joseph H. *Hawaiian Family Life During the Monarchy* (Salt Lake City: Corporation of the President, 1980, fiche 6085823).

Takaki, Ronald. "They Also Came: The Migration of Chinese and Japanese Women to Hawaii and the Continental United States." *Chinese American History and Perspectives* (1991): 30–48.

— . *Pau Hana: Plantation Life and Labor Hawaii, 1835–1920* (Honolulu: University of Hawaii Press, 1983).

Young, Nancy Foon. *The Chinese in Hawaii: An Annotated Bibliography* (Honolulu: Social Science Research Institute, University of Hawaii Press, 1973).

Zwiep, Mary. *Pilgrim Path: The First Company of Women Missionaries to Hawaii* (Madison: University of Wisconsin Press, 1991).

SELECTED RESOURCES FOR WOMEN'S HISTORY

Archives of Hawaii
Iolani Palace
478 South King Street
Honolulu, HI 96813

Bernice Pauahi Bishop Museum Library
1525 Bernice Street
PO Box 19000-A
Honolulu, HI 96817-0916

D.A.R. Memorial Library
1914 Makiki Heights Drive
Honolulu, HI 96822

Daughters of Hawaii
2913 Pali Highway
Honolulu HI, 96817

Hawaii Chinese History Center
111 North King Street, Room 410
Honolulu, HI 96817

Hawaiian Historical Society
560 Kawaiahao Street
Honolulu, HI 96813

Hawaiian Mission Children's Society Library
553 South King Street
Honolulu, HI 96813

Historical Records Repositories in Hawaii, available online at **<www.aloha.com/~mem/hrr.html>**

Wash day (Kansas State Historical Society)

IDAHO

IMPORTANT DATES IN STATE HISTORY

1818 U.S. and Great Britain jointly occupy the area by treaty.
1834 Fort Hall is built on the Snake River by fur traders.
1843 Under the laws of the Oregon territory (not officially organized).
1846 The 49th Parallel becomes the boundary between British North America and the U.S.
1848 Part of the Oregon Territory (officially organized).
1853 Northern part of Idaho becomes part of the Washington Territory.
1859 Southern part of Idaho becomes part of the Washington Territory.
1860 Mormon settlement founded in Cache Valley; gold discovered at Orofino Creek.
1863 Created as a separate territory from the Washington and Dakota territories.
1864 Territorial legislature adopts statutes of common law.
1866 Snake War.
1890 Statehood.

MARRIAGE AND DIVORCE

1864 dower and curtesy are recognized; premarital agreements are allowed as long as they do not "alter the legal order of descent [repealed in 1887]."

1873 in divorce, the division of community property is "in such proportions as the court . . . may deem just," for grounds of extreme cruelty; property shall be distributed equally in all other cases (§ 32-712).

1895 county recorders are required to issue marriage licenses.

Where to Find Marriage and Divorce Records

Marriage records have been recorded by the county clerk since 1860. There are statewide marriage indexes to 1900 in the Special Collections at Ricks College in Rexburg. Divorces have been under the jurisdiction of the county district courts. Statewide marriage and divorce registration began in 1947. Some county records have been filmed, such as:

- Oneida County Court marriage register, 1865-1941, index, 1865-1976, and certificates, 1887-95 (film 1450637 ff.).
- Oneida County District Court calender, including divorces, 1874-9 (film 1502903), and court records, 1879-84 (film 1450649 ff.), at the Oneida County Courthouse in Malad.

See also compiled sources, such as:

- CD-ROM: *Territorial Vital Records: Births, Divorces, Guardianships, Marriages, Naturalizations, Wills; 1800s Thru 1906 Utah Territory, Arizona, Colorado, Idaho, Nevada, Wyoming, Indian Territory; LDS Branches, Wards; Deseret News Vital Records; J.P. Marriages; Methodist Marriages* (Saint George, UT: Genealogical CD Publishing, 1994).
- The Marriage License Card Index (film 0820155 ff.), compiled by members of the LDS Church from marriage license records in the following county courthouses: Franklin and Lemhi.

PROPERTY AND INHERITANCE

1867 territorial legislature adopts community property system of marital law (Territory of Idaho Laws, Ch. 9).

1887 a married woman may devise a will, but she may not devise her half of community property, which is inherited in entirety by her husband; as a widow, a wife receives only one-half of the community property.

1915 a married woman may control the income from her earnings and separate property (both are community property in Idaho).

1919 a married woman controls the disposition of her separate estate, but she may not enter into contracts, except in the management of that estate, which is vested in the husband. Curtesy and dower are abolished.

SUFFRAGE

1896 Idaho women receive complete suffrage.

CITIZENSHIP

1846 when Great Britain cedes its claims to the Oregon Territory, all residents who are not already citizens of the U.S. become citizens by treaty, except for Native Americans, whose tribes are considered a separate nation until 1924.

CENSUS INFORMATION

The first federal census for Idaho is in 1870; part of Idaho is enumerated in Utah Territory. There are no state censuses for Idaho.

OTHER

1919–11 midwife records of Mary Ann Butler, southeastern Idaho and northern Utah (film 1082337).

BIBLIOGRAPHY

Attebery, Louie W. *Idaho Folklife: Homesteads to Headstones* (Salt Lake City: University of Utah Press, 1985).

Bennet, Dana. "Mormon Polygamy in Early Southeastern Idaho." *Idaho Yesterdays* 28 (Spring 1984): 24–30.

Donaldson, Thomas. *Idaho of Yesterday* (Caldwell, ID: The Caxton Printer, 1941).

Hawley, James H. *History of Idaho: The Gem of the Mountains*. 4 Vols. (Chicago: S.J. Clarke Publishing, 1920, film 1000165 ff.).

Idaho Genealogical Society. *Footprints Through Idaho: A Centennial Tribute to the Pioneers by Their Descendants*. 3 Vols. (Boise: Idaho Genealogical Society, 1989).

Penson-Ward, Betty. *Idaho Women in History* (Boise: Northwest Publishing Co., 1991).

Rahder, Bobbie and Mary Reed. *Idaho Ethnic Heritage*. 3 Vols. (Boise: Idaho Centennial Commission and Idaho State Historical Society, 1990).

Ruckman, Jo Ann. "Knit, Knit, and Then Knit: The Women of Pocatello and the War Effort of 1917–1918." *Idaho Yesterdays* 26 (Spring 1982): 26–36.

SELECTED RESOURCES FOR WOMEN'S HISTORY

Eli M. Oboler Library
Idaho State University
PO Box 8089
Pocatello, ID 83209-8089

Idaho State Historical Society and Archives
325 West Main Street
Boise, ID 83702

McKay Library
Ricks College
525 South Center
Rexburg, ID 83460-0405

University Library
University of Idaho
Moscow, ID 83848

Pioneer Women of the West: A Brief Listing of Holdings in Special Collections and Archives, University of Idaho Library, Moscow, available online at **<www.lib.uidaho.edu/special-collections/pionwom.htm>**

MOTHERHOOD.

"The mother, in her office, holds the key
Of the soul; and she it is who stamps the coin
Of character."

From Perfect Womanhood, by C.K.T. Boland (1903)

ILLINOIS

IMPORTANT DATES IN STATE HISTORY

1673 Claimed by France, under laws of the French Custom of Paris.
1699 French settlement founded at Cahokia.
1703 French settlement founded at Kaskaskia.
1721 Under French military law.
1763 Ceded from France to Great Britain.
1769 Migration of settlers from Virginia begins.
1774 Part of Quebec.
1779 Virginia claims all land north of the Ohio River; first settlement founded at Bellefontaine.
1784 Virginia cedes Illinois claims to the U.S.
1787 Part of the Northwest Territory; French law is repealed; parts of the Illinois country where settlers are citizens of Virginia are exempted from the Northwest Territorial Government.
1800 Part of the Indiana Territory.
1809 Created as a separate territory.
1818 Statehood.
1846 Mormons are driven out of Illinois.
1848 Illinois-Michigan Canal opened.
1871 Great Chicago Fire.

MARRIAGE AND DIVORCE

1825 law prohibits persons who obtain a divorce to remarry for a two-year period.
1845 dower rights are recognized.
1877 marriage licenses are required by law.
1887 county clerks may require a marriage affidavit.
1903 county clerks are required to issue a marriage license.

Where to Find Marriage and Divorce Records

Marriages have been recorded in the county records since about 1791. The Illinois State Archives in Springfield has copies of the county records from 1791 to 1921: see the county marriage records index, 1763–1916 (fiche 6334564 ff.). In 1809, the first divorces were granted by acts of the territorial legislature and also by the county circuit courts. Separations before this date were recorded in the records of the Indiana Territory. The records have been kept by the county clerks and the clerk of the superior court in Cook County. Statewide marriage and divorce registration did not begin until 1962. Many county records have been filmed, such as:

- Gallatin County Clerk marriage certificates, 1813–96 (film 0969484 ff.), at the Gallatin County Courthouse in Carbondale.
- Randolph County Clerk marriage records, 1807–1927 (film 0975007 ff.), at the Randolph County Courthouse in Chester.
- Cook County Clerk marriage licenses, 1871–1920, and index, 1871–1916 (film 1288817 ff.), at the Cook County Courthouse in Chicago.

See also compiled publications, such as:

- Sanders, Walter R. *Marriages from Illinois Counties*. 6 Vols. (Litchfield, IL: The Author, 1976, film 0823698 ff.). Covers at least the following counties: Bond (1817–28), Brown (1839–41), Clay (1825–34), Edwards (1815–16), Fayette (1827–33), Greene (1821–32), Lawrence (1821–4), Macon (1829–32), Macoupin (1829–33), Madison (from 1812), Monroe

(1816–19), Montgomery (1821–34), Perry (1827–30), Randolph (1809–12), Schuyler (1825–31), Union (1819–26), Wayne (1819–24), and White (1816–19).

- Alguire, Joan L. *Some Cook County Marriages Prior to Fire [1871]* (South Holland, IL: South Suburban Genealogical & Historical Society, 1987, fiche 6050058).
- Sanders, Walter R. *Marriages from Illinois Counties [1809–1841]*. 6 Vols. (Litchfield, IL: The Author, 1976, film 0823698 ff).

PROPERTY AND INHERITANCE

1845 a widow's dower entitles her to one-third of her husband's real estate; widows of aliens are entitled to same dower as widows of native-born husbands.

1861 a married woman may hold separately property that was owned before marriage. A deed to a husband and wife no longer makes them tenants by the entirety.

1869 a married woman's earnings are her separate property.

1872 a married woman may devise a will.

1874 a married woman's separate estate is free from the debts of her husband.

SUFFRAGE

1919 women become eligible to vote in presidential elections.

1920 Illinois women receive complete suffrage by passage the 19th Amendment to the Constitution.

CITIZENSHIP

1783 all residents of Illinois become U.S. citizens by legislation, except for Native Americans, whose tribes are considered a separate nation until 1924.

CENSUS INFORMATION

The first surviving federal census for Illinois is an 1810 census for Randolph County only.

1845 state census for Cass, Putnam, and Tazewell counties (film 0976178) at the Illinois State Archives.

OTHER

1827 a woman convicted of procuring an abortion may be sentenced to one month's imprisonment. Those who are convicted of administering abortions may be imprisoned for three years.

1867 a state board of charities is established.

1872 state law prohibits sexual discrimination in employment.

1904 the Soldiers and Sailors Home in Quincy begins accepting some widows, daughters, and mothers of veterans of the Mexican War and the Civil War.

1895–1963 Wilmington Widows' Home also accepts widows of veterans.

The Home records are at the Illinois State Archives.

BIBLIOGRAPHY

Barber, Rita Barrow. *Somewhere in Between: Quilts and Quilters of Illinois* (Paducah, KY: American Quilters Society, 1986).

Beck, Nelson. *Resources for the Study of Women's History Located in the Illinois Historical Survey Library* (Urbana: Illinois Historical Survey Library, 1979).

Bogue, Allen C. *From Prairie Belt to Corn Belt: Farming on the Illinois and Iowa Prairies in the Nineteenth Century* (Chicago: University of Chicago Press, 1963).

Clinton, Katherine. "Pioneer Women in Chicago, 1833–1837." *Journal of the West* 12 2 (1973): 317–24.

Elbert, E. Duane and Rachel Kemp Elbert. *History from the Heart: Quilt Paths Across Illinois* (Nashville: Rutledge Hill Press, 1993).

The Genealogical Index of the Newberry Library. 4 Vols. (Boston: G.K. Hall, 1960, film 0928135 ff.).

Gilman, Agnes Geneva and Gertrude M. Gilman. *Who's Who in Illinois: Women, Makers of History* (Chicago: The Eclectic Publishers, 1927, film 1674246).

Goodwin, Joanne L. *Gender and the Politics of Welfare Reform: Mothers' Pensions in Chicago, 1911–1929* (Chicago: University of Chicago Press, 1997).

Higgs, David L. "Tenancy by the Entirety in Illinois: A Reexamination." *Southern Illinois University Law Journal* 1980 (Fall 1980): 83–106.

Hine, Darlene Clark. *The Black Women in the Middle West Project: A Comprehensive Resource Guide, Illinois and Indiana; Historical Essays, Oral Histories, Biographical Profiles, and Document Collections* (Indianapolis: Indiana Historical Bureau, 1986).

McCormick, Henry. *The Women of Illinois* (1913. Reprint. Washington, DC: Library of Congress Photoduplication Service, 1990, film 1674246).

Perryman, F.M. *Pioneer Life in Illinois* (Pana, IL: Kerr's Printing House, 1907, fiche 6101678).

Schweitzer, George K. *Illinois Genealogical Research* (Knoxville, TN: The Author, 1997).

Szucs, Loretto Dennis. *Chicago and Cook County: A Guide to Research* (Salt Lake City: Ancestry, Inc., 1996).

Tilson, Christiana. *A Woman's Story of Pioneer Illinois* (Chicago: R.R. Donnelly, 1919).

Travis, Anthony R. The Origin of Mothers' Pensions in Illinois." *Journal of the Illinois State Historical Society* 68 5 (1975): 421–8.

University of Illinois at Urbana-Champaign Archives. *Guide to Women's History Sources* (Urbana: The University, 1989).

Wheeler, Adade Mitchell and Marlene Steen Wortman. *The Roads They Made: Women in Illinois History* (Chicago: Charles H. Kerr, 1972).

SELECTED RESOURCES FOR WOMEN'S HISTORY

Chicago Area Women's History Conference
400 E. Randolph, #3910
Chicago, IL 60601

Daughters of Union Veterans of the Civil War
503 S. Walnut Street
Springfield, IL 62704

Helen Matthes Library
100 Market Street
Effingham, IL 62401

Illinois State Archives
Capitol Complex
Springfield, IL 62756

Illinois State Historical Society
Old State Capitol
Springfield, IL 62701

Newberry Library
60 West Walton Street
Chicago, IL 60610

Oral History Offices
Sangamon State University
Shepherd Road
Springfield, IL 62708

INDIANA

IMPORTANT DATES IN STATE HISTORY

1679 Claimed by France.
1732 Vincennes founded.
1763 Ceded from France to Great Britain.
1784 Clarksville founded.
1787 Part of the Northwest Territory.
1800 Created as the Territory of Indiana, including the remainder of the Northwest Territory.
1814 Separate Indiana Territory organized.
1816 Statehood; constitution drafted with basis in common law.
1846 National Road is extended across Indiana.

MARRIAGE AND DIVORCE

1852 dower and curtesy are abolished.
1905 a written application for a marriage license must be filed with the clerk of the circuit court in the county of the bride's residence.

Where to Find Marriage and Divorce Records

The earliest marriage records were recorded in the parish registers of the Catholic Church, beginning in 1749. See the following records:

- Saint Francois Xavier de Oubache parish registers, 1749–86 (film 1026606), at the French National Archives, Section Outre-Mer, in Paris, and transcripts at the National Archives of Canada in Ottawa, Ontario; and parish registers, 1780–1960 (film 1433361 ff.), at Saint Francis Xavier Church in Vincennes.

Marriages have been recorded by the county clerks since about 1817. Statewide registration did not begin until 1958. The first divorces were granted by the state legislature from 1817 to 1851. The county courts of common pleas have held jurisdiction for divorce cases since 1852. Some county records have been filmed, such as:

- Marion County Clerk of Circuit Court marriage records, 1822–1944 (film 0499367 ff.), marriage returns, 1892–1907, 1910–21, and WPA index to marriages, 1822–50, 1856–60, and 1866–1915 (film 0413535 ff.).
- Marion County Clerk of the Superior Court marriage returns, 1882–91 (film 0382748).
- Marion County Court of Common Pleas issue docket, 1853–73 (film 0522982 ff.), and judgment docket, 1853–72 (film 0522980 ff.), divorces are mixed with the other cases.
- Fountain County Clerk of the Circuit Court marriage records, 1826–1921 (film 1321668 ff.), at the Fountain County Courthouse in Covington.

The State Library has a database index of marriages based on county records through 1850, available online at **<www.state.lib.in.us/indiana/genealogy/mirr.html>**, which, at present, does not include Clay, Jasper, Madison, Newton, Noble, and Starke counties. See also indexes and compiled publications, such as:

- Indiana State Board of Health. *Indiana Marriage Index*. 2 Vols. (Indianapolis: The Board, 1960, fiche 6105310 ff.). Indexes give names of brides and grooms, names of spouses, county of residence, and date of marriage.
- Newhard, Malenda E.E. *Divorces and Name Changes Granted by the Indiana General Assembly Prior to 1852* (Harlan, IN: The Author, 1981).
- Newspaper divorce notices, Indianapolis, 1848–88 (film 1476959), at the Indiana State

Library in Indianapolis. Includes names of persons, date of event, page and column of newspaper, and a code for the newspaper.

- Wolfe, Barbara A. *Index, Divorces, Cass County, Indiana, November, 1829 to October 1872* (Logansport, IN: The Author, 1993). Abstracted from county court records.

PROPERTY AND INHERITANCE

1852 lands and profits "of a married woman shall be her separate property as fully as if she were unmarried (§ 5)." Dower and curtesy are abolished.

1852 married women may devise wills "to their heirs, which they may have in any lands . . . or in any personal property (§ 1)," and in intestacy gives widows one-third of her husband's real estate "in fee simple, free from all demands of creditors (§ 16–17)."

1879 a married woman's separate property is her separate estate.

SUFFRAGE

1913 women become eligible to vote in presidential elections.

1920 Indiana women receive complete suffrage by passage of the 19th Amendment to the Constitution.

CITIZENSHIP

1783 all residents of Indiana become U.S. citizens by treaty, except for Native Americans, whose tribes are considered a separate nation until 1924.

CENSUS INFORMATION

The 1800 and 1810 federal censuses for Indiana Territory are missing.

1807 territorial census, see *Census of Indiana Territory for 1807* (Indianapolis: Indiana Historical Society, 1980, film 1033927).

1853, 1856, 1857, 1877 state census fragments (not at FHL).

1886, 1890, 1894 enumerations of veterans and widows (not at FHL).

The territorial and state censuses are at the Indiana State Library.

OTHER

1866–94 Indiana Adjutant General enrollment of the late soldiers, their widows, and orphans of the late armies of the U.S. residing in the state of Indiana (film 1605057 ff.), at the Indiana State Library.

1873 Indiana becomes the first state to open an all-women's prison (in Indianapolis).

BIBLIOGRAPHY

Arnold, Eleanor. *Memories of Hoosier Homemakers*. 6 Vols. (Bloomington: Indiana University Press, 1993).

Beatty, John D. *Research in Indiana* (Arlington, VA: National Genealogical Society, 1992).

Blee, Kathleen M. *Women of the Klan: Racism and Gender in the 1920s* (Berkeley: University of California Press, 1991). Substantial body of information on Indiana Klanswomen from archives at Ball State University, the Indiana State Library, the Indiana Historical Society, and the Fort Wayne-South Bend Roman Catholic Archdiocese.

Brown, Avis Bryant and Ethel Alice Vinnedge. *Pioneer Women of Lake County, Indiana, 1834–1850* (Lowell, IN: The Authors, 1979).

Hine, Darlene Clark. *The Black Women in the Middle West Project: A Comprehensive Resource Guide, Illinois and Indiana; Historical Essays, Oral Histories, Biographical Profiles, and Document Collections* (Indianapolis: Indiana Historical Bureau, 1986).

—— . *When the Truth is Told: A History of Black Women's Culture and Community in Indiana, 1875–1950* (Indianapolis: Council of Negro Women, 1981).

Indiana Quilt Registry Project. *Quilts of Indiana: Crossroads of Memories* (Bloomington: Indiana University Press, 1991).

Montgomery, Pauline. *Indiana Coverlet Weavers and Their Coverlets* (Indianapolis: Hoosier Heritage Press, 1974).

O'Byrne, Mrs. Roscoe C. *Roster of the Soldiers and Patriots of the American Revolution Buried in Indiana* (1938. Reprint. Baltimore: Clearfield Co., 1994). Includes pension information and names of wives and widows.

Pottinger, David. *Quilts from the Indiana Amish* (New York: E.P. Dutton & Co., 1983).

Robinson, Mona. *Who's Your Hoosier Ancestor: Genealogy for Beginners* (Bloomington: Indiana University Press, 1992).

Siegel, Peggy Brase. "She Went to War: Indiana Women Nurses in the Civil War." *Indiana Magazine of History* 86 (March 1990): 1–27.

Thornbrough, Emma Lou. "The History of Black Women in Indiana." *Black History News and Notes* 13 (May 1983): 4–8 and 14 (August 1983): 4–7.

Wires, Richard. *The Divorce Issue and Reform in Nineteenth-Century Indiana* (Muncie, IN: Ball State University Press, 1967).

Women's History Collections Bibliography (Indianapolis: Indiana Historical Society Library, 1994).

SELECTED RESOURCES FOR WOMEN'S HISTORY

Allen County Public Library
900 Webster Street
Box 2270
Fort Wayne, IN 46801

Indiana Historical Society
315 West Ohio Street
Indianapolis, IN 46202

Indiana State Archives / Indiana State Library
140 North Senate Street
Indianapolis, IN 46204-2215

Lewis Historical Library
Vincennes University
Vincennes, IN 47951

THE HOUSEHOLD.

☞ *(For other Household Items, see "Basket" pages.)*

How we Bake our Bread.

Fig. 1.—BAKING BEFORE THE FIRE.

Fig. 2.—BAKING IN A BAKE-KETTLE.

Fig. 3.—THE DETACHED OVEN.

American Agriculturist June, 1873

IOWA

IMPORTANT DATES IN STATE HISTORY

1682 Claimed by France.
1762 Ceded to Spain.
1788 First white settlement founded near present-day Dubuque (abandoned in 1810).
1800 Ceded to France.
1803 Part of the Louisiana Purchase.
1804 Part of the Indiana Territory.
1805 Part of the Louisiana Territory.
1812 Part of the Missouri Territory.
1821 Part of unorganized Indian territory.
1833 Area opened for white settlement by the Black Hawk Purchase Treaty.
1834 Part of the Michigan Territory.
1836 Part of the Wisconsin Territory.
1838 Created as a separate U.S. territory.
1848 Statehood.
1870 The Iowa frontier is closed by the Bureau of the Census.

MARRIAGE AND DIVORCE

1838 first divorce law is written.

1845 divorce may be granted "when it shall be made fully apparent to the satisfaction of the court, that the parties cannot live in peace or happiness together, and their welfare requires a separation between them (Ch. 659)."

1851 a judge may award a wife a share of the husband's property as alimony.

1882 marriage licenses are required to be issued and recorded by the clerk of court.

Where to Find Marriage and Divorce Records

County clerks began recording marriages in 1834. Statewide marriage registration began in 1880 and is indexed from 1919 at the State Department of Health in Des Moines. Divorce has been under the jurisdiction of county district and chancery courts. Statewide divorce registration began in 1906. Many county records have been filmed, such as:

- Linn County Clerk of the District Court marriage records, 1840–1928 (film 0985981 ff.), at the Linn County Courthouse in Cedar Rapids and at the Iowa State Historical Society in Des Moines.
- Des Moines County Clerk of the District Court index to marriage records, 1921–77, and marriage records, 1835–1930 (film 1543920 ff.).
- Des Moines County Court records, including applications for marriage licenses, 1849–57 (film 0956337), at the Des Moines County Courthouse in Burlington.
- Des Moines County District Court chancery records including divorces, 1839–55 (film 0956331), and divorce records, 1835–1950 (film 1547826 ff.), at the Des Moines County Courthouse.

See also indexes and compiled publications, such as:

- Iowa marriages, 1844–1900 (film 1023609 ff.), at the Iowa State Historical Society, contain abstracts, licenses, newspaper items, etc. for the counties of Buena Vista, Chicaksaw, Des Moines, Floyd, Freemont, Greene, Mills, Osceola, Plymouth, Pottawattamie, and Story.
- Des Moines County Genealogical Society. *Des Moines County, Iowa, Index to Dissolution of Marriages, 1835–1930* (Des Moines: The Society, 1992, fiche 6101897).

- Fretwell, Sheila. S. *Iowa Marriages Before Statehood, 1835–1846* (Waterloo, IA: The Author, 1985).
- Riley, Glenda. "Divorce Records: Linn County, Iowa, 1928–1944." *Annals of Iowa* 50 (Winter 1991): 787–800.

PROPERTY AND INHERITANCE

1840 a married woman is granted *feme sole* status to administer her separate property.
1846 a married woman's separate property is free from the debts of her husband.
1866 a married woman's earnings are her separate property if she is living separately from her husband.
1870 a married woman's earnings are her separate property.
1919 a married woman many enter into contracts without restriction.

SUFFRAGE

1919 women become eligible to vote in presidential elections.
1920 Iowa women receive complete suffrage by passage of the 19th Amendment to the Constitution.

CITIZENSHIP

1803 all residents of Iowa become U.S. citizens by legislation, except for Native Americans, whose tribes are considered a separate nation until 1924.

CENSUS INFORMATION

For the 1830 federal census, see Michigan.
1836 see Shambaugh, Benjamin F. *Wisconsin Territory: The First Census of the Original Counties of Dubuque and Des Moines (Iowa) Taken in July, 1836* (Des Moines: Historical Department of Iowa, 1897, film 1022202). Comprises the present states of Iowa, Minnesota, and parts of North and South Dakota.
1838 territorial census (available on microfiche from the University of Northern Iowa Library).
1846 territorial census of Louisa, Polk, and Wapello counties (film 1022202).
1847 territorial census of Clinton, Davis, Louisa, Marion, Scott, Van Buren, and Wapello counties (film 1022202).
1849 state census of Benton, Boone, Clinton, Jackson, Louisa, Madison, Poweshiek, Scott, Van Buren, and Washington counties (film 1022202).
1851 state census of Cedar, Clinton, Decatur, Guthrie, Iowa, Jackson, Jasper, Jefferson, Johnson, Madison, Mahaska, Page, Pottawattamie, Poweshiek, Scott, and Washington counties (film 1022203).
1852 state census of various counties, Appanoose through Wayne (film 1022204 ff.).
1854 state census of various counties, Adams through Winneshiek (film 1022206 ff.).
1856 state census (film 1021290 ff.).
1859 state census (film 1022208).
1862, 1867, 1869 state censuses, statistical information only.
1915 state census (film 1379445 ff.).
1925 census (film 1429191 ff. and index on film 1430705 ff.).
The territorial and state censuses are at the Iowa State Historical Society.

OTHER

1919–26 Des Moines County Treasurer ledger, including widows' pension records, (film 1710479), at the Des Moines County Courthouse in Burlington. Records of assistance for other counties are also on microfilm.

Century Farm Applications (film 1023895 ff.), at the Iowa State Historical Society, of farms that have remained in Iowa families for more than 100 years.

BIBLIOGRAPHY

Cordier, Mary Hurlbut. *Schoolwomen of the Prairies and Plains: Personal Narratives from Iowa, Kansas, and Nebraska, 1860s–1920s* (Albuquerque: University of New Mexico Press, 1997).

Dolan, John P. and Lisa Lacher. *Guide to Public Records of Iowa Counties* (Des Moines: Connie Wimer, 1986).

Farrell, Jane A. "Clothing for Adults in Iowa, 1850–1899." *Annals of Iowa* 46 2 (1981): 100–20.

Fink, Deborah. *Open Country, Iowa: Rural Women, Tradition, and Change* (Albany: State University of New York Press, 1986).

Gallaher, Ruth A. *The Legal and Political Status of Women in Iowa: An Historical Account of the Rights of Women in Iowa from 1838 to 1918* (Iowa City: State Historical Society of Iowa, 1918).

Hanft, Ethel W. *Remarkable Iowa Women* (Muscatine, IA: River Bend Publishing, 1983).

Hawbaker, Becky Wilson. "Oral History Interviews with Iowa Women: A Survey of Collections in Iowa." *Annals of Iowa* 53 2 (1994): 246–64.

Reeves, Winona Evans. *The Blue Book of Iowa Women: A History of Contemporary Women* (1914. Reprint. Tucson: W.C. Cox Co., 1974, film 0934928).

Riley, Glenda. *The Female Frontier: A Comparative View of Women on the Prairie and on the Plains* (Lawrence: University of Kansas Press, 1988).

—. *Frontierswoman: The Iowa Experience* (1981. Reprint. Ames: Iowa State University Press, 1994).

—. "Not Gainfully Employed: Women on the Iowa Frontier, 1833–1870." *Pacific Historical Review* (Mary 1980): 237–64.

— . *Prairie Voices: Iowa's Pioneering Women* (Ames: Iowa State University Press, 1996).

Swierenga, Robert P. *Pioneers and Profits: Land Speculation on the Iowa Frontier* (Ames: Iowa State University Press, 1968). Contains information on ethnic settlement patterns on the Iowa frontier.

Wilson, Jennie L. *Legal Status of Women in Iowa* (Des Moines: Iowa Printing Co., 1894).

SELECTED RESOURCES FOR WOMEN'S HISTORY

Amana Heritage Society
PO Box 81
Amana, IA 52203

Archives of Women in Science and Engineering
Special Collections
Iowa State University
403 Parks Library
Ames, IA 50011-2140

CWSHA
History Department
University of Northern Iowa
Cedar Falls, IA 50614

State Archives of Iowa
State Historical Society of Iowa
600 East Locust, Capitol Complex
Des Moines, IA 50319

Iowa Women's Archives
University of Iowa Library
100 Main Library
Iowa City, IA 52242

Iowa Women's Archives, available online at **<www.lib.uiowa.edu/iwa>**, is an index to the Women's History Archives at the University of Iowa Library.

KANSAS

IMPORTANT DATES IN STATE HISTORY

1803 Part of the Louisiana Purchase.
1812 Part of Missouri Territory.
1821 Part of unorganized Indian Territory; Santa Fe Trail opened.
1827 Fort Leavenworth established.
1854 Created as a U.S. territory by the Kansas-Nebraska Act.
1861 Statehood; constitution written.
1863 Confederate irregulars sack and burn Lawrence; Indian wars with the Cheyenne, Arapahoe, Kiowa, and Comanche (end in 1869).
1872 Dodge City founded.
1879 10,000 African Americans migrate from the "Deep South" to Kansas.

MARRIAGE AND DIVORCE

1868 county judges of probate are required to issue and record marriage licenses. Dower and curtesy are abolished.

Where to Find Marriage and Divorce Records

County marriage records began in about 1855 and have been kept by the county recorders and the clerks of the courts of probate. Statewide marriage registration began in 1913 and records are kept at the State Department of Health in Topeka. Divorces have been under the jurisdiction of the county district courts. Many county records have been filmed, such as:

- Bourbon County Probate Court marriage records, 1855–1919 (film 1434854 ff.), at the Bourbon County Courthouse in Fort Scott. The marriage returns were registered mainly with the county clerk, with a few registered under the probate judge.
- Jackson County District Court civil appearance dockets and divorce case files, 1858–1919 (film 1650985 ff.), at the Clerk of the District Court, Jackson County Courthouse, in Holton.

There are also marriages in the Bureau of Indian Affairs records, such as:

- Bureau of Indian Affairs, Pottawatomie Agency register of marriage licenses, 1901–5 (film 1015900), at the NARA Midwest Region in Kansas City, Missouri.

See also compiled publications, such as:

- Ostertag, John A. *Births, Marriages, Deaths, and Other News Items and Events [1857–1896]*. 9 Vols. (Saint Joseph, MO: The Author, 1989-96, fiche 6093681 ff.). Information was abstracted from the *White Cloud Kansas Chief* and the *Weekly Kansas Chief*.
- *Marriage Notices from Kansas Territorial Newspapers, 1854–1861* (Cheney, KS: Midwest Historical and Genealogical Society, 1983, film 1320825). Marriages are reprinted from the *Kansas Historical Quarterly* 21 (Summer 1955).

PROPERTY AND INHERITANCE

1858 a married woman may devise a will.
1859 a woman's property rights are written into the territorial constitution. A married woman is guaranteed control over her separate earnings and separate estate.
1861 Kansas drafts the first state constitution to give a married woman equal control of her children and marital property.

1862 in intestacy, a widow has a right to choose dower or one half of her husband's estate absolutely, both real and personal (Ch. 83).

1868 a married woman may sue and be sued, "carry on any trade or business, and perform any labor or services, on her sole and separate account; and the earnings of any married woman, from her trade . . . shall be her sole and separate property, and may be invested by her in her own name (Ch. 62 § 1-7)." The widow of a deceased husband, or husband of a deceased wife, are "entitled to the same rights or portion in the estate of the other (Ch. 34 § 28)."

SUFFRAGE

1861 women may vote in school elections.
1887 women may vote in city and bond elections.
1912 Kansas women receive complete suffrage.

CITIZENSHIP

1803 all residents of Kansas become U.S. citizens by legislation, except for Native Americans, whose tribes are considered a separate nation until 1924.

CENSUS INFORMATION

The first federal enumeration of Kansas was in 1860.
1855 territorial census (film 0570188).
1856–8 territorial censuses (film 1405337).
1859 territorial census (film 1654575).
1865 state census (film 0570189 ff.).
1875 state census (film 0570198 ff.).
1885 state census (film 0975699 ff.).
1895 state census (film 0570221 ff.).
1905–1925 state censuses (not at FHL).
The territorial and state censuses are at the Kansas Historical Society in Topeka, and most are available on microfilm through ILL.

❧ *"Kansas women look at the legal status of the Massachusetts women, and can scarce refrain from praying the prayer of the Pharisee, but their presumption is checked when they look westward to Colorado and Wyoming, where there are women who not only can earn and hold property but also have a voice in the question of the taxation of the same. Kansas women have learned that there is nothing too good for Kansas people, so they are asking why not give us full suffrage? And the almost universal answer is: there is no reason not."*

Ella W. Brown, of Holton, Kansas, "The Women and the Law." *The Plebian* 1 6 (May 1894): 15.

OTHER

1842–1907 records of the Delaware Indians in Kansas, transcribed in Arellano, Faye L. *Delaware Trails: Some Tribal Records, 1842–1907* (Baltimore: Clearfield Co., 1996). Includes tribal censuses, allotments, trading post records, medical records, annuity payments, school records, removal records, etc.

1873 a state board of charities is established.

BIBLIOGRAPHY

Brackman, Barbara. *Kansas Quilts & Quilters* (Lawrence: University of Kansas Press, 1993).

Cordier, Mary Hurlbut. *Schoolwomen of the Prairies and Plains: Personal Narratives from Iowa, Kansas, and Nebraska, 1860s–1920s* (Albuquerque: University of New Mexico Press, 1997).

Dick, Everett. *The Sod House Frontier, 1854–1890: A Social History of the Northern Plains from the Creation of Kansas & Nebraska to the Admission of the Dakotas* (1954. Reprint. Lincoln: University of Nebraska, 1979).

Kansas

Dobler, Grace. "Oil Field Camp Wives and Mothers." *Kansas History* 10 (Spring 1987): 29–42.

Flott, Mary M. *Directory of Historical & Genealogical Societies, Museums, & Cultural Organizations in Kansas* (Topeka: Kansas Historical Society, 1995).

Goldberg, Michael. *An Army of Women: Gender and Politics in Gilded Age Kansas* (Baltimore: Johns Hopkins University Press, 1997).

Haywood, C. Robert. *Victorian West: Class and Culture in Kansas Cattle Towns* (Lawrence: University of Kansas Press, 1991).

Holt, Marilyn , Bobbie Pray, and Dot E. Taylor. *Textile Diaries: Quilts as Cultural Markers* (Topeka: Kansas State Historical Society, 1990).

Katz, William Loren. "Exodus to Kansas," in *Black Women of the Old West* (New York: Atheneum Books, 1995), 41–7.

Madden, Mary. "Textile Diaries: Kansas Quilt Memories." *Kansas History* 13 1 (Spring 1990).

Malin, James C. *Doctors, Devils, and the Women: Fort Scott, Kansas, 1870–1890* (Lawrence: Coronado Press, 1975).

Oringderff, Barbara. *True Sod* (North Newton, KS: Mennonite Press, 1976).

Orpen, Mrs. *Memories of the Old Emigrant Days in Kansas, 1862–1865* (London: William Blackwood and Sons, 1926).

Robertson, Clara H. *Kansas Territorial Settlers of 1860 Who Were Born in Tennessee, Virginia, North Carolina, and South Carolina* (Baltimore: Genealogical Publishing Co., 1976).

Shortridge, James R. *Peopling the Plains: Who Settled Where in Frontier Kansas* (Lawrence: University of Kansas Press, 1995).

Smith, Patricia Douglass. *Kansas Biographical Index: State-Wide and Regional Histories: Citing More Than 35,500 Biographies from Sixty-eight Volumes of Kansas Biographical Sources* (Garden City, KS: The Author, 1994, film 1698049).

Stratton, Joanna L. *Pioneer Women: Voices from the Kansas Frontier* (New York: Simon & Schuster, 1983).

Thomas, M. Evangeline. "The Role of Women Religious in Kansas History, 1841-1891." *Kansas History* 4 1 (1981): 53–63. Women's Catholic orders in Kansas.

Underwood, June. "Civilizing Kansas: Women's Organizations, 1880–1920." *Kansas History* 7 (Winter 1984): 291–306.

Whittemore, Margaret. *Historic Kansas: A Centenary Sketchbook* (Lawrence: University of Kansas Press, 1954).

SELECTED RESOURCES FOR WOMEN'S HISTORY

Argonia and Western Sumner Historical Society
Salter House Museum
PO Box 203
510 South Main Street
Argonia, KS 67004

Agricultural Hall of Fame and National Center
630 North 126th Street
Bonner Springs, KS 66012

Boot Hill Museum
Front Street
Dodge City, KS 67801

Kansas Collection
Kenneth Spencer Research Library
University of Kansas
Lawrence, KS 66045

Kansas State Historical Society Library
6425 SW 6th Avenue
Topeka, KS 66615-1099

Learning Resource Center
Coffeyville Community College
11th and Willow Streets
Coffeyville, KS 67337

Mennonite Library and Archives
Western District of the General Conference,
Mennonite Church
Bethel College
300 East 27th Street
North Newton, KS 67117

Notable Kansas Women, available online at **<history.cc.ukansas. edu/heritage/ksjs/people/women.html>**

KENTUCKY

IMPORTANT DATES IN STATE HISTORY

1763 Area ceded from France to Great Britain; attached to Virginia; first settlers come from Virginia, North Carolina, Maryland, and Pennsylvania.

1774 Harrodsburg settled.

1775 Boonesborough settled; Transylvania Company from North Carolina purchases most of western Kentucky.

1776 Kentucky County formed from Fincastle County, Virginia.

1790 Virginia cedes its claims to Kentucky; part of Southwest Territory.

1792 Statehood; state constitution based on the common laws of Virginia.

MARRIAGE AND DIVORCE

1783 because of the lack of ordained ministers, civil marriages are allowed.

1785 all marriages require a certificate to be filed by the minister or clerk. Marriage bonds require a male relative or guardian to sign for the bride, since women may not enter into contracts.

1809 defendants in divorce cases are not allowed to remarry during the lifetime of the spouse.

1883 county clerks are required to issue marriage licenses.

Where to Find Marriage and Divorce Records

Marriages have been recorded in county records since their creation. Statewide registration did not begin until 1958. The first divorces were granted by the Kentucky State Legislature. From 1849 to 1959 county circuit courts held jurisdiction for divorces, which are mixed among the other records of the court. Many county records have been filmed, such as:

- Fayette County Clerk marriage bonds, 1803–98, and minister marriage returns, 1795–1851 (film 0009014 ff.), at the Margaret I. King Library, University of Kentucky, in Lexington.
- Floyd County Circuit Court order books, 1808–1934 (film 1843752 ff.), at the Floyd County Courthouse in Prestonburg.
- Lincoln County Clerk of the County Court marriage records, 1781–1961 (film 1904116 ff.), at the Lincoln County Courthouse in Stanford.

See also compiled publications, such as:

- Garrison, Gwendolyn. *Black Marriage Bonds of Fayette County, Kentucky, 1866–1876* (Lexington: Kentucky Tree-Search, 1985).
- Clift, Garrett Glenn. *Kentucky Marriages, 1797–1865* (Baltimore: Genealogical Publishing Co., 1966, film 1320550).
- *Kentucky Marriage Records, from the Register of the Kentucky Historical Society* (Baltimore: Genealogical Publishing Co., 1983).

PROPERTY AND INHERITANCE

1822 in intestacy, a widow inherits one-third of her husband's real and personal property.

1838 a married woman is allowed a separate estate, free from the debts of her husband, and she may devise a will with the permission of her husband.

1843 a married woman is allowed to have a separate estate and is granted *feme sole* status in the management of that estate.

1846 a "marriage shall give to the husband, during the lifetime of the wife, no estate or interest in her real estate, chattels real, or slaves owned at the time or acquired by her after marriage, except the use thereof, with power to rent the real estate for not more than three years at a time, and hire the slaves in like manner for not more than one year, and receive the rent and hire (§ 1)." A married woman "who shall come to this from another state or country, without her husband, he never having resided here, may function legally as a *feme sole*." Upon his arrival, however, this power is revoked (§ 3). Married women may convey their separate estates created since 1 July 1852, those antedating this time must be conveyed "under the superintendence of a court of equity."

1852 dower rights (one-third of the deceased husband's real estate in fee simple, for life use only) are recognized, and a married woman may dispose of her separate estate "secured to her by deed or devise" by will, recorded in chancery courts, and by the clerk of the county court (Art. IV § 3).

1867 a married woman may devise her separate estate with the permission of her husband.

1894 regarding her separate estate, a married woman may make contracts, sue and be sued, and devise a will without restriction.

SUFFRAGE

1920 Kentucky women receive complete suffrage by passage of the 19th Amendment to the Constitution.

CITIZENSHIP

Within the jurisdiction of the original Thirteen Colonies.

CENSUS INFORMATION

Federal censuses for 1790 and 1800 have been destroyed; county tax lists may be used as substitutes to establish residency. Kentucky has no state censuses, but county school censuses were taken between 1870 and 1932, many of which have been filmed, such as:

- Boone County school censuses, 1896–1902 (film 10551021), at the Boone County Courthouse in Burlington.
- Elliott County school censuses, 1902–32 (film 0839947 ff.), at the Elliott County Courthouse in Sandy Hook.

OTHER

1818–53 slave importation certificates of slaves brought into Kentucky by their masters, at the Kentucky State Archives.

1912–46 Confederate veterans' and widows' pensions (film 1670795 ff.), at the Kentucky State Archives, indexed by Simpson, Alicia. *Index of Confederate Pension Applications, Commonwealth of Kentucky* (Frankfort: Division of Archives, 1981).

BIBLIOGRAPHY

Clarke, Mary Washington. *Kentucky Quilts and Their Makers* (Paducah: University Press of Kentucky, 1993).

Drake, Daniel. *Pioneer Life in Kentucky* (Cincinnati: Robert Clarke & Co., 1870).

Farr, Sidney S. *Appalachian Women: An Annotated Bibliography* (Lexington: University Press of Kentucky, 1981).

Genealogies of Kentucky Families: From the Register of The Kentucky Historical Society. 2 Vols. (Baltimore: Genealogical Publishing Co., 1981).

Genealogies of Kentucky Families: From the Register of The Filson Club History Quarterly. 2 Vols. (Baltimore: Genealogical Publishing Co., 1981).

Kentucky

Giesen, Carol A.B. *Coal Miner's Wives: Portraits of Endurance* (Lexington: University Press of Kentucky, 1995).

Greene, Janet W. "Strategy for Survival: Women's Work in the Southern Coal Camps." *West Virginia History* 49 (1990): 37-54.

Hartman, Margaret S. "Annulments and Divorces in Kentucky." *Kentucky Genealogist* 20 (1978): 60-4.

Hehir, Donald M. *Kentucky Families: A Bibliographic Listing* (Bowie, MD: Heritage Books, 1993).

Hogan, Roseann Reinemuth. *Kentucky Ancestry: A Guide to Genealogical and Historical Research* (Salt Lake City: Ancestry, Inc., 1992).

Irvin, Helen Deiss. *Women in Kentucky* (Lexington: University Press of Kentucky, 1979).

Johnson, W.D. *Biographical Sketches of Prominent Negro Men and Women of Kentucky* (1897. Reprint. Lexington: University of Kentucky, 1953, film 0156894).

Kentucky Quilt Project. *Kentucky Quilts, 1800–1900* (New York: Pantheon Books, 1982).

Kleber, John E. *The Kentucky Encyclopedia* (Lexington: University Press of Kentucky, 1992).

Kozee, William Carlos. *Early Families of Eastern and Southeastern Kentucky and Their Descendants* (Baltimore: Genealogical Publishing Co., 1973).

McAdams, Ednah Wilson. *Kentucky Pioneer and Court Records: Abstracts of Early Wills, Deeds, and Marriages from Court House Records of Old Bibles, Churches, Grave Yards, and Cemeteries Copied by American War Mothers, Genealogical Material Collected from Authentic Sources, Records from Anderson, Bourbon, Boyle, Clark, Estill, Fayette, Garrard, Harrison, Jessamine, Lincoln, Madison, Mercer, Montgomery, Nicholas, and Woodford Counties* (1929. Reprint. Baltimore: Genealogical Publishing Co., 1975).

Moore, Marat. *Women in the Mines: Stories of Life and Work* (New York: Twayne, 1996).

Sears, Richard. "Working Like a Slave: Views of Slavery and the Status of Women in Antebellum Kentucky." *The Register of the Kentucky Historical Society* 87 (Winter 1989): 1-19.

Smith, W.T. *A Complete Index to the Names of Persons, Places, and Subjects Mentioned in Littel's Laws of Kentucky: A Genealogical and Historical Guide* (1931. Reprint. Baltimore: Clearfield Co., 1994).

Taney, Mary Florence. *Kentucky Pioneer Women* (1893. Reprint. Washington, DC: Library of Congress Photoduplication Service, 1990, film 1688874).

Thompson, Lawrence S. "Marriage and Courtship Customs in the Ohio Valley." *Kentucky Folklore Record* 9 3 (1963): 47-50.

SELECTED RESOURCES FOR WOMEN'S HISTORY

Camden-Carroll Library
Morehead State University
Morehead, KY 40351

The Filson Club Historical Society
1310 South Third Street
Louisville, KY 40208

Frontier Nursing Service in Kentucky
PO Box 4
Wendover, KY 41775

Kentucky State Archives
300 Coffee Tree Road
PO Box 537
Frankfort, KY 40602-0537

Margaret I. King Library
University of Kentucky
Euclid Avenue and Rose Street
Lexington, KY 40506

Women's History Coalition of Kentucky
Blazer Library
Kentucky State University
East Main Street
Frankfort, KY 40601

LOUISIANA

IMPORTANT DATES IN STATE HISTORY

1699 France founds its first settlements.

1712 Chartered as a province; French civil law adopted.

1714 Natchitoches founded.

1720 Becomes a Crown Colony of France.

1763 Ceded to Spain.

1769 Spanish military forces arrive and take possession of the colony; French civil law is abolished and replaced with laws of Spain.

1800 Ceded back to France.

1803 In the Louisiana Purchase from France, the U.S. purchases land that includes the future states of Arkansas, Iowa, Louisiana, Missouri, Nebraska, North Dakota, Oklahoma, and South Dakota, and the major portions of Colorado, Idaho, Kansas, Montana, and Wyoming; and parts of Minnesota, New Mexico, and Texas (about 50,000 people). The territorial governor creates the court of common pleas and allows trial by jury.

1804 Organized as the U.S. territory of Orleans and the District of Louisiana.

1805 Louisiana Territory is reorganized (encompasses the size of the future state).

1808 Louisiana Civil Code adopted, containing elements of French and Spanish civil law and English common law; but mostly based on the Code of Napoleon.

1812 Statehood; first constitution adopted (nine more will be adopted by 1921). Louisiana's regional geographic divisions are parishes, not counties.

1861 26 January secedes from the Union.

1868 11 June readmitted to the Union.

MARRIAGE AND DIVORCE

1807 marriage licenses must be obtained from a parish judge, to be performed only by ordained priests or ministers, or a justice of the peace.

1808 marriage is defined "in no other view than as a civil contract (Art. 1)."

1825 marriage between slaves is prohibited.

1856 in divorce, a woman may claim half of the community property.

Where to Find Marriage and Divorce Records

Marriages were recorded in parish records beginning in about 1735 and are available from the original parishes. Some colonial-era marriages were also recorded in the French *Conseil Superior* and Spanish *Cabildo* records, which can be found at the Louisiana Historical Center Library in New Orleans. Until about 1870, the Recorders of Births, Deaths, and Marriages issued marriage licenses. After 1880 city courts also issued marriage licenses (some were also issued by city courts from 1807 to 1808). Divorces were first granted by act of legislature from 1805 to about 1846. In 1818, the Orleans Parish District Court held coterminous jurisdiction for divorces, as did all the parish district courts by 1827. There is no statewide registration of marriage or divorce. See the following indexes:

- Marriage records index and contracts, 1718–1900 (New Orleans: Louisiana State Museum, 1980, film 1292185), a card file index of marriage records and contracts from various newspapers in Louisiana.
- Justice of the Peace marriage licenses and certificates card index, 1846–70, at the New Orleans Public Library.

- Name card index to records of the French Superior Council and judicial records of the Spanish *Cabildo* (film 1276244 ff.), at the Louisiana Historical Center Library.

There are forty-eight parishes with civil records on microfilm at the FHL and at the New Orleans Public Library. For a list of these parishes, see **<www.gnofn.org/~nopl/guide/genguide/loucivil.htm>**. Many of the individual parishes have been filmed, such as:

- Orleans Parish Eighth District Court cases, 1866-72 (film 1822282 ff.), and Orleans Parish First District case papers, 1813-46 (film 1710492 ff.), at the New Orleans Public Library, including divorces, separations of bed and board, successions, emancipations, and separations of property. Other Orleans Parish district court records have also been filmed.
- Assumption Parish Clerk of Court marriage records (certificates, bonds, licenses), 1790-1926, and index, 1800-1971 (film 0876511 ff.), at the Assumption Parish Courthouse in Napoleonville.
- Natchitoches Parish Clerk conveyance records, including marriage contracts, administration of estates, intestate settlements, etc., 1738-1900 (film 0279036 ff.), and Natchitoches Parish Clerk of the District Court marriages, 1855-1900; index, 1855-1939 (film 0279004 ff.), at the Natchitoches Parish Courthouse in Natchitoches.

The Florida Parishes (present parishes of East Baton Rouge, East Feliciana, Livingston, Saint Helena, Tammany, Tangipahoa, Washington, and West Feliciana) have been transcribed for the years 1782 to 1810 in the *Archives of the Spanish Government of West Florida*. 19 Vols. (Baton Rouge: Works Progress Administration, 1939). This includes marriage contracts and many court records and other legal documents.

See also compiled publications, such as:

- De Ville, Winston. *Marriage Contracts of the Attakapas Post, 1760-1803: Colonial Louisiana Marriage Contracts, Volume V* (Saint Martinville, LA: Attakapas Historical Association, 1966).
- De Ville, Winston. *The New Orleans French, 1720-1733: A Collection of Marriage Records Relating to the First Colonists of the Louisiana Province* (Baltimore: Genealogical Publishing Co., 1973).
- Forsyth, Alice Daly and Ghislaine Pleasanton. *Louisiana Marriage Contracts: A Compilation of Abstracts from Records of the Superior Council of Louisiana During the French Regime, 1725-1769*. 2 Vols. (New Orleans: Polyanthos Press, 1980).

PROPERTY AND INHERITANCE

1769 Spanish civil law requires a married woman to file a release of dower before land owned as common property can be sold.

1815 the property of married persons is described as being divided into "separate" and "common," and the separate property of the wife into "dotal" and "extra dotal," or "paraphernal," dotal being what the wife brings to the husband to assist him in bearing the expenses of the marriage establishment (Art. 2314-7). The management of community property is vested in the husband.

1825 "the wife has a legal mortgage on her husband's immovables, which he may release by giving a special mortgage to the satisfaction of a family meeting, or in accordance with the marriage contract, but it shall not be lawful to stipulate that no mortgage exists (Art. 2360-8)." Common property is defined as "that which is acquired by the husband and wife during marriage, in any manner different from that above declared."

1856 a wife has privileges on her husband's immovables for restitutions of her dower, in lieu of dower, and is seventh in the order of preference.[27] A "partnership or community of acquests or gains exist

[27] In other words, if the husband defaults in the marriage contract, the wife is seventh in line, after creditors, etc., who take preference in a claim.

by operation of the law in all cases (Art. 3321)." Community property consists of "the profits of all the effects of which the husband has the administration . . . and of the estates which they may acquire during marriage, wither by donations made jointly to them both, or by purchase, or in any similar way, even though the purchase be in the name of one and not of both. The husband is the head and master of the community; administers its effects, disposes of the revenue, and may alienate by unencumbered title, without the wife's consent (Art. 2313, 2369, 2370, 2393–8)." The wife "cannot appear in court without the authority of the husband, though she may be a public merchant, or hold property separate from him. Even then she cannot alienate, mortgage, or acquire . . . title without his written consent . . . but may be authorized by the judge of probate upon his refusal," or if she is legally separated (Art. 2372–3). A married woman may make a will without her husband's consent, but she cannot become executrix without his consent, or the court's (Art. 1659). If a husband or wife dies intestate, without ascendants or descendants, his or her share in the community property is held by the survivor for life, or until remarriage (Art. 65). A wife is considered a public merchant if she "carries on a separate trade, but not if she retails only the merchandise of the commerce carried on by him [her husband] (Art. 2371–3)."

1870 a "husband and wife can in no case enter into an agreement . . . which would be to alter the legal order of descents, either with respect to themselves in what concerns the inheritance of their children or posterity (Art. 2326)."

1916–28 Emancipation Acts allow a married woman to control her separate estate, appear in court, and bring suit as a single woman.

SUFFRAGE

1920 Louisiana women receive complete suffrage by passage of the 19th Amendment to the Constitution.

CITIZENSHIP

1803 all residents of Louisiana become U.S. citizens by legislation, except for Native Americans, whose tribes are considered a separate nation until 1924.

CENSUS INFORMATION

The first federal census for Louisiana is in 1810.

1699–1732 censuses, see Maudell, Charles R. *The Census Tables for the French Colony of Louisiana from 1699 Through 1732* (Baltimore: Genealogical Publishing Co., 1972).

1766–1803 censuses, see Platt, Lyman D. *Census Records for Latin America and the Hispanic United States* (Baltimore: Genealogical Publishing Co., 1998).

1844–6 City of Lafayette censuses of licensed merchants, at the New Orleans Public Library. Lafayette was annexed to New Orleans in 1852.

1855–6 New Orleans censuses of "Merchants and Persons Following Professions Requiring Licenses," at the New Orleans Public Library, give name, residence or place of business, profession, license number, amount paid, and remarks.

OTHER

1813–43 petitions for emancipations of slaves, in the records of the parish district civil courts. The Orleans Parish Court emancipation petitions are indexed online **at <www.gnofn.org˜nopl/guides/genguide/circts.htm>**.

1827–51 Orleans Parish Police Jury emancipation records include some children emancipated with their mothers.

1818–65 passports issued by the Mayor of New Orleans to free blacks traveling to and from the city, and slaves traveling with their masters.

1840–64 Free Persons of Color Registers are lists of black people allowed to remain in the state (film 1309932).

1858–70 House of Refuge minutes and releases (film 0906701 ff).

1869–91 Touro Infirmary patient records (film 1064455).

The above records are at the New Orleans Public Library.

1898–1944 applications for Confederate veterans' and widows' pensions (film 1412743 ff.), at the Louisiana State Archives in Baton Rouge.

1912–36 Confederate veterans' and widows' pensions (film 1704156), at the Louisiana National Guard, Jackson Barracks, New Orleans.

BIBLIOGRAPHY

Adams, Donna Burge. *Women in the Florida Parishes.* 5 Vols. (Baton Rouge: The Author, 1985–91). Abstracts from court records, probate records, vital records, newspaper clippings, deeds and other land records, oral traditions, and correspondence about women residing in Louisiana and Mississippi from 1780 to 1971.

Beers, Henry Putney. *French and Spanish Records of Louisiana: A Bibliographical Guide to Archives and Manuscript Sources* (Baton Rouge: Louisiana State University Press, 1989).

Batiza, Rodolfo. "The Louisiana Civil Code of 1808: Its Actual Sources and Present Relevance." *Tulane Law Review* 46 4 (1971).

Dart, Henry P. "Marriage Contracts of French Colonial Louisiana." *Louisiana Historical Quarterly* 17 (1934): 229–41.

Gehman, Mary. *Women and New Orleans: A History* (New Orleans: Margaret Media, 1988).

Glasgow, Vaughn L. "Textiles of the Louisiana Acadians." *Antiques* (August 1981).

Malone, Ann Patton. "Searching for Family and Household Structure of Rural Louisiana Slaves, 1810–1864." *Louisiana History* 28 (Fall 1987): 357–80.

Roach-Lankford, Susan. *Gifts from the Hills: North Central Louisiana Folk Traditions* (Rustin: Louisiana Tech University, 1984).

Schafer, Judith K. "Open and Notorious Concubinage: The Emancipation of Slave Mistresses by Will and the Supreme Court in Antebellum Louisiana." *Louisiana History* 28 (Spring 1987): 165–82.

Scott, Anne Firor. *Southern Women and Their Families in the 19th Century, Papers and Diaries* (Bethesda, MD: University Publications of America, 1997). A guide to the microfilm edition, Series E, holdings of the Louisiana and Lower Mississippi Valley Collections, Louisiana State University Libraries.

Simpson, Vaughan B. "Cherchez les Femmes: Some Glimpses of Women in Early Eighteenth-Century Louisiana." *Louisiana History* 31 (Winter 1990): 21–37.

—— . "Women in Louisiana History," in *A Guide to the History of Louisiana* (Westport, CT: Greenwood Press, 1982).

Tucker, Susan. *The New Orleans Guide to Collections on Women* (New Orleans: Newcomb College, Tulane University, 1989).

SELECTED RESOURCES FOR WOMEN'S HISTORY

Hill Memorial Library
Louisiana State University
Baton Rouge, LA 70803

Howard-Tilton Memorial Library
Tulane University
New Orleans, LA 70118-5682

Louisiana Historical Center Library
751 Chartres Street
New Orleans, LA 70176

New Orleans Public Library
Louisiana Division
219 Loyola Avenue
New Orleans, LA 70140

Louisiana State Archives and Records
3851 Essen Lane
PO Box 94125
Baton Rouge, LA 70804-9125

State Library of Louisiana
760 North Third Street
Baton Rouge, LA 70821

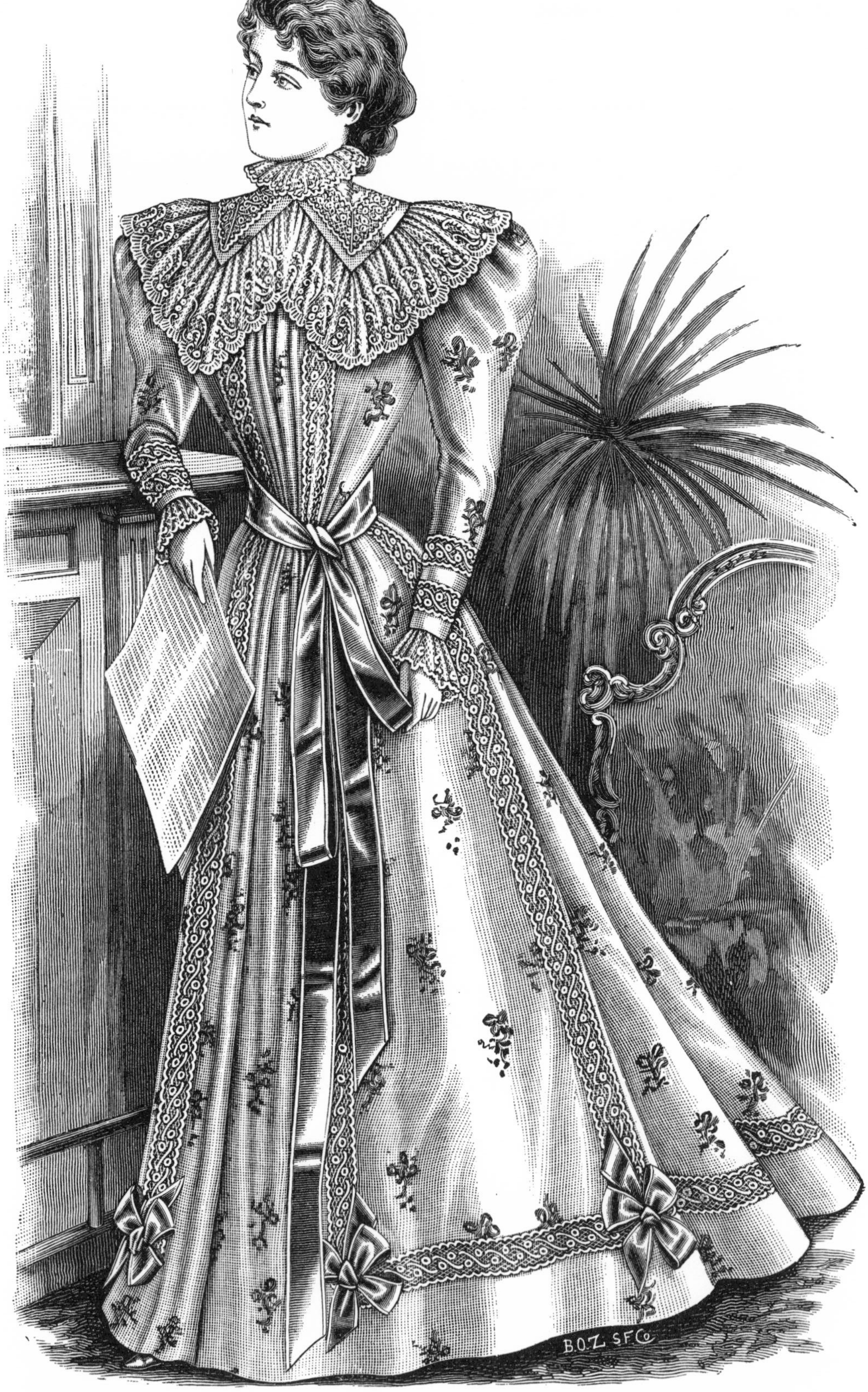

The Standard Designer, June, 1897

MAINE

IMPORTANT DATES IN STATE HISTORY

1620 Most of Maine is part of the Plymouth Colony grant.
1622–4 Settlements made at Monhegan, Saco, and York.
1639 Chartered as the Province and County of Maine.
1658 County of Yorkshire is formed in the Province of Maine.
1675–7 Many settlements are destroyed during King Phillip's War.
1716 Becomes York County, Massachusetts.
1760 Becomes the District of Maine.
1769 Lincoln and Cumberland counties formed in the District of Maine.
1819 Constitution written.
1820 Separates from Massachusetts and gains statehood.
1838 Aroostook War.
1842 Border with Canada (British territory) settled.

MARRIAGE AND DIVORCE

1820 under the laws of Massachusetts until this time.

1850 a provision is added to the divorce law, allowing a divorce on "any facts tending to show that divorce would be reasonable and proper, conducive to domestic harmony, for the good of the parties, and consistent with the peace and morality of Society (Ch. 171 § 2)."

1891 town clerks are required to record marriages within six days of the ceremony.

Where to find Marriage and Divorce Records

Marriage records have been recorded in town records since 1639. All town records have been filmed and are available through the FHL and at the Maine State Archives in Augusta. Marriages and divorces since 1892 have been filed with the Maine Office of Vital Statistics in Augusta. There is a searchable index of marriages, 1892–1966, online at **<www.state.me.us/sos/arc/genealog/marriage.htm>**. Since Maine was a part of Massachusetts until 1820 some court records can be found in Massachusetts records. Indexes at the State Archives include:

- Bride's index, 1895–1953 (film 0010261 ff.), also giving the name of the groom and marriage date.
- Index to delayed registration of marriage bonds, 1670–1891 (1002375 ff.).
- Index to vital records, 1892–1907 (film 0009884 ff.).
- Index to vital records, 1908–22 (film 0010068 ff.).
- Index to vital records of towns prior to 1892 (film 0009743 ff.).

See also compiled publications, such as:

- Frost, John E. and Joseph Crook Anderson II. *York County, Maine, Marriage Returns Prior to 1892* (Camden, ME: Picton Press, 1993).
- Kelley, Judith H. *Marriage Returns of Cumberland County, Maine, to the Year 1892* (Camden, ME: Picton Press, 1998).
- Rohrback, Lewis B. *Maine Marriages, 1892–1966* (Portland: Maine Genealogical Society, 1996). Also available on CD-ROM from Picton Press in Camden, Maine.
- Young, Elizabeth Keene. *Marriage Notices from the Maine Farmer, 1833–1852* (Bowie, MD: Heritage Books, 1995).
- —— . *Vital Records from Maine Newspapers, 1785–1820* (Bowie, MD: Heritage Books, 1993).

Divorce cases prior to 1892 have been centralized at the Maine State Archives. The Archives also has an index to divorces, 1892 to 1983. The original records from 1892 remain in the custody of the district court where the divorce was granted.

PROPERTY AND INHERITANCE

1821 a married woman deserted by her husband may be empowered by the court "to have and hold property as if unmarried (Ch. 57)."

1828 a married woman is given *feme sole* status to manage her separate property.

1844 a married woman may retain all property she owned prior to marriage and possess an estate separate from her husband.

1860 a married woman's separate earnings are her separate property.

SUFFRAGE

1919 women become eligible to vote in presidential elections.

1920 Maine women receive complete suffrage by passage of the 19th Amendment to the Constitution.

CITIZENSHIP

Within the jurisdiction of the original Thirteen Colonies.

CENSUS INFORMATION

For 1790 to 1810 federal censuses, see Massachusetts.

1837 state census, at the Maine State Archives and the Maine Historical Society in Portland. For a list of towns enumerated, see Lainhart, Ann S. *State Census Records* (Baltimore: Genealogical Publishing Co., 1992), 49–52.

OTHER

House, Charles J. *Names of Soldiers of the American Revolution [from Maine] Who Applied for State Bounty ...* (1893. Reprint. Baltimore: Clearfield Co., 1996). Includes 500 widows who made applications for pensions.

BIBLIOGRAPHY

Agger, Lee. *Women of Maine* (Portland: Gannet Books, 1982).

Beedy, Helen Coffin. *Mothers of Maine* (Portland: The Thurston Print, 1895).

Bourne, Miriam Anne. *The Ladies of Castine: From the Minutes of the Castine, Maine Woman's Club* (New York: Arbor House, 1986).

Davis, Walter Goodwin. *Massachusetts and Maine Families* (Baltimore: Genealogical Publishing Co., 1996).

Estes, Marie. *Name Index to Maine Local Histories* (Portland: Maine Historical Society, 1985, film 1698019).

Gray, Ruth, et al. *Maine Families in 1790.* 5 Vols. (Camden, ME: Picton Press, 1988–96).

Litoff, Judy Barret and Hal Litoff. "Working Women in Maine: A Note on Sources." *Labor History* 17 (Winter 1976): 88–95.

Medeiros, Phyllis P. *The Seeds of the Soil: The Planting of the Freewill Baptist Church in Hollis, Buxton, and Gorham, Maine, 1780–1820* (Lanham, MD: University Press of America, 1997).

Meyer, Susan H. *Women's Quilts, Women's Lives: A Study of Maine Quilts and Their Makers* (Waterville, ME: Colby College, 1981).

Nitkin, Nathaniel. "Year of the Penobscot." *New England Galaxy* 14 4 (1973): 8–15. Courtship, marriage, and other customs of the Penobscot Indians.

Noyes, Sybil, Charles T. Libby, and Walter G. Davis. *Genealogical Dictionary of Maine and New Hampshire* (1928–39. Reprint. Baltimore: Genealogical Publishing Co., 1996).

Ostroff, Susan. *A Woman's Place . . . The Maine Point of View* (Augusta: Maine State Museum, 1977).

Pope, Charles Henry. *Pioneers of Maine and New Hampshire* (1908. Reprint. Baltimore: Genealogical Publishing Co., 1996).

Ring, Betty. "Samplers and Silk Embroideries of Portland, Maine." *Antiques* (September 1988).

Spencer, Wilbur D. *Pioneers on Maine Rivers* (1930. Reprint. Baltimore: Genealogical Publishing Co., 1996).

SELECTED RESOURCES FOR WOMEN'S HISTORY

Maine Historical Society
485 Congress Street
Portland, ME 04101

Maine State Archives / Maine State Library
L.M.A. Building
State House Station
Number 84 (archives) /Number 64 (library)
Augusta, ME 04333

Driving the reaper

MARYLAND

IMPORTANT DATES IN STATE HISTORY

1634 First English settlements founded at Saint Mary's City; becomes a proprietary colony; from now until the end of the century, most unmarried women immigrating to Maryland are indentured servants from the English ports of Bristol, Liverpool, and London.

1649 Act of Toleration grants religious freedom in Maryland (repealed in 1654, reinstated in 1657).

1657 First Quakers immigrate to Maryland.

1664 Slavery is sanctioned by law.

1670s First Germans immigrate to Maryland.

1680s Scotch-Irish immigration to Maryland begins.

1691 Becomes a Royal colony.

1692 The Anglican Church becomes the official church in Maryland.

1704 Men outnumber women four to one.

1715 Proprietary government restored.

1718 Catholics and Quakers are disenfranchised (cannot practice their religion).

1732 Boundary line established with three lower counties of Pennsylvania (to become Delaware).

1763–7 The Mason-Dixon Line becomes the border between Maryland and Pennsylvania.

1791 Land ceded to form the District of Columbia.

1861 Federal troops occupy Annapolis.

1862 Battle of Antietam.

MARRIAGE AND DIVORCE

1640 clergy are required to post marriage banns and keep marriage registers.

1661 act prohibits interracial marriage.

1691 marriage between a white woman and a black man is illegal; any children may be bound into service until they reach the age of thirty years.

1701 the recording of marriages is required.

1777 county clerks are required to issue marriage licenses.

1890 clerks of court are required to record marriages.

❧ *Because of the shortage of women in seventeenth-century Maryland, few free women remained single or widowed for long. An indentured female over twelve years of age could have her time purchased by a prospective husband. Most women married after age twenty-two. One-fifth of the children born to female servants were illegitimate. If the mother remained indentured, the children could be bound out by the court as orphans. Some of these pregnant women did marry. In Somerset County, in the seventeenth century, one-third of the women were pregnant at the time of their marriages.*

For more information, see Lois Green Carr and Lorena S. Walsh, "The Planter's Wife: The Experience of White Women in Seventeenth-Century Maryland." *William and Mary College Quarterly* 34 (1977): 542–71.

Where to Find Marriage and Divorce Records

County marriage records began in 1777, although there are some registers and banns from as early as 1640. Records from 1777 have been filed with the clerks of the circuit courts in the counties, and the clerk of the Court of Common Pleas in Baltimore. The records from 1777 to 1950 are also at the Hall of Records in Annapolis. Also at the Hall of Records is the *Maryland Indexes Maryland Marriage References*, available online at **<www.mdarchives.state.md.us/msa/refserv/stager/ssu1500/html/ssu1527.html>**, with references taken from county land and probate records, Maryland inventories, administration accounts, will books, patent libers, etc.; Provincial Court records, and other primary sources. There are other online indexes relating to marriage records (under construction).

Maryland did not grant absolute divorce until 1848. The earliest divorces were in fact legal separations and private agreements to divide property, awarded by the legislature from 1634 to 1854. Beginning in 1829 chancery and county courts also held jurisdiction for divorces. After 1853, the county circuit courts (and the court of common pleas in Baltimore) handled divorce cases. Many county records have been filmed, such as:

- Baltimore County Clerk of the Circuit Court marriage licenses, 1777–1851 (film 0013693 ff.), at the Hall of Records.
- Maryland Land Office official transcription of register for Charles County of births, marriages, and burials, 1654–1726 (film 0013759), at the Maryland Historical Society in Baltimore. Some of the original records are in Charles County Circuit Court land records, 1658–1770, including vital records, 1654–1706 (film 0013746 ff.), at the Hall of Records.

See also indexes and compiled publications, such as:

- Index to the record of Maryland marriages, 1777–1804 (film 0013148), at the Maryland Historical Society.
- Card index to marriages, 1760–95 and 1777–1886, at the Hall of Records.
- Soundex index to marriages, 1914–30, at the Hall of Records.
- Barnes, Robert. *Maryland Marriages, 1634–1820*. 3 Vols. (Baltimore: Genealogical Publishing Co., 1975, 1993).
- —— . *Marriages and Deaths from the Baltimore, Maryland Gazette, 1727–1829* (Baltimore: Genealogical Publishing Co., 1973).
- Bell, Annie W.B. *Maryland Marriage Records*. 23 Vols. (Annapolis: The Author, 1938, fiche 6046950). These records cover the late 1600s and the 1700s.
- Meyer, Mary K. *Divorces and Names Changed in Maryland: By Act of the Legislature, 1634–1867* (Mount Airy, MD: Pipe Creek Publications, 1991).

PROPERTY AND INHERITANCE

1648 first land grant issued to a woman.

1658 a wife is prohibited from acting as her husband's attorney in his absence.

1670 in intestacy, a widow receives one-third of her husband's real and personal property (in the seventeenth century over seventy-five percent of Chesapeake men did not devise a will).[28] A widow may also serve as executrix of her deceased husband's estate.

❧ *Because of the great number of remarriages in colonial Maryland, it is important to look for records of marriage settlements, which were agreements entered into prior to marriage, establishing a woman's separate property from her first husband.*

1674 "any married woman, or *feme covert*, shall happen to be named a Party, Grantor, in any such Writing indented, the same shall not be of Force to debar her, or her Heirs. The Person or Persons taking such, her Acknowledgment, shall examine her privately and secretly, out of the Hearing of her Husband . . ." In land conveyances, a married woman must be examined "privately and secretly" to determine if she is acting of her own free will. All trust estates are required to be registered.

1715 in intestacy, a widow receives one-third of her husband's personal estate absolutely, and one-third of the real estate for life.

1860 a married woman "may devise this separate estate [real and personal property held prior to marriage] as if she were fully unmarried. All property real and personal prior to marriage and all acquired after shall beheld for her separate use (Art. 45 § 1)."

---

[28] Carol Berkin, *First Generations: Women in Colonial America* (New York: Hill & Wang, 1996), 16.

SUFFRAGE

1920 Maryland women receive complete suffrage by passage of the 19th Amendment to the Constitution.

CITIZENSHIP

One of the original Thirteen Colonies.

CENSUS INFORMATION

1776 census, see Brumbaugh, Gaius Marcus. *Maryland Records, Colonial, Revolutionary, County, and Church from Original Sources*. 2 Vols. (1915–28. Reprint. Baltimore: Genealogical Publishing Co., 1967).

OTHER

1661 terms of indentured service for women are set at age twenty-two and over (four years), ages eighteen to twenty-one (five years), ages fifteen to seventeen (six years), and under fifteen (until age twenty-one).

1666 terms of indentured service for women are set at age twenty-two and over (five years), ages eighteen to twenty-one (six years), ages fifteen to seventeen (seven years), and under fifteen (until age twenty-two).

1902 the first workmen's compensation law in the U.S. is enacted in Maryland.

BIBLIOGRAPHY

Allen, Gloria Seaman, et al. *A Maryland Album: Quilting Traditions* (Nashville: Rutledge Hill Press, 1995).

— . "Bed Coverings, Kent County, Maryland, 1710–1820," in *Uncoverings 1985* (Mill Valley, CA: American Quilt Study Group, 1986).

Breen, T.H. *Tobacco Culture: The Mentality of the Great Tidewater Planters on the Eve of the Revolution* (Princeton: Princeton University Press, 1985).

Carr, Lois Green and Lorena S. Walsh. "The Planter's Wife: The Experience of White Women in Seventeenth-Century Maryland." *William and Mary College Quarterly* 34 (1977): 542–71.

Chused, Richard H. *Private Acts in Public Places: A Social History of Divorce in the Formative Era of American Family Law* (Philadelphia: University of Pennsylvania Press, 1994). The focus of this book is colonial Maryland.

Coldham, Peter W. *Settlers of Maryland, 1679–1783*. 5 Vols. (Baltimore: Genealogical Publishing Co., 1996).

Dorsey, Clement. *The Statutory Testamentary Laws of Maryland: With the Decisions of the Courts Thereof, Explanatory of the Same* (Baltimore: F. Lucas, 1838, fiche 6125856).

Goldsborough, Jennifer F. *Legacies: Baltimore Album and Related Quilts in the Collection of the Maryland Historical Society* (Baltimore: Maryland Historical Society, 1994).

Jacob, Kathryn A. "The Woman's Lot in Baltimore Town: 1729–1797." *Maryland History Magazine* 71 3 (1976): 283–95.

Kulikoff, Allan. *Tobacco and Slaves: The Development of Southern Cultures in the Chesapeake, 1680–1800* (Chapel Hill: University of North Carolina Press, 1986).

Land, Aubrey C., Lois Green Carr, and Edward C. Papenfuse. *Law, Society, and Politics in Early Maryland* (Baltimore: Johns Hopkins University Press, 1977).

Luckett, Margie H. *Maryland Women* (Baltimore: The Author, 1931).

Main, Gloria L. *Tobacco Colony* (Princeton: Princeton University Press, 1982).

McDaniel, George W. *Hearth & Home: Preserving a People's Culture* (Philadelphia: Temple University Press, 1983). Black culture and homes in Maryland.

Meyer, Mary K. *Genealogical Research in Maryland* (Mount Airy, MD: Pipe Creek Publications, 1992).

Requardt, Cynthia Horsburgh. "Women's Deeds in Women's Words: Manuscripts in the Maryland Historical Society." *Maryland Historical Society Magazine* 73 (Summer 1978): 186–204.

Sionssat, Anna. "Colonial Women of Maryland." *Maryland Historical Magazine* 2 (1907): 214–6, 379–80.

Smith, Daniel Blake. *Inside the Great House: Planter Life in Eighteenth-Century Chesapeake Society* (Ithaca: Cornell University Press, 1980).

Steward, David and Francis Casey. *A Digest of the Law of Husband and Wife in Maryland* (Baltimore: n.p., 1881).

The Study of Women: Resources in the Special Collections of the University of Maryland at College Park Libraries (College Park: University of Maryland Libraries, 1992).

Van Ness, James S. "On Untiing the Knot: The Maryland Legislature and Divorce Petitions." *Maryland Historical Magazine* 67 (1972): 171–5.

SELECTED RESOURCES FOR WOMEN'S HISTORY

Maryland Historical Society
201 West Monument Street
Baltimore, MD 21201

Maryland State Archives
Hall of Records
350 Rowe Boulevard
Annapolis, MD 21401

National Women's Studies Association
University of Maryland at College Park
College Park, MD 20742

Sojourner Truth Room
Prince George's County Memorial Library
6200 Oxon Hill Road
Oxon Hill, MD 20745

Historical and Biographical Information at the Maryland State Archives: Women in Maryland, available online at **<www.mdarchives.state.md.us/speccol/3520/html/womenbios/html>**

MASSACHUSETTS

IMPORTANT DATES IN STATE HISTORY

1620 New Plymouth Colony settlement begun, Mayflower Compact drafted.
1632 Massachusetts Bay Company receives a charter.
1648 The Laws and Liberties of Massachusetts are drafted.
1691 Massachusetts Bay Colony and New Plymouth Colony are united.
1692 Nineteen women are hanged as witches in Salem.
1770 Boston Massacre.
1773 Boston Tea Party.
1775 Battles of Lexington and Concord; Battle of Bunker Hill.
1780 State constitution drafted.
1820 Maine separates from Massachusetts.

MARRIAGE AND DIVORCE

1621 in New Plymouth Colony, marriage is a civil contract.
1631 Bay Colony law makes adultery punishable by death.
1639 the first divorce in English North America is granted by the Court of Assistants in the Massachusetts Bay Colony.
1658 law in New Plymouth Colony states that "if any shall make any motion of marriage to any man's daughter or maid servant, not having first obtained leave . . . he shall be punished with by fine or corporal punishment . . . (Ch. 25). "
1692 clergymen are given the authority to perform marriages, which have been only civil ceremonies to this date.
1693 act requires the recording of marriages (37 [1693] and 68 [1695]).
1695 a "Bill against Incest" prohibits a widower to marry his deceased wife's sister or niece; a widow may marry her deceased husband's brother or nephew.
1705 interracial marriage is prohibited.
1845 marriage settlements are permitted by law.
1855 divorce law is amended to "make [it] more equitable for women."
1892 town clerks are required to make returns of marriage certificates.

Where to Find Marriage and Divorce Records

Marriages have been recorded in the town records and early colony records since 1620. Births, marriages, and deaths were recorded by the county courts from 1657 until 1692 and by the Court of General Sessions of the Peace thereafter. The original records are available on microfilm and many have also been published. Before 1841, the town records must be searched. Marriages, 1841 to 1901 (film 0961262 ff.), and 1901 to 1905 (film 2057533 ff.), organized by county, are at the Massachusetts State Archives in Boston. Records from 1902 to the present are recorded with the State Registrar of Vital Records and Statistics in Boston. Most county records have been filmed, such as:

- Essex County Court records of births, marriages, and deaths, 1636–1795 (film 0877432 ff.), at the Essex County Courthouse in Salem.
- Middlesex County Clerk of Courts card index to births, deaths, wills, and miscellaneous court records, 1600–1799 (film 1420474), at Clerk of Courts, Middlesex Courthouse in Cambridge.

Massachusetts had no law providing for absolute divorce until 1786, although they were granted.

In 1639, the Court of Assistants (Massachusetts Bay Colony) was given jurisdiction for divorces. The General Court in the Bay Colony granted the first legislative divorce in 1650. After the two colonies united, the Court of Assistants held jurisdiction, although the Governor and Council continued to grant divorces until 1785. Beginning in 1738, the superior courts of judicature also held jurisdiction for divorces. Beginning in 1786, primary jurisdiction shifted from the General Court to the Supreme Judicial Courts in the counties. Beginning in 1887, divorces were heard concurrently by the superior and probate courts, and probate courts were given jurisdiction in 1922. See also:

- Massachusetts Council divorce records, 1760–86 (film 0946895), of various counties, at the Massachusetts State Archives.
- Supreme Judicial Court index cards to divorce records, 1812–67 (film 2027325), at the Massachusetts State Archives.
- Hampshire County Superior Court index to divorces, 1758–1960 (film 2027325 ff.), at the Superior Court in Northampton.
- General Court, colony records, 1629–1777 (film 0954385 ff.), at the Statehouse in Boston.

See also compiled publications, such as:

- American Antiquarian Society. *Index of Marriages in the Massachusetts Centinel and Columbian Centinel, 1784 to 1840*. 4 Vols. (Boston: G.K. Hall, 1961, fiche 6051397 ff.).
- Bailey, Frederic W. *Early Massachusetts Marriages Prior to 1800*. 3 Vols. in 1 (1897–1914. Reprint. Baltimore: Genealogical Publishing Co., 1991, fiche 6051393).
- Noble, John and John F. Cronin. *The Records of the Court of Assistants of the Colony of the Massachusetts Bay, 1630–1692* (Boston: State Printer, 1901–28).
- Roser, Susan E. *Mayflower Marriages: From the Files of George Ernest Bowman at the Massachusetts Society of Mayflower Descendants* (Baltimore: Genealogical Publishing Co., 1990). Contains upward of 10,000 entries and spans five centuries.
- Shurtleff Nathaniel B. and David Pulsifer. *Records of the Colony of New Plymouth, in New England*. 12 Vols. in 10 (Boston: William White, 1855–61, fiche 6046866). Includes General Court and Court of Assistants orders, 1633–91, judicial acts, 1636–92, and miscellaneous records including marriages, 1633–89.

PROPERTY AND INHERITANCE

1641 if a husband's estate does not provide adequately for his widow, the General Court can give relief.

1647 "every woman in the colony who was either married and living with her husband, or married and not living with him as a result of his consent or inevitable providence, or divorced and she was the innocent party; the rights conferred by the act accrued upon marriage; the widow's interest was an estate for her life, after the death of her husband, in one-third of all realty of which her husband had been seised . . . she could not be deprived of her inchoate right during the marriage by any act of her husband . . . her interest might be barred only by a jointure before marriage . . . her estate was free from the claims of her husband's creditors . . . if the lands were not assigned to her within a month after her demand, she was entitled to a writ of dower . . ." A widow also receives one-third of her husband's personalty.

1649 act repeals provision on personalty and charges the county courts to assign what "they shall conceive just and equal."

1787 a deserted wife can petition the court for the right to sell land as a *feme sole*.

1818 Supreme Court decision denies a widow's dower rights over unimproved lands in her husband's estate.

1833 a married woman's separate property is free from the debts of her husband, and she is granted *feme sole* status to manage her separate property.
1835 an abandoned woman may obtain power from the court to sell or convey her property.
1845 property acquired by a married woman that does not derive from her husband is her separate estate.
1854 a married woman may devise a will.
1855 Married Women's Property Act applies to women who marry after 1855; a married woman's separate earnings are her separate property.
1887 courts of probate are given jurisdiction over married women's petitions for separate estates (Ch. 332 § 2).

SUFFRAGE

1780 state constitution denies women the right to vote.
1920 Massachusetts women receive complete suffrage by passage of the 19th Amendment to the Constitution.

CITIZENSHIP

One of the original Thirteen Colonies.

CENSUS INFORMATION

1855, 1865 state censuses (film 0953973 ff.).
1915 state census (not at FHL).
The state censuses are at the Massachusetts State Archives.

OTHER

1636 Boston ordinance establishes the first warning-out policy to prevent strangers from becoming public dependents.
1642 New Plymouth Colony statute defines the status for non-residents and warnings out.
1692 towns become accountable for welfare of the poor.
1767 the warning-out system is abolished.
1863 Massachusetts becomes the first state to create a state welfare agency, called a Board of State Charities.
1862–4 records of nurses enlisted in the Civil War, at the Commonwealth of Massachusetts Military Archives and Museum in Worcester.

BIBLIOGRAPHY

Beattie, Mary E. *Obligation and Opportunity: Single Maritime Women in Boston, 1870 to 1930* (Orono: University of Maine Press, 1994).

Boyer, Paul and Stephen Nissenbaum. *Salem Possessed: The Social Origins of Witchcraft* (Cambridge: Harvard University Press, 1974).

Cott, Nancy F. "Divorce and the Changing Status of Women in Eighteenth-Century Massachusetts." *William and Mary College Quarterly* 33 (1976): 586–614.

—. "Eighteenth-Century Family and Social Life Revealed in Massachusetts Divorce Records." *Journal of Social History* 10 1 (1976): 20–43.

Davidson, Mary M. *Plimoth Colony Samplers* (Marion, MA: The Channings, 1975).

Demos, John P. *A Little Commonwealth: Family Life in Plymouth Colony* (New York: Oxford University Press, 1970).

—— . *Entertaining Satan: Witchcraft and the Culture of Early New England* (New York: Oxford University Press, 1982).

Dublin, Thomas. *Women at Work: The Transformation of Work and Community in Lowell, Massachusetts, 1826–1860* (New York: Columbia University Press, 1979).

Eisler, Benita. *The Lowell Offering: Writings by New England Mill Women [1840–1845]* (New York: W.W. Norton & Co., 1998).

Haskins, George Lee. *Law and Authority in Early Massachusetts: A Study in Tradition and Design* (Lanham, MD: University Press of America, 1960).

Hull, N.E. *Female Felons: Women and Serious Crime in Colonial Massachusetts [1673–1774]* (Urbana: University of Illinois Press, 1987).

Keyssar, Alexander. "Widowhood in Eighteenth-Century Massachusetts: A Problem in the History of the Family." *Perspectives in American History* 8 (1974): 83–122.

Konig, David Thomas. "Community Custom and the Common Law: Social Change and the Development of Land Law in Seventeenth-Century Massachusetts." *American Journal of History* 18 (1974): 137–77.

Lee, Charles R. "The Poor People: Seventeenth-Century Massachusetts and the Poor." *Historical Journal of Massachusetts* 9 (January 1981): 41–50.

—— . "Public Poor Relief and the Massachusetts Community, 1620–1715." *New England Quarterly* 55 (December 1982): 564–85.

Matthews, Nathan. "Early Files of the County Courts of Massachusetts." *Massachusetts Law Quarterly* 10 (1925): 46.

Menand, Catherine S. *A Research Guide to the Massachusetts Courts and Their Records* (Boston: Massachusetts Supreme Judicial Court, Archives and Records, 1987).

Norkunas, Martha K. "Women, Work, and Ethnic Industry: Personal Narratives and the Ethnic Enclaves in the Textile City of Lowell, Massachusetts." *Journal of Ethnic Studies* 15 (Fall 1987): 27–48.

Noyes, Ethel J.R.C. *The Women of the Mayflower and Women of Plymouth Colony* (Ann Arbor, MI: Gryphon, 1971).

Porter, Susan L. *Women of the Commonwealth: Work, Family and Social Change in Nineteenth-Century Massachusetts* (Boston: University of Massachusetts Press, 1996).

Sanborn, Melinde Lutz. "Maiden Names from the Essex County, Massachusetts, General Sessions." *New England Historical and Genealogical Register* CXLIV (January 1990).

Winterhalter, Cynthia E. "Repatriations of Women from the Records of U.S. District Court at Boston, Massachusetts." *NEXUS* XII 1 (1995): 199.

SELECTED RESOURCES FOR WOMEN'S HISTORY

American Antiquarian Society
185 Salisbury Street
Worcester, MA 01609-1634

Archives of the Commonwealth
220 Morrisey Boulevard
Boston, MA 02125

Berkshire Athenaeum
1 Wendell Avenue
Pittsfield, MA 01201

Fall River Historical Society
451 Rock Street
Fall River, MA 02720

Library of the Boston Athenaeum
10 Beacon Street
Boston, MA 02108

Massachusetts Historical Society
1154 Boylston Street
Boston, MA 02215

New England Historic Genealogical Society
99–101 Newbury Street
Boston, MA 02116

Plymouth Public Library
132 South Street
Plymouth, MA 02360

Sophia Smith Collection
William Allan Neilson Library
Smith College
Northampton, MA 01063

Schlesinger Library
Radcliffe College
3 James Street
Cambridge, MA 02138

Williston Memorial Library
Mount Holyoke College
South Hadley, MA 01075

The Schlesinger Library on the History of Women in America, available online at **<www.radcliffe.edu/schles/libcolls/index.htm>**

Sophia Smith Collection of Smith College, available online at **<www.smith. edu/libraries/ssc/home/html>**

Evelyn Schaefer and Mary Herr, Red Cross volunteers, Rochester, New York, 1918 (Courtesy of Dorothy Driscoll Armstrong, cousin of the Author)

MICHIGAN

IMPORTANT DATES IN STATE HISTORY

1668 First permanent French settlement at Sault Sainte Marie.
1701 French territory, under the French Custom of Paris; Fort Ponchartrain (Detroit) established.
1763 Ceded from France to Great Britain.
1774 Part of Quebec.
1783 Ceded from Great Britain to the U.S., except for Detroit and Michilimackinac.
1787 Part of the Northwest Territory.
1796 Great Britain cedes the remainder of Michigan to the U.S. in Jay's Treaty.
1800 Part of the Indiana Territory.
1805 Created as a separate territory.
1812 Detroit surrenders to the British during the War of 1812.
1813 U.S. forces retake Detroit.
1835 Territorial constitution written based on the common laws of New York.
1837 Statehood.
1855 Sault Saint Marie canal is opened.

MARRIAGE AND DIVORCE

1805 territorial legislature recognizes dower and curtesy.
1832 a divorce granted in favor of the husband gives him possession of all of his wife's property, and her dower rights are forfeit (Ch. 218 § 1).
1855 curtesy is abrogated.
1887 county clerks are required to issue and record marriage licenses.

Where to Find Marriage and Divorce Records

County clerks began recording marriages as early as 1815. State registration began in 1867, and is kept at the Department of Public Health in Lansing. The earliest divorces were granted by the Supreme Court, followed in jurisdiction by the county chancery and circuit courts. The Supreme Court cases, 1819 to 1857 (film 0955819 ff.), are at the Bentley Library, University of Michigan, in Lansing. There is a index to marriages and divorces, 1867 to 1914, at the Library of Michigan in Lansing. Many county records have been filmed, such as:

- Mackinac County Clerk marriages, 1820–32 (film 0926733), at the Library of Michigan, marriage records, 1867–1948, marriage index, 1867–1972 (film 1007362), at the Mackinac County Courthouse in Saint Ignace, and Mackinac County Circuit Court marriages, 1805–20 (film 0955819), at the Bentley Library, University of Michigan.
- Wayne County Clerk marriage records, 1836–1913, and index, 1836–1937 (film 1377627 ff.), at the City County Building in Detroit.
- Kent County Circuit Court chancery files (including divorces), 1880–1921 (film 1984352), at Western Michigan University in Kalamazoo.

See also indexes, such as:

- Grand Rapids Public Library brides' names index, 1850–69 (film 1002012), at the Public Library in Grand Rapids. Includes grooms' names and marriage dates. Most are Kent County marriages, but some are from other counties in Michigan.

PROPERTY AND INHERITANCE

1811 in intestacy, a widow receives one-third of her husband's personal property and no real estate.

1818 a son or daughter not given an inheritance by will may claim a portion of his or her parent's estate.

1844 a married woman's inheritance is her separate estate and she has powers of *feme sole* over that estate.

1846 property acquired after marriage shall remain the wife's to the same extent as property acquired before marriage. In intestacy, a widow inherits one-third of her husband's real estate, for life use only.

1850 a married woman may devise a will.

1855 a married woman's property owned prior to marriage is her sole and separate estate. A married woman may devise her separate estate.

1909 in intestacy, a widow receives one-third of her husband's estate, both real and personal (Title X Ch. 218 §27).

1911 a married woman's wages are part of her separate estate and free from the debts of her husband.

SUFFRAGE

1918 Michigan women receive complete suffrage.

CITIZENSHIP

1783 all residents of Michigan become U.S. citizens by treaty, except for Native Americans, whose tribes are considered a separate nation until 1924.

CENSUS INFORMATION

The 1810 federal census for Michigan Territory is missing.

1710–1830 colonial and territorial censuses, see Russell, Donna Valley. *Michigan Censuses, 1710–1830* (Detroit: Detroit Society for Genealogical Research, 1982).

1834, 1837, 1845 territorial and state censuses (not at FHL, all except 1837 have published indexes).

1854–1904 decennial censuses (not at FHL).

1884 and 1894 state censuses are organized by county, such as Kent County, 1884, 1894 (film 0984118 ff.).

The territorial and state censuses are at the Library of Michigan.

OTHER

1843 the Colored Ladies Benevolent Society is founded at Detroit to provide aid to the elderly, poor, and orphaned.

1871 a state board of charities is established.

Sillman, Sue I. *Michigan Military Records* (1920. Reprint. Baltimore: Clearfield Co., 1996). Includes pension information, name of wife, and place and date of birth, if known.

BIBLIOGRAPHY

Bibliography of Resources Relating to Women (Lansing: Michigan History Division, Michigan Department of State, 1975).

Brehm, Victoria. *The Women's Great Lakes Reader* (Minneapolis: Holy Cow Press, 1998).

Callard, Carole. *Sourcebook of Michigan Census, County Histories, and Vital Records* (Lansing: Library of Michigan, 1986, fiche 6101261).

Coratheru, Alice T. *In Detroit . . . Courage Was the Fashion: The Contributing of Women to the Development of Detroit from 1701 to 1951* (Detroit: Wayne State University Press, 1953).

Michigan

Harley, Rachel Brett and Betty MacDowell. *Michigan Women: Firsts and Founders*. 2 Vols. (Lansing: Michigan Women's Studies Association, 1995).

Hine, Darlene Clark. *Black Women in the Middle West: The Michigan Experience* (Indianapolis: Indiana Historical Bureau, 1986).

Lankton, Larry D. *Beyond the Boundaries: Life and Landscape at the Lake Superior Copper Mines, 1840–1875* (New York: Oxford University Press, 1997).

—. *Cradle to Grave: Life, Work, and Death at the Lake Superior Copper Mines* (New York: Oxford University Press, 1991).

Massie, Larry B. *Birchbark Belles: Women on the Michigan Frontier* (Alleghan Forest, MI: Priscilla Press, 1993).

McDowell, Marsha. *African American Quiltmaking in Michigan* (East Lansing: Michigan State University Press, 1998).

—. *Michigan Quilts: 150 Years of a Textile Tradition* (East Lansing: Michigan State University Press, 1987).

—. "A Stitch in Time: Michigan's Women Folk Artists." *Michigan History* 66 4 (1982): 8–13.

McGinnis, Carol. *Michigan Genealogy: Sources & Resources* (Baltimore: Genealogical Publishing Co., 1987).

Michigan Pioneer and Territorial Collections. 40 Vols. (Lansing: Michigan Pioneer and Historical Society, 1877–1929).

Michigan Women: Biographies, Autobiographies, and Reminiscences (Lansing: State Library Services, 1975).

Michigan Women in the Civil War (Lansing: Michigan Civil War Centennial Observance Commission, 1963).

Motz, Marilyn Ferris. *True Sisterhood: Michigan Women and Their Kin, 1820–1920* (Albany: State University of New York Press, 1983).

Quigley, Maud. *Index to Family Names in Genealogical Periodicals* (Grand Rapids: Western Michigan Genealogical Society, 1979).

Richards, R. Owen. "Michigan's Law of Coverture." *Detroit College of Law Review* 3 (Fall 1982): 649–700.

Sourcebook of Michigan Census, County Histories, and Vital Records (Lansing: Library of Michigan, 1986, fiche 6101261).

Troester, Rosalie Riegle. *Historic Women of Michigan: A Sesquicentennial Celebration* (Lansing: Michigan Women's Studies Association, 1987).

Vander Hill, C. Warren. *Settling the Great Lakes Frontier: Immigration to Michigan, 1837–1924* (Lansing: Michigan Historical Commission, 1970).

Women in Grand Rapids History: A Guide to Resources in the Local History Department of the Grand Rapids Public Library (Grand Rapids: Greater Grand Rapids Women's History Council, 1995).

SELECTED RESOURCES FOR WOMEN'S HISTORY

Ella Sharp Museum
3225 Fourth Street
Jackson, MI 49203

Michigan Women's History Center
213 West Main Street
Lansing, MI 48933

Library of Michigan
State Archives of Michigan
717 West Allegan Street
Lansing, MI 48919

Michigan Women's Historical Center and Hall of Fame, available online at **<scnc.leslie.k12.mi.us/~mwhfame>**

MINNESOTA

IMPORTANT DATES IN STATE HISTORY

1680 Sparsely settled by French fur traders and missionaries.
1763 Eastern Minnesota ceded from France to Great Britain.
1774 Part of Quebec.
1783 Eastern Minnesota is ceded from Great Britain to the U.S.
1787 Part of the Northwest Territory.
1803 Western Minnesota is part of the Louisiana Purchase.
1820 Fort Snelling is established at the site of Saint Paul.
1830 Part of the Michigan Territory.
1836 Part of the Wisconsin Territory.
1849 Created as a separate U.S. territory.
1858 Statehood.
1862 Santee Sioux Rebellion in Minnesota and the Dakota Territory (ends 1863).
1890 Mesabi Range iron ore deposits discovered.

MARRIAGE AND DIVORCE

1849 dower is recognized.
1875 dower is abolished.
1905 the clerk of the district court is required to record marriage returns.

Where to Find Marriage and Divorce Records

Marriages have been recorded in the county district courts since 1856. Sometimes marriage certificates were filed many years after the marriage licenses were filed. Information from the original licenses and certificates were usually copied into the registers. The marriage records from 1871 for Hennepin County are at the Vital Records Office in Minneapolis. Divorces have also been recorded in the county district courts. Many county records have been filmed, such as:

- Blue Earth County Clerk of the District Court marriage licenses, 1865–1917, and applications for marriage licenses, 1870–1915 (film 1309275 ff.), at the Blue Earth County Courthouse in Mankato.
- Faribault County Clerk of the District Court marriage registers and returns, 1857–1917 (film 1673580 ff.), at the Faribault County Courthouse in Blue Earth.

PROPERTY AND INHERITANCE

1849 dower is recognized; in intestacy a widow receives one-third of the real estate for life.
1860 a married woman's earnings are her separate property.
1874 a married woman is given *feme sole* status to manage he separate property.
1875 dower is abolished; a husband and a wife both inherit the homestead property in full, and one-third of all lands as held in fee-simple, or as held at time of death (Ch. 407).
1878 all property owned by a married woman shall be her separate property.

SUFFRAGE

1919 women become eligible to vote in presidential elections.
1920 Minnesota women receive complete suffrage by passage of the 19th Amendment to the Constitution.

CITIZENSHIP

1803 all residents of Minnesota become U.S. citizens by legislation, except for Native Americans, whose tribes are considered a separate nation until 1924.

CENSUS INFORMATION

For pre-territorial federal censuses, see Michigan (1830) and Wisconsin (1840).

1836 see Shambaugh, Benjamin F. *Wisconsin Territory: The First Census of the Original Counties of Dubuque and Demoines (Iowa) Taken in July, 1836* (Des Moines: Historical Department of Iowa, 1897, film 1022202). Comprises the present states of Iowa, Minnesota, and parts of North and South Dakota.

1849 territorial census, published in "Census of the Minnesota Territory, June 11, 1849." *Minnesota Genealogist* 11 (September 1980): 121–32.

1857 special federal territorial census (film 0944283 ff./M1175).

1865 state census (film 0565714 ff.).

1875 state census (film 0565717 ff.).

1885 state census (film 0565334 ff.).

1895 state census (film 0565761 ff.).

1905 state census (film 0928767 ff.).

The territorial and state censuses are at the Minnesota Historical Society Research Center in Saint Paul. The decennial censuses have every-name indexes available at the research centers for the corresponding geographical areas.

OTHER

1905–50 Indian War pension records of veterans of the Dakota War and their widows, and pension register, 1905–37.

1918 alien registration records of all non-U.S. citizens in Minnesota.

The above records are at the Minnesota Historical Society Research Center.

BIBLIOGRAPHY

Beito, Gretchen. *Women of Thief River Falls at the Turn of the Century: A Study of Life in a Boom Town, 1895–1905* (Thief River Falls, MN: Pennington County Historical Society, 1977).

Blatti, Jo. *Women's History in Minnesota: A Survey of Published Sources and Dissertations* (Saint Paul: Minnesota Historical Society Press, 1993).

Buffalohead, Priscilla K. "Farmers, Warriors, Traders: A Fresh Look at Ojibway Women." *Minnesota History* 48 6 (1983): 236–44.

Burris, Evandene A. "Keeping House on the Minnesota Frontier." *Minnesota History* 14 (September 1933): 263–82.

Foster, Mary Dillon. *Who's Who Among Minnesota Women: A History of Women's Work in Minnesota from Pioneer Days to Date . . .* (n.p.: The Author, 1924).

Kreidberg, Marjorie. "Corn Bread, Portable Soup, and Wrinkle Cures." *Minnesota History* 41 3 (1968): 105–16.

—. *Food on the Frontier: Minnesota Cooking from 1856 to 1900* (Saint Paul: Minnesota Historical Society, 1975).

Lind, Marilyn. *Research in Minnesota* (Washington, DC: National Genealogical Society, 1992).

Martin, Janet and Allen Todnem. *Lutheran Church Basement Women* (Hastings, MN: Redbird Productions, 1992).

Palmquist, Bonnie B. "Women in Minnesota History, 1915–1976: An Annotated Bibliography of Articles Pertaining to Women." *Minnesota History* 45 (1977): 187–91.

Peavy, Linda and Ursula Smith. *The Gold Rush Widows of Little Falls* (Saint Paul: Minnesota Historical Society Press, 1990).

Spector, Janet D. *What This Awl Means: Feminist Archeology at the Wahpeton Dakota Village* (Saint Paul: Minnesota Historical Society, 1993).

Steinmetz, Cheryl Fales. *Business Women of Minneapolis, 1870–1880* (Minneapolis: The Author, 1989).

Stuhler, Barbara and Gretchen Kreuter. *Women of Minnesota: Selected Biographical Essays* (Saint Paul: Minnesota Historical Society Press, 1977).

Tsuchida, Nobuya. *Reflections: Memoirs of Japanese American Women in Minnesota* (Covina, CA: Pacific Asia Press, 1994).

Upham, Warren. "The Women and Children of Fort Saint Anthony, Later Named Fort Snelling." *The Magazine of History* (New York) 21 (July 1915): 25–39.

Wanless, Dorothy, L. *Century Farms of Minnesota: One Hundred Years of Changing Lifestyles on the Farms* (Dallas: Taylor Publishing Co., 1985).

Warren, Paula S. *Continuing Your Genealogical Research in Minnesota* (Saint Paul: Minnesota Historical Society Press, 1991).

Webb, Anne B. "Forgotten Persephones: Women Farmers on the Frontier." *Minnesota History* 50 (Winter 1986): 134–8.

—. "Minnesota Women Homesteaders: 1863–1889." *Journal of Social History* 23 (1989): 115–36.

SELECTED RESOURCES FOR WOMEN'S HISTORY

American Lutheran Church Archives
Lutheran Northwestern Theological Seminary
2481 Como Avenue
Saint Paul, MN 55108

Minnesota Historical Society
345 Kellogg Boulevard
Saint Paul, MN 55012

Otter Tail County Historical Society
1110 Lincoln Avenue West
Fergus Falls, MN 56537

Upper Midwest Women's History Center
Hamline University
1536 Hewitt Avenue
Saint Paul, MN 55104-1284

[EDITION OF 1917.]

[FORM FOR NATIVE CITIZEN.]

Issued ....

UNITED STATES OF AMERICA

~~STATE OF~~ United States District Court.
~~COUNTY OF~~ Middle District of Tennessee. ss:

(Mrs. A.C.Lackey)
I, Mrs. Della Tankaley Lackey, a NATIVE AND LOYAL citizen of the UNITED STATES, hereby apply to the Department of State, at Washington, for a passport

I solemnly swear that I was born at Waverly Tennessee, on or about the 5th day of March, 1880; that my {~~father~~ husband} A.C.Lackey was born in Trigg Co. Kentucky, and is now residing at Nashville, Tennessee. ~~that he emigrated to the United States from the port of~~ .... ~~on or about~~ .... 1....; ~~that he resided~~ ~~the United States, from 1~~ .... ~~to 1~~ ...., ~~at~~ .... ~~naturalized as a citizen of the United States before the~~ .... ~~of~~ .... ~~at~~ .... ~~on~~ ...., 1...., ~~as shown by the accompanying~~ .... ~~that I have resided outside the United States at the following places~~: .... from .... from .... and that I am domiciled in the United States, my permanent residence being at Nashville, in the State of Tennessee, where I follow the occupation of ---------. ~~My last passport was obtained from~~ ...., on ...., ~~and was~~ .... (Disposition of passport.) I ~~am about to~~ go abroad temporarily; and I intend to return to the United States within 3 {months ~~years~~} with the purpose of residing and performing the duties of citizenship therein; and I desire a passport for use in visiting the countries hereinafter named for the following purpose:

Panama (Name of country.)	To bring my daughter back to (Object of visit.)
(Name of country.)	the United States - she having been (Object of visit.)
(Name of country.)	there on account of her health. (Object of visit.)

I intend to leave the United States from the port of New York (Port of departure.) sailing on board ~~the~~ one of the United Fruit Boats (Name of vessel.), about April 1st, 1918 (Date of departure.) or as soon thereafter as I obtain my passport.

DESCRIPTION OF APPLICANT.

Age: 38 years. Mouth: Small
Stature: 5 feet, 8 Chin: Medium
Forehead: High Hair: Brown
Eyes: Blue Complexion: Fair
Nose: Medium Face: Round
Distinguishing marks: Third finger of right hand off.

OATH OF ALLEGIANCE.

Further, I do solemnly swear that I will support and defend the Constitution of the United States against all enemies, foreign and domestic; that I will bear true faith and allegiance to the same; and that I take this obligation freely, without any mental reservation or purpose of evasion: So help me God.

x Mrs Della Tankesley Lackey
(Signature of applicant.)

Sworn to before me this 19th day of March, 1918

[SEAL OF COURT]

H.M.Doak
W. A. McKinnon Jr. ~~Clerk of the~~ U.S.District Court at Nashville, Tenn.

Passport application of Mrs. Della Tankaley Lackey, of Nashville, Tennessee, 19 March 1918

MISSISSIPPI

IMPORTANT DATES IN STATE HISTORY

1699 First French settlement at Biloxi.
1763 Ceded from France to Great Britain.
1781 Part of Mississippi ceded to Spain.
1783 Most of Mississippi claimed by Georgia.
1795 The Pinckney Treaty with Spain gives the U.S. all of West Florida above the 31st parallel (does not include Biloxi, Mississippi and Mobile, Alabama).
1796 U.S. takes possession of the area claimed by Georgia.
1798 Organized as a territory; laws are similar to those of the Northwest Territory, except for Article IV prohibiting slavery.
1802 Georgia cedes its claims to the area.
1812 Coastal portion (West Florida) ceded to the U.S. by Spain; called the District of Mobile.
1817 Statehood; constitution based on common law.
1831 Choctaw-Chickasaw Indian removals.
1861 9 January secedes from the Union.
1863 Battle of Vicksburg.
1870 3 February readmitted to the Union.

MARRIAGE AND DIVORCE

1817 constitution provides that "divorces from the bonds of matrimony shall not be granted, but in cases provided for by law, by suit on chancery; provided, that no decree for such divorces shall have effect until the same shall be sanctioned by two thirds of both branches of the General Assembly (Art. VI § 17)."

1892 marriages without licenses are found void. Clerks of the circuit court are required to issue and record marriage licenses.

Where to Find Marriage and Divorce Records

Marriages have been recorded by the clerks of the county circuit courts since about 1800. State registration of marriages began in 1926 and is kept at the State Department of Health in Jackson. The Russell Soundex Index of marriages prior to 1926 is at the Mississippi Department of Archives and History in Jackson, and through ILL from the Mississippi Library Commission in Jackson. Divorces were first granted by the Mississippi State Legislature from 1817 to 1859. The county chancery courts have held jurisdiction for divorces since 1859. Many county records have been filmed, such as:

- Chickasaw County Circuit Clerk marriage records of the First District, 1863–1918; index, 1866–1972 (film 0893474 ff.), at the Chickasaw County Courthouse in Houston.
- Leflore County Circuit Clerk marriage records and bonds, 1844–1916 (film 0889879 ff.), at the Leflore County Courthouse in Greenwood.

See also compiled publications, such as:

- Humphreys, Rena and Mamie Owen. *Index of Mississippi Session Acts, 1817–1865* (Jackson: Tucker Printing House, 1937).
- Wiltshire, Betty Couch. *Marriages and Deaths from Mississippi Newspapers [1801–1863]*. 4 Vols. (Bowie, MD: Heritage Books, 1987).

PROPERTY AND INHERITANCE

1839 a married woman may hold real and personal property in her own name "by direct bequest, demise, gift, purchase, or distribution, provided the same does not come from the husband during coverture." Slaves owned by a *feme covert* at the time of her marriage, and those acquired after, are her separate estate; however, they may only be sold by joint deed of husband and wife. The control and management of the slaves is also in the husband.

1846 a married woman is granted separate use of real estate owned at the time of her marriage.

1871 all property owned by a woman prior to marriage shall be her separate estate.

SUFFRAGE

1920 Mississippi women receive complete suffrage by passage of the 19th Amendment to the Constitution.

CITIZENSHIP

1796 all residents of Mississippi become U.S. citizens by legislation, except for Native Americans, whose tribes are considered a separate nation until 1924.

CENSUS INFORMATION

The federal censuses for 1800 and 1810 are missing.

1792–1816 see Gillis, Norman E. *Early Inhabitants of the Natchez District* (Baton Rouge: The Author, 1963). The 1792 census includes maiden names.

1792–1866 colonial, territorial, and state censuses (film 0899868 ff.), at the Mississippi Department of Archives and History.

OTHER

1878 yellow fever epidemic victims lists, transcribed in Power, J.L. *The Epidemic of 1878 in Mississippi* (Jackson: Clarion Steam Publishing Co., 1879).

1900–1950s Confederate pension applications of soldiers, sailors, and widows (film 0902556 ff.), at the Mississippi Department of Archives and History. See also Wiltshire, Betty C. *Mississippi Confederate Pension Applications* (Carrollton, MS: Pioneer Publishing Co., 1994).

For land records, see also Georgia records (prior to 1802), British West Florida records (prior to 1798), and Spanish records (prior to 1797).

BIBLIOGRAPHY

Adams, Donna Burge. *Women in the Florida Parishes.* 5 Vols. (Baton Rouge: The Author, 1985-91). Abstracts from court records, probate records, vital records, newspaper clippings, deeds, other land records, oral traditions, and correspondence about women residing in Louisiana and Mississippi from 1780 to 1971.

Brown, Elizabeth G. "Husband and Wife: Memorandum on the Mississippi Women's Law of 1839." *Michigan Law Review* 42 (June 1944): 1110-24.

Freeman, Ronald L. *Something to Keep You Warm: The Roland Freeman Collection of Black American Quilts from the Mississippi Heartland* (Jackson: Mississippi Department of Archives and History, 1981).

Kerns, Gloria L. *Early Newspapers of Natchez, Mississippi, 1800–1828* (Shreveport, LA: J & W Enterprises, 1993). Information includes probate and marriage notices. The Natchez District comprised the present-day counties of Adams, Claiborne, Jefferson, Warren, and Wilkinson, plus sections of Franklin and Amite counties.

Lipscomb, Anne S. and Kathleen S. Hutchinson. *Tracing Your Mississippi Ancestors* (Jackson: University Press of Mississippi, 1994).

Lohrenz, Mary Edna. *Mississippi Homespun: Nineteenth-Century Textiles and the Women Who Made Them* (Jackson: Mississippi Department of Archives and History, 1989).

Pearce, Charles. *Index to the Laws of the Mississippi Territory* (Jackson: Mississippi Department of Archives and History, 1985).

United Daughters of the Confederacy. *Reminiscences of Columbus, Mississippi and Elsewhere, 1861–1865* (West Point, MS: Sullivan's, 1961).

SELECTED RESOURCES FOR WOMEN'S HISTORY

Mississippi Department of Archives and History
100 State Street
PO Box 571
Jackson, MS 39205-0571

Mississippi Historical Society
PO Box 571
Jackson, MS 39205-0571

University of Mississippi
Sarah Isom Center for Women's Studies
University, MS 38677

First black kindergarten, Topeka, Kansas, 1893
(Kansas State Historical Society)

MISSOURI

IMPORTANT DATES IN STATE HISTORY

1700 French civil law and the Custom of Paris in effect (date approximate).
1763 Ceded from France to Spain; French law replaced by Spanish law.
1764 City of Saint Louis organized.
1800 Ceded from Spain to France.
1803 Part of the Louisiana Purchase.
1804 Part of the District of Louisiana attached to the Indiana Territory.
1805 Part of the Louisiana Territory.
1812 Created as a separate territory.
1820 Missouri Compromise allows slavery to be legal in the state.
1821 Statehood.

MARRIAGE AND DIVORCE

1807 under Louisiana law, the Louisiana Territorial Legislature adopts statutes recognizing dower and curtesy.

1889 all persons performing marriages must issue a certificate and keep a record of the marriage. This record must be filed with the county recorder within ninety days.

Where to Find Marriage and Divorce Records

The earliest marriage records in Missouri were recorded in the Basilica of Saint Louis, King of France, Saint Louis Catholic Church beginning in 1766 (fiche 6075777 ff.). Marriages have been recorded by the county clerks and recorders of deeds since about 1805. For a list of the dates of the organization of Missouri's 114 counties, see **<mosl.sos.state.mo.us/rec-man/archives/croll1.html>**. Statewide registration began in 1881. Divorces were granted by the Missouri State Legislature from 1833 to 1849, followed and preceded by the court of common pleas and the circuit court. Many county records have been filmed, such as:

- Cape Girardeau County Recorder of Deeds marriage records, 1805–1950 (film 0925660 ff.), records, 1808–1950, and indexes, 1808–1959 (film 2026829 ff.), at the Cape Girardeau County Courthouse in Jackson.
- Saint Louis County Court, Saint Louis City Archives records: French, Spanish, and English deeds, land grants, marriage contracts, powers of attorney, and notarial records, 1816–48 (film 0466341 ff.), at the City Hall in Saint Louis.

See also compiled publications, such as:

- Brooks, Linda Barber. *Missouri Marriages to 1850*. 3 Vols. (Saint Louis: Ingmire Publications, 1983–).
- Ormesher, Susan. *Missouri Marriages Before 1840* (Baltimore: Genealogical Publishing Co., 1982, fiche 6051425).
- Rising, Marsha Hoffman. *The Springfield Advertiser, Greene County, Missouri, 1844–1850* (Decorah, IA: Anundsen Publishing, 1984, fiche 6125835). Includes death notices, marriages, estate settlements, divorces, legal notices, and letters. Includes items from present-day counties of Barry, Bates, Benton, Cedar, Christian, Dade, Dallas, Douglas, Greene, Jasper, LaClede, Lawrence, McDonald, Newton, Ozark, Polk, Pulaski, Shannon, Stone, Taney, Webster, and Wright.
- Saint Louis County Genealogical Society. *Saint Louis Genealogical Society Index of Saint Louis Marriages, 1804–1876*. 2 Vols. (Saint Louis: The Society, 1973).

- Wilson, George F. *1,300 "Missing" Missouri Marriage Records from Newspapers, 1812–1853* (Decorah, IA: Anundsen Publishing, 1982, film 1421793).
- Blattner, Theresa. *Divorces, Separations, and Annulments in Missouri, 1769–1850* (Bowie, MD: Heritage Books, 1992).
- Stanley, Lois. *Divorces and Separations in Missouri, 1808–1853* (Greenville, SC: Southern Historical Press, 1990).

PROPERTY AND INHERITANCE

1849 a married woman's separate property is free from the debts of her husband.
1865 married women are granted *feme sole* status with regard to their separate property.
1879 a married woman's separate property is her separate estate.

SUFFRAGE

1919 women become eligible to vote in presidential elections.
1920 Missouri women receive complete suffrage by passage of the 19th Amendment to the Constitution.

CITIZENSHIP

1803 all residents of Missouri become U.S. citizens by legislation, except for Native Americans, whose tribes are considered a separate nation until 1924.

CENSUS INFORMATION

The 1810 and 1820 federal censuses are missing.
1814, 1817, and 1819 territorial censuses (not at FHL).
1821 state census (not at FHL).
1824–63 state censuses (not at FHL).
1868 and 1876 state censuses, organized by county, such as Cape Girardeau County (film 1006666 ff.)
The territorial and state censuses are at the State Historical Society of Missouri in Columbia.

OTHER

1869–1905 Saint Louis Health Department register of midwives and physicians (film 0981607).
1876–1906 Saint Louis Female Hospital registers (film 0980624 ff.).
1911 Missouri adopts the first widows' pension law in the U.S.; it gives aid to mothers of dependent children; counties can provide financial assistance for mothers with dependent children.
Confederate pension applications and soldiers' home admission applications (including widows) (film 1021101), at the Missouri Department of Records and Archives in Jefferson City.

BIBLIOGRAPHY

Beck, W.G. "Survivals of Old Marriage Customs Among the Low Germans of Missouri." *Journal of American Folklore* 21 (1908): 60–7.

Bishop, Beverly D. and Deborah W. Boats. *In Her Own Write: Women's History Resources in the Library and Archives of the Missouri Historical Society* (Saint Louis: Missouri Historical Society, 1983).

Blattner, Teresa. *People of Color: Black Genealogical Records and Abstracts from Missouri Sources.* 2 Vols. (Bowie, MD: Heritage Books, 1993, 1998).

Corbett, Katherine T. *In Her Place: A Guide to St. Louis Women's History, 1764–1965* (Saint Louis: Missouri Historical Society Press, 1999).

Dains, Mary K. *Show Me Missouri Women, Selected Biographies: Missouri Women's History Project* (Kirksville, MO: Thomas Jefferson University Press, 1989).

Eddleman, Sherida K. *Missouri Genealogical Records and Abstracts*. 6 Vols. (Bowie, MD: Heritage Books, 1990–6).

Flynn, Jan F. *Kansas City Women of Independent Minds* (Kansas City, MO: Fifield Publishing, 1992).

Foley, William E. *The Genesis of Missouri: From Wilderness Outpost to Statehood* (Saint Louis: University of Missouri Press, 1989).

Gentlzer, Lynn Wolf. *Guide to Women's Collections, Western Historical Manuscript Collection, State Historical Society of Missouri* (Columbia: Western Historical Manuscript Collection, 1989).

Giffin, Jerena E. "Add a Pinch and a Lump: Missouri Women in the 1820s." *Missouri History Review* 65 (July 1971): 478–504. French and American families in early Missouri.

Having, Betty. *Missouri Heritage Quilts* (Paducah, KY: American Quilters Society, 1986).

Hehir, Donald M. *Missouri Family Histories and Genealogies: A Bibliography* (Bowie, MD: Heritage Books, 1996).

Missouri Division, United Daughters of the Confederacy. *Reminiscences of Women of Missouri During the Sixties* (Jefferson City: Hugh Stephens Printing Co., 1925).

Peters, Virginia B. *Women of the Earth Lodges: Tribal Life on the Plains* (Hamden, CT: Archon Books, 1997).

Schweitzer, George. *Missouri Genealogical Research* (Knoxville, TN: The Author, 1997).

Stanley, Lois. *Death Records of Pioneer Missouri Women, 1808–1853* (Greenville, SC: Southern Historical Press, 1990). Contains records from the old *Missouri Gazette Newspaper.*

Wall, Carla and Barbara Oliver Korner. *Hardship and Hope: Missouri Women Writing About Their Lives, 1820–1920* (Saint Louis: University of Missouri Press, 1997).

SELECTED RESOURCES FOR WOMEN'S HISTORY

Blanche Skiff Ross Memorial Library
Cottey College
225 South College
Nevada, MO 64772

Missouri Historical Society
Jefferson Memorial Building
225 South Skinner
Saint Louis, MO 63112-1099

Missouri State Archives
600 West Main Street
PO Box 778
Jefferson City, MO 65102

The State Historical Society of Missouri
1020 Lowry Street
Columbia, MO 65201

Western Historical Manuscript Collection
University of Missouri, Saint Louis
8001 Natural Bridge Road
Saint Louis, MO 63121

The Saint Louis Ladies' Union Aid Society, available at **<fv.stlcc.cc.mo.us/ mfuller/luas>**, describes the work of the Society in Missouri during the Civil War.

MONTANA

IMPORTANT DATES IN STATE HISTORY

1803	Most of Montana is part of the Louisiana Purchase.
1812	Most of Montana is part of the Missouri Territory.
1821	Part of unorganized Indian territory.
1846	Extreme northwestern Montana is part of the Oregon Territory.
1853	Extreme northwestern Montana is part of the Washington Territory.
1854	Most of Montana is part of the Nebraska Territory.
1861	Most of Montana is part of the Dakota Territory.
1863	Extreme northwestern Montana is part of the Idaho Territory.
1864	Created as a separate U.S. territory from parts of the Dakota and Idaho territories.
1876	Battle of Little Big Horn.
1889	Statehood.

MARRIAGE AND DIVORCE

1887 in divorce, minor children are to be left in the custody of the mother; county clerks are required to issue marriage licenses.

1895 companionate marriage is recognized in Montana (§ 795).

Where to Find Marriage and Divorce Records

Marriages have been recorded by the county clerk of the district court since 1865. State registration did not begin until 1943 and is an index only. From 1863 to 1865 divorces were recorded as acts in the records of the Montana Territorial Legislature. Divorce cases have been under the jurisdiction of the county district courts since 1865. Many county records have been filmed, such as:

- Custer County Clerk of the District Court marriage records, 1877–1950 (film 1940923 ff.), at the Custer County Courthouse in Miles City.
- Lewis and Clark County Clerk of the District Court marriage records, 1865–1959 (film 1906337 ff.), at the Lewis and Clark County Courthouse in Helena.

See also the Bureau of Indian Affairs records, such as:

- Flathead Indian rolls for marriages and divorces, 1936 (film 0576471), at the National Archives in Washington, DC.

PROPERTY AND INHERITANCE

1889 a married woman's separate property is her separate estate, free from the debts of her husband; her separate earnings are her own property; she is granted *feme sole* status to manage her separate estate; a widow also has access to her husband's personal estate.

SUFFRAGE

1914 Montana women receive complete suffrage.

CITIZENSHIP

1803 all residents of Montana become U.S. citizens by legislation, except for Native Americans, whose tribes are considered a separate nation until 1924.

CENSUS INFORMATION

For pre-territorial federal censuses, see Washington Territory (1860) and Nebraska Territory (1860, unorganized area). In addition to federal censuses, see Bureau of Indian Affairs records, such as the census rolls for the Flathead Indians, 1886-1939 (film 0575799 ff.), at the National Archives in Washington, DC. There are no state censuses for Montana.

OTHER

1917 Montana is the first state to elect a woman to the U.S. Congress.

BIBLIOGRAPHY

Cole, Judith K. "A Wide Field for Usefulness: Women's Civil Status and the Evolution of Women's Suffrage on the Montana Frontier, 1864-1914." *American Journal of Legal History* 34 (July 1990): 262-94.

Emmons, David M. *The Butte Irish: Class and Ethnicity in an American Mining Town, 1875-1925* (Urbana: University of Illinois Press, 1990).

Foley, Jodie and Dave Walter. "Montana Women as Community Builders," in *Speaking of Montana: A Guide to the Oral History Collection at the Montana Historical Society* (Helena: The Society, 1998).

Malone, Michael P., et al. *Montana: A History of Two Centuries*. Rev. ed. (Tacoma: University of Washington Press, 1991).

Murphy, Mary. *Mining Culture: Men, Women, and Leisure in Butte, 1914-1941* (Urbana: University of Illinois Press, 1997).

Petrick, Paula. *No Step Backward: Women and Family on the Rocky Mountain Mining Frontier, Helena, Montana, 1865-1900* (Helena: Montana Historical Society Press, 1987).

—. "If She Be Content: The Development of Montana Divorce Law, 1865-1907." *Western Historical Quarterly* 18 (July 1987): 262-92.

Richards, Dennis L. *Montana's Genealogical and Local History Records: A Selected List of Books, Manuscripts, and Periodicals* (Detroit: Gale Research, 1981, fiche 6019973).

Shirley, Gayle C. *More Than Petticoats: Montana's Remarkable Women* (Helena: Twodot, 1995).

Stevenson, Elizabeth. *Figures in a Western Landscape: Men and Women of the Northern Rockies* (Baltimore: Johns Hopkins University Press, 1994).

Stewart, Edgar. "The Custer Battle and Widow's Weeds." *Montana Magazine of Western History* 22 1 (1972): 52-9. The families of the men killed at the Battle of Little Big Horn, 1876.

West, Carroll Van. *A Traveler's Companion to Montana History* (Helena: Montana Historical Society, 1996).

SELECTED RESOURCES FOR WOMEN'S HISTORY

Montana State Archives
Montana Historical Society
225 North Roberts Street
Helena, MT 59620

Montana Women's History Project
Mansfield Library
University of Montana
2626 Garland
Missoula, MT 59812

NEBRASKA

IMPORTANT DATES IN STATE HISTORY

1795 French build trading post in northeastern Nebraska.
1803 Part of the Louisiana Purchase.
1812 Part of the Missouri Territory.
1819 Fort Atkinson first settled.
1820 Unorganized territory.
1823 Fort Bellevue established as a fur-trading post.
1834 Nebraska area is divided among Arkansas, Michigan, and Missouri.
1854 Created as a separate territory from parts of Arkansas, Michigan, and Missouri; the new territory includes the future states of Colorado, Montana, Nebraska, North and South Dakota, and Wyoming.
1861 Boundaries of Nebraska established.
1863 Union Pacific railroad connects to Omaha; Indian wars with the Cheyenne, Arapahoe, Kiowa, and Comanche (end 1869).
1864 Statehood.
1871 First white settlers arrive in Boone County.

MARRIAGE AND DIVORCE

1855 county clerks begin recording marriages.
1885 a probate or county judge is required to issue a marriage license; marriages are to be recorded with the probate judge within one month.

Where to Find Marriage and Divorce Records

Marriage records have been recorded by the county clerks and county judges of probate; some from 1855 to 1915 are at the Nebraska State Historical Society in Lincoln. Statewide registration began in 1909 and is kept at the State Department of Health in Lincoln. Divorces have been under the jurisdiction of the territorial and state county district courts. The clerk of the district court has custody of the records; after 1909 there are also copies at the State Department of Health. Between 1887 and 1906, 114 divorces were recorded in Boone County.[29] Many county records have been filmed, such as:

- Cheyenne County Judge marriage licenses and certificates, 1870–1914 (film 1940948 ff.), at the Nebraska State Historical Society.
- Dakota County Probate Court marriage records, 1851–1993 (film 2021908 ff.), at the Dakota County Courthouse in Dakota City.

See also compiled publications, such as:

- Cline, Martha Jane Adamson. *Golden Weddings of Nebraskans* (Lincoln: The Author, 1986, film 1421791). Excerpted from issues of the *Nebraska Farmer*, 1930–65.

PROPERTY AND INHERITANCE

1881 all property owned by a woman at her marriage "shall be and remain her sole and separate property free from the disposal or debts of her husband."
1904 Congress enacts the Kinkaid Act homestead law, applying only to western and central Nebraska, allowing homesteads of up to 640 acres.

---

[29] Deborah Fink, *Agrarian Women: Wives and Mothers in Rural Nebraska, 1880–1940* (Chapel Hill: University of North Carolina Press, 1992), 82.

SUFFRAGE

1867 women may vote in school elections.
1918 women become eligible to vote in presidential elections.
1920 Nebraska women receive complete suffrage by passage of the 19th Amendment to the Constitution.

CITIZENSHIP

1803 all residents of Nebraska become U.S. citizens by legislation, except for Native Americans, whose tribes are considered a separate nation until 1924.

CENSUS INFORMATION

1854–6 territorial censuses, see Cox, Evelyn E. *1854, 1855, 1856 Nebraska Territory Censuses* (Ellensburg, WA: The Author, 1977, fiche 6051283).
1865 census of Otoe and Cuming counties (not at FHL).
1869 census of Butler and Stanton counties (not at FHL).
1885 state census (film 0499529 ff.).
The territorial and state censuses are at the Nebraska State Historical Society.

OTHER

Counties in Nebraska territorial court districts, 1855–67:

- *First District, 1855*: Douglas and Washington
- *Second District, 1855*: Cass, Clay, Gage, Greene, Johnson, Lancaster, Nemaha, Otoe, Pawnee, Richardson, Saline, and York
- *First District, 1856*: Burt, Dakotah, Dodge, Douglas, Washington, and territory to the west
- *Second District, 1856*: Cass, Clay, Lancaster, and Otoe
- *Third District, 1856*: Johnson, Nemaha, Pawnee, Richardson, and territory to the west
- *First District, 1857–67*: Calhoun, Cass, Douglas, Dodge, and Sarpy
- *Second District, 1857–67*: Clay, Johnson, Nemaha, Otoe, Pawnee, and Richardson
- *Third District, 1857–67*: Burt, Dakotah, and Washington

BIBLIOGRAPHY

Alberts, Francis Jacobs. *Sod House Memories: A Compilation of Sod House Experiences Including a Definitive History of the Period in Nebraska* (Hastings, NE: The Sod House Society, 1973).

Cordier, Mary Hurlbut. *Schoolwomen of the Prairies and Plains: Personal Narratives from Iowa, Kansas, and Nebraska, 1860s–1920s* (Albuquerque: University of New Mexico Press, 1997).

Crewes, Patricia Cox. *Nebraska Quilts and Quiltmakers* (Lincoln: University of Nebraska Press, 1991).

Everett, Dick. *The Sod House Frontier, 1854–1890* (New York: Appleton-Century, 1937).

—. "Sunbonnet and Calico, the Homesteader's Consort." *Nebraska History* 47 (May 1966): 3–13.

Fink, Deborah. *Agrarian Women: Wives and Mothers in Rural Nebraska, 1880–1940* (Chapel Hill: University of North Carolina Press, 1992).

Governor's Commission on the Status of Women. *Nebraska Women Through the Years, 1867–1967* (Lincoln: Johnsen Publishing Co., 1967).

Hodd, Jane Renner. "A Readers's Guide to Women in the *Nebraska History Magazine*, 1918–1977." *Nebraska History* 59 1 (1978): 70–83.

Loewen, Royden K. and Eden K. Loewen. *Family, Church, and Market: A Mennonite Community in the Old and New Worlds, 1850–1930* (Urbana: University of Illinois Press, 1993).

Mattes, Merrill J. *The Great Platte River Road: The Covered Wagon Mainline via Fort Kearney to Fort Laramie.* Vol. 25 *Nebraska State Historical Society Publications* (Lincoln: The Society, 1969).

—. *Platt River Road Narratives* (Urbana: University of Illinois Press, 1988).

Nebraska, A Guide to Genealogical Research (Lincoln: Nebraska State Genealogical Society, 1984).

Nebraska State Historical Society. *A Guide to the Manuscript Division of the State Archives*. 2 Vols. (Lincoln: The Society, 1956).

Nimmo, Sylvia and Mary Culter. *Nebraska Local History and Genealogy Reference Guide: A Bibliography of County Research Materials in Selected Repositories, Library of Congress, National DAR Library, Omaha Public Library, Grand Island Public Library, University of Nebraska Library, Nebraska State Historical Society, Genealogical Department of the Church of Jesus Christ of Latter-day Saints* (Pappillion, NE: The Authors, 1986).

Pickle, Linda S. "Rural German-Speaking Women in Early Nebraska and Kansas." *Great Plains Quarterly* 9 (Autumn 1989): 239–51.

Rife, Janet Warkentin. *Germans and German-Russians in Nebraska* (Lincoln: Center for Great Plains Studies, 1980). Contains bibliographic chapters on church records, ethnic newspapers, communities, etc.

Sheldon Memorial Art Gallery. *Quilts from Nebraska Collections* (Lincoln: The Gallery, 1974).

White, John Browning. *Published Sources on Territorial Nebraska: An Essay and Bibliography* (Lincoln: Nebraska State Historical Society, 1983).

SELECTED RESOURCES FOR WOMEN'S HISTORY

American Quilt Study Group
35th and Holdrege Street, East Campus Loop
PO Box 4737
Lincoln, NE 68504-0737

Bennet/Martin Public Library
136 South 14th Street
Lincoln, NE 68508

Nebraska Jewish Historical Society
333 South 132nd Street
Lincoln, NE 68144

Nebraska State Historical Society
1500 R Street
PO Box 82554
Lincoln, NE 68501-2553

Special Collections, University of Nebraska
308 Love Library
Lincoln, NE 68588-0333

Stuhr Museum of the Prairie Pioneer
3133 West Highway 34
Grand Island, NE 68801

McCall's, September 1925

NEVADA

IMPORTANT DATES IN STATE HISTORY

1763 Claimed by both Spain and France.
1821 Claimed by Mexico.
1848 Acquired from Mexico in the Treaty of Guadalupe-Hildago; no settlements exist.
1849 First white settlement founded by Mormons at Mormon Station (Genoa).
1850 Part of Utah Territory.
1858 Carson City founded.
1859 Comstock Lode discovered.
1860 10,000 settlers come from California to prospect for silver and gold.
1861 Created as a U.S. territory from the Utah Territory; first laws are based on Texas law.
1863 Southern part of Nevada added from New Mexico Territory.
1864 Statehood; adopts the community property system of marital law based on the constitution of California.
1906 Ely copper deposit discovered.

MARRIAGE AND DIVORCE

1861 premarital agreements are allowed without restriction.
1864 dower and curtesy are abolished.
1882 in divorce, the court shall divide community property "as shall appear just and equitable [considering] the party through whom the property was acquired (§ 125.150, 125.210)."
1885 county clerks are required to issue marriage licenses.
1899 the county recorder of deeds must receive a return of a marriage within thirty days.

Where to Find Marriage and Divorce Records

County clerks began recording marriages in 1860. The earliest divorce cases were heard in the county probate courts (these records are at the Nevada State Library and Archives in Carson City). After 1864, the county district courts were given jurisdiction for divorces. Many county records have been filmed, such as:

- Elko County Clerk marriage licenses, 1886–1951 (film 1943268 ff.), at the Elko County Courthouse in Elko.
- Storey County Clerk marriage license applications and affidavits, 1874–1950 (film 1901583 ff.), at the Storey County Courthouse in Virginia City.

See also:

- CD-ROM: *Territorial Vital Records: Births, Divorces, Guardianships, Marriages, Naturalizations, Wills; 1800s Thru 1906 Utah Territory, Arizona, Colorado, Idaho, Nevada, Wyoming, Indian Territory; LDS Branches, Wards; Deseret News Vital Records; J.P. Marriages; Methodist Marriages* (Saint George, UT: Genealogical CD Publishing, 1994).

PROPERTY AND INHERITANCE

1861 only the portion of an estate not included in a premarital agreement may be included in a will of a deceased spouse. Nevada becomes first territory to enact a marital property law, providing that all property owned or claimed by a married woman at the time of her marriage shall be her separate property after marriage. Both husband and wife may hold property as joint-tenants, tenants in common, or as community property.
1864 a married woman's separate estate is liable for her antenuptial debts, and she must support her husband if he cannot support himself. "All property, both real and personal, of the wife, owned or claimed by her before marriage, and that acquired afterward by gift, devise, or descent, shall be her

separate property; and laws shall be passed more clearly defining the rights of the wife in relation as well to her separate property as to that held in common with her husband. Laws shall also be passed providing for the registration of the wife's separate property (Art. IV § 31)."

1867 a married woman is granted *feme sole* status to manage her separate estate.

1873 a married woman may devise a will, except for community property, which the husband inherits in entirety; a widow inherits only one-half of community property.

1883 a widow has access to her husband's personal estate.

SUFFRAGE

1914 Nevada women receive complete suffrage.

CITIZENSHIP

1848 all residents of Nevada become U.S. citizens by legislation of Congress, except for Native Americans, whose tribes are considered a separate nation until 1924.

CENSUS INFORMATION

For the 1860 federal census, see Utah, Saint Mary's County (for Elko County), and Carson County (for Douglas, Lyon, Ormsby, and Storey counties).

1861–4 territorial censuses (film 1689341) of the following counties: Buena Vista, Churchill, Douglas, Humboldt, Leander, Lyon, Ormsby, Storey, and Washoe.

1875 censuses for Washoe County (film 1689341).

1875 state census has been published in manuscripts based on the census:

- *Census of the Inhabitants of the State of Nevada, 1875.* 2 Vols. (1877. Reprint. Millwood, NY: Kraus-Thomson, 1984, fiche 6016536 ff.).
- Jensen, Genevieve S. *Index to Nevada State Census of 1875, Appendix to Journals of the Senate and Assembly, 8th Session, Volumes 2–3, Head of Family and Other Names* (Las Vegas: Las Vegas, Nevada Multi-Regional Family History Center, 1994, film 1598226).

The territorial and state censuses are at the Nevada State Library and Archives.

OTHER

Index to materials collected from bank and safe deposit boxes, Unclaimed Property Division, Department of Commerce, State of Nevada (film 1421665), at the Las Vegas Family History Center in Las Vegas. Materials collected in 1986 include birth and death certificates, marriage licenses, divorce records, court records, military records, tax records, business records, church records, wills and other probate records, and deeds and land records. The land records are mostly from Lyon, Storey, and Washoe counties.

BIBLIOGRAPHY

Brown, Marjorie and Hugh Brown. *A Lady in Boomtown: Miners and Manners on the Nevada Frontier* (Reno: University of Nevada Press, 1991).

Comstock, David A. "Proper Women at the Mines: Life at Nevada City in the 1850s." *Pacific Historian* 28 (Fall 1984): 65–73.

Ellison, Marion. *An Inventory & Index to the Records of Carson County, Utah & Nevada Territories, 1855–1861* (Reno: Grace Dahlberg Foundation, 1984).

Greene, Diane E. *Nevada Guide to Genealogical Records* (Baltimore: Clearfield Co., 1998).

James, Ronald and C. Elizabeth Redmond. *Comstock Women: The Making of a Mining Community* (Reno: University of Nevada, 1998).

—. *Temples of Justice: County Courthouses of Nevada* (Reno: University of Nevada, 1994).

King, R.T. *Women, Children & Family Life in the Nevada Interior, 1900–1930s* (Reno: University of Nevada Oral History Project, 1987).

Lee, Joyce C. *Genealogical Prospecting in Nevada: A Guide to Nevada Directories* (Carson City: Nevada State Library, 1984).

Loverin, Janet I. *To Clothe Nevada Women, 1860–1920* (Las Vegas: Nevada State Museum, 1990).

Nevada Historical Society. *Quilts in Nevada* (Reno: The Society, 1984).

Seagraves, Anne. *Women of the Sierra* (Lakeport, CA: Wesanne Publications, 1990).

Spiros, Joyce V. Hawley. *Genealogical Guide to Arizona and Nevada* (Gallup, NM: Verlene Publishing, 1983, fiche 6049613).

SELECTED RESOURCES FOR WOMEN'S HISTORY

Nevada Historical Society
1650 North Virginia Street
Reno, NV 89503

Nevada State Library and Archives
100 Stewart Street
Carson City, NV 89710

Nevada Women's Archives
James R. Dickinson Library
University of Nevada, Las Vegas
4504 Maryland Parkway
Box 457010
Las Vegas, NV 89154-7010

Nevada Women's Archives
University Library
University of Nevada, Reno
Reno, NV 89557-0044

Nevada Women's History Project
1048 N. Sierra, #A
Reno, NV 89503

Nevada Women's Archives, available online at **<www.nscee.edu/unlv/Libraries/women/womarch.html>**

Nevada Women's History Project, available online at **<www.unr.edu/unr/sb204/mwhp>**

Women's calling cards, New Hampshire, 1880s (Author collection)

NEW HAMPSHIRE

IMPORTANT DATES IN STATE HISTORY

1623 First settlement at Dover.
1641 Part of the Massachusetts Bay Colony.
1679 Becomes a separate Royal colony.
1759 Western New Hampshire opened for white settlement.
1764 New Hampshire's western boundary becomes the Connecticut River.
1784 State constitution written.
1842 New Hampshire-Quebec boundary resolved.

MARRIAGE AND DIVORCE

1679 under the laws of Massachusetts Bay Colony until this time.
1774 British Privy Council disallows legislative divorces in New Hampshire.
1880 town clerks begin issuing marriage certificates.
1891 town clerks are required to issue marriage licenses.

Where to Find Marriage and Divorce Records

Marriages have been recorded in town records since 1639. Colony-wide registration began in 1686. The original town records or transcripts have been filmed and are available through the FHL and at the New Hampshire Historical Society in Concord. The earliest divorces were granted by the colonial legislature beginning in 1680, when New Hampshire separated from Massachusetts. The county superior courts of judicature and county supreme judicial courts handled divorces until the 1850s. The county supreme courts held jurisdiction until 1900, when they were replaced by the county superior courts. The clerk of the county superior court has custody of divorce cases from 1774. The available state indexes at the State Department of Health in Concord are:

- Brides' index, 1640–1900 (film 0975678 ff.), to brides, mothers of brides, and mothers of grooms.
- Marriage index, early to 1900, by grooms' surname (film 1001120 ff.).
- Index to divorces and annulments prior to 1938 (film 1001323 ff.).

Most county court records have been filmed but are not cataloged as divorce records. Some county divorce records have been filmed, such as:

- Grafton County Superior Court of Judicature court records, 1774–1821, 1836–7; court dockets, 1774–1819, 1833–51 (film 1763455 ff.), including divorce cases, at the Grafton County Courthouse in Woodsville. From 1813 to 1816, records were kept by the Supreme Judicial Court.
- Grafton County Supreme Court equity records, 1881–1918 (film 1763365 ff.), including divorce records. Records were kept by the Supreme Court from 1881 to 1900 and the Superior Court from 1901 to 1918.

See also indexes and compiled publications, such as:

- Card file index to publishments of marriage intentions prior to 1900 (film 1001439), at the New Hampshire Historical Society.
- Canney, Robert S. *The Early Marriage Records of Strafford County, New Hampshire, 1630–1860* (Bowie, MD: Heritage Books, 1997).
- Hammond, Otis G. *Notices from the New Hampshire Gazette, 1765–1800* (Lamberstville, NJ: Hunterdon House, 1970, fiche 6051306).
- Oesterlin, Pauline J. *New Hampshire Marriage Licenses and Intentions, 1709–1961* (Bowie, MD:

Heritage Books, 1991).

- Roberts, Richard P. *New Hampshire Name Changes, 1768–1923* (Bowie, MD: Heritage Books, 1990). Includes some name changes in divorce proceedings.
- New Hampshire miscellaneous province and state papers, 1641–1800 (film 0983682 ff.), at the New Hampshire Historical Society.

PROPERTY AND INHERITANCE

1718 in intestacy, a widow receives one-third of her husband's personal estate absolutely, and one-third of the real estate for life.

1761 in intestacy, a widow receives one-third of her husband's real and personal estate in addition to dower.

1822 a widow has access to her husband's personal estate.

1841 a married woman may devise a will, with her husband's consent.

1842 a married woman had sole and separate use of all property when she has been deserted by her husband. She may also apply for *feme sole* status six months after abandonment.

1854 a married woman may devise a will.

1867 "all property earned, acquired, or inherited by, or bequeathed to a woman before or after her marriage shall be to her own use, free from the control or interference of her husband, if the same did not include his payment or pledge."

1871 a married woman may control her separate estate without restriction.

SUFFRAGE

1784 state constitution denies women the right to vote.

1920 New Hampshire women receive complete suffrage by passage of the 19th Amendment to the Constitution.

CITIZENSHIP

One of the original Thirteen Colonies.

CENSUS INFORMATION

There are no state censuses for New Hampshire, except for an 1786 enumeration of the heads of families of Peterborough, published in Vol. 10 of the *State Papers* (film 1033737).

OTHER

1719 Act for Regulating Townships establishes a three-month "warning-out" period for non-resident poor in communities.

BIBLIOGRAPHY

Dodge, Timothy. *Poor Relief in Durham, Lee, and Madbury, New Hampshire, 1732–1891* (Bowie, MD: Heritage Books, 1995).

Evans, Helen F. *Index of References to American Women in Colonial Newspapers, Through 1800*. 3 Vols. (Bedford, NH: The Bibliographer, 1979). This covers New Hampshire women, 1756–1800.

Federal Writers' Project. *Hands That Built New Hampshire: Spinning and Weaving in New Hampshire* (Brattleboro, VT: Stephen Daye Press, 1940).

Galloway, Colin G. *North Country Captives: Selected Narratives of Indian Captivity from Vermont to New Hampshire* (Hanover, NH: University Press of New England, 1992).

Hareven, Tamara K. *Family Time and Industrial Time: The Relationship Between the Family and Work in a New England Industrial Community* (Cambridge: Cambridge University Press, 1982). Study of the Amoskeag Manufacturing Company in Manchester.

Harriman, Alice Stratton. *A History of the New Hampshire Federation of Women's Clubs, 1895–1940* (Bristol, NH: Musgrave Printing House, 1941).

Hood Museum of Art. *Lessons Stitched in Silk: Samplers from the Canterbury Region of New Hampshire* (Hanover, NH: Dartmouth College, 1990).

LaBrance, John F. and Rita F. Conant. *In Female Worth and Elegance: Sampler and Needlework Students and Teachers in Portsmouth, New Hampshire, 1741–1840* (Portsmouth: Portsmouth Museums, Portsmouth Naval Shipyard Museum, 1996).

Noyes, Sybil, Charles T. Libby, and Walter G. Davis. *Genealogical Dictionary of Maine and New Hampshire* (1928–39. Reprint. Baltimore: Genealogical Publishing Co., 1996).

Pope, Charles Henry. *Pioneers of Maine and New Hampshire* (1908. Reprint. Baltimore: Genealogical Publishing Co., 1996, fiche 6049825).

Tardiff, Olive. *They Paved the Way: A History of New Hampshire Women* (Exeter, NH: Women for Women Weekly Publishing, 1980).

Towle, Laird. *New Hampshire Genealogical Research Guide* (Bowie, MD: Heritage Books, 1983).

SELECTED RESOURCES FOR WOMEN'S HISTORY

Dimond Library
University of New Hampshire
Durham, NH 03824

New Hampshire Division of Records
Management and Archives
71 South Fruit Street
Concord, NH 03301-2410

New Hampshire Historical Society
30 Park Street
Concord, NH 03301

New Hampshire State Library
20 Park Street
Concord, NH 03301

Special Collections
Baker Library
Dartmouth College
Hanover, NH 03755

A New-Fashioned Girl
Ladies' Home Journal, 1909

NEW JERSEY

IMPORTANT DATES IN STATE HISTORY

1618 Dutch trading post established at Bergen (Jersey City).
1623 Dutch settlement founded at Fort Nassau (Gloucester).
1640 First Swedish settlements founded at Racoon Creek and Cape May.
1641 First English settlement founded at Salem Creek (not permanent).
1655 Dutch forces conquer the New Sweden colony.
1664 Established as a proprietary English colony.
1665 Concessions and Agreements of 1665 drafted; the Duke's Laws are published.
1666 Newark founded by Puritans from Connecticut.
1674 Divided into the provinces of East Jersey and West Jersey.
1676 West Jersey purchased as a refuge for persecuted Quakers.
1677 West Jersey Concessions issued, including a coded based on Quaker jurisprudence.
1682 Quaker proprietors purchase East Jersey.
1683 Court of Common Right created by the East Jersey Assembly (civil, criminal, common law, and equity jurisdiction).
1685 Board of Proprietors of East Jersey organized.
1688 Council of the Proprietors of West Jersey organized; New York and both Jersey provinces annexed to the Dominion of New England (dissolved in 1692).
1693 East Jersey counties divided into townships; county courts established in both provinces (Gloucester County Court established in 1686).
1702 Two Jersey provinces unite as a single Royal colony.
1769 Boundary dispute with New York is resolved.
1776 Battle of Trenton.
1777 Battle of Princeton.
1778 Battle of Monmouth.

MARRIAGE AND DIVORCE

1669 first divorce is granted in New Jersey by the governor.
1673 law requires town clerks to keep marriage records (not widely practiced).
1675 only qualified ministers or justices of the peace may solemnize marriages.
1682 in East Jersey, marriages are forbidden unless banns have been published and the governor has issued a license.
1711 marriage bonds are required to be filed with the colonial governor (not widely practiced).
1719 no one under twenty-one can be married without consent of parent or guardian.
1774 British Privy Council disallows legislative divorce in New Jersey.
1795 requirement for marriage licenses is repealed.
1897 marriage licenses are required.

Where to Find Marriage and Divorce Records

The earliest marriage bonds were recorded from the 1660s to 1795. From 1795 to 1848 county clerks recorded marriages. The records are at the original counties, except for Atlantic and Somerset counties (at the New Jersey State Archives in Trenton) and Middlesex County (at Rutgers University Archives in New Brunswick). Statewide registration began in 1848. State records before 1878 are at the New Jersey State Archives, and those after 1878 are in the custody of the Department of Health in Trenton. In the seventeenth century, some divorces were granted by the colonial governor; the Middlesex County Court of Sessions granted at least one divorce in 1692. From 1743 to 1850 divorces were granted by the state legislature and court of chancery. The Superior Court of New Jersey in Trenton has held jurisdiction since that time. Records and indexes at the New Jersey State Archives are:

- New Jersey marriages, 1711–1878 (film 0888701 ff.), from various counties and are arranged in groups by surname.
- New Jersey marriage bonds, WPA marriage records, 1670–1800 (film 0542533 ff.).
- Marriage bonds, 1736-97, licenses, 1711-94, Monmouth County marriage records, 1794–1878, marriages, 1727–1878 (film 0802936 ff.).
- Typescript of New Jersey marriage bonds of the 1700s (film 0540682 ff.).
- Legislative and chancery court divorce petitions, 1743–1850.

Many county records have been filmed, such as:

- Morris County Clerk marriage records, 1795–1919 (film 1314453 ff.), at the Morris County Courthouse in Morristown.
- Cape May County Clerk marriages, 1694–1830 (film 0441460 ff.), at the Historical Society of Pennsylvania in Philadelphia.

See also compiled publications, such as:

- Gibson, George and Florence Gibson. *Marriages of Monmouth County, New Jersey, 1795–1843* (1981. Reprint. Baltimore: Clearfield Co., 1992).
- Nelson, William. *New Jersey Marriage Records, 1665–1800* (1900. Reprint. Baltimore: Genealogical Publishing Co., 1973). Reprinted from the *New Jersey Archives*, 1st Series, Vol. 22.
- Hood, John. *Index of Colonial and State Laws of New Jersey, Between the Years 1663–1903 Inclusive* (Camden: Sinnickson & Sons, 1905).
- Jones-Reichman, Beth. "Divorces by Legislative Acts, 1778–1844." *The Genealogical Magazine of New Jersey* 53 (January 1978): 1–10.
- McCracken, George E. "New Jersey Legislative Divorces, 1778–1844." *The American Genealogist* 34 (1958): 107–12.

PROPERTY AND INHERITANCE

1664 New Jersey land records begin; before this date, see New York.

1676 in West Jersey, in intestacy a widow receives one-third of her husband's personal estate absolutely and one-third of his real estate for life.

1698 East Jersey Proprietors require that to be valid, deeds must be recorded with the register in Perth Amboy within six months of execution.

1714 counties must keep a record of lands deeded and conveyances (disallowed by the King in 1721).

1716 law requires "road returns," which enumerate property owners along the routes where roads are to be laid (revised in 1744 and 1760).

1727 act similar to act of 1714 is passed (disallowed by the King in 1731).

1743 justices of the peace and county judges may register deeds (amounting to about twenty-five percent of all land transactions).[30]

1785 jurisdiction for probate is transferred from the state prerogative court to the county orphans' courts.

1804 jurisdiction for probate is now held by the county surrogate's courts.

[30] Peter O. Wacker, *Land & People: A Cultural Geography of Preindustrial New Jersey* (New Brunswick: Rutgers University Press, 1975), 337.

1852 statute secures a separate legal estate to a married woman (copied from the New York statute of 1848), providing that any woman who married after 4 July 1852 who owns property at the time of marriage "shall continue to own said property as if she were a single woman."
1864 a married woman may devise a will.
1878 a married woman's separate earnings are her own, if she is living separately from her husband.

SUFFRAGE

1776 state constitution gives all free inhabitants, including widows and spinsters (unmarried women) who own property, the right to vote.
1807 election reforms strip women of the right to vote.
1920 New Jersey women receive complete suffrage by passage of the 19th Amendment to the Constitution.

CITIZENSHIP

One of the original Thirteen Colonies.

CENSUS INFORMATION

The federal censuses for 1790, 1800, 1810, and 1820 are missing.
1855–65 state censuses (film 0802944 ff.).
1885 state census (film 0865449 ff.).
1895 state census (film 0888644 ff.).
1905 state census (film 1688587 ff.).
1915 state census (film 1465501 ff.).
State censuses are at the New Jersey State Archives. Some are incomplete.

OTHER

A widow who needed to go into business to support herself would sometimes open a tavern in her home. The New Jersey State Archives has tavern licenses for the following counties: Bergen (1760– 1866), Camden (1828–75), Cumberland (1807–1920), Essex (1726–1871), Hunterdon (1738–1870), Middlesex (1742–1826), Ocean (1850–95), Somerset (1782–1876), and Sussex (1753–1860). Most of these records are indexed. There are also peddlers' and shopkeepers' licenses for some counties.

BIBLIOGRAPHY

Burstyn, Joan, M. *Past and Promise: Lives of New Jersey Women* (Metuchen, NJ: Scarecrow Press, 1990).

Cook, Margaret. "New Jersey's Charitable Cooks: A Checklist of Fund-raising Cookbooks Published in New Jersey (1879–1915)." *Journal of the Rutgers University Library* 35 1 (1971): 15–26.

Curtis, Phillip. *American Quilts in the Newark Museum Collection* (Newark: The Newark Museum, 1973).

DePauw, Linda G. *Fortunes of War: New Jersey Women and the American Revolution* (Trenton: New Jersey Historical Commission, 1975).

Epperson, Gwenn F. *New Netherland Roots* (Baltimore: Genealogical Publishing Co., 1994).

Epstein, Bette Marie, et al. *Guide to Family History Sources in the New Jersey State Archives*. 3rd ed. (Trenton: The Archives, 1994).

Heritage Quilt Project of New Jersey. *New Jersey Quilts, 1777 to 1950: Contributions to an American Tradition* (Paducah, KY: American Quilters Society, 1992).

Miller, George J. "Chancery Courts in New Jersey in the Seventeenth Century." *New Jersey Law Journal* 58 (1935): 3–5, 273.

Morris Museum of Arts and Sciences. *New Jersey Quilters: A Timeless Tradition* (Morristown: The Museum, 1984).

Murrin, Mary R. *Women in New Jersey History* (Trenton: New Jersey Historical Commission, 1985).

Nelson, William. *The Law and the Practice of New Jersey from the Earliest Times: Concerning the Probate of Wills, the Administration of Estates, the Protection of Orphans and Minors, and the Control of Their Estates; the Prerogative Court, the Ordinary, and the Surrogates* (Paterson, NJ: Paterson History Club, 1909).

—— . *New Jersey Index of Wills*. 3 Vols. (1912. Reprint. Baltimore: Genealogical Publishing Co., 1969). Indexes New Jersey wills prior to 1901.

Philbrook, Mary. "Women's Suffrage in New Jersey Prior to 1807." *Proceedings of the New Jersey Historical Society* LVII (1939): 870–98.

Rutgers University Libraries Special Collections and Archives. *A Guide to Women's History Archives at Rutgers* (New Brunswick: The Libraries, 1990).

Shinn, Henry. "An Early New Jersey Poll List." *Pennsylvania Magazine of History and Biography* XLIV (1920): 77–81.

Steiner-Scott, Elizabeth and Elizabeth Pearce Wagle. *New Jersey Women, 1770–1970: A Bibliography* (Rutherford, NJ: Farleigh Dickinson University Press, 1978).

SELECTED RESOURCES FOR WOMEN'S HISTORY

Messler Library
Farleigh Dickinson University
Montross Avenue
Rutherford, NJ 07070

New Jersey Historical Society Library
230 Broadway
Newark, NJ 07104

New Jersey State Archives
New Jersey State Library
185 West State Street
CN 307 (archives) / CN 520 (library)
Trenton, NJ 086250307

Special Collections and Archives
Rutgers University
New Brunswick, NJ 08903

NEW MEXICO

IMPORTANT DATES IN STATE HISTORY

1598 Spanish settlement of Santa Fe founded.
1610 Santa Fe becomes provincial capital.
1680 Pueblo Indian revolt drives all settlers out of the area.
1693 Settlers return to Santa Fe.
1706 Albuquerque founded.
1821 Becomes province of Mexico.
1846 U.S. forces occupy Santa Fe; military government established.
1848 Acquired from Mexico in the Treaty of Guadalupe-Hildago.
1850 Organized as a U.S. territory; includes the future states of Arizona and parts of Utah and Nevada (about 85,000 people).
1850 First territorial acts adopt some procedures of common law.
1853 Gadsen Purchase adds territory from Mexico south of the Gila River.
1864 Navajo Long Walk: 8,000 Navajos held as prisoners of war at For Sumner (until 1867).
1868 Navajo reservations established.
1870 Apache reservations established.
1876 Territorial legislature adopts common law.
1911 Constitution adopted.
1912 Statehood.

MARRIAGE AND DIVORCE

1557 (pre-settlement) Royal Edict of Spain declares "no Indian Chieftain, even if he is an infidel, can marry more than once, nor keep women locked up, nor deprive them of their freedom to join with a person of their choice." Law is confirmed again in 1595, 1596, 1638, and 1680.

1563 (pre-settlement) Council of Trent declares that marriage must be solemnized by a priest before two witnesses to be valid and must be recorded in the parish register.

1776 Spanish Crown issues the Royal Pragmatic on Marriage, which takes exclusive control of marriage away from the Catholic Church and gives parents rights under civil law to prevent marriages against their wishes; parents are allowed to disinherit children who marry against their wishes.

1778 the Royal Pragmatic becomes law in New Mexico.

1884 the community property system of marital law is adopted.

1905 an Act of Congress requires county clerks of probate to issue and record marriage licenses.

Where to Find Marriage and Divorce Records

From 1693 to 1846 marriage investigations of the Catholic Church, *diligencias matrimoniales*, can be found in the Archives of the Archdiocese of Santa Fe at the University of New Mexico in Albuquerque. For other early marriages, see church records and compiled publications, such as:

- San Juan de los Caballeros Catholic Church, San Juan, parish records, 1726–1956 (film 0016981 ff.), at the Church in San Juan, Rio Arriba County.
- Chávez, Angelico. *New Mexico Roots, LTD: A Demographic Perspective from Genealogical, Historical, and Geographical Data Found in the Diligencias Matrimoniales, or Pre-Nuptial Investigations [1678–1869]*. 11 Vols. (n.p., 1982, fiche 6051367).
- *New Mexico Marriages: Santa Fe, Saint Francis Parish and Military Chapel of Our Lady of Light, 1728–1857* (Albuquerque: New Mexico Genealogical Society, 1997).
- Salas, Raymond P. and Maragaret L. Windham. *New Mexico Marriages: Church of San Antonion de Sandia, 1771–1864* (Albuquerque: New Mexico Genealogical Society, 1993).

Marriages have been recorded by the county clerks beginning as early as 1863. There are also some pre-1912 marriages at the New Mexico Records Center and Archives in Santa Fe. Divorces have been under the jurisdiction of the county district courts. Very few of these records have been filmed, and have to be examined in the original. There are published compilations, such as:

- Lofgreen, June and Margaret L. Windham. *New Mexico Marriages: Union County, 1893–1940* (Albuquerque: New Mexico Genealogical Society, 1994).
- Mannen, Eunice M. *Marriage Records of Doña Ana County, New Mexico [1869–1916]*. 3 Vols. (Dona Ana: Doña Ana Chapter, Daughters of the American Revolution, 1980, fiche 6019986 ff.).
- Weiss, Iva Hartsell. *Sierra County, New Mexico, Marriage Records [1884–1920]* (Truth or Consequences, NM: Sierra County Genealogical Society, 1990).
- Reithel, Louise and Robert J. Reithel. *Marriage Records (1909–1915), Curry County Courthouse, Clovis, New Mexico* (Clovis: The Authors, 1988, film 1597655).
- *Some Marriage Records of the State of New Mexico, 1880–1920*. 2 Vols. (n.p.: New Mexico Daughters of the American Revolution, 1971, film 0908289 ff.). Covers the counties of Bernalillo, Chaves, Curry, Eddy, Otero, Quay, Roosevelt, and San Juan.

PROPERTY AND INHERITANCE

1884 first statutes dealing with community property law are enacted (§ 1410 et seq.); community property laws of Spain and Mexico have been extended through the territorial period.

1907 spouses are given separate control of community property acquired by each of them individually; a married woman may devise a will, but not with regard to community property, which her husband inherits in entirety. A widow inherits only one-half of the community property.

SUFFRAGE

1920 New Mexico women receive complete suffrage by passage of the 19th Amendment to the Constitution.

CITIZENSHIP

1848 all residents of New Mexico become U.S. citizens by treaty, except for Native Americans, whose tribes are considered a separate nation until 1924.

CENSUS INFORMATION

1750–1830 censuses, see Olmsted, Virginia Langham. *Spanish and Mexican Censuses of New Mexico, 1750–1830* (Albuquerque: New Mexico Genealogical Society, 1981).

1790, 1823, and 1845 censuses, see *New Mexico Spanish and Colonial Censuses, 1790, 1825, 1845* (Albuquerque: New Mexico Genealogical Society, 1979).

1642–1815 censuses, see Platt, Lyman D. *Census Records for Latin America and the Hispanic United States* (Baltimore: Genealogical Publishing Co., 1998).

OTHER

The Spanish Archives of New Mexico cover records of Spain's administration of the area from 1621 to 1820. See *Guide to the Microfilm of the Spanish Archives of New Mexico, 1697–1821* (Santa Fe: New Mexico Records Center and Archives, 1967, film 0468381 ff.). The Mexican Archives of New Mexico are records of the Mexican government from 1821 to 1846. There is a filmed guide (film 0962163). Both series are at the New Mexico Records Center and Archives and the Center for Southwest Research, University of New Mexico, Albuquerque. See also Vigil, Julian Josue. *The Vigil Index: Spanish and Mexican Archives of New Mexico, 1681–1846 (SANM 1:10)* (Albuquerque: Center for Southwest Research, 1994).

BIBLIOGRAPHY

Barnes, Thomas C. *Northern New Spain: A Research Guide* (Tucson: University of Arizona Press, 1981).

Benson, Nancy C. "Pioneering Women of New Mexico." *El Palacio* 85 (Summer 1979): 8-13, 34-8.

Chávez, Fray Angelico. *Origins of New Mexico Families* (1954. Reprint. Santa Fe: Museum of New Mexico Press, 1992).

—— . *Archives of the Archdiocese of Santa Fé, 1678–1900* (Washington, DC: Academy of American Franciscan History, 1957).

Clark, Gerald. *Community Property and the Family in New Mexico* (Albuquerque: University of New Mexico Press, 1956).

Craver, Rebecca M. *The Impact of Intimacy: Mexican-Anglo Intermarriage in New Mexico, 1821–1846* (El Paso: Texas Western Press, 1982).

Cutter, Charles R. *The Legal Culture of Northern New Spain, 1700–1810* (Albuquerque: University of New Mexico Press, 1995).

Foote, Cheryl, J. "The History of Women in New Mexico: A Selective Guide to Published Sources." *New Mexico Historical Review* 57 (1982): 387-94.

——. *Women of the New Mexico Frontier, 1846–1912* (Niwot: University Press of Colorado, 1990).

García, Nasario. *Comadres: Hispanic Women of the Río Puerco Valley* (Albuquerque: University of New Mexico Press, 1997).

Guitierriez, Ramon A. *When Jesus Came, the Corn Mothers Went Away: Pioneer and Sexuality in New Mexico, 1580–1846* (Stanford: Stanford University Press, 1991).

Jenson, Joan M. and Doris A. Miller. *New Mexico Women: Intercultural Perspectives* (Albuquerque: University of New Mexico Press, 1986).

Kent, Kate Peck. *Pueblo Indian Textiles: A Living Tradition* (Santa Fe: School of American Research Press, 1983).

Lecompte, Janet. "The Independent Women of Hispanic New Mexico, 1821-1846." *Western Historical Society Quarterly* 12 (January 1981): 17-36.

Mock, Charlotte. *Bridges: New Mexican Black Women, 1900–1950* (Albuquerque: New Mexico Commission on the Study of Women, 1985).

Noble, David Grant. *Pueblos, Villages, Forts, and Trails: A Guide to New Mexico's Past* (Albuquerque: University of New Mexico Press, 1994).

Rock, Rosalind Z. "Pido y Suplico: Women and the Law in Spanish New Mexico." *New Mexico Historical Review* 65 (April 1990): 145-60.

Schackel, Sandra. *Social Housekeepers: Women Shaping Public Policy in New Mexico, 1920–1940* (Albuquerque: University of New Mexico Press, 1982).

Spiros, Joyce V. Hawley. *Handy Genealogical Guide to New Mexico* (Gallup, NM: Verlene Publishing, 1986, fiche 6051310).

Weigle, Marta. *Women of New Mexico: Depression Era Images* (Santa Fe: Ancient City Press, 1993).

Wiltsey, Thomas E. "Territorial Court Records and Local History: New Mexico as a Case Study." *Prologue* (Spring 1983).

SELECTED RESOURCES FOR WOMEN'S HISTORY

Albuquerque Public Library
423 Central Avenue NE
Albuquerque, NM 87102

Center for Southwest Research
Zimmerman Library
University of New Mexico
Albuquerque, NM 87131

Museum of New Mexico History Library
PO Box 2087
110 Washington Avenue
Santa Fe, NM 87504-2087

New Mexico State Records Center and Archives
404 Montezuma Street
Santa Fe, NM 87501

New Mexico State Library
325 Don Gaspar Avenue
Santa Fe, NM 87503

Rio Grande Historical Collections
New Mexico State University
Box 3475
Las Cruces, NM 88003

NEW YORK

IMPORTANT DATES IN STATE HISTORY

1612 First Dutch trading post built on Manhattan Island.
1614 Dutch post built near site of Albany.
1621 Dutch West India Company receives a charter for New Netherland.
1624 First Dutch colonists arrive on Manhattan Island and at the Albany area.
1629 Patroonship of Rennselaerwyck founded.
1640 English Puritans from Massachusetts and Connecticut found settlements on Long Island.
1654 Dutch forces conquer New Sweden.
1664 New Netherland colony captured by the English.
1673 Dutch forces retake New York /New Netherland.
1674 English forces recapture New York.
1683 Charter of Libertyes drafted; twelve original counties formed.
1688 Annexed by the Dominion of New England.
1689 Leisler Rebellion (ends 1691).
1708 Palatine Germans establish Germantown in the Hudson Valley.
1776 British forces occupy New York City (surrendered in 1783); Battle of Long Island; Battle of Saratoga.
1825 Erie Canal opened.

MARRIAGE AND DIVORCE

1624 under Dutch civil law, married women retain their maiden names.
1655 first known divorce is granted in New Netherland.
1664 act legalizes justice of the peace marriages (from old Dutch law of 1590).
1670–2 four divorces are granted by the Governor and Council (New York Jurisprudence, Evidence § 870).
1675 absolute divorce is disallowed.
1685 law allows remarriage after separation (for the first time).
1787 first law to permit absolute divorce, on grounds of adultery only (not amended until 1966).
1881 clergy, county judges, justices of the peace, mayors, aldermen, and Indian peacemakers may perform marriages.
1889 New York City police justices may perform marriages (until 1896).
1893 Brooklyn police justices may perform marriages (until 1896).

Where to Find Marriage and Divorce Records

As New York was settled by different groups with different legal traditions, records have been kept on different levels of government. The colonial towns established by New Englanders have marriages recorded in the town records. There were also marriage bonds and licenses issued from 1639 to about 1783. State and county registration was in effect from 1847 to 1853 in some places and began again in 1881. Some county clerks have justice of the peace dockets prior to 1847. Most county records from 1908 to 1935 have been filmed. The State Health Department has records for most localities (except Albany, Buffalo, the boroughs of New York City, and Yonkers) beginning in 1881. Faster replies are usually obtained by writing to the county clerks. For the other localities, see:

- New York City marriage register, 1829–87 (film 1671684 ff.), New York City index to marriages in all boroughs (Manhattan, Bronx, Brooklyn, Queens, and Staten Island [Richmond]), 1888–1937 (film 1653852 ff.), at the Municipal Archives in New York City.
- Brooklyn marriage certificates, 1866–1937 (film 1543711 ff.), and 1908 to present, at the

City Clerk's Office in Brooklyn, also marriages, 1847–65, at the Kings County Clerk's Office in Brooklyn.

- Manhattan marriage records and index, 1866–1937 (film 1522995 ff.), and 1908 to present, at the Municipal Archives in New York City. The Archives does not accept search requests for records that are not indexed.
- Queens marriage records, 1881–1937 (film 1908328 ff.), and 1908 to present, at the City Clerk's Office in Kew Gardens, and some, 1908–19, at the Queens County Clerks's Office in Jamaica.
- Bronx marriage indexes, 1898–1937 (film 1983782 ff.), and 1908 to present, at the City Clerk's Office in Bronx.
- Staten Island, 1908 to present, at the City Clerk's Office in Staten Island.
- Albany (city) marriages, 1847, 1870–1917, and Albany County, 1908–36, at the County Clerk's Office in Albany; Albany (city) marriages, 1920 to present, at the City Clerk's Office in Albany.
- Buffalo County marriages, 1811–1935, at the Erie County Clerk's Office in Buffalo (records, 1811–36 may be missing), and 1935 to the present at the City Hall in Buffalo.
- Yonkers marriages, 1870 to the present (records, 1870–1900 may be missing), at the Health Center Building in Yonkers.

There were a few divorces granted by the colonial governor and council in the 1670s, but absolute divorce was disallowed in 1675. The county chancery courts were given jurisdiction for divorce cases in 1787. In 1846 the Supreme Court was given jurisdiction for divorces. See Supreme Court records (holding terms in the counties), such as:

- Dutchess County Supreme Court records, 1847–67 (film 0923905 ff.), at the Dutchess County Courthouse in Poughkeepsie, and records, 1863–84 (film 0940246 ff.), at the Adriance Memorial Library in Poughkeepsie.
- Albany County divorce decrees, 1884–1919 (film 1301982), at the City Hall in Albany.

See also compiled publications, such as:

- New York Secretary of State. *Names of Persons for Whom Marriage Licenses Were Issued by the Secretary Of the Province of New York, Previous to 1784* (Albany: Weed, Parsons & Co., 1860, film 0514675). Reprinted as *New York Marriages Previous to 1784: A Reprint of the Original Edition of 1860 with Additions and Corrections Including: Supplementary List of Marriage Licenses; New York Marriage Licenses, by Robert H. Kelby; New York Marriage Licenses, 1639–1706, with Index by Kenneth Scott* (Baltimore: Genealogical Publishing Co., 1968).
- Bowman, Fred Q. *10,000 Vital Records of Central New York, 1813–1850* (Baltimore: Genealogical Publishing Co., 1986).
- —— . *10,000 Vital Records of Eastern New York, 1777–1834* (Baltimore: Genealogical Publishing Co., 1987).
- —— . *10,000 Vital Records of Western New York* (Baltimore: Genealogical Publishing Co., 1985).
- —— . *8,000 More Vital Records of Eastern New York State, 1804–1850* (Rhinebeck, NY: Kinship, 1991).

PROPERTY AND INHERITANCE

1624 under Dutch law, a married woman may enter into contracts, operate a business in her own name, buy and sell her separate property, and devise her own will. Sons and daughters inherit equally from a parent's estate.

1664 Dutch inheritance laws are to remain in place for all Dutch residents (after 1695, only two Dutch-language wills are probated in New York City).

1665 in intestacy, a widow receives one-third of her deceased husband's personal property, after his creditors have been paid; and one-third of his real property, for life use.

1683 the Charter of Libertyes provides "that a Widdow after the death of her husband shall have her Dower and shall and may tarry in the Chiefe house of her husband forty days after the death of her husband within which forty days her Dower shall be assigned her and for her Dower shall be assigned unto her the third part of all the Lands of her husband dureing Coverture, Except she were endowed of Lesse before Marriage . . . No estate of a *feme covert* shall be sold or conveyed but by Deed acknowledged by her in Some Court of Record the Woman being secretly Examined if she doth it freely without threats or Compulsion of her husband."

1771 private examinations and the practice of requiring a signature on a deed are enforced.

1774 the intestacy law is changed from the right of primogeniture, to giving a widow one-third of her husband's personal estate; no provision is made for real estate.

1786 in intestacy, both sons and daughters inherit equal shares of real property.

1848 real and personal property owned by a woman at the time of her marriage "shall continue her sole and separate property free from the disposal or debts of her husband as if she were a single female."

1849 "any married female may . . . convey and devise real and personal property, and any interest on estate therein, and the rents, issues, and profits thereof in same manner and with like effect as if she were unmarried . . ."

1860 "the property, both real and personal, which any married woman now owns, as her sole and separate property; that which comes to her by descent, devise, bequest, gift, or grant; that which she acquires by her trade, business, labor, or services . . . and the rents, issues, and proceeds of all such property, shall, not withstanding her marriage, be and remain her sole and separate property."

1887 "any transfer or conveyance of real estate hereafter made by a married man directly to his wife [or] by a married woman to her husband, shall not be invalid because such transfer or conveyance was made directly from one to the other without the intervention of a third person."

SUFFRAGE

1777 state constitution denies women the right to vote.

1917 New York women receive complete suffrage by state constitutional amendment.

CITIZENSHIP

One of the original Thirteen Colonies.

CENSUS INFORMATION

1663 and later colonial censuses, see Meyers, Carol M. *Early New York State Census Records, 1663–1772* (Gardena, CA: RAM Publishers, 1965, fiche 6111479).

Most of the surviving records have been filmed and can be found in the Family History Library Catalog under individual counties in New York state. The original records are at the New York State Library in Albany. The following films for Tioga County are *examples* of such records:

- 1825, 1835 state censuses (film 0816363).
- 1855 state census (film 0816364).
- 1865 state census (film 0816365).
- 1865 state census (film 0816366).
- 1875 state census (film 0816367).
- 1885 state census (film 0816368).
- 1892–1905 state censuses (film 0816369).
- 1915 state census (film 0523351).
- 1925 state census (film 0529016).

OTHER

1662 a New Amsterdam court has a man flogged and his right ear cut off, for selling his wife.
1802 The Society for the Relief of Poor Widows with Small Children is incorporated in New York City.
1814 An Association for the Relief of Respectable, Aged, Indigent Females is incorporated in New York City.
1824 "Act for Relief and Settlement of the Poor" establishes poorhouses (workhouses) in each county.
1824–7 Supreme Court of Judicature writs of dower, at the New York State Archives in Albany.
1867–1921 state board of charities records, at the State Archives.
1875–1904 Western House of Refuge, Rochester, Female Department records, at the State Archives.

BIBLIOGRAPHY

Atkins, Jacqueline M. and Phyllis A. Tepper. *New York Beauties: Quilts from the Empire State* (New York: Dutton Studio Books, 1992).

Austin, John D. *Court Records as Family History Resources: New York State as an Example* (Salt Lake City: World Conference on Records, 1969, fiche 6070698).

Basch, Norma. *In the Eyes of the Law: Women, Marriage and Property in 19th Century New York* (Ithaca: Cornell University Press, 1982).

Biemer, Linda Briggs. *Women and Property in Colonial New York: The Transition from Dutch to English Law, 1643–1727* (Ann Arbor: University of Michigan Press, 1983).

Bullock, William E. *A Treatise on the Law of Husband and Wife in the State of New York Including Chapters on Divorce and Dower* (Albany: n.p., 1897).

Cohen, Miriam. *Workshop to Office: Two Generations of Italian Women in New York City, 1900–1950* (Ithaca: Cornell University Press, 1993).

DePauw, Linda Grant. *Four Traditions: Women of New York During the Revolution* (Albany: New York State American Revolution Bicentennial Commission, 1974).

Epperson, Gwenn. *New Netherland Roots* (Baltimore: Genealogical Publishing Co., 1994).

Ernst, Roberts. *Immigrant Life in New York City* (New York: Columbia University Press, 1949).

Ewen, Elizabeth. *Immigrant Women in the Land of Dollars: Life and Culture on the Lower East Side, 1890–1925* (New York: Monthly Review Press, 1985).

Gunderson, Joan R. and Gwen Victor Gampel. "Married Women's Legal Status in Eighteenth-Century New York and Virginia." *William and Mary College Quarterly* 39 (1982): 114–43.

Guzik, Estele M. *Genealogical Resources in the New York Metropolitan Area* (New York: Jewish Genealogical Society, 1989, fiche 6100654).

Hewitt, Nancy A. *Women's Activism and Social Change: Rochester, New York, 1822–1872* (Ithaca: Cornell University Press, 1984).

Hoare, Steve and Carter Houck. *The Unbroken Thread: A History of Quilt-Making in the Catskills* (Hensonville, NY: Black Dome Press, 1996).

Kessner, T. and B.B. Caroli. "New Immigrant Women at Work: Italians and Jews in New York City, 1880–1905." *Journal of Ethnic Studies* (Winter 1978).

McKee, Samuel. *Labor in Colonial New York, 1664–1776* (New York: Columbia University Press, 1935).

Narrett, David Evan. *Inheritance and Family Life in Colonial New York* (Ithaca: Cornell University Press, 1992).

New York Women's History Aid: More Than 100 Record Series Pertaining to Women (Albany: New York State Archives, 1985).

O'Connell, Lucille. "Travelers' Aid for Polish Immigrant Women." *Polish American Studies* 31 1 (1974): 15–19.

Osterud, Nancy Grey. *Bonds of Community: The Lives of Farm Women in Nineteenth-Century New York* (Ithaca: Cornell University Press, 1991).

Richardson, Dorothy. *The Long Day: The Story of a New York Working Girl* (Charlotte: University Press of Virginia, 1990).

Stansell, Christene. *City of Women: Sex and Class in New York, 1789–1860* (Urbana: University of Illinois Press, 1987).

Tompsett, Christine H. "A Note on the Economic Status of Widows in Colonial New York." *New York History* 55 (1974): 319–32.

Yeager, Edna J. "Long Island's Unsung Revolutionary Heroines." *DAR Magazine* 109 8 (1975): 908–15.

SELECTED RESOURCES FOR WOMEN'S HISTORY

Adirondack Women in History
5 Middle Road
PO Box 565
Willsboro, NY 12996

James Wheelock Clark Library
Russell Sage College
45 Ferry Street
Troy, NY 12180

National Women's Hall of Fame
PO Box 335
Seneca Falls, NY 13148-0335

New York Public Library
U.S. History, Local History, and Genealogy Division
Fifth Avenue and 42nd Street
New York, NY 10018

New York State Archives
New York State Library
Cultural Education Center
Empire State Plaza
Albany, NY 12230

Thomas J. Shanahan Library
Marymount Manhattan College
221 East 71st Street
New York, NY 10021

Upstate New York Women's History Conference
1202 East State Street
Ithaca, NY 14850

Wollman Library
Barnard College
606 West 120th Street
New York, NY 10027

Women's Studies Collection
Brooklyn College Library
Brooklyn College of the City University of New York
Bedford Avenue and Avenue H
Brooklyn, NY 11210

Guide to Women's History Collections at the University at Buffalo Archives, available online at **<ublib.buffalo.edu/libraries/units/archives/womhis>**

Records in the New York State Archives Relating to Women: An Overview, available online at **<unrx6.nysed.gov/holding/fact/women-fa.htm>**

NORTH CAROLINA

IMPORTANT DATES IN STATE HISTORY

1653 First settlers migrate from Virginia to Albemarle Sound.
1663 Area granted to eight proprietors.
1665 Concessions and Agreements of Albemarle Province drafted.
1669 Fundamental Constitutions of Carolina drafted.
1691 Albemarle Province recognized as the Province of North Carolina.
1711 Tusacarora War.
1712 The British Crown divides Carolina into two provinces.
1719 South Carolina becomes a Royal Colony.
1729 North Carolina becomes a Royal Colony.
1771 Regulator wars.
1780 Battle of King's Mountain.
1781 Battle of Guilford Courthouse.
1861 21 May secedes from the Union.
1866 More than 9,000 former slaves record their marriages in county records.
1868 11 June readmitted to the Union.

MARRIAGE AND DIVORCE

1669 constitution states that "no marriage shall be lawful, whatever contract and ceremony thy have used till both the parties mutually own it, before the Register of the place where they were married, and he register it, with the names of the father and the mother of each party [not widely practiced]."

❧ *According to the North Carolina State Archives, there are no known surviving Church of England parish registers for North Carolina.*

1701 common-law marriages are not recognized in North Carolina.
1715 marriages are to be recorded by the Secretary of State or in a county register of deeds; marriages could be performed by clergy of the Anglican Church, the Governor, or his Councilors.
1741 law to prevent clandestine marriages requires that parties to be married must either file a marriage bond in the bride's county of residence or post banns for three weeks prior to marriage; interracial marriages are declared to be illegal (not abolished until the 1960s).
1766 Presbyterian ministers are allowed to solemnize marriages.
1851 ministers shall file a marriage return and have it recorded in the county marriage register.
1866 marriage bonds are abolished and are replaced with licenses and certificates; dower rights are reinstated.
1872 law requires parents to be named on marriage certificates.
1937 a woman receiving a divorce decree may petition the court to have her maiden name restored (these are recorded in separate registers, such as Pasquotank County Superior Court maiden names of divorced women, 1937–59 (film 0259369).

Where to Find Marriage and Divorce Records

The earliest county marriages date from 1669 to 1742. Marriage banns or bonds were required from 1741 to 1868 and are at the North Carolina State Archives in Raleigh, except for Granville and Davie counties. The county courts of pleas and quarter sessions were abolished in 1868. Marriages after this date were filed with the Register of Deeds until 1962. From 1783 until 1835, divorces were under the jurisdiction of the state legislature. From 1806 to 1835, the county superior courts could also grant divorces. After 1835, all divorces were under the jurisdiction of the county superior courts. Many records have been deposited at the North Carolina State Archives. An index to marriage bonds, 1741–1868 (fiche 6330241), is available for purchase on microfiche. Many county records have been filmed, such as:

- Craven County Court of Pleas and Quarter Sessions marriage bonds, 1782–1865 (film 0296803 ff.), and Craven County Register of Deeds marriage licenses, 1892–1960; marriage bond abstracts, 1740–1868 (film 0288285 ff.), at the North Carolina State Archives.
- Currituck County Superior Court Negro cohabitation certificates, 1866 (film 1689140), at the North Carolina State Archives. These certificates were issued before marriage was legalized.

See also compiled publications, such as:

- Clemens, William M. *North and South Carolina Marriage Records: From the Earliest Colonial Days to the Civil War* (1927. Reprint. Baltimore: Genealogical Publishing Co., 1981).
- White, Barnetta M. *Somebody Knows My Name: Marriages of Freed Slaves in North Carolina, County by County*. 3 Vols. (Athens, GA: Iberian Publishing Co., 1995).
- McBride, B. Ronan. "Divorces and Separations Granted by Act of the North Carolina Assembly from 1790 to 1818." *North Carolina Genealogical Society Journal* 3 (February (1977): 43–7. For other records, see the "Legislative Papers" at the State Archives and the printed session laws of the North Carolina General Assembly.

PROPERTY AND INHERITANCE

1663 in intestacy, a widow receives a dower of one-third of her husband's real estate owned at the time of marriage or acquired during coverture.

1715 in intestacy, a widow is to receive one-third of her husband's personal estate and one-third of her husband's real estate absolutely. In the conveyance of deeds, a married woman must be examined privately to determine if she is acting of her own free will (reconfirmed in 1749 and 1762).

1784 "the real estates of persons dying intestate should undergo a more general and equal distribution than has hitherto prevailed in this State, be it therefore Enacted . . . when any person shall die seized or possessed of, or having right, title or interest in . . . inheritance of land, or other real estate in fee simple, and such person shall die intestate, his or her estate or inheritance, shall descend in the following manner, to wit: to all the sons to be equally divided amongst them, and for want of sons, to all the daughters to be divided amongst them equally . . . as tenants in common in severalty, not as joint tenants . . ." Dower rights are abolished. If a husband is living, a wife cannot make a will without his permission.

1795 in intestacy, realty is divided among all heirs in the same degree, both sons and daughters.

1796 in intestacy, a widow may request food and necessities during the probate period from funds of the estate.

1849 "all real estate owned by a married woman at the time of marriage shall not be subject to be sold or leased by the husband for the term of his life or for a less term, except by consent of his wife." The wife's consent shall be ascertained by private examination.

1851 a married woman may be given power by will, deed, etc. to devise a will to dispose of any property.

1868 the property of any female acquired before her marriage "shall remain the sole and separate estate of such female and may not be liable for debts, obligations, or engagements of her husband."

1869 a wife's dower rights are reinstated (not abolished again until 1960).

SUFFRAGE

1920 North Carolina women receive complete suffrage by passage of the 19th Amendment to the Constitution.

North Carolina

CITIZENSHIP
One of the original Thirteen Colonies.

CENSUS INFORMATION
1785-7 state census, see Register, Alvaretta K. *State Census of North Carolina, 1784–1787.* 2nd ed. (Baltimore: Genealogical Publishing Co., 1978, film 0897274).

OTHER
1869 a state board of charities is established.

1885- 1953 Confederate veterans' and widows' pensions (film 0175779 ff.). Widows were eligible to file applications after 1887.

Records of widows' years' support, such as those for Pasquotank County, 1882-1960 (film 0260251). The pension and widows' support records are at the North Carolina State Archives.

BIBLIOGRAPHY
Anderson, Lucy L. *North Carolina Women of the Confederacy* (Charlotte: The United Daughters of the Confederacy, 1926).

Coates, Albert. *By Her Own Bootstraps: A Saga of Women in North Carolina* (n.p.: The Author, 1975).

Hathaway, James R.B. *The North Carolina Genealogical and Historical Register* (1900-3. Reprint. Baltimore: Clearfield Co., 1998).

Hehir, Donald M. *Carolina Families: A Bibliography of Books About North and South Carolina Families* (Bowie, MD: Heritage Books, 1994).

Johnson, Guion G. "Courtship and Marriage Customs in Antebellum North Carolina." *North Carolina Historical Review* 8 (1931): 384–402.

Jordan, Paula S. *Women of Guilford County, North Carolina: A Study of Women's Contributions, 1740–1979* (Greensboro, NC: Women of Guilford, 1979).

Leary, Helen F.M. "The Better Half: North Carolina Women's Genealogy." *On to Richmond!* FGS/VGS Conference, 1994.

—. *North Carolina Research: Genealogy and Local History.* 2nd ed. (Raleigh: North Carolina Genealogical Society, 1996).

—. "Marriage, Divorce, and Widowhood: A Study of North Carolina Law Governing the Property and Person of Married Women, 1663-1869." *North Carolina Genealogical Society Journal* 16 (August 1990).

Mitchell, Thornton W. *North Carolina Wills, A Testator Index, 1665–1900.* 2 Vols. Rev. ed. (Baltimore: Genealogical Publishing Co., 1992).

North Carolina Country Quilts: Regional Variations (Chapel Hill: The Ackland Museum, University of North Carolina, 1979).

Parker, Freddie L. *Stealing a Little Freedom: Advertisements for Slave Runaways in North Carolina, 1791–1840* (New York: Garland Publishing, 1994). Abstracts for almost 2,700 slaves.

Resources for Women's Studies in the University of North Carolina at Chapel Hill (Chapel Hill: The University, 1984).

Robeson, Ruth. *North Carolina Quilts* (Chapel Hill: University of North Carolina Press, 1988).

Rodman, Lida T. "Patriotic Women of North Carolina in the Revolution." *DAR Magazine* 45 2/3 (August/September 1914): 145–52.

Semonche, John E. "Common-Law Marriage in North Carolina: A Study of Legal History." *American Journal of Legal History* 9 (1965): 320–49.

Spindel, Donna. *Crime and Society in North Carolina* (Baton Rouge: Louisiana State University Press, 1989).

Thompson, Catherine E. *A Selective Guide to Women-Related Records in the North Carolina State Archives* (Raleigh: The Archives, 1977).

Watson, Alan D. "Women in Colonial North Carolina: Overlooked and Underestimated." *North Carolina Historical Review* 58 (1981): 1–22.

SELECTED RESOURCES FOR WOMEN'S HISTORY

Afro-American Women's Collection
Thomas F. Holgate Library
900 East Washington Street
Greensboro, NC 27420

Joyner Library
East Carolina University
Greenville, NC 27858

Museum of Early Southern Decorative Arts
924 South Main Street
Winston-Salem, NC 27108

North Carolina State Archives
State Library of North Carolina
109 East Jones Street
Raleigh, NC 27601-2807

Triangle Multicultural Women's History Project
605 Germaine Street
Apex, NC 27502

Wilson Library
University of North Carolina at Chapel Hill
Chapel Hill, NC 27514-8890

William Madison Randall Library
University of North Carolina at Wilmington
601 South College Road
Wilmington, NC 28403

Women's Studies Reference Archivist
William R. Perkins Library
Duke University
Box 90185
Durham, NC 27708-0185

African American Women Online Archival Collections, available online at **<scriptorium.lib.duke.edu/collections/african-american-women-.html>**

NORTH DAKOTA

IMPORTANT DATES IN STATE HISTORY

1803 Southwestern North Dakota is part of the Louisiana Purchase.
1804 Part of the District of Louisiana.
1805 Part of the Louisiana Territory.
1812 Part of the Missouri Territory; Scots colonists found Pembina.
1818 Northeastern North Dakota ceded from Great Britain to the U.S. by treaty.
1821 Part of unorganized Indian territory.
1834 Part of the Michigan Territory.
1836 Part of the Wisconsin Territory.
1838 Part of the Iowa Territory.
1849 Part of the Minnesota Territory.
1854 Part of the Nebraska Territory.
1859 Left unorganized.
1861 Reorganized as the Dakota Territory, including Montana and northern Wyoming.
1864 Montana and Wyoming separate from Dakota.
1871 The Northern Pacific Railroad crosses the Red River; white settlement begins in the Red River area.
1889 Dakota Territory divides and becomes two separate states.

MARRIAGE AND DIVORCE

1881 counties begin recording marriages.

1885 marriage "must be followed by a solemnization, or by a mutual assumption of marital rights, duties, or obligations." A marriage certificate must be issued upon request.

1889 common-law dower and curtesy are abolished; neither spouse has any interest in the property of the other (§ 14).

1890 "marriage is a personal relation arising out of a civil contract . . . maintained, annulled, or dissolved only as provided by law." County judges are required to issue and record marriage licenses.

Where to Find Marriage and Divorce Records

County clerks and clerks of the county district courts and some towns began recording marriages in 1881. Statewide registration began in 1925 and is kept at the Division of Vital Records in Bismarck. Divorces have been under the jurisdiction of the county district courts, and the Dakota Territorial Legislature also granted divorces from 1862 to 1866. There are no county records for North Dakota on film at the FHL. Most county records have been centralized at the North Dakota State Historical Archives and Research Library in Bismarck.

Bureau of Indian Affairs records, at the NARA Midwest Region in Kansas City, Missouri also contain marriage records, such as:

- Pine Ridge Agency marriage records, including licenses and certificates, 1888–1936 (film 1014637 ff.), contains records of Oglala and Dakota Indians.
- Spotted Tail Agency marriage register, 1847–78 (film 1012661), contains records of Dakota Indians. Spotted Tail Agency became Rosebud Agency in 1878.
- Fort Totten Agency police records, including marriages and divorces, 1881–1919 (film 1023369).

PROPERTY AND INHERITANCE

1877 a married woman may devise a will.

1899 a married woman's separate property is her separate estate, and she has *feme sole* powers in the management of that estate.

1906 Congress prohibits married women living on reservations in North and South Dakota to hold grazing lands (H. Doc. 257, 59th Cong., 2nd Sess., 1906. Serial 5153).

SUFFRAGE

1917 women become eligible to vote in presidential elections.

1920 North Dakota women receive complete suffrage by passage of the 19th Amendment to the Constitution.

CITIZENSHIP

1803 all residents of North Dakota become U.S. citizens, except for Native Americans, whose tribes are considered a separate nation until 1924.

CENSUS INFORMATION

For federal censuses, see Iowa (1840), Minnesota (Pembina District for 1850), and Dakota Territory (1860, 1870, and 1880). The Pembina censuses have been published in the *Collections of the State Historical Society of North Dakota*, Vol. 1.

1836 see Shambaugh, Benjamin F. *Wisconsin Territory: The First Census of the Original Counties of Dubuque and Des Moines (Iowa) Taken in July, 1836* (Des Moines: Historical Department of Iowa, 1897, film 1022202). Comprises the present states of Iowa, Minnesota, and parts of North and South Dakota.

1857 census of Pembina District only (not at FHL).

1885 Dakota Territory census (film 0547583), covers the present North Dakota counties of Bowman, Dunn, McIntosh, McKenzie, Mercer, Mountrail, Renville, Ward, and Wells. The census is also available as a searchable database online at **<www.state.nd.us/hist/infcens.htm>**.

1884–1940 censuses of Indian reservations. All censuses provide every name in Indian and English (if given), age, sex, tribal enrollment number, and relationship to the head of household. Enumerations after 1913 also include the date of birth; enumerations taken after 1929 also include marital status and degree of blood. The censuses are available through the FHL and the National Archives (M595).

1915 state census (film 1731408 ff.).

1925 state census (film 1731393 ff.).

Unless otherwise noted, the state and territorial censuses are at the North Dakota State Archives and Historical Research Library.

OTHER

The *Collections of the State Historical Society of North Dakota*. 7 Vols. (Bismarck: The Society, 1905–25, film 1697422 ff.), contain published accounts of the history of the settlement of North Dakota. These are some of the topics in the collections:

- Danish settlement of Cass County
- Bohemian settlement of Richland County
- Icelandic settlement of Pembina County
- Norwegian settlement of Griggs County and the Red River Valley area
- Swedish, Mennonite, and Dunker settlements in North Dakota
- Canadian history of the Selkirk settlement, the Red River Colony, the Northwest Company, and Rupert's Land and Hudson's Bay Company
- History of the Arikara, Dakota, Grosventre, Hidatsa, Mandan, Ojibway, Sioux, and Turtle Mountain Chippewa tribes
- A gazetteer of old settlers prior to 1862

- Survivors of the smallpox epidemic of 1837
- The Medora Black Hills Stage Line
- Fort Totten and Fort Abercrombie
- Pembina County property valuation for 1873

BIBLIOGRAPHY

Benson, Bjorn, Elizabeth Hampsten, and Kathryn Sweeney. *Day In, Day Out: Women's Lives in North Dakota* (Bismarck: University of North Dakota, 1988).

Coulter, John Lee. "Marriage and Divorce in North Dakota." *American Journal of Sociology* 12 (1906–7): 398–416.

Hampsten, Elizabeth. *To All Inquiring Friends: Letters, Diaries, and Essays in North Dakota* (Grand Forks: Department of English, University of North Dakota, 1979).

—. "Writing Women's History in North Dakota." *North Dakota History* 63 (Spring/Summer 1996): 2–6.

Jameson, Elizabeth. "Washburn, Chickens, and Crazy Quilts: Piecing a Common Past." *North Dakota History* 63 (Spring/Summer 1996): 11–16.

Levorsen, Barbara. *The Quiet Conquest: A History of the Lives and Times of the First Settlers of Central North Dakota* (Hawley, MN: The Hawley Herald, 1974).

Lindgren, H. Elaine. *Land in Her Own Name: Women as Homesteaders in North Dakota* (1991. Reprint. Norman: University of Oklahoma Press, 1996).

Lounsbury, Clement. *North Dakota History and People.* 3 Vols. (Chicago: S.J. Clarke, 1917, film 0982024 ff.).

Lysengen, Janet D. and Ann M. Rathke. *The Centennial Anthology of North Dakota History* (Fargo: North Dakota Institute for Regional Studies, 1996).

Miller, Rose Seelye. "Women Farmers of Dakota." *Nebraska Farmer* 20 (1896): 568–9, 588–9.

Riley, Glenda. "Women's History from Women's Sources: Three Examples from Northern Dakota." *North Dakota History* (Spring 1985): 2–9.

Rylanee, Daniel and J.F.S. Simeall. *Reference Guide to North Dakota History and North Dakota Literature* (Grand Forks: University of North Dakota, 1979).

Sherman, William C. *Prairie Mosaic: An Ethnic Atlas of Rural North Dakota* (Fargo: North Dakota Institute for Regional Studies, 1983).

Snortland, J. Signe. A *Traveler's Companion to North Dakota State Historic Sites* (Fargo: North Dakota Institute for Regional Studies, 1996)

Stutenroth, Stella Marie. *Daughters of Dacotah* (Mitchell, SD: Education Supply Co., n.d.).

SELECTED RESOURCES FOR WOMEN'S HISTORY

Barns County Historical Museum
PO Box 188
Valley City, ND 58072

North Dakota Institute for Regional Studies
North Dakota State University Library
PO Box 5599
Fargo, ND 58105-5599

State Historical Society of North Dakota
North Dakota Heritage Center
612 East Boulevard Avenue
Bismarck, ND 58505-0830

Chester Fritz Library
University of North Dakota
Grand Forks, ND 58202

OHIO

IMPORTANT DATES IN STATE HISTORY

1747 Ohio Land Company of Virginia organized.
1763 Ceded by France to Great Britain.
1778 U.S. Army post built at Fort Laurens.
1781 New York cedes its claims to Ohio to the federal government.
1783 Great Britain cedes the Ohio Valley to the U.S.
1784 Virginia cedes its claims to Ohio to the federal government, except the lands in the Virginia Military District.
1785 U.S. Congress Land Ordinance establishes townships. Massachusetts donates its claims in Ohio to the federal government.
1786 Connecticut abnegates its claims to Ohio to the federal government, except the lands of the Connecticut Western Reserve.
1787 Part of the Ordinance of 1787, also known as the Northwest Ordinance, establishes the Northwest Territory.
1788 First settlement at Marietta.
1799 Created as a separate territory.
1803 Statehood.

MARRIAGE AND DIVORCE

1787 territorial constitution recognizes both dower and curtesy.

1795 general and circuit courts hold jurisdiction for divorce and separation (Ch. LXVII § 5).

1880 a marriage license is required, unless notice or banns are published on two different days in the county of residence of the bride, at least ten days prior to the marriage.

1889 in addition to ordained ministers and justices of the peace, a mayor of any city or incorporated village may perform a marriage ceremony. A marriage certificate must be returned to the probate judge within three months of the ceremony.

Where to Find Marriage and Divorce Records

County probate judges began recording marriages in 1797. A statewide index for marriages and divorces began in 1949 and is kept at the Department of Health in Columbus. Records are in the original county courthouses, except for Marion County, 1824–1920 (at the Ohio Historical Society in Columbus), and Stark County, 1809–1916 (at the Stark County District Library in Canton). Divorces were under the jurisdiction of the state supreme court until 1852 and thereafter under the county courts of common pleas. Divorces from 1804 to 1852 required an act of legislation and may be found in the records of the cases of the state supreme court and also the county chancery courts (succeeded by the courts of common pleas). Many county records have been filmed, such as:

- Allen County Probate Court marriage records, 1831–1917 (film 0901410 ff.), at the Allen County Courthouse in Lima.
- Scioto County Probate Court marriage records, 1804–1911 (film 0292694 ff.), at the Scioto County Courthouse in Portsmouth.

See also:

- Smith, Marjorie. *Ohio Marriages Extracted from The Old Northwest Genealogical Quarterly* (1977. Reprint. Baltimore: Genealogical Publishing Co., 1980, fiche 6051390).
- Caccamo, James F. *Marriage Notices from the Ohio Observer Series, 1827–1855* (Apollo, PA: Closson Press, 1994).

- Bell, Carol Willsey. *Ohio Divorces: The Early Years* (Boardman, OH: Bell Books, 1994).
- Null, David G. "Ohio Divorces, 1803–1852." *National Genealogical Society Quarterly* 69 (March 1981): 109–14.

PROPERTY AND INHERITANCE

1787 the territorial government recognizes both common law and dower rights (one-third of husband's personal estate in intestacy); and the statutes of descent and accession.

1808 a married woman may devise a will.

1811 a married woman is granted *feme sole* status to manage her separate property.

1846 the property of a wife shall not be liable for payment of her husband's debts during her life or the lives of the heirs of her body. Her separate property is her separate estate.

1861 any interest in real property owned by a woman at the time of her marriage shall remain her separate property, under her own control, and free from the debts of her husband.

1871 a married woman's separate earnings are her own.

SUFFRAGE

1919 women become eligible to vote in presidential elections.

1920 Ohio women receive complete suffrage by passage of the 19th Amendment to the Constitution.

CITIZENSHIP

1783 all residents of Ohio become U.S. citizens, except for Native Americans, whose tribes are considered a separate nation until 1924.

CENSUS INFORMATION

The 1800 and 1810 federal censuses are missing. There are no state censuses for Ohio.

OTHER

1790 towns are required to administer and care for the poor.

1803 state constitution continues the territorial poor law.

1867 a state board of charities is established.

BIBLIOGRAPHY

Baumann, Roland M. *Guide to the Women's History Sources in the Oberlin College Archives* (Oberlin: Gertrude F. Jacob Archival Publications Fund, 1990).

Bowers, Ruth and Anita Short. *Gateway to the West*. 2 Vols. (Baltimore: Genealogical Publishing Co., 1989).

Christian, Donna. "Women's Studies Archives in Northwest Ohio." *Northwest Ohio Quarterly* 56–7 (1984/1985), a series of articles on various libraries and archives.

Clark, Ricky, et al. *Quilts in Community: Ohio's Traditions* (Nashville: Rutledge Hill Press, 1991).

Clinefelter, Ruth W., et al. *Women of Summit County: A Guided Tour* (Akron: Women's History Project, 1991).

Frost, John. *Pioneer Mothers of the West; Or Daring and Heroic Deeds of American Women* (1859. Reprint. New York: Arno Press, 1974).

Fry, Mildred Corey. "Women on the Ohio Frontier: The Marietta Area." *Ohio History* (Winter 1981): 54–73.

Genealogical Data Relating to Women in the Western Reserve Before 1840 (Cleveland: Cleveland Centennial Commission, 1943). See also *Index to the Microfilm Edition of Genealogical Data Relating to Women in the Western Reserve Before 1840* (Cleveland: Western Reserve Historical Society, 1976, fiche 6087501).

Green, Karen M. *Pioneer Ohio Newspapers, 1793–1810 and 1802–1818.* 2 Vols. (Galveston, TX: Frontier Press, 1988).

Hehir, Donald M. *Ohio Families: A Bibliographic Listing of Books About Ohio Families* (Bowie, MD: Heritage Books, 1993).

Ingham, Mrs. W.A. *Women of Cleveland and Their Work* (Cleveland: The Author, 1893).

Laws, Annie. *History of the Ohio Federation of Women's Clubs, 1894–1924* (Cincinnati: Ebbert and Richardson, 1924).

Morton, Marian J. *Women In Cleveland: An Illustrated History* (Bloomington: Indiana University Press, 1995).

Neely, Ruth. *Women in Ohio: A Record of Their Achievements in the History of the State.* 3 Vols. (Chicago: Clarke Publishing Co., n.d.).

Newell, Linda King and Valeen T. Avery. "Sweet Counsel and Seas of Tribulation: The Religious Life of Women in Kirtland." *Brigham Young University Studies* 20 2 (1980): 151–62. Mormon women in Kirtland, 1831–8.

Petty, Gerald McKinney. *Index of the Ohio Girls Industrial School: Inmates' Case Records, 1869–1911* (n.p.: Petty's Press, 1984).

Remember the Ladies: A Bibliography on Women in Montgomery County History (Dayton: Dayton and Montgomery County Public Library, 1986).

Sperry, Kip. *Genealogical Research in Ohio* (Baltimore: Genealogical Publishing Co., 1997).

Studebaker, Sue. *Ohio Samplers, Schoolgirl Embroideries* (Lebanon, OH: Warren County Historical Society, 1988).

Whitlock, Marta. *Women in Ohio History* (Columbus: Ohio Historical Society, 1976).

SELECTED RESOURCES FOR WOMEN'S HISTORY

Center for Women's Studies
University of Cincinnati
155 McMicken Hall
Cincinnati, OH 45221-0164

Mennonite Historical Library
Bluffton College
Bluffton, OH 45817

Oberlin College Archives
420 Mudd Center
Oberlin, OH 44074

Ohio Historical Society
1982 Vienna Avenue
Columbus, OH 43211-2497

Western Reserve Historical Society
10825 East Boulevard
Cleveland, OH 44106

William O. Thompson Memorial Library
Ohio State University
1800 Cannon Drive
Columbus, OH 43210

Women's Studies Archives
Jerome Library
Bowling Green State University
Bowling Green, OH 34303

Women in History, available online at **<ww.kwdpl.org/wiohio>**

OKLAHOMA

IMPORTANT DATES IN STATE HISTORY

1803 Most of Oklahoma is part of the Louisiana Purchase.
1812 Part of the Missouri Territory.
1819 Part of the Arkansas Territory.
1821 Remainder of Oklahoma ceded from Spain to Mexico (becomes part of Texas in 1836).
1830 Organized as Indian Territory.
1831 Five Civilized Tribes forcibly relocated to Indian Territory.
1850 Panhandle becomes unattached U.S. territory.
1854 Cherokee, Chickasaw, Choctaw, Muscogee, and Seminole Indians form a federation.
1860 Greer County is created by Texas within Oklahoma.
1861 Most of the Five Civilized Tribes side with the Confederacy.
1866 U.S. begins to relocate other tribes to Oklahoma.
1889 Part of Oklahoma is opened for white settlement.
1890 Organized as the Oklahoma Territory; the eastern portion of Oklahoma is Indian Territory under the jurisdiction of Arkansas; the Oklahoma Panhandle is opened for settlement. Oklahoma Territory law follows that of Nebraska: Indian Territory law follows that of Arkansas.
1893 Cherokee Outlet lands opened for settlement; the Dawes Commission liquidates tribal governments.
1901 Congress passes the Five Civilized Tribes Citizenship Act.
1906 Most tribal governments and reservations are liquidated.
1907 Territory reorganized to combine the Oklahoma and Indian territories; becomes the state of Oklahoma.

MARRIAGE AND DIVORCE

1881 Cherokee National Council passes a divorce statute.
1890 in Indian territory, tribal law applies to all until this time, when the statutes of Arkansas applied to non-tribal members (tribal law remains in force for members of Indian tribes until 1898). At this time, counties in Oklahoma Territory begin to issue marriage licenses. Oklahoma Territory courts also begin to hear divorce cases. In Oklahoma Territory, "Indians contracting marriage according to the Indian custom, and cohabitating as husband and wife, are lawfully married."
1897 "all Indians who have taken allotments of land in severalty, and who have taken their homes in this territory, and who are living together as husband and wife, and who have before that date [12 March 1897] been married according to Indian custom, are hereby declared lawfully married. After the passage of this act, marriages among Indians, or among their descendants, according to the Indian custom, shall be unlawful . . . such Indians and their descendants shall procure marriage licenses in the same county and have their marriages solemnized by the same persons, and returns thereof made in the same manner as . . . other persons."

Where to Find Marriage and Divorce Records

Marriages have been recorded by county clerks since the creation of the county. There is no state registration. Some earlier marriage records were also recorded in the Indian Territory district courts. Divorce records began in the territorial district and the probate courts in 1890 and were confined only to the district courts in 1893, although probate courts continued to grant divorces until about 1895. Many county, territorial, and district records have been filmed, such as:

- Illinois District marriage licenses and certificates, 1868–98 (film 1666334), at the Oklahoma

Historical Society in Oklahoma City, many of which are for U.S. citizens marrying Cherokee citizens.

- Cooweescoowee District marriage records and divorces, 1867-93 (film 1666317 ff.).
- Going Snake District Circuit and Supreme Court cases, 1876-98 (film 1666333), at the Oklahoma Historical Society, including divorces and marriage licenses and certificates.
- Blaine County Probate Court, marriage records, 1892–1908 (film 1313695 ff.), and Blaine County Court Clerk marriage records, 1908-30, and index, 1892–1982 (film 1313693 ff.), at the Blaine County Courthouse in Watonga.
- U.S. District Court, Second Division and Central District, South McAlester, Indian Territory marriage records, 1890–1907 (film 1671218 ff.), at the Oklahoma Historical Society.

See also compiled publications, such as:

- Bode, Frances Murphy. *Oklahoma Territory Weddings* (Geary, OK: Pioneer Book Committee, 1983, fiche 6104367).
- Bogle, Dixie and Dorothy Nix. *Cherokee Nation Marriages, 1884–1901, Abstracted from the Indian Chieftain* (Owensboro, KY: Cook & McDowell Publications, 1980).
- Hutchins, Alma. *Indian Territory Marriages, 1867–1898* (Tahlequah, OK: The Author, 1988).
- Littlefield, Daniel F. Jr. and Lonnie E. Underhill. "Divorce Seekers' Paradise: Oklahoma Territory, 1890–1897." *Arizona and the West* 17 1 (1975): 21-34.
- Oklahoma Genealogical Society. *Index to Marriage Records, Oklahoma County, Oklahoma Territory, 1889–1907* (Oklahoma City: The Society, 1993).
- Tiffe, Ellen. *Oklahoma Marriage Records, Choctaw Nation, Indian Territory [1890–1907]*. 10 Vols. (Howe, OK: The Author, n.d., film 1321223). Abstracts from federal court records in eleven counties.

The Cherokee Indian Nation maintained its own government for many years. See the Indian Archives Division records at the Oklahoma Historical Society, such as:

- Cherokee Nation records (film 1666294 ff.), including the following district marriages: Canadian (1879-98), Delaware (1867-98), Flint (1893), Illinois (1859-98), Saline (1866-98), Sequoyah (1870-98), and Tahlequah (1839-1910). There are also divorce records in this series.

PROPERTY AND INHERITANCE

1889 the U.S. Government begins to sell unassigned Indian land in central Oklahoma.

1901 reservation land in western Oklahoma is sold through a lottery.

1906 more reservation land is sold at auction.

❧ *As of 1976, tribal membership in the Cherokee Nation requires proof of direct descent from an ancestor on the Dawes Rolls, taken between 1902 and 1907. The Dawes Rolls are available on the CD-ROM,* The Native American Collection, *from the Friends of the Oklahoma Historical Society Archives and Gen Ref.*

SUFFRAGE

1918 Oklahoma women receive complete suffrage.

CITIZENSHIP

1803 all residents of the area become U.S. citizens by legislation, except for Native Americans, whose tribes are considered a separate nation until 1924.

For records of the Choctaw-Chickasaw Citizenship Court, see the "Introduction" to this book under Bureau of Indian Affairs Records. The case file enrollment records of the Five Civilized Tribes are now available online at **<www.nara.gov/nara/nail. html>**.

CENSUS INFORMATION

For pre-territorial federal censuses, see Arkansas (1860, does not enumerate Native Americans). The 1870 to 1890 federal censuses have been lost or destroyed.

1835–1900s Indian censuses for the Cherokee Nation, Kiowa Agency, etc., many of which have been filmed (T496, M595). Some of these rolls cover other states, such as Alabama, Georgia, North Carolina, and Tennessee (Cherokee Nation East).

1890 territorial census for some counties (film 0227282/M1811) is indexed at the Oklahoma Historical Society. The Cherokee Nation census records for 1890 have also been filmed. See also, *An Index to the 1890 United States Census of Union Veterans and Their Widows in Oklahoma and Indian Territories: Including Old Greer County and Soldiers Stationed at Military Installations in the Territories (Section I) Also an Index to Records from the Oklahoma Union Soldiers' Home Including Civil War Veterans and Their Dependents* (Oklahoma City: Oklahoma Genealogical Society, 1970, film 0496937).

1907 federal census of Seminole County (M595).

OTHER

1865–1909 Female Seminary documents, Cherokee Nation (film 1666294 ff.).

1915– Confederate pension applications (film 1001529 ff.). See also *Index to Applications for Pensions from the State of Oklahoma Submitted by Confederate Soldiers, Sailors, and Their Widows* (Oklahoma City: Oklahoma Genealogical Society, 1969, fiche 6046932).

List of persons who are Indians or their widows to whom money is due by the U.S. (film 1666295).

The above are at the Oklahoma Historical Society.

BIBLIOGRAPHY

Ashton, Sharon S. *Indians and Intruders*. 2 Vols. (Norman: Ashton Books, 1997–8). Abstracts from Manuscripts in the Oklahoma Historical Society Archives.

—. *Marriages and Deaths, 1838–1840: Army and Navy Chronicle* (Norman: Ashton Books, n.d.). Includes marriages at frontier posts, outside the jurisdiction of established courts.

Carlile, Glenda. *Buckskin, Calico, and Lace: Oklahoma's Territorial Women* (Oklahoma City: Southern Hills Publishing Co., 1990).

—. *Women of Oklahoma, 1890–1920* (Norman: University of Oklahoma Press, 1997).

DuPriest, Maud Ward. *Cherokee Recollections: The Story of the Indian Women's Pocahontas Club and Its Members in the Cherokee Nation & Oklahoma, Beginning in 1899* (Stillwater, OK: Thales Microuniversity Press, 1976).

Garrett, Sandi. A.K.A. *(Also Known As)* (Spavinaw, OK: Cherokee Woman Publishing, 1998). Contains explanations of reservations, old settlers, treaties, strip payment, the Dawes Roll, etc.

Gormley, Myra V. *Cherokee Connections: Introduction to Genealogical Sources Pertaining to Cherokee Ancestors* (Baltimore: Genealogical Publishing Co., 1998).

Hamilton, Kenneth M. *Black Towns and Profit* (Chicago: University of Illinois Press, 1991). Includes material on African American women in Oklahoma.

Holway, Hope. "The American Indian and His Name." *Chronicles of Oklahoma* 43 3 (1965): 340–4.

King, James Barry. *Women as Affected by the Laws of Oklahoma* (Oklahoma City: n.p., 1930).

Lindsey, Lilah D. *Study Course in Citizenship on Federal and Oklahoma Laws Pertaining to Women and Children* (Muskogee: The Bowman Press, 1924).

McClure, Tony M. "Pre-Colonial and Colonial-Era Intermarriages," in *Cherokee Proud: A Guide for Tracing and Honoring Your Cherokee Ancestors* (Somerville, TN: Chunannee Books, 1997).

Noever, Janet Hulsly. *Women in Oklahoma Territory, 1889–1907* (Midwest City, OK: History Department, Rose State College, 1989).

Oklahoma Heritage Quilt Project. *Oklahoma Heritage Quilts: A Sampling of Quilts Made in and Brought to Oklahoma before 1940* (Paducah, KY: American Quilters Society, 1989).

Reese, Linda Williams. *Women of Oklahoma* (Norman: University of Oklahoma Press, 1997).

Riley, Glenda. "Divorce in Oklahoma." *Chronicles of Oklahoma* 67 (Winter 1989/90): 392–413.

Smith's First Directory of Oklahoma Territory: For the Year Commencing August 1st, 1890 (Guthrie, OK: James W. Smith, 1890, film 1307628).

Thurman, Melvena. *Women in Oklahoma: A Century of Change* (Oklahoma City: Oklahoma Historical Society, 1982).

Underhill, Lonnie E. and Daniel F. Littlefield. "Women Homeseekers in Oklahoma Territory, 1889–1901." *Pacific Historian* 17 3 (1973): 36–47.

Wilson, Terry P. "Osage Indian Women During a Century of Change, 1870–1980." *Prologue* 14 4 (1982): 185–201.

Wright, Muriel H. A *Guide to the Indian Tribes of Oklahoma* (Norman: University of Oklahoma Press, 1987).

SELECTED RESOURCES FOR WOMEN'S HISTORY

Museum of the Great Plains
601 Ferris
PO Box 68
Lawton, OK 73502

Office of Archives and Records
Oklahoma Department of Libraries
220 NE 18th Street
Oklahoma City, OK 73105-3298

Oklahoma Historical Society
Wiley Post Historical Building
2100 North Lincoln Boulevard
Oklahoma City, OK 73105-4997

Pioneer Woman Museum
701 Monument Road
Ponca City, OK 74604

Oklahoma

Sac and Fox National Public Library
Route 2, Box 246
Stroud, OK 74079

University Library
Oklahoma State University
Stillwater, OK 74078

University of Tulsa
Research in Women's Literature
600 South College
Tulsa, OK 74104

Western History Collections
University of Oklahoma
Room 452
Monnett Hall
Norman, OK 73109

Will Rogers Memorial Library
PO Box 157
Claremore, OK 74018

So Your Grandmother Was a Cherokee Princess? available online at **<www.powersource.com/powersource/cherokee/gene.html>**

Women's Archives: A Guide to the Collections Held by Special Collections and University Archives, Oklahoma State University Library, available online at **<www.library.okstste.edu/dept/scua/guide.htm>**

ALL WROUGHT UP!

Mrs. Pinkham's words to nervous women—How she helped two of them.

"Everything irritates me; I am a bundle of nerves; I ache all over and can't sleep; I don't want to be cross, but I can't help it, and then I get the blues. Little household matters work me up so that I don't know what I am saying or doing."

This extract from one of the letters to Mrs. Pinkham describes the condition of many women.

Nine-tenths of the nervous despondency and irritability in women arises from some trouble with the organs that make her a woman.

Nothing will relieve this distressing condition so surely as Lydia E. Pinkham's Vegetable Compound; it soothes, strengthens, heals and tones up the delicate female organism.

Mrs. Pinkham invites you to write her for advice. You can tell every detail of your illness to her, because she is a woman—anyway, it is better to address a woman, for a man does not understand, simply because he is a man.

Here are two letters from women who wrote to Mrs. Pinkham, followed her advice, and are now well and happy:

Mrs. W. L. ELLIOTT, of Liscomb, Iowa, writes:

Dear Mrs. Pinkham:—I doctored nearly all the time for two years. I spent several hundred dollars without receiving much benefit. Last June I wrote to you, and described all my aches and pains. Such a list as there was!—headache, backache, constipation, dizziness and feeling of extreme lassitude. But you answered my letter and told me just what to do. I followed your advice. After taking several bottles of the Vegetable Compound, three bottles of Blood Purifier, I am glad to write you that I have not enjoyed such good health for years.

Mrs. CARRIE BURGESS, Box 115, South Gardiner, Me., writes:

Dear Mrs. Pinkham:—For six years I have suffered with female weakness. At times I suffered so that I would have to have hot applications applied and take morphine to ease the pain. The pains I had were almost unbearable. I tried all kinds of patent medicine, also was treated by several doctors. Last October I had a very bad sick spell. I had one of the best doctors in the city, but he failed to help me. I was advised to take Lydia E. Pinkham's Vegetable Compound, which I did after writing to Mrs. Pinkham for advice. I have taken the Compound and Blood Purifier, and consider myself a new woman. I can never thank you enough for your advice to me. It would take a lifetime to tell the benefit I have received from your medicine. I would advise all suffering women to take this wonderful medicine, which has no equal.

Lydia E. Pinkham's Vegetable Compound. A Woman's Remedy for Woman's Ills.

The Delineator, 1898

OREGON

IMPORTANT DATES IN STATE HISTORY

1811 Trading post established at Astoria.
1818 Treaty permits joint occupation of area by U.S. and Great Britain.
1830s First American settlers begin to arrive from New England.
1841 First court system organized, based on the laws of New York.
1843 Laws of Oregon Territory adopted (not officially organized); based on the Iowa Territory laws of 1839.
1847 Cayuse Indian War (ends 1848).
1848 Organized as a territory; includes the future states of Idaho and Washington and parts of Montana and Wyoming.
1849 First statutes adopted, based on the Iowa constitution of 1843.
1851 Oregon Land Donation Act; Rogue River Indian wars (end 1856).
1857 Constitution adopted.
1859 Statehood.
1872 Modoc War (ends 1873).
1883 The Northern Pacific Railway reaches Oregon.

MARRIAGE AND DIVORCE

1849 dower and curtesy are recognized.
1859 curtesy is abolished.
1887 marriage licenses are required to be issued in the county of residence of the bride.
1903 marriages must be recorded in both the county where the license is issued and the county where the marriage is performed if different.

Where to Find Marriage and Divorce Records

County clerks and recorders began recording marriages in 1849. Many records, 1849–1935, are at the Oregon State Archives in Salem. The Archives also has a marriage index from 1906 to 1942. Statewide registration of marriages began in 1906, and records are kept at the State Department of Human Resources in Portland. Divorces from 1848 to 1853 were granted by the territorial legislature and are at the Oregon State Archives. The county circuit courts have held jurisdiction for divorce cases since 1853; records prior to 1859 were created by the U.S. district courts. Statewide registration began in 1925. County marriage records include marriage licenses, ministerial certificates, and marriage certificates for couples who married outside the county and wanted to create a county record. A descriptive inventory of the records of all thirty-six Oregon counties is available online at **<accweb.sos.or.gov/county/cphome.html>**. Some county records have been filmed, such as:

- Wasco County Court marriage certificates and licenses, 1856-98 (film 2057573), at the Oregon State Archives.
- Wasco County Circuit Court divorce records, 1859–1916 (film 2056577 ff.), at the Wasco County Courthouse in The Dalles, extracted from the series of case files, with name index.

Most county records are not available on film through the FHL, but are at facilities in Oregon, such as:

- Multnomah County marriage license index and records, 1855–1903, and marriage license index, 1903–60, on film at the Oregon State Archives.
- Multnomah County marriage licenses, 1855–1961, marriage records of licenses outside the county, 1920–68, and marriage license index, 1855–1944, on film at the Oregon Commonwealth Center Building in Portland.

- Multnomah County marriage certificates, 1879–1913, and miscellaneous recordings, 1850–1908, in manuscript, at the Oregon Historical Society Library in Portland.
- Multnomah County judgment and execution records, 1849–1919, containing instructions to sheriffs regarding divorces and other civil cases.
- Multnomah County Circuit Court records, 1859–1919, at the Multnomah County Court Records Center in Portland.

PROPERTY AND INHERITANCE

1843 territorial law adopts the common-law system of marital property law; a married woman may not write a will unless specified in an antenuptial agreement.

1851 Oregon Donation Land Act finds women eligible to receive property.

1852 territorial legislature adopts "An Act to Exempt the Wife's Portion of Lands Donated in Oregon Territory by Act of Congress . . . From the Debts and Liabilities of Her Husband" exempts donation lands from the claims of husbands (p. 64).

1853 a married woman may devise "real estate held in her own right, subject to any rights which her husband may have as a tenant by the curtesy (§ 354–55)."

1857 a woman's property from before marriage shall not be subject to the debt or contract of her husband.

1859 a married woman is granted *feme sole* status to manage her separate property. "The property and pecuniary rights of every married woman, at the time of marriage, or afterwards, acquired by gift, devise, or inheritance, shall not be subject to the debts or contracts of the husband; and laws shall be passed providing for the registration of the wife's separate property (Art. XV § V)."

1872 a married woman can open a business independent of her husband.

1880 a married woman's separate earnings are her own.

SUFFRAGE

1912 Oregon women receive complete suffrage.

CITIZENSHIP

1846 when Great Britain cedes it claims to the Oregon Territory, all residents who are not already citizens of the U.S. become citizens by treaty, except for Native Americans, whose tribes are considered a separate nation until 1924.

CENSUS INFORMATION

The first federal census for Oregon was in 1850.

1842–59 territorial and state censuses (film 0899786).

1865, 1885, 1895, 1905 state censuses (not at FHL).

State and territorial censuses are at the Oregon State Archives.

OTHER

1851–1903 U.S. General Land Office, Oregon and Washington donation land files (film 1028543/M815) at the National Archives in Washington, DC, are arranged alphabetically by name of state and thereunder by name of land office. For each office there is a main series for approved claims, arranged by final certificate number. The records for a typical donation claim are filmed as follows: the endorsement on the outer page, final certificate, the notification, and the other documents, in chronological order. See also:

- Genealogical Forum of Oregon. *Index [to] Oregon Donation Land Claims*. 2nd ed. (Portland: The Forum, 1987).

- Genealogical Forum of Oregon. *Genealogical Material in Oregon Donation Land Claims*. 5 Vols. (Portland: The Forum, 1957–75, fiche 6051173).

Counties maintained separate registers for married women's property. These were registrations of separate property, usually provided in conjunction with a marriage or divorce settlement. Most are on microfilm at the Oregon State Archives, such as those for Multnomah County, 1859 to 1923.

Widows' pension journals are at the Oregon State Archives, such as those for Multnomah County, 1913 to 1921.

BIBLIOGRAPHY

Allen, Eleanor. *Canvas Caravans* (Portland: Bindford & Mort, 1946).

Blair, Karen J. *Northwest Women: An Annotated Bibliography of Sources on the History of Oregon and Washington Women, 1787–1970* (Pullman: Washington State University Press, 1997).

Brandt, Patricia and Nancy Guilford. *Oregon Biography Index* (Corvallis: Oregon State University, 1976, film 1321470).

Butruille, Susan G. and Kathleen Petersen. *Women's Voices from the Oregon Trail: The Times That Tried Women's Souls and a Guide to Women's History Along the Oregon Trail* (Boston: Tamarack Books, 1994).

Chusted, Richard H. "The Oregon Donation Act of 1850 and Nineteenth-Century Federal Married Women's Property Law." *Law and History Review* 2 (Spring 1984): 44–78.

Cross, Mary Bywater. *Treasures in the Trunk: Quilts of the Oregon Trail* (Nashville: Rutledge Hill Press, 1993).

Glenn, Judith A. *Select Bibliography of Women's Studies: Holdings of the Women's Center Library at Oregon State University* (Corvallis: Oregon State University Press, 1988).

Holmes, Kenneth L. *Covered Wagon Women: Diaries and Letters from the Western Trails, 1852: The Oregon Trail.* Vol. 5 (Lincoln: University of Nebraska Press, 1997).

Leasher, Evelyn M. *Oregon Women: A Bio-Bibliography* (Corvallis: Oregon State University Press, 1981).

White, Kris and M.C. Cuthill. *Overland Passages: A Guide to Overland Documents in the Oregon Historical Society* (Portland: The Society, 1993).

SELECTED RESOURCES FOR WOMEN'S HISTORY

Archives Division, Secretary of State
880 Summer Street NE
Salem, OR 97310

Center Oregon Community College Library
NW College Way
Bend, OR 97701

Coordinating Committee for Women Historians
Western Oregon State University
Monmouth, OR 97361

Oregon Historical Society
1200 SW Park Avenue
Portland, OR 97205

Oregon State Library
Winter and Court Streets NE
Salem, OR 97310

Oregon State Records Center
Archives Division
1005 Broadway NE
Portland, OR 97310

Women's Center Library
Oregon State University
Corvallis, OR 97333

PENNSYLVANIA

IMPORTANT DATES IN STATE HISTORY

1681 Area granted to proprietor William Penn.
1682 Frame of Government, the Pennsylvania charter, drafted; first English Quakers arrive; three original counties established.
1683 Germantown settlement begins.
1688 Welsh Baptist settlement begins.
1708 "Pennsylvania-Dutch" groups from Alsace-Lorraine, Baden, Wurttemburg, the Rhineland, and Switzerland begin to immigrate to Pennsylvania.
1717 Scotch-Irish from Ulster begin to immigrate to Pennsylvania.
1730 Moravians migrate from Georgia to Pennsylvania.
1750 Connecticut claims land in the Susquehanna area.
1753 French troops build Fort Duquesne (Pittsburgh).
1754 French and Indian War begins in Pennsylvania.
1758 British forces capture Fort Duquesne.
1763–7 Mason-Dixon Line is established as the boundary line between Maryland and Pennsylvania.
1777 State constitution drafted; British troops occupy Philadelphia (evacuated in 1778).
1787 Constitutional Convention meets at Philadelphia.
1790 Philadelphia is capital of the U.S. (until 1800).
1863 Battle of Gettysburg.

MARRIAGE AND DIVORCE

1682 county registrars are required to keep marriage registers. A "Bill of Divorcement" allows divorce on grounds of adultery.
1700 marriages must be performed before twelve witnesses.
1701 "An Act to Prevent Clandestine Marriages" states that all marriages must be solemnized by a justice of the peace and recorded in the county register. Female indentured servants who marry without their master's consent must serve an additional year beyond the original contract of indenture. Those marrying contrary to this act are required to pay a £ 5 fee to the proprietary and the governor, in any court of record.
1690 religious societies are required to keep marriage registries.
1729 for a justice of the peace to perform a marriage, at least one of the parties must reside in the county where the justice dwells; if the parties are under twenty-one years of age, a certificate of parental consent is required.
1773 the British Privy Council disallows legislative divorces.
1785 a divorce law is passed.
1849 individuals authorized to perform marriages must, upon application, furnish a certified transcript for fifty cents.

Where to Find Marriage and Divorce Records

From the beginning of the colony until 1851 marriage registration, although required, was not widely practiced. There are some justice of the peace registers that were kept in counties. From 1852 to 1854, county registers of wills kept marriage records and were also required to send a copy to the state. This was also not uniformly practiced. Beginning in 1884, county clerks of the orphans' courts began recording marriages. Statewide registration did not begin until 1941. For the period prior to 1852, check records for specific counties and churches, and see:

- *Record of Pennsylvania Marriages, Prior to 1810*. 2 Vols. (1880. Reprint. Baltimore: Genealogical Publishing Co., 1987, fiche 6049248 ff.). In addition to marriages from church records, this includes marriages recorded by the Registrar General of the Province, 1685–9. Reprinted from *Pennsylvania Archives*, Series 2, Vols. VIII and IX.
- *Pennsylvania Marriages Prior to 1790* (1890. Reprint. Baltimore: Genealogical Publishing Co., 1968, film 1036417). Reprinted from *Pennsylvania Archives*, Series 2, Vol. II.
- *Pennsylvania Marriage Licenses, 1784–1786*, in *Pennsylvania Archives*. Series 6, Vol VII: 283–310 (fiche 6051534).
- *Pennsylvania Vital Records from The Pennsylvania Genealogical Magazine and The Pennsylvania Magazine of History and Biography*. 3 Vols. (Baltimore: Genealogical Publishing Co., 1983, also available on CD-ROM). Comprises all the articles on births, baptisms, marriages, and deaths ever published in *The Pennsylvania Magazine of History and Biography*, and *The Pennsylvania Genealogical Magazine*.
- Extracts from Common Pleas and Quarter Sessions courts and abstracts from justice docket of Buckingham: indentures of servants and marriages, 1684–1805 (film 0387839), at the Historical Society of Pennsylvania in Philadelphia.
- Lancaster County Justice of the Peace docket book, 1784–91 (film 1032470), at the Pennsylvania State Archives in Harrisburg.

From 1852 to 1885, see records for specific counties, such as:

- Record and indexes of marriages, 1852–4 (film 1016403), at the Pennsylvania State Archives.
- Bucks County Register of Wills, marriages, 1852–69, index, 1852–69 (film 0927590), at the Bucks County Courthouse in Doylestown.
- Lancaster Mayor's Record Book, marriages, 1858–61, at the Pennsylvania State Archives.
- Philadelphia marriage registers, 1860–85 (film 0978997 ff.), and returns, 1860–85 (film 1764889 ff.), at the City Hall in Philadelphia.
- Pittsburgh marriage records, 1875–1909 (film 1299316 ff.), at the City-County Building in Pittsburgh.

For records after 1885, see:

- Marriage records, 1885–9 (film 1027957 ff.), at the Pennsylvania State Archives, include all counties, grouped by names of brides and grooms.
- County records, such as Bucks County Clerk of the Orphans' Court marriage license dockets, 1885–1906, and index, 1885–1946 (film 0927053 ff.), at the Bucks County Courthouse in Doylestown.

From 1682 to 1847, the legislature held jurisdiction for divorces, along with other bodies. From 1682 to 1773, the Governor and Council could also grant divorces. From 1773 to 1785, the legislature alone held jurisdiction for divorces. From 1785 to 1804, the Supreme Court held conterminous jurisdiction. From 1804, the courts of common pleas also heard divorce cases. After 1846, only the county courts of common pleas held jurisdiction. For more information, see:

- County records, such as Philadelphia County Court of Common Pleas divorce docket, 1851–74 (film 0963387 ff.), at the Philadelphia City Archives.
- Pennsylvania Supreme Court, Eastern District divorce papers, 1786–1815 (film 1023001 ff.), at the Pennsylvania State Archives.
- *Divorces Granted by the Pennsylvania Supreme Court, December, 1785–1801* (1900. Reprint. Bedminster, PA: Adams Apple Press, 1992, film 1698098).
- Livengood, C.C. *Genealogical Abstracts of Pennsylvania and the Statutes at Large* (Westminster, MD: Family Line Publications, 1990).

- Throop, Eugene F. *Lancaster County, Pennsylvania, Divorces, 1786–1832* (Bowie, MD: Heritage Books, 1995).

PROPERTY AND INHERITANCE

1682 in intestacy, a widow shall receive one-third of her husband's estate by dower.

1688 a widow's dower is confined to realty only, for life use.

1697 dower is defined as both personalty and realty (for life).

1705 "Act for the Better Settling of Intestate's Estates" provides that, in intestacy, a widow shall receive one-third of her husband's personal estate.

1706 "Act for the Better Settling of Intestate's Estates" provides that dower is amended to include only realty for life.

1718 a married woman is granted the status of *feme sole* trader when her husband is absent for long periods of time, "that where any mariners or others are gone, or hereafter shall go, to sea, leaving their wives at shop-keeping, or to work for their livelihood at any other trade in this province, all such wives shall be deemed adjudged and taken, and are hereby declared to be, as *feme sole* traders, and shall have the ability, and are by this act enabled, to sue and be sued, plead and implead, at law in any court or courts of this province . . ."

1748 "Act for Amending the Laws Relating to the Partition and Distribution of Intestate's Estates" states that, in intestacy, a widow receives one-third of her husband's personal estate and one-third of his real estate for life use.

1770 private examinations for women are required, and the practice of requiring a signature on a deed is enforced.

1832 a husband cannot collect an award to his wife without giving security (a bond) in orphans' court; to be paid to his wife after his death. The wife is entitled to a separate examination to state that she does not require the money to be secured.

1833 in the distribution of estates (both male and female) a wife is entitled to a dower of one-third of the real estate for life use and one-third of the personal estate absolutely. A bequest by a husband may be taken in lieu of dower, by the choice of the widow.

1845 a married woman may hold property to use as a *feme covert*, not a *feme sole*.

1848 a married woman's separate estate is created, and she is conferred with certain powers of disposition and contract, allowing her full use of property brought into the marriage, and granting her the status of *feme sole*. A married woman may dispose of separate property, real, personal, or mixed, acquired before or during coverture, by will (§ 6).

1850 a married woman's property may not be subject to the debts of her husband (§ 20).

1855 "Act to Amend Certain Defects of the Law for the More Just and Safe Transmission and Secure Enjoyment of Real and Personal Estate" provides that "illegitimate children shall take and be known by the name of their mother, and they and their mothers shall respectively have capacity to take or inherit from each other personal estate as next of kin, and real estate as heirs in fee simple."

1856 a married woman may receive a legacy from a personal estate as a *feme sole*.

1859 a married woman may become incorporated, with others or with an institution.

1872 "Act Securing to Married Women Their Separate Earnings" codifies a married woman's property rights.

1881 "An Act to Enable Mother in Certain Cases to Appoint Testamentary Guardians" allows a woman to appoint guardians for her minor children for the first time.

SUFFRAGE

1920 Pennsylvania women receive complete suffrage by passage of the 19th Amendment to the Constitution.

CITIZENSHIP
One of the original Thirteen Colonies.

CENSUS INFORMATION
There are no state censuses for Pennsylvania.

OTHER
1771 "Act for the Relief of the Poor" provides that a married woman who has been deserted by her husband may have her property attached by the Overseers of the Poor to "protect her interests"; the property is not put in her own name until her husband has been absent for many years.

1838 there are 119 mutual aid societies in Philadelphia, half of them founded by women.

County records, such as Bedford County widows' appraisements, 1876–1953, Chester County soldiers' widows burial dockets, 1917–61, Dauphin County midwife register, 1921–4, Lancaster County Almshouse admissions and discharges, 1866–1912, Mifflin County Relief Board dockets of payments to families of Civil War soldiers, 1861–5 (Pennsylvania Archives RG 47).

1913–17 Mothers' pension accounts, (Pennsylvania Archives RG 28).

BIBLIOGRAPHY
Bartlett, Virginia K. *Keeping House: Women's Lives in Western Pennsylvania, 1790–1850* (Pittsburgh: Historical Society of Western Pennsylvania and University of Pittsburgh Press, 1994).

Bethke, Robert D. "Chester County Widow Wills (1714–1800): A Folklife Source." *Pennsylvania Folklife* 18 1 (1968): 16–20.

Biddle, Gertrude B. and Sarah Dickinson Lowrie. *Notable Women of Pennsylvania* (Philadelphia: University of Pennsylvania Press, 1942).

Brouwer, Merle G. "Marriage and Family Life Among Blacks in Colonial Pennsylvania." *Pennsylvania Magazine of History and Biography* 99 (1975): 368–72.

Burke, Susan M. and Matthew H. Hill. *From Pennsylvania to Waterloo: Pennsylvania-German Folk Culture in Transition* (Kitchner, ON: Joseph Schneider Haus, 1991).

Butler, Elisabeth. *Women and the Trades: Pittsburgh, 1907–1908* (1909. Reprint. Pittsburgh: University of Pittsburgh Press, 1984).

Calvo, Janis. "Quaker Women Ministers in Nineteenth-Century America." *Quaker History* 63 (1974): 75–93.

Chmielewski, Wendy E. *Guide to Sources on Women in the Swarthmore College Peace Collection* (Swarthmore, PA: Swarthmore College, 1988).

Develin, Mrs. John F. "Pennsylvania's Patriotic Women During the Revolution." *DAR Magazine* 46 4 (April 1915): 252–57.

Dructor, Robert M. *Guide to Genealogical Sources at the Pennsylvania State Archives* (Harrisburg: Pennsylvania Historical and Museum Commission, 1998).

Pennsylvania

Egle, William H. *Some Pennsylvania Women in the American Revolution* (Harrisburg: Harrisburg Publishing Co, 1898).

Gehret, Ellen and Alan G. Keyser. *The Homespun Textile Tradition of the Pennsylvania Germans* (Harrisburg: Pennsylvania Historical Commission, 1976).

—. *Rural Pennsylvania Clothing* (York, PA: Liberty Cap, G. Shumway, 1976).

Granick, Eve Wheatcroft. *The Amish Quilt* (Intercourse, PA: Good Books, 1989).

Hawbaker, Gary T. *Runaways, Rascals, and Rogues: Missing Spouses, Servants, and Slaves. Abstracts from Lancaster County, Pennsylvania Newspapers* (Hershey, PA: The Author, 1987).

Heffner, William C. *History of Poor Relief Legislation in Pennsylvania, 1682–1913* (Cleona, PA: Holzapfel, 1913).

Krause, Corinne A. "Italian, Jewish, and Slavic Grandmothers in Pittsburgh: Their Economic Roles." *Frontiers II* (Summer 1977): 18–28.

Kriebel, Martha B. "Women, Servants, and Family Life in America." *Pennsylvania Folklife* 28 1 (1978): 2–9. Schwenkfelder women in colonial Pennsylvania.

Lasansky, Jeanette. *A Good Start: The Aussteier or Dowry* (Lewisburg, PA: Oral Traditions Project, 1990).

—. *In the Heart of Pennsylvania: 19th and 20th Century Quiltmaking Traditions* (Lewisburg, PA: Oral Traditions Project, 1985).

Luder, Hope E. *Women and Quakerism* (Wallingford, PA: Pendle Hill, 1974).

McElroy, Janice H. *Our Hidden Heritage: Pennsylvania Women in History* (Washington, DC: Pennsylvania Division, American Association of University Women, 1983).

Meehan, Thomas R. "Not Made Out of Levity: Evolution of Divorce in Early Pennsylvania." *Pennsylvania Magazine of History and Biography* 92 4 (1968): 441–64.

Meier, Judith Ann. *Runaway Women: Elopements and Other Miscreant Deeds of Women, As Advertised in the Pennsylvania Gazette* (Apollo, PA: Closson Press, 1993).

Rich, E.S. *Mennonite Women: A Story of God's Faithfulness, 1683–1983* (Kitchner, ON: Kitchner Herald, 1983).

Rowe, G.S. "The Role of Courthouses in the Lives of Eighteenth-Century Pennsylvania Women." *Western Pennsylvania Historical Magazine* 68 (Jan 1985): 5–24.

—. "Femes Covert and Criminal Prosecution in Eighteenth-Century Pennsylvania." *American Journal of Legal History* 32 2 (April 1988): 138–56.

Schiffer, Margaret B. *Historical Needlework of Pennsylvania* (New York: Charles Scribner's Sons, 1968).

—. *Arts and Crafts of Chester County, Pennsylvania* (Exton, PA: Schiffer Publishing Ltd., 1980).

Sergeant, Thomas. *View of the Land Laws of Pennsylvania* (1838. Reprint. Laughlin: Southwest Pennsylvania Genealogical Services, 1992).

Soderlund, Jean R. "Black Women in Colonial Pennsylvania." *Pennsylvania Magazine of History and Biography* 107 (January 1983): 49–68.

Stoltzfus, Louise. *Amish Women: Lines and Stories* (Intercourse, PA: Good Books, 1997).

Turner, Kristen D. A *Guide to Materials on Women in the Pennsylvania State University Archives* (University Park: University Libraries, 1993).

Vaux, Trina. *Guide to Women's History Resources in the Delaware Valley Area* (Philadelphia: University of Pennsylvania Press, 1983).

Virdin, Donald O. *Pennsylvania Genealogies and Family Histories: A Bibliography of Books About Pennsylvania Families* (Bowie, MD: Heritage Books, 1992).

Wells, R.V. "Quaker Marriage Patterns in a Colonial Perspective." *William and Mary College Quarterly* 29 (1972).

Wilson, Lisa. *Life After Death: Widows in Pennsylvania, 1750–1850* (Philadelphia: Temple University Press, 1992).

SELECTED RESOURCES FOR WOMEN'S HISTORY

American Quilt Museum
Market and New Haven Streets
Marietta, PA 17547-0065

Friends Historical Library
Swarthmore College
500 College Avenue
Swarthmore, PA 19081-1905

Historical Society of Pennsylvania
1300 Locust Street
Philadelphia, PA 19107-5699

Pennsylvania State Archives
Third and Forster Streets
PO Box 1026
Harrisburg, PA 17108-1026

Philadelphia College of Textiles and Science
Pastore Library
School House Lane and Henry Avenue
Philadelphia, PA 19144

Temple University Libraries
Temple University
13th and Berks Street
Philadelphia, PA 19122

University of Pennsylvania Library
3420 Walnut Street
Philadelphia, PA 19104

Women's Studies Collection
Cressman Library
Cedar Crest College
Cedar Crest Boulevard
Allentown, PA 18104

RHODE ISLAND

IMPORTANT DATES IN STATE HISTORY

1636 First Rhode Island settlement founded at Providence.

1638 Anne Hutchinson, banned as a heretic from Massachusetts Bay Colony, founds Pocasset (Portsmouth).

1643 The Rhode Island Patent, called "Incorporation of Providence Plantations in the Narragannsett Bay in New England," is drafted.

1647 The Rhode Island Colony unites with the Warwick Colony.

1658 Jewish settlement established at Newport.

1664 Block Island admitted as part of the Colony.

1657 First Quakers arrive in Rhode Island.

1664 Seventh-Day Baptist movement begins in Westerly.

1685 French Huguenot refugees settle in Rhode Island.

1747 Towns of Bristol, Little Compton, Tiverton, and Warren are annexed from Massachusetts to Rhode Island.

1763 Touro Synagogue founded at Newport.

1776 British Army occupies Newport (not evacuated until 1779).

MARRIAGE AND DIVORCE

1647 marriages by agreement (self-betrothal, common law) are declared to be illegal. Marriages must be published at town meetings and confirmed in the town records.

1767 "Act Empowring justices . . . to give Sentence of Divorce for the relief of such persons as are injured in the Breach of the Marriage Covenant" states that because of the great number of mariners who disappear, divorce on the grounds of desertion is allowed, and the innocent party has the right to remarry (p. 74).

1882 all clergy are required to register their names in their towns of residence.

1896 town clerks are required to issue marriage licenses.

Where to Find Marriage and Divorce Records

The basic unit of government in Rhode Island is the town, which has handled all recording of vital records, land, probate, and other civil matters. The earliest marriages date from 1636. Most town records have been published and filmed. Statewide registration began in 1853 and was practiced by 1915. The first divorces were granted by the General Assembly in 1644. The first divorce law was written in 1650. Most legislative divorces were granted before 1749, but the practice continued until 1851. The Superior Court of Judicature and its successors held jurisdiction from 1749 to 1961. Divorce records prior to 1749 are at the Rhode Island State Archives in Providence. Cases from 1749 to 1992 are at the Rhode Island Judicial Records Center in Pawtucket (records to 1902 are in the archives, records from 1902 to 1992 are in the records center unit). See:

- Original town and city records, such as Providence City Registrar marriages, 1636–1880 (film 0914402 ff.), intentions of marriages, 1881–94 (film 2028007 ff.), and returns of marriages, 1879–92 (film 2027972 ff.), at the City Archives in Providence.
- Marriage indexes of brides and grooms, 1853–1900 (film 1822288 ff.), at the Rhode Island State Historical Society in Providence.
- Published vital records, such as *Alphabetical Index of the Births, Marriages and Deaths Recorded in Providence*. 32 Vols. (Providence: Sidney S. Rider, 1879–1946, fiche 6051317).

- Statewide published records, the most important being Arnold, James N. *Vital Records of Rhode Island, 1636–1850: A Family Register for the People*. 21 Vols. (Providence: Narragansett Historical Society, 1891-1912, fiche 6046912). Includes records from the town records in all the counties, church records, and newspaper abstracts. This contains errors.
- Other individual town records, such as Portsmouth Town Clerk town records, 1638-1850 (film 0945382), at the Town Hall in Portsmouth, containing records of town meetings 1638–1797, including deeds, indentures, wills, inventories, vital records, 1638–1799, and earmarks of livestock, 1638–1850.

PROPERTY AND INHERITANCE

1711 a married woman whose husband has been absent for three years may apply to the town council for "power to demand, sue, recover, possess, and improve all lands and houses or other real estate or property."

1719 in intestacy, a widow shall receive one-third of her husband's personal estate absolutely and one-third of his real estate for life.

1730 "Act for Granting Administration to the Wives of Persons Three Years Absent and Unheard Of" reaffirms the law of 1711.

1767 "Act for the Probate of Wills, and Granting Administration" provides that intestacy will be settled at the discretion of the town councils (pp. 214–17).

1844 a married woman's separate property, acquired before or after marriage, is secured for her own use.

1872 a married woman "may devise her separate estate, but cannot impair the husband's right of curtesy thereby, nor his right to administer on her personal property without account."

SUFFRAGE

1824 property ownership is a qualification to vote, but women who own property are excluded.

1917 Rhode Island women receive complete suffrage.

CITIZENSHIP

One of the original Thirteen Colonies.

CENSUS INFORMATION

1782 state census, see Holbrook, Jay Mack. *Rhode Island 1782 Census* (Oxford, MA: Holbrook Research Associates, 1979).

1865 state census (film 1008371 ff.) and every-name card index (film 0934776 ff.)

1875 state census (film 0947361 ff.).

1885 state census (film 0953910 ff.).

1915 state census (film 1763723 ff.).

1925 state census (film 1769232 ff.).

1936 state census (film 1753773 ff.).

The state censuses are at the Rhode Island State Historical Society.

OTHER

1647 town Overseers of the Poor are elected.

1682 first warning-out law is written.

1769 a notice in the *Newport Mercury* calls for the donation of 50 to 100 spinning wheels to poor women "almost starving for want of employ."

1774 because of the number of deaths at sea, twenty percent of the households in Newport are headed by women.[31]

1827 a lace school at Newport employs 500 young women.

1869 a state board of charities is established.

BIBLIOGRAPHY

Austin, John D. *Genealogical Dictionary of Rhode Island* (1858. Reprint. Baltimore: Genealogical Publishing Co., 1984).

—. "A Few Wills of Newport Women." *Narragansett Historical Register* VII (1889): 302–3. Abstracts of eighteenth-century wills.

Cohen, Sheldon S. "The Broken Bond: Divorce in Providence County, 1749–1809." *Rhode Island History* 44 3 (August 1985): 67–79.

Coughtry, Jay. *The Notorious Triangle: Rhode Island and the African Slave Trade, 1700–1807* (Philadelphia: Temple University Press, 1981).

Crane, Elaine F. *A Dependent People: Newport Rhode Island in the Revolutionary Era* (New York: Fordham University Press, 1985).

Dailey, Charlotte F. *Rhode Island Women's Directory for the Columbian Year 1892* (Providence: Rhode Island Women's World Fair Advisory Board, 1893).

Dunigan, Kate, et al. "Working Women at Work in Rhode Island, 1880–1925." *Rhode Island History* 38 (February 1979): 3–23.

Lamphere, Louise. *From Working Daughters to Working Mothers: Immigrant Women in a New England Industrial Community* (Ithaca: Cornell University Press, 1987).

Palmer, Mrs. F.P. *List of Rhode Island Literary Women, 1726–1892* (Providence: n.p., 1892).

Ring, Betty. *Let Virtue Be a Guide to Thee: Needlework in the Education of Rhode Island Women, 1730–1830* (Providence: Rhode Island State Historical Society, 1983).

Sperry, Kip. *Rhode Island Sources for Family Historians* (Logan, UT: Everton Publishers, 1986).

Strom, Sharon Hartman. "Old Barriers and New Opportunities: Working Women in Rhode Island, 1900–1940." *Rhode Island History* 39 (May 1980): 43–56

SELECTED RESOURCES FOR WOMEN'S HISTORY

Newport Historical Society
82 Touro Street
Newport, RI 02840

John Hay Library
Brown University
20 Prospect Street
Providence, RI 02912

---

[31] Elaine F. Crane, *A Dependent People: Newport, Rhode Island in the Revolutionary Era* (New York: Fordham University Press, 1985), 69.

Rhode Island State Historical Society
110 Benevolent Street
Providence, RI 02906

Rhode Island State Library
Rhode Island State Archives
337 Westminster Street
Providence, RI 02903

What Did You Do in the War, Grandma? available online at **<www.stg.brown.edu/projects/WWII_Women/tocCS.html>**

SOUTH CAROLINA

IMPORTANT DATES IN STATE HISTORY

1663 Area granted to eight proprietors.
1669 Fundamental Constitutions of Carolina drafted; first settlement is at Charles Town (Charleston).
1706 Province divided into twelve parishes.
1712 The British Crown divides Carolina into two provinces.
1715 Yamassee War.
1719 South Carolina becomes a Royal colony.
1760 Cherokee Wars.
1769 1795, and 1798 divided into twenty-four districts.
1771 Regulator wars.
1780 British forces occupy Charleston (evacuated in 1782); Battle of King's Mountain.
1781 Battle of Cowpens.
1828 Twenty-four districts are changed to counties.
1860 20 December secedes from the Union.
1865 Union troops burn Columbia.
1868 11 June readmitted to the Union.

MARRIAGE AND DIVORCE

1669 "no marriage shall be lawful, whatever contract and ceremony they have used till both the parties mutually own it, before the Register of the place where they were married, and he register it, with the names of the father and the mother of each party [not widely practiced]."

1866 "Act to Establish and Regulate the Domestic Relations of Persons of Color" provides that "the relation of husband and wife amongst persons of color is established. Those who now live as such are declared to be husband and wife (§ 1–2)."

1868–78 divorce is allowed, but none are granted.

1949 divorce is legalized.

Where to Find Marriage and Divorce Records

Early marriage records for South Carolina are few and far between. The Ordinary (ecclesiastical judge) of the province recorded the earliest marriages. In the early 1800s, a few probate courts began recording marriages. From 1911 to 1950, county marriage licenses were first issued by county probate judges. Marriage settlements (pre- and post-marital agreements) were contracts for women who had been previously married and were recorded from the 1760s to 1889. Alternate record sources, such as church records and newspaper abstracts, must be used. Divorces were illegal in South Carolina until 1949, when jurisdiction was given to the county courts. Some county records from 1911 have been filmed, such as:

- Edgefield County Probate Judge proof of marriages prior to 1 July 1911, marriage registers, 1911–47 (film 1429858 ff.), at the Edgefield County Courthouse in Edgefield.
- Laurens County Probate Judge marriage registers, 1911–51 (film 0024100 ff.), at the Laurens County Courthouse in Laurens.

See also indexes and compiled sources, such as:

- South Carolina marriage settlements, 1785–1889 (film 0022512 ff.), at the South Carolina Department of Archives and History in Columbia.

- Manuscript of South Carolina county records, Charleston County Court records containing renunciation of dowers, land, probate, and miscellaneous court actions, 1740–87 (film 0370945 ff.), at the South Caroliniana Library, University of South Carolina, in Columbia.
- Clemens, William M. *North and South Carolina Marriage Records: From the Earliest Colonial Days to the Civil War* (1927. Reprint. Baltimore: Genealogical Publishing Co., 1981).
- Holcomb, Brent. *South Carolina Marriages, 1688–1820.* 2 Vols. (Baltimore: Genealogical Publishing Co., 1980). Abstracted from newspapers, church records, district marriage bonds and licenses, probate records, deed books, and journals of the Ordinary.
- — . *Marriage and Death Notices from the Charleston Observer, 1827–1845* (Bowie, MD: Heritage Books, 1980).
- Langdon, Barbara R. *South Carolina Marriages.* 5 Vols. (n.p., 1991). Almost 10,000 marriages reference from vital, court, and public records, including marriages, 1749–1867, implied in South Carolina equity reports; 1735–1885, implied in South Carolina law reports; 1671–1791, implied in the provincial and miscellaneous records; 1787–1875, implied in miscellaneous records; and 1749–1853, implied in South Carolina marriage settlements.
- Lucas, S. Emmett Jr. *Abbeville District, South Carolina Marriages, 1777–1852* (Easley, SC: Southern Historical Press, 1979). Abbeville District became the present-day counties of Abbeville, Greenwood, and McCormick.

PROPERTY AND INHERITANCE

1712 "Act for Better Securing the Payment of Debts" provides that a widow shall receive one-third of her husband's personal estate, and one-third of his real estate for life; a married woman in business may be sued as a *feme sole*, "for securing of debts due from any person . . . and to subject a *Feme Covert* that is a *Feme Sole* Trader to be arrested and Sued for any debt contracted by Her as a Sole Trader."

1731 conveyancing statute is continuation of the present practice.

1744 married women are granted the status of *feme sole* trader in business, "to empower and enable a *Feme Covert* that is a Sole Trader to Sue for and Recover such debts as shall be contracted with Her as a Sole Trader, and to subject such *Feme Covert* to be arrested and Sued for any debt contracted by Her as a Sole Trader . . ."

1791 "Act for the Abolition of the Rights of Primogeniture and for Giving an Equitable Distribution of the Real Estate of Intestates" abolishes curtesy (Stat. 5 § 162–3).

1823 "no woman having a husband living shall be entitled, either at law or in equity, to the rights of a free dealer, unless she shall give notice by publications in a public newspaper, of her intention to trade as a sole trader, which notice shall be published at least one month; and in case there is no newspaper published in the district, then the notice shall be published in the same way as sheriff's sales. And be it further enacted that no marriage settlement shall be valid until recorded in the office of the Secretary of State . . ."

1868 "all the property held by her [a married woman] at the time of marriage, shall be her separate property, free from her husband's debts, and may be bequeathed, devised, or alienated by her in the same manner as if she were unmarried."

SUFFRAGE

1920 South Carolina women receive complete suffrage by passage of the 19th Amendment to the Constitution.

CITIZENSHIP

One of the original Thirteen Colonies.

CENSUS INFORMATION

1800–70 miscellaneous state censuses (film 0954248), covering the districts/counties of Anderson, Chester, Fairfield, Horry, Laurens, Pickens, Richland, Spartanburg, Sumter, and York.

1848 census, city of Charleston (film 08238835).

All state censuses are at the South Carolina Department of Archives and History.

OTHER

1726–1887 renunciations of dower, South Carolina Court of Common Pleas.

1919–26 card file index to Confederate veteran application files. The first pensions to widows of disabled Confederate veterans were awarded in 1895. Pensions are filmed by county, such as those for Abbeville, 1916–36 (film 0818614), Charleston, 1916–59 (film 0201831), Laurens, 1899, 1933–68 (film 1029317), and Union, 1919–20 (film 0255051). Few applications survive for the period 1888 to 1918.

1925–50 Confederate Home applications for wives, sisters, and daughters.

The above are at the South Carolina Department of Archives and History, except for pension records, which are in the records of individual counties.

BIBLIOGRAPHY

Bodie, Idella. *South Carolina Women* (Orangeburg, SC: Sandlapper Publishing, 1978).

Carlton, David. *Mill and Town in South Carolina, 1880–1920* (Baton Rouge: Louisiana State University Press, 1982).

Chepsuik, Ron. "The Winthrop College Archives and Special Collections: Selected Resources for the Study of Women's History." *South Carolina History Magazine* 82 (April 1981): 142–72.

Cody, Cheryll Ann. "Naming, Kinship, and Estate Dispersal: Notes on Slave Family Life on a South Carolina Plantation, 1786 to 1833." *William and Mary College Quarterly* 39 (January 1982): 192–211.

Côté, Richard N. *Local and Family History in South Carolina: A Bibliography* (Easley, SC: Southern Historical Press, 1981).

Farley, M. Foster. "South Carolina Women in the American Revolution." *DAR Magazine* 113 (April 1979): 309–12.

Frierson, J. Nelson. "Divorce in South Carolina." *North Carolina Law Review* 93 (April 1931): 271–82.

Hehir, Donald M. *Carolina Families: A Bibliography of Books About North and South Carolina Families* (Bowie, MD: Heritage Books, 1994).

Holcomb, Brent H. "Women in South Carolina Records: When, Where, and Why?" *On to Richmond!* FGS/VGS Conference, 1994.

—. *Probate Records of South Carolina [1746–1821].* 3 Vols. (Easley, SC: Southern Historical Press, 1977). Records prior to 1732 were kept by the Provincial Secretary.

Horton, Laurel and Lynn Robertson Myers. *Social Fabric: South Carolina's Traditional Quilts* (Columbia: University of South Carolina, 1986).

Houston, Martha L. *Indexes to the County Wills of South Carolina* (1939. Reprint. Baltimore: Genealogical Publishing Co., 1964, fiche 6046877). The index covers pre-1860 wills; there are no records for Beaufort, Chesterfield, Colleton, Georgetown, Lancaster, and Orangeburg districts. This does not include Charleston.

Mays, Harriet Anderson and Harry Roy Mays. *Daring Hearts and Spirits Free: South Carolina Women in the United Methodist Tradition* (Franklin, TN: Providence House Publishers, 1995).

McCurry, Stephanie. *Masters of Small Worlds: Yeoman Households, Gender Relations, and the Political Culture of the Antebellum South Carolina Low Country* (New York: Oxford University Press, 1995).

Moore, Caroline T. *Abstracts of the Wills of the State of South Carolina.* 3 Vols. (1969. Reprint. Baltimore: Genealogical Publishing Co., 1969).

Our Women in the War: The Lives They Lived and the Deaths They Died (Charleston: News and Courier Book Presses, 1885).

Salmon, Marylynn. "Women and Property in South Carolina: The Evidence from Marriage Settlements, 1730–1830." *William and Mary College Quarterly* 39 (1982): 655–85.

Schwalm, Leslie A. *A Hard Fight for We: Women's Transition from Slavery to Freedom in South Carolina* (Champaign: University of Illinois Press, 1997).

Shankman, Arnold. "A Jury of Her Peers: The South Carolina Woman and Her Campaign for Jury Service." *South Carolina History Magazine* (April 1980): 100–21.

South Carolina Daughters of the Confederacy. *South Carolina Women of the Confederacy.* 2 Vols. (Columbia: State Printing Co., 1903–7).

Weiner, Marli F. *Mistresses and Slaves: Plantation Women in South Carolina, 1830–1880* (Champaign: University of Illinois Press, 1997).

SELECTED RESOURCES FOR WOMEN'S HISTORY

Association of Black Women Historians
Department of History
South Carolina State University
Orangeburg, SC 29117

Ida Jane Dacus Library
Winthrop College
Oakland Avenue
Rock Hill, SC 29733

South Carolina Department of Archives
and History
1430 Senate Street
PO Box 11669
Columbia, SC 29211-1669

South Carolina Historical Society
100 Meeting Street
Charleston, SC 29401

South Caroliniana Library
University of South Carolina
Columbia, SC 29208-0103

SOUTH DAKOTA

IMPORTANT DATES IN STATE HISTORY

1803 Part of the Louisiana Purchase.
1804 Part of the District of Louisiana.
1805 Part of the Louisiana Territory.
1812 Part of the Missouri Territory.
1821 Part of unorganized Indian territory.
1834 Part of the Michigan Territory.
1836 Part of the Wisconsin Territory.
1838 Part of the Iowa Territory.
1849 Part of the Minnesota Territory.
1854 Part of the Nebraska Territory.
1858 White settlements established at Yankton and Vermillion.
1859 Left unorganized.
1861 Reorganized as the Dakota Territory, including Montana and northern Wyoming.
1864 Montana and Wyoming separate from Dakota.
1875 Gold is discovered in the Black Hills; they are opened for white settlement.
1876 Sioux War.
1889 Dakota Territory divides and becomes two separate states.
1890 Massacre of Lakota Indians at Wounded Knee.

MARRIAGE AND DIVORCE

1862 counties begin recording marriages.

1885 marriage "must be followed by a solemnization, or by a mutual assumption of marital rights, duties, or obligations."

1890 marriage licenses are required. Marriages may be solemnized by a minister or priest of any denomination, a judge of supreme or probate court, a justice of the peace, a mayor, the parties themselves by joint declaration; in the case of Indians, by the peacemakers, their agents, or superintendent of Indian affairs.

Where to Find Marriage and Divorce Records

Marriages have been recorded by the county clerk in probate and other county records since 1862. Divorces have been under the jurisdiction of the county courts and also granted by the Dakota Territorial Legislature from 1862 to 1866. County records for South Dakota have not been filmed by the FHL. Statewide registration began in 1905, and records are kept at the Department of Health in Pierre. Records prior to 1905 must be obtained from the county. There are some published compilations and indexes, such as:

- Long, Rita. *Early Marriage Records, Meade County, South Dakota [1889–1928]*. 3 Vols. (Rapid City, SD: Rapid City Society for Genealogical Research, 1985, fiche 6049386). Taken from county probate books.
- Sioux Valley Genealogical Society, Sioux Falls marriage index files of Minnehaha, 1879–93 (film 1710502 ff.), at the Sioux Valley Genealogical Society in Sioux Falls.
- Toms, Donald D. *Births, Marriages, Deaths, Burials, 1876 Through 1880 and 1881 [Lawrence County]* (n.p., n.d., film 1036951). Extracted from the *Black Hills Pioneer*, 1876, *Black Hills Daily Times*, 1877–81, and *Black Hills Weekly Times*, 1887–81, published in Deadwood, Lawrence County.

Bureau of Indian Affairs records at the NARA Midwest Region in Kansas City, Missouri also contain marriage records, such as:

- Pine Ridge Agency marriage records, including licenses and certificates, 1888–1936 (film 1014637 ff.), contain records of Oglala and Dakota Indians.
- Spotted Tail Agency marriage registers, 1847–78 (film 1012661), contain records of Dakota Indians. Spotted Tail Agency became Rosebud Agency in 1878.

PROPERTY AND INHERITANCE

1887 a married woman may devise a will conveying her separate property.

1889 a married woman is granted *feme sole* status regarding her separate property; property acquired before or after marriage is her separate estate, free from the debts of her husband.

1899 law abolishes common-law dower and curtesy; neither spouse has any interest in the property of the other (§ 25).

1906 Congress prohibits married women living on reservations in North and South Dakota to hold grazing lands (H. Doc. 257, 59th Cong., 2nd Sess., 1906. Serial 5153).

SUFFRAGE

1918 South Dakota women receive complete suffrage.

CITIZENSHIP

1803 all residents of the South Dakota area become U.S. citizens by legislation, except for Native Americans, whose tribes are considered a separate nation until 1924.

CENSUS INFORMATION

For pre-statehood federal censuses, see Iowa (1840), Minnesota (1850, Pembina District), and Dakota Territory (1860, 1870, and 1880).

1836 see Shambaugh, Benjamin F. *Wisconsin Territory: The First Census of the Original Counties of Dubuque and Des Moines (Iowa) Taken in July, 1836* (Des Moines: Historical Department of Iowa, 1897, film 1022202). Comprises the present states of Iowa, Minnesota, and parts of North and South Dakota.

1885 Dakota Territory census (film 0547583).

1884–1940 censuses of Indian reservations. All censuses provide every name in Indian and English (if given), age, sex, tribal enrollment number, and relationship to the head of household. Enumerations after 1913 also include the date of birth; enumerations taken after 1929 also include marital status and degree of blood. The censuses are available through the FHL and the National Archives (M595).

❧ *To obtain copies of the maiden names given in the 1905 to 1945 state censuses, a for-fee search by the South Dakota State Archives can be ordered with the form* **<www.state.sd.us/state/executive/deca/cultural/archform.htm>**, *available online.*

1895 state census (film 1405183), mostly destroyed.

1905–45 decennial state censuses, *including* maiden names (not at FHL).

Unless otherwise stated, territorial and state censuses are at the South Dakota State Archives in Pierre.

OTHER

The South Dakota State Archives has microfilmed 1,000 newspapers dating from 1861, and the films are available through ILL from the Archives. There is also a search service for obituaries and other articles, if the date and location are known. Research forms are available online at **<www.state.sd.us/executive/deca/cultural/anewform/htm>**.

BIBLIOGRAPHY

Hazel, Harry and S.L. Lewis. *The Divorce Mill: Realistic Sketches of the South Dakota Divorce Colony* (Kansas City, MO: Sheed & Ward, 1987).

Holley, Frances C. *Once Their Home: Or Our Legacy from the Dahkotans* (Chicago: Donohue & Henneberry, 1892, film 1000589).

Houghland, Lonnie R. "South Dakota Divorce Legislation and Reform, 1862–1908." *The Region Today: A Quarterly Journal of the Social Science Research Associates* 2 3 (May 1975): 48–65.

Jones, Clifton H. "Manuscript Sources in Women's History at the Historical Resource Center." *South Dakota History* 7 1(1976): 57–65.

Klock, Irma. *Black Hill Ladies: The Frail and the Fair* (Deadwood, SD: The Author, 1980).

Nelson, Paula M. *After the West Was Won: Homesteaders and Town-Builders in Western South Dakota, 1900–1917* (Iowa City: University of Iowa Press, 1986).

—. "No Place for Clinging Vines: Women Homesteaders on the South Dakota Frontier, 1900–1915." Thesis, University of South Dakota, 1978.

—. *The Prairie Winnows Out Its Own: The West River Country of South Dakota in the Years of Depression and Dust* (Iowa City: University of Idaho Press, 1996).

Peterson, Susan and Courtney A. Vaughan-Robertson. *Women with Vision: The Presentation Sisters in South Dakota* (Urbana: University of Illinois Press, 1988).

Prairie Progress in West Central South Dakota (Sioux Falls: Historical Society of Old Stanley County, 1968, film 1036396).

Reyer, Carolyn. *Cante ohitika Win (Brave-hearted Women): Images of Lakota Women from the Pine Ridge Reservation, South Dakota* (Vemillion: University of South Dakota Press, 1991).

Riley, Glenda. "Farm Women's Roles in the Agricultural Development of South Dakota." *South Dakota History* 13 (Spring/Summer 1983): 55–62.

Rose, LaVera. "Dakota Resources: Women's History Resources in the State Archives at the South Dakota State Historical Society." *South Dakota History* 28 (Spring/Summer 1998).

Schell, Herbert S. *History of South Dakota*. 2nd ed. (Lincoln: University of Nebraska Press, 1968).

South Dakota Commission on the Status of Women. *South Dakota Women, 1850–1919: A Bibliography* (Pierre: The Commission, 1975).

Spector, Janet D. *What This Awl Means: Feminist Archeology at the Wahpeton Dakota Village* (Saint Paul: Minnesota Historical Society, 1993).

Wagner, Sally R. *Daughters of Dakota*. 6 Vols. (n.p.: Sky Carrier, 1990).

—— . "The Pioneer Daughters Collection of the South Dakota Federation of Women's Clubs." *South Dakota History* 19 (Spring 1989): 95–109.

Wyman, Walker, D. *Frontier Woman: The Life of a Woman Homesteader on the Dakota Frontier* (River Falls: University of Wisconsin-River Falls Press, 1972).

SELECTED RESOURCES FOR WOMEN'S HISTORY

Center for Western Studies
Mikkelsen Library
Augustana College
29th and Summit Avenue
Sioux Falls, SD 57197

I.D. Weeks Library
Richardson Archives
University of South Dakota
Spearfish, SD 57069

South Dakota State Archives
South Dakota State Historical Society
900 Governors Drive
Pierre, SD 57501-2294

Women's Studies Program
South Dakota State University
Political Science Department
Brookings, SD 57007

TENNESSEE

IMPORTANT DATES IN STATE HISTORY

1663 Part of French territory.
1763 Area ceded by France to Great Britain; settlers begin to migrate from the Carolinas and Virginia; North Carolina claims sovereignty of the area.
1771 Watauga (Valley) Association formed.
1776 Becomes Washington County, Tennessee.
1779 Nashville founded.
1780 Battle of Kings Mountain.
1784 Ceded from North Carolina to the U.S.; State of Franklin organized (dissolved in 1788).
1789 Under jurisdiction of North Carolina.
1790 North Carolina again cedes area to the U.S.; becomes part of the Southwest Territory.
1796 Separated from North Carolina; statehood, constitution written adopting the common law of North Carolina.
1861 24 June secedes from the Union.
1863 Battle of Chickamauga; Battle (and siege) of Chattanooga.
1866 July readmitted to the Union.

MARRIAGE AND DIVORCE

1815 a husband is exempted from liability for the debts of his wife incurred during separation.
1858 grounds for divorce are expanded (§ 2448-9).
1884 the clerk of the county court in the bride's jurisdiction is required to issue a marriage license.

Where to Find Marriage and Divorce Records

Marriages were first recorded in county records in 1787. Statewide marriage registration began in 1945. Under early Tennessee divorce laws, the state legislature granted divorces from 1797 to 1858. The district superior courts also held jurisdiction from 1799 to 1809. From 1809 to 1835, the county circuit courts also handled divorces. After 1835, divorces were heard in county circuit and chancery courts, and records are in the custody of the clerks of the county circuit courts. Many county records have been filmed, and there is also a collection of twentieth-century marriage records at the Tennessee State Library and Archives in Nashville. Many county records have been filmed, such as:

- Marriages, 1919–74, and Anderson County index, 1838–1987 (film 1928596 ff.), listed by county, at the Tennessee State Library and Archives.
- Davidson County Clerk marriage records, 1789–1951, and licenses and bonds, 1789–1856 (film 1994117 ff.), at the Metropolitan Government Archives in Nashville.
- Benton County Clerk marriage records, 1838–1968 (film 0557642 ff.), at the Tennessee State Library and Archives.

See also compiled publications, such as:

- Sistler, Byron and Barbara Sistler. *Early East Tennessee Marriages*. 2 Vols. (Nashville: B. Sistler & Associates, 1987, film 1597922).
- —. *Early Middle Tennessee Marriages*. 2 Vols. (Nashville: B. Sistler & Associates, 1988, film 1597922).
- —. *Early West Tennessee Marriages*. 2 Vols. (Nashville: B. Sistler & Associates, 1989, fiche 6100916 ff.).

  Bamman, Gale W. and Debbie W. Spero. *Tennessee Divorces, 1797–1858* (Thorndike, MA: Van Volumes Unlimited, 1990).

PROPERTY AND INHERITANCE

1796 a married woman cannot bring a suit to court in her own name; *feme sole* status may only by granted by an act of legislature.

1835 a married woman is empowered to act as *feme sole* regarding her separate property.

1850 a married woman may devise her separate property.

1870 a married woman's separate property is her separate estate.

SUFFRAGE

1919 women become eligible to vote in presidential elections.

1920 Tennessee women receive complete suffrage by passage of the 19th Amendment to the Constitution.

CITIZENSHIP

Within jurisdiction of original Thirteen Colonies.

CENSUS INFORMATION

The federal censuses for 1790, 1800, most of 1810, and almost half of 1820 have been destroyed. County tax lists, such as those for Washington County, 1778–1846 (film 0825545), at the Washington County Courthouse in Jonesboro, can be used as substitutes to fill in the missing years. There are no state censuses for Tennessee. See also:

- McGhee, Lucy Kate. *Partial Census of 1787 to 1791 of Tennessee as Taken from the North Carolina Land Grants*. 3 Vols. (Washington: The Author, 1930, film 1728882 ff.).
- Creekmore, Pollyanna. *Early East Tennessee Taxpayers* (Easley, SC: Southern Historical Press, 1980, film 1486601).

OTHER

1891–1965 Confederate veterans' and widows' pension applications (film 0978497 ff.), at the Tennessee State Library and Archives. See also Wiefering, Edna. *Tennessee's Confederate Widows and Their Families: Abstracts of 11,190 Confederate Widows' Pension Applications* (Cleveland, TN: Cleveland Public Staff & Volunteers, 1992, fiche 6051232). An index to Soldiers Home applications (includes information on family members) is available online at **<www.state.tn.us/sos/statelib/pubsos/csh_intr.htm>**.

1934–54 Tennessee Valley Authority population relocation files (film 2033011 ff.), at the NARA Southeast Region in East Point, Georgia. The files are for the Norris Project (Anderson and Campbell counties), giving name, address, marital status, birthplace of parents, number and ages of children, occupation, real estate, and religion for those who were relocated.

BIBLIOGRAPHY

Avendale, Marirose. "Tennessee and Women's Rights." *Tennessee Historical Quarterly* 39 (Spring 1980): 62–78.

Crawford, Margaret L. "The Legal Status of Women in Early Tennessee: Knox, Jefferson, and Blount Counties, 1792–1843." Master's Thesis, University of Tennessee, 1992.

Dykeman, Wilma. *Tennessee Women, Past and Present* (Memphis: Tennessee Committee for the Humanities, 1977).

Goodheat, Lawrence B., Neil Hanks, and Elizabeth Johnson. "An Act for the Relief of Females . . .:

Divorce and the Changing Legal Status of Women in Tennessee, 1796–1860." *Tennessee Historical Quarterly* 44 3 (Fall 1985): 318–39, 44 4 (Winter 1985): 402–16.

Hahn, Nicolas F. "Female State Prisoners in Tennessee, 1831–1979." *Tennessee Historical Quarterly* 19 (Winter 1980): 485–97.

Hehir, Donald M. *Tennessee Families: A Bibliography of Books About Tennessee Families* (Bowie, MD: Heritage Books, 1996).

Hoobler, James A. *Distinctive Women on Tennessee* (Nashville: Tennessee Historical Association, n.d.).

Kendrick, Robert E. "Information Marriages in Tennessee: Marriages by Estoppel, by Prescription, and by Ratification." *Vanderbilt Law Review* 3 (1950): 610–26.

Lane, Patricia G. Birth, Marriage, and Death: Past and Present Customs in East Tennessee." *Tennessee Folklore Society Bulletin* 48 2 (1982): 53–60.

Mack, Thura. *Shaping of a State: The Legacy of Tennessee Women* (Nashville: Cuningson Women's Center, 1995).

Marshall, Martha. *Quilts of Appalachia: The Mountain Woman and Her Quilt* (Bluff City: TN: Tri-City, 1972).

Ramsey, Bets and Merikay Waldvogel. *The Quilts of Tennessee: Images of Domestic Life Prior to 1930* (Nashville: Rutledge Hill Press, 1986).

Schweitzer, George K. *Tennessee Genealogical Research* (Knoxville, TN: The Author, 1993).

Smith, Jessie Carney. "Colorful Women, Women of Color: African American Women and Tennessee History." *Tennessee Business* 6 2 (1995): 13–20.

Tennessee Federation of Women's Clubs. *Woman's Work in Tennessee* (Memphis: Jones-Briggs Co., 1916).

Wiefering, Edna. *Tennessee's Confederate Widows and Their Families* (Cleveland: Tennessee Library Association, 1992).

Williams, Samuel C. *History of the Lost State of Franklin* (1933. Reprint. Baltimore: Clearfield Co., 1993).

SELECTED RESOURCES FOR WOMEN'S HISTORY

Archives of Appalachia, Sherrod Library
East Tennessee State University
Johnson City, TN 37614-0002

Tennessee Collection
Andrew L. Todd Library
Middle Tennessee State University
Murfreesboro, TN 37132

Tennessee State Library and Archives
403 Seventh Avenue, North
Nashville, TN 37243-0312

Tennessee Women's Network
5632 Meadowcrest Lane
Nashville, TN 37209

Women in Tennessee History: A Bibliography, available online at **<www.mtsu.edu/~library/wtn/wtn-home.html>**

TEXAS

IMPORTANT DATES IN STATE HISTORY

1641 Spanish Governor appointed for Texas.
1682 First permanent Spanish settlement near the site of El Paso.
1691 Part of the Viceroyalty of Nueva España.
1700 Mission of San Juan Bautista founded.
1718 Presidio of San Antonio de Bejár founded.
1749 Laredo founded.
1779 Nacogdoches founded.
1813 Spain crushes rebellion for independence at the Alamo (San Antonio).
1821 Ceded from Spain to Mexico; becomes a province; Austin Colony established.
1827 10,000 Americans have settled in Texas. Constitution of Coahuila and Texas calls for trial by jury in criminal cases (normally not provided for under Spanish civil law).
1830 Civil pleading courts implemented by decree.
1835 35,000 Americans have settled in Texas.
1836 Battle of the Alamo; Texas becomes a Republic; Spanish and Mexican law retained; the civil court pleading system of *demanda y repuesta* (petition and answer) established.
1840 Texas Congress adopts common law and repeals Spanish and Mexican civil laws.
1845 Statehood.
1861 1 February secedes from the Union.
1870 15 March readmitted to the Union.

MARRIAGE AND DIVORCE

1600s Spanish Civil Code and the civil law of Spain prevails.

1776 Spanish Crown issues the Royal Pragmatic on Marriage, which takes exclusive control of marriage away from the Catholic Church and gives parents rights under civil law to prevent marriages against their wishes; parents are allowed to disinherit children who marry against their wishes.

1840 premarital agreements are allowed, but must "contain no provisions which would alter the legal orders of descent . . . and that no matrimonial agreement shall be altered after marriage [repealed in 1856]."

1895 in divorce, the court shall "order a division of the estate of all parties in such a way as the court shall deem just and right . . ." and it is not required "to divest himself or herself of the title to real estate (Art. 4638)."

Where to Find Marriage and Divorce Records

Before 1836 only the Catholic Church could solemnize marriages. Some of the early parish registers have been filmed, such as:

- San Fernando Cathedral Missions, San Antonio, parish registers, 1731–1860 (El Paso: Golightly Co., 1957, film 0025433 ff.), at the Archdiocese of San Antonio, including Misión de la Purisima Concepcion, Misión de la San Jose, San Juan y San Francisco, and Misión de San Antonio de Valero.
- San Fernando Cathedral, San Antonio, parish registers, 1703–1957 (El Paso: Golightly Co., 1957, film 0025438 ff.), at the Archdiocese of San Antonio.
- See also Guerra, Raul J., Nadine M. Vasquez, and Baldomero Vela. *Index to the Marriage Investigations of the Diocese of Guadalajara Pertaining to the Former Provinces of Coahuila, Nuevo León, Nuevo Santander, and Téxas* (Edinburg, TX: The Authors, 1989). Includes Coahuila, Nuevo León, Nayarit, and Jalisco, Mexico.

The early county marriage records generally began in 1837 and are in the custody of the county clerks. The Texas Congress granted divorces as acts from 1837 to 1841. In 1846 the county district courts were given jurisdiction for divorce cases. For an inventory of county records available on microfilm at the Texas State Library and Archives in Austin, see **<www.tsl.state.tx.us/lobby/ local/locrmenu.htm>**. Many county records have been filmed, such as:

- Nacogdoches County Court marriage contracts, 1824-38 (film 1003764), and marriage records, 1837-1918 (film 1003581 ff.), at the Nacogdoches County Courthouse in Nacogdoches.

There are also compiled publications, including early marriage bonds, such as:

- Grammar, Norma Rutledge. *Marriage Records of Early Texas, 1824–1846* (Fort Worth: Fort Worth Genealogical Society, 1971, film 0982117).
- Ladd, Kevin. *Gone to Texas: Genealogical Abstracts from The Telegraph and Texas Register, 1835–1841* (Bowie, MD: Heritage Books, 1994).
- Partin, SheRita and Kae Vaughan Roberts. *Marriages of Nacogdoches County, Texas, 1830–1895* (Nacogdoches: Partin Publications, 1994).
- Smith, Bennett L. *Marriage by Bond in Colonial Texas* (Fort Worth: Branch-Smith, 1972). The appendix includes indexes of bonds in Austin, Brazoria, and Gonzales counties.
- Swenson, Helen S. *8,800 Texas Marriages, 1824–1850*. 2 Vols. (Round Rock, TX: The Author, 1981).

PROPERTY AND INHERITANCE

1716 the first Spanish land grants are made in Texas (last Spanish grants issued in 1836).

1823 land offices are opened under the jurisdiction of the Republic of Mexico (closed in 1830).

1836 the community property system of marital law is retained from Spanish and Mexican law.

1837 the General Land Office for the Republic of Texas is opened in Austin (issued Republic grants until 1845, state land grants thereafter).

1840 first marital property laws, based on civil and common law, state that a woman's personalty, realty, and slaves owned at the time of marriage or acquired during marriage "shall not become the property of the husband, but remain the property of the wife (§ 3)." The husband shall have the sole management of such land and slaves and "full powers of ownership over the community property . . . during coverture [the common property] may be sold or otherwise disposed of by the husband only (§ 4)."

1845 "all property both real and personal, of the wife, owned or claimed by her before marriage, and that acquired afterward by gift, devise, or descent, shall be her separate property . . . and laws shall be passed more clearly defining the rights of the wife, in relation as well to her separate property held in common with her husband. Laws shall also be passed for the registration of the wife's separate property (§ 19)."

1848 the registration of a wife's separate property is required by statute.

1895 a married woman's separate property is free from the debts of her husband; she may devise a will conveying her half of the community property.

1913 a married woman may manage her earnings and income from her separate property, which was formerly considered community property.

SUFFRAGE

1918 women are found eligible to vote in primary elections.

1920 Texas women receive complete suffrage by passage of the 19th Amendment to the Constitution.

CITIZENSHIP

1845 all residents of Texas become U.S. citizens by legislation, except for Native Americans, whose tribes are considered a separate nation until 1924.

CENSUS INFORMATION

The first federal census for Texas was in 1850. There are early census records at the Archivo General de Indias in Seville, Spain. They have been abstracted in:

- Salazar, J. Richard. *El Paso Census, 1684* (Albuquerque: The Author, 1992).
- Salazar, J. Richard. *1692 Population Census of El Paso* (Albuquerque: The Author, 1992).

1680–1825 censuses, see Platt, Lyman D. *Census Records for Latin America and the Hispanic United States* (Baltimore: Genealogical Publishing Co., 1998).

1829–45 censuses, see Mullins, Marion D. *The First Census of Texas, 1829–1836: To Which Are Added Texas Citizenship Lists, 1821–1845, and Other Early Records of the Republic of Texas* (Washington, DC: National Genealogical Society, 1962, film 0844966).

OTHER

1835–88 Republic of Texas donation lands granted to widows and surviving veterans.
1863–5 list of Confederate indigent families of Texas soldiers.
1870–1930 Confederate pension index (film 2031526).
1899–1964 Confederate pension applications (film 0960279 ff.).
1908–64 Confederate Women's Home records.
The above records are at the Texas State Library and Archives in Austin. See also White, Virgil D. *Index to Texas CSA Pension Files* (Waynesboro, TN: National Historical Publishing Co., 1989). There is also an online index of the 54,634 pension applications: **<link.tsl.state.tx.us/c/compt/index.html>**.

1736–1838, the Bexar Archives of the Province of Texas and the Mexican State of Coahuila y Texas, (film 1019360 ff.), at the Texas History Center, University of Texas at Austin, and at the Bexar County Courthouse in San Antonio. The records taken from the papers of the viceroys of New Spain and the governors of Texas include census records, deeds, slave sales, trade reports, tax lists, judicial records, mission records, militia reports and pay lists, soldiers' petitions for marriage, arrest warrants, marriage records, wills and estates, land grants and records, contracts, agreements, receipts, powers of attorney, protocol, and an index to the Archives. They are described in Benavides, Adán. *The Bexar Archives, 1717–1836* (San Antonio: University of Texas at Austin, 1989). Localities documented in the records include La Bahía, Nacogdoches, and the Texas-Louisiana border. See also Kielman, Chester Valls. *Guide to the Microfilm Edition of the Bexar Archives*. 3 Vols. (Austin: University of Texas, 1967–71). The microfilmed records cover the years 1717 to 1836.

BIBLIOGRAPHY

Beeman, Cynthia. *Women in Texas History: They Made a Difference* (Austin: Texas Historical Commission, 1989).

Blackwelder, Julia K. *Women of the Depression: Caste and Culture in San Antonio, 1929–1939* (College Station: Texas A & M University Press, 1984).

Bresenhan, Karoline P. and Nancy O. Puentes. *Lone Star: A Legacy of Texas Quilts* (Austin: University of Texas Press, 1986).

Burnett, Georgellen. *We Just Toughed It Out: Women Heads of Household on the Llano Estacado, 1880–1935* (El Paso: Texas Western Press, 1989).

Carrington, Evelyn M. *Women in Early Texas* (Austin: Jenkins Publishing Co., 1975).

Downs, Fane and Nancy Baker Jones. *Women and Texas History: Selected Essays* (Austin: Texas State Historical Association, 1993).

Gould, Florence, C. *Claiming Their Own Land: Women Homesteaders in Texas* (El Paso: Texas Western Press, 1991, fiche 6125888).

Gruben, Karl T. and James E. Hambleton. *A Reference Guide to Texas Law and Legal History: Sources and Documentation.* 2nd ed. (Austin: Butterworth Legal Publishers, 1987).

Kelsey, Michael. *Miscellaneous Texas Newspaper Abstracts [1839–1882].* 5 Vols. (n.p.: Dataplex, 1988-92).

Kennedy, Imogene K. *Genealogical Records in Texas* (Baltimore: Genealogical Publishing Co., 1987).

Lazarou, Kathleen E. *Concealed Under Petticoats: Married Women's Property and the Law of Texas, 1840–1913* (New York: Garland Publishing, 1986).

Malone, Anne Paton. *Women on the Texas Frontier* (El Paso: Texas Western Press, 1983).

Marks, Paula Mitchell. *Hands to Spindle: Texas Women & Home Textile Production, 1822–1880* (College Station: Texas A & M University Press, 1996).

McKnight, Joseph W. "The Spanish Legacy to Texas Law." *American Journal of Legal History* 3 (1959): 222–41.

Mills, Betty J. Savage. *Calico Chronicle: Texas Women and Their Fashions, 1830–1910* (Lubbock: Texas Tech Press, 1985).

Munnerlyn, Tom. *Texas Local History: A Source Book for Available Town and County Histories, Local Memoirs, and Genealogical Records* (Austin: Eakin Press, 1983).

Olien, Diana Davids. "Keeping House in a Tent: Women in the Early Permian Basin Oil Fields." *Permian History Association* 22 (1982): 3–14. Permian Basin, 1920s to 1930s.

Paulson, James W. "Community Property and the Early American Women's Rights Movement: The Texas Connection." *Idaho Law Review* 32 4 (Fall 1996): 641–90.

Pickerell, Annie Doom. *Pioneer Women in Texas* (1929. Reprint. Austin: Jenkins Publishing Co., 1970).

Ragsdale, Crystal Sasse. *The Golden Free Land: The Reminiscences and Letters of Women of the American Frontier* (Austin: Landmark Press, 1976). German pioneer women in Texas.

Residents of Texas, 1782–1836. 3 Vols. (San Antonio: University of Texas Press, 1984).

Ruiz, Vicki L. "Dead Ends or Gold Mine? Using Missionary Records in Mexican American Women's History," in Ruiz, Vicki and Ellen Carol DuBois, *Unequal Sisters: A Multi-Cultural Reader in U.S. Women's History*. 2nd ed. (London: Routledge, 1994), 298–315. Case study using the records of the Houchen Settlement, El Paso.

Silverthorne, Elizabeth. *Plantation Life in Texas* (College Station: Texas A & M University Press, 1986).

Snapp, Elizabeth. *Read All About Her! Texas Women's History: A Working Bibliography* (Denton: Texas Woman's University Press, 1996).

Texas Heritage Quilt Society. *Texas Quilts, Texas Treasures* (Paducah, KY: American Quilters Society, 1986).

Turner, Elizabeth Hayes. *Women, Culture, and Community: Religion and Reform in Galveston, 1880–1920* (New York: Oxford University Press, 1997).

Williams, Villamae. *Stephen F. Austin's Register of Families* (Baltimore: Genealogical Publishing Co., 1989).

Winegarten, Ruth. *Black Texas Women: A Sourcebook* (Austin: University of Texas Press, 1996).

Women and Texas History: An Archival Bibliography (Austin: Texas State Historical Association, 1990).

Yabsey, Suzanne. *Texas Quilts, Texas Women* (College Station: Texas A & M University Press, 1984).

SELECTED RESOURCES FOR WOMEN'S HISTORY

Daughters of the Republic of Texas Library
PO Box 1401
San Antonio, TX 78295-1401

De Goyler Library and Methodist Historical Library
Souther Methodist University
Dallas, TX 75275

Eugene C. Barker Texas History Center
University of Texas, Austin
Austin, TX 78713-7330

Foundation for Women's Resources
3500 Jefferson, Suite 210
Austin, TX 78731

Texas and Local History Division
Dallas Public Library
Dallas, TX 75201

Texas State Library and Archives
Capitol Station, Box 12927
Austin, TX 78711

Panhandle-Plains Historical Museum
Box 967, W.T. Station
Canyon, TX 79016

University Library, Special Collections
University of Texas, El Paso
El Paso, TX 79968-0582

UTSA Archives
University of Texas, San Antonio
801 South Bowie Street
San Antonio, TX 78205-3296

Women's Collection
Blagg-Huey Library
Texas Women's University
TWU Station
Box 23925
Denton, TX 76204

Archives for Research on Women and Gender, available online at **<www.lib. utsa.edu/Archives/index.htm>**

Daughters of the Republic of Texas Library, available online at **<www.drtl.org/>**

Genealogy Research at the Texas State Archives, available online at **<www.tsl.state.tx.us.lobby/arcgen/htm>**

UTAH

IMPORTANT DATES IN STATE HISTORY

1847 First Mormon settlers arrive in Salt Lake Valley; Provisional (ecclesiastical) Government organized by the Church of Jesus Christ of Latter-day Saints, outside U.S. territory.[32]

1848 Acquired from Mexico in the Treaty of Guadalupe-Hildago.

1849 Provisional Government of the State of Deseret created.

1850 Organized as the Utah Territory, which included most of Nevada, western Colorado, and southwestern Wyoming; federal district courts established.

1852 Iron mine established near Cedar City.

1857 Utah War.

1862 Congress makes polygamy illegal in all U.S. territories by the Morrill Act.

1865 Ute-Black Hawk War.

1874 The Poland Act increases federal oversight of territorial courts.

1882 The Edmunds Act makes cohabitation with more than one woman illegal.

1887 The Edmunds-Tucker Act unincorporates the LDS Church, confiscates the assets of the Church, and requires test oaths.

1895 Constitution drafted.

1896 Statehood.

MARRIAGE AND DIVORCE

1852 the LDS Church publicly adopts polygamy, although it has been practiced for years. The territorial legislature, to "protect plural marriages," passes a law allowing a registry of plural marriages to be kept by the Church rather than civil courts.

1884 Congress requires all marriages in Utah Territory to be registered (H. Rept. 1351, 48th Cong., 1st Sess., 1884. Serial 2257).

1885 2,400 Mormon men (two percent of men in the Church) are practicing polygamy.

1888 clerks of the probate court must issue and record marriage licenses.

1890 the LDS Church renounces polygamy.

1895 the Utah constitution makes polygamy illegal.

1896 county clerks assume the issuing and recording of marriage licenses.

1904 the LDS Church promises to excommunicate any male members of the Church who enter into polygamous unions from this time forward.

Where to Find Marriage and Divorce Records

The first civil government in Utah was an ecclesiastical one, which existed from 1847 to 1849. The Provisional State of Deseret which existed from 1849 to 1851 also had Church courts of justice. During the territorial period, federal district courts, county probate courts (usually presided over by a bishop of the LDS Church), justice of the peace courts, and Church courts existed. After statehood in 1896, the probate courts were abolished, county district courts were established, and justice of the peace courts were continued. Marriages from 1847 to 1852 were recorded in Church membership and temple records. In 1852, marriages were first recorded by probate judges and justices of the peace. As part of the anti-polygamy laws, the federal government required marriage certificates to be filed with the courts of probate in 1887. In 1893, the county clerks took over recording marriages from the probate courts.

[32] Hereafter known as the LDS Church.

The Church membership records are restricted, but many baptisms and marriages (sealings) have been indexed in the *International Genealogical Index,*© available on CD-ROM at the FHL, Family History Centers, and many public and private libraries. Justice of the peace records are at the original county courts, at the Utah State Archives in Salt Lake City, and in private possession. Probate court records are at the county courthouses and the State Archives. A few county records have been filmed, such as:

- Salt Lake County Clerk alphabetic marriage listing, index to males and females, 1887–1987 (fiche 6052848 ff.), marriage records, 1887–1965 (film 0429035 ff.), at the City and County Building in Salt Lake City.

See also indexes and compiled publications, such as:

- Marriage License Card Index (film 0820155 ff.) compiled by members of the LDS Church from marriage license records in the following county courthouses: Box Elder, Millard, Morgan, Salt Lake, Sanpete, Sevier, Summit, Utah, Wayne and Weber.
- CD-ROM: *Marriage License Information System* (Salt Lake City: Ja-Ne't Global-Data Search, 1993), covering the counties of Davis and Salt Lake, 1800s–1992.
- CD-ROM: *Territorial Vital Records: Births, Divorces, Guardianships, Marriages, Naturalizations, Wills; 1800s Thru 1906 Utah Territory, Arizona, Colorado, Idaho, Nevada, Wyoming, Indian Territory; LDS Branches, Wards; Deseret News Vital Records; J.P. Marriages; Methodist Marriages* (Saint George, UT: Genealogical CD Publishing, 1994).

Divorces granted by the LDS Church between 1847 and 1852 are available on a restricted basis only to descendants. Federal district court divorces, granted from 1852 to 1896, have been filmed and are at the Utah State Archives, the National Archives in Washington, DC, and are also available from the county clerk in the county where the divorce was granted. Salt Lake City, Ogden, Provo, and Beaver were seats of the four U.S. judicial districts that existed in the territorial period. County probate records are in the custody of the county clerk where the divorce was granted. District court records from 1896 are also kept by the county clerk. For more information, see:

- U.S. District Court for the Territory of Utah case files, 1870 (film 1616325 ff./M1401), at the National Archives in Washington, DC. The cases involve mostly polygamy, or cohabitation, but also include various other crimes.
- U.S. District Court for the Territory of Utah, First Judicial District (Salt Lake City), journal, 1851–6 (film 0431224), at the State Capitol Building in Salt Lake City.
- County records, such as Salt Lake County Probate Court divorce records, 1852–56, 1877–87 (film 0431227), at the City and County Building in Salt Lake City.

❧ *Since polygamy was not recognized by law, the LDS Church granted many divorces in plural marriages. Brigham Young granted at least 1,645 divorces during his presidency, most if not all involving plural marriages.*

Jessie L Embrey, *Mormon Polygamous Families: Life in the Principle* (Salt Lake City: University of Utah Press, 1987).

PROPERTY AND INHERITANCE

1852 since polygamous wives are not recognized by law, the territorial legislature provides that "illegitimate children and their mothers inherit in like manner from the father, whether acknowledged by him or not, provided it shall be made to appear to the satisfaction of the court that he was the father of such illegitimate child or children." Disputed estates not receiving redress through civil law may be heard in Church courts.

1862 the federal Morrill Act voids the territorial inheritance law.

1882 the federal Edmunds Act legitimizes all children born of plural marriages prior to 1 January 1883. All children born after this date are declared to be illegitimate.

1887 the federal Edmunds-Tucker Act states "no illegitimate child shall hereafter be entitled to inherit from his or her father or to receive any distributive share in the estate of his or her father."

1895 a married woman may devise a will regarding her separate property, which is her separate estate. Her separate earnings are her own property.

1896 children from polygamous marriages are declared legitimate by the state constitution. A married woman's separate estate is free from the debts of her husband.

SUFFRAGE

1870 women in the Utah Territory receive complete suffrage.

1887 the Edmunds-Tucker Act of U.S. Congress abolishes female suffrage.

1894/6 women in the state of Utah receive complete suffrage.

CITIZENSHIP

1848 all residents of Utah who are not already U.S. citizens become citizens, except for Native Americans, whose tribes are considered a separate nation until 1924.

CENSUS INFORMATION

The first federal census for Utah was in 1850. For an index (heads of households only) to the 1850, 1860, and 1870 federal censuses, see Kearl, J.R. *Index to the 1850, 1860, and 1870 Censuses of Utah* (Baltimore: Genealogical Publishing Co., 1981, fiche 6051336).

1856 territorial census (film 0505913), at the Historical Department of the LDS Church in Salt Lake City.

OTHER

1895 the state constitution outlaws the labor of women and children in mines.

BIBLIOGRAPHY

Arrington, Leonard J. and Susan Arrington Madsen. *Sunbonnet Sisters: True Stories of Mormon Women and Frontier Life* (Salt Lake City: Bookcraft Press, 1981).

Bartholomew, Rebecca and Ralph Bartholomew. *Audacious Women: Early British Mormon Immigrants* (Salt Lake City: Signature Books, 1995).

Beecher, Maureen U. "Under the Sunbonnets: Mormon Women with Faces." *Brigham Young University Studies* 16 4 (1976): 471–84.

Brown, Edwin F. and Richard C. Mangrum. *Zion in the Courts: A Legal History of the Church of Jesus Christ of Latter-day Saints, 1830–1900* (Urbana: University of Illinois Press, 1988).

Burgess-Olson, Vicky. *Sister Saints* (Salt Lake City: The Author, 1978).

Bushmam, Claudia. *Mormon Sisters: Women in Early Utah* (1976. Reprint. Salt Lake City: Utah State University Press, 1997, film 1059488).

Campbell, Eugene E. *Establishing Zion: The Mormon Church in the American West, 1847–1869* (Salt Lake City: Signature Books, 1988).

Campbell, Eugene E. and Bruce L. Campbell. "Divorce Among Mormon Polygamists: Extent and Explanations." *Utah Historical Society Quarterly* 46 1 (1978): 4–23.

Chambers, Antonette. *Manuscripts Collection Guide to Western Women* (Salt Lake City: University of Utah Libraries, 1984). Pertains mostly to the women of Utah.

Coleman, Ronald G. "Blacks in Utah History: An Unhuman Legacy," in Papanikolas, Helen, *People of Utah* (Salt Lake City: Utah State Historical Society, 1976). Slavery was legal in Utah until 1862.

Covington, Kae. *Gathered in Time: Utah Quilts and Their Makers, Settlement to 1950* (Salt Lake City: University of Utah Press, 1997).

Cross, Mary Bywater. *Quilts & Women of the Mormon Migrations* (Nashville: Rutledge Hill Press, 1996). Contains migration tables of pioneer companies that crossed the oceans and the plains.

DeLafosse, Peter H. *Trailing the Pioneers, A Guide to Utah's Emigrant Trails, 1829–1869* (Logan: Utah State University Press, 1994).

Embrey, Jessie L. "Divorce and Inheritance in Plural Families," in *Mormon Polygamous Families: Life in the Principle* (Salt Lake City: University of Utah Press, 1987).

Foster, Lawrence. "Polygamy and the Frontier: Mormon Women in Early Utah." *Utah Historical Quarterly* 50 (Summer 1982): 268–89.

Fox, Sandi. *Quilts in Utah: A Reflection of the Western Experience* (Salt Lake City: Salt Lake City Art Center, 1981).

Gates, Susan Young. *History of the Young Ladies' Mutual Improvement Association of The Church of Jesus Christ of Latter-day Saints: From November 1869 to June 1910* (Salt Lake City: The Deseret News, 1911, film 0928257).

Godfrey, Kenneth W., Audrey M. Godfrey, and Jill M. Derr. *Women's Voices: An Untold History of the Latter-day Saints, 1830–1900* (Salt Lake City: Deseret Book Co., 1982).

Jaussi, Laureen Richardson. *Genealogical Records of Utah* (Salt Lake City: Deseret Book Co., 1974).

Larson, Gustive O. "An Industrial Home for Polygamous Wives." *Utah Historical Quarterly* 38 3 (Summer 1970).

Linford, Orma. "The Mormons, the Law, and the Territory of Utah." *American Journal of Legal History* 23 (1979): 213–35.

Magnum, R. Collin. "Furthering the Cause of Zion: An Overview of the Mormon Ecclesiastical Court System in Early Utah." *Journal of Mormon History* 10 (1973): 79–90.

Murphy, Miriam B. "If Only I Shall Have the Right Stuff: Utah Women in World War I." *Utah Historical Quarterly* 58 (Fall 1990): 334–50.

Noall, Claire. *Guardians of the Hearth: Utah's Pioneer Midwives and Doctors* (Bountiful, UT: Horizon Publishers, 1974).

Thatcher, Linda. *Guide to the Women's History Holdings at the Utah State Historical Society Library* (Salt Lake City: The Library, 1985).

University of Utah Libraries. *Marriott Library Special Collections: Women in Utah, Mormon, and Western History* (Salt Lake City: The Libraries, 1975).

SELECTED RESOURCES FOR WOMEN'S HISTORY

Brigham Young University
Women's Research Institute
945 SWKT
Provo, UT 84602

Family History Library of the Church of Jesus
Christ of Latter-day Saints
35 North West Temple
Salt Lake City, UT 84150

Utah State Archives and Record Services
Archives Building
State Capitol
Salt Lake City, UT 84114

Marriott Library
University of Utah
Salt Lake City, UT 84112

Merrill Library Special Collections
Utah State University
College Hill
Logan, UT 84321

Utah State Historical Society
300 Rio Grande
Salt Lake City, UT 84101

Women in uniform, Barber's Point Naval Air Station, Oahu, Hawaii, 1943, by Peter Mason (Courtesy of Peter Mason, cousin of the Author)

VERMONT

IMPORTANT DATES IN STATE HISTORY

1724 First white settlement in Vermont made by Massachusetts at Fort Dummer (Brattleboro).
1764 New York claims Vermont as part of Albany County: Green Mountain Boys formed by Connecticut and Massachusetts settlers to protect the existing land grants.
1772 Scottish colonists found Ryegate and Barnet.
1775 Green Mountain Boys capture Fort Ticonderoga.
1777 Vermont Declaration of Independence; becomes an independent republic.
1786 Vermont constitution drafted.
1791 Statehood.
1793 State constitution drafted.

MARRIAGE AND DIVORCE

1779 first divorce law is enacted.
1798 a divorce may be granted on the grounds of impotence, adultery, intolerable cruelty, or three years' willful desertion or absence with presumption of death.
1902 marriage certificates must be recorded by the town clerk.
1906 town paupers are not allowed to marry without consent of the selectman or overseer of the poor.

Where to Find Marriage and Divorce Records

Marriages have been recorded in the earliest town records since about 1760. State registration began in 1896. The town records have been filmed and are available through the FHL and at the Vermont Pubic Records Division in Montpelier. There is a series of indexes at the Division:

- Statewide index vital records, 1760–1870 (film 0027455 ff.).
- Statewide index to vital records, 1871–1908 (film 0540051 ff.).
- Statewide index to vital records, 1909–41 (not at the FHL).
- Statewide index to vital records, 1942–52 (film 1953789 ff.).

Divorces have been granted by the district courts of probate since 1760. State filing began in 1860. Divorce cases are also at the Vermont Public Records Division, except for the last ten years, which are at the Department of Health in Montpelier. Most of the district probate courts have been filmed, such as:

- Bennington District Probate Court records, 1778–1851 (film 0027955 ff.), at the Bennington Probate Court in Bennington, and on film at the Vermont Public Records Division.
- Rutland District Probate Court records, 1784–1850 (film 0028782 ff.), at the Rutland Probate Court in Rutland, and on film at the Vermont Public Records Division.

See also compiled publications, such as:

- Jackson, Mary S. and Edward F. Jackson. *Marriage Notices from Washington County, New York, Newspapers, 1799–1880* (Bowie, MD: Heritage Books, 1995). Contains marriage notices from Washington County, New York newspapers from 1799 to 1880 for all the surrounding counties and the state of Vermont.

PROPERTY AND INHERITANCE

1821 a widow is given access to her husband's personal estate.
1846 a married woman is granted powers of *feme sole* regarding her separate property.
1847 a wife's property is exempted from the debts and liabilities of her husband and prohibits his conveyance, unless she is joint with him on the deed.

1866 a married woman's separate earnings are her separate property.
1867 a married woman's separate property is said to be her separate estate.
1881 "all personal property acquired during coverture shall be her [a married woman's] sole and separate estate."

SUFFRAGE

1920 Vermont women receive complete suffrage by passage of the 19th Amendment to the Constitution.

CITIZENSHIP

Within the jurisdiction of the original Thirteen Colonies.

CENSUS INFORMATION

The federal census of 1790 was taken in Vermont in 1791, after Vermont became the fourteenth state. There are no state censuses for Vermont. Gloucester and Cumberland counties are enumerated in the 1771 New York census. See Holbrook, Jay Mack. *Vermont 1771 Census* (1983. Reprint. Baltimore: Clearfield Co., 1997).

OTHER

1860 the *Vermont Quarterly Gazetteer* is published by a Ludlow woman, and she is criticized for her effort being "unsuitable for a woman." See Hemenway, Abby Maria. *The Vermont Historical Gazetteer: A Magazine Embracing A History of Each Town, Civil, Ecclesiastical, Biographical, and Military*. 6 Vols. in 9 (Burlington: The Author, 1868–1923, film 0873674 ff.).

Rollins, Alden M. *Vermont Warnings Out*. 2 Vols. (Camden, ME: Picton Press, 1995). Includes names of women warned out of Vermont towns; often gives marital status.

BIBLIOGRAPHY

Blackwell, Marilyn. "Women in Vermont: A Bibliography." *Vermont History* 56 (1988): 84–101.

Carter, Christie. "Sources of Women's History at the Vermont State Archives." *Vermont History* 59 (1991): 30–48.

Cleveland, Richard L and Donna Bister. *Plain and Fancy: Vermont's People and Their Quilts as a Reflection of America* (San Francisco: Quilt Digest, 1991).

Eichholz, Alice. *Collecting Vermont Ancestors* (Montpelier: New Trails, 1986).

McGovern, Constance M. "Women's History: The State of the Art." *Vermont History* 56 (1988): 69–83.

Morrissey, Charles T. "Green Mountain Girls." *Vermont Life* (Summer 1973).

Oliver, Cecilia Y. *Enduring Grace: Quilts from the Shelburne Museum Collection* (Lafayette, CA: C & T Publishing, 1997).

Pepe, Faith L. "Toward a History of Women in Vermont: An Essay and Bibliography." *Vermont History* 45 (Spring 1977): 69–101.

Sharrow, Greg. *From Before My Grandmother: Artists from the Vermont Traditional Arts* (Montpelier: Vermont Historical Society, 1997).

Smith, Jean K. *Those Intriguing, Indomitable Vermont Women* (Montpelier: Vermont State Division of the American Association of University Women, 1980).

Vermont State Archives. *A Guide to Vermont's Repositories*. Rev. ed. (Montpelier: The Archives, 1987).

Vermont General Assembly. *Laws of Vermont [1777–1799]*. 6 Vols. (Montpelier: Secretary of State, 1964–68).

Zonderman, David. "From Mill Village Industrial City: Letters for Vermont Factory Operatives." *Labor History* 27 (Spring 1986): 265–85.

SELECTED RESOURCES FOR WOMEN'S HISTORY

Bailey/Howe Memorial Library
University of Vermont
Burlington, VT 05405

Shelburne Museum
Shelburne Road
Shelburne, VT 05482

Vermont Public Records Division
Reference Research
Drawer 33
Montpelier, VT 05633-7601

Vermont Historical Society
109 State Street
Montpelier, VT 05609-0901

Women's Studies Program
Middlebury College
Munroe Hall
Middlebury, VT 05753

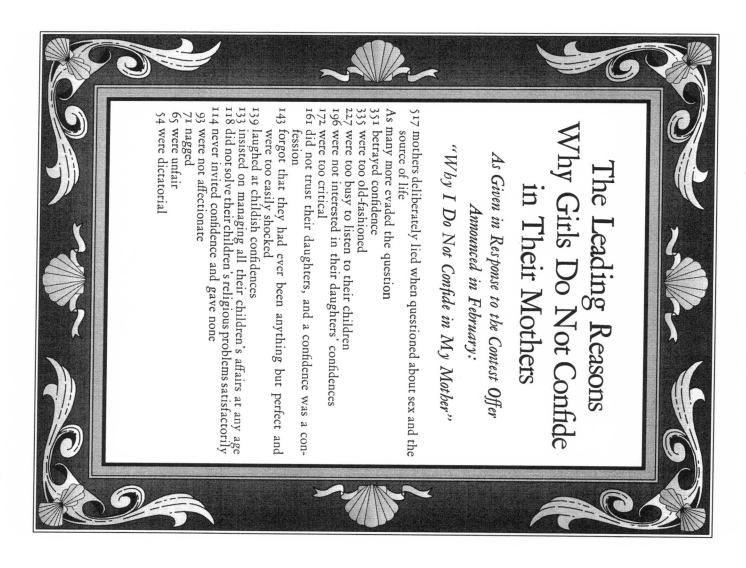

The Leading Reasons Why Girls Do Not Confide in Their Mothers

As Given in Response to the Contest Offer Announced in February:

"Why I Do Not Confide in My Mother"

517 mothers deliberately lied when questioned about sex and the source of life
As many more evaded the question
351 betrayed confidence
335 were too old-fashioned
227 were too busy to listen to their children
196 were not interested in their daughters' confidences
172 were too critical
161 did not trust their daughters, and a confidence was a confession
143 forgot that they had ever been anything but perfect and were too easily shocked
139 laughed at childish confidences
133 insisted on managing all their children's affairs at any age
118 did not solve their children's religious problems satisfactorily
114 never invited confidence and gave none
93 were not affectionate
71 nagged
65 were unfair
54 were dictatorial

Woman's Home Companion, July, 1926

VIRGINIA

IMPORTANT DATES IN STATE HISTORY

1607 First English settlers found Jamestown.
1624 Virginia Company dissolved; Virginia becomes a Royal Colony.
1634 Eight shires established.
1643 The eight shires become counties.
1676–7 Bacon's Rebellion.
1700 French Huguenots immigrate to Virginia.
1714 German colonists establish the Germanna Colony on the Rappahanock River.
1725 German colonists found a settlement in the Valley of Virginia.
1730s The Shenandoah Valley settlement is begun by Ulster Scots and Germans.
1770s The Wilderness Road opens settlement in Kentucky.
1776 State constitution drafted, including the Virginia Declaration of Rights.
1781 Battle of Yorktown.
1861 16 April secedes from the Union; Battle of Bull Run (Manassas).
1862 Battle of Shiloh; Second Battle of Bull Run; Battle of Harper's Ferry; Battle of Fredericksburg
1863 Battle of Chancellorsville.
1864 Battle of the Wilderness; Battle of Spotsylvania; Battle of Cold Harbor; Battle (and siege) of Petersburg; Battle of Cedar Creek.
1865 Confederate forces surrender at Appomattox Courthouse.
1870 15 January readmitted to the Union.

MARRIAGE AND DIVORCE

1624 ministers shall make returns of births, marriages, and deaths in the parish registers.

1631 "no minister shall celebrate matrimony between any person without a license granted by the Governor, except the banns of matrimony have been first published three several Sundays or holy days . . . in the parish churches where the said persons dwell . . . in every parish church within this colony shall be kept by the minister a book wherein shall be written the day and year of every christening, wedding, and burial [vestry records]."

1660 either the posting of banns or the posting of a marriage bond with the clerk of the county court is required by law.

1705 persons living in different parishes must publish banns in both parishes before they are married (reaffirms 1631 law); only a clerk of court in the county of the residence of the bride may issue a marriage license. Interracial marriage is prohibited.

1780 in addition to Anglican ministers, Quaker and Mennonite ministers may solemnize marriages; all marriages must be recorded in the county court order books within three months of the ceremony; Quaker and Mennonite marriages are not recorded in county registers.

1784 all Christian ministers may solemnize marriages.

1803 the first legislative divorce declares that a divorced wife is a *feme sole*.

1825 county courts are required to record marriages.

1827 absolute divorce may be granted without an act from the General Assembly (Ch. 165).

1853 recording of all births, marriages, and deaths in county records is required by law (practiced until 1896).

1912 vital registration resumes.

Where to Find Marriage and Divorce Records

Marriages were first recorded in the parish vestry records in lieu of a civil court and began about 1646. In addition to the county government, the local parishes of the Anglican Church also functioned as part of the civil government, even writing bylaws until 1679. After 1660, marriage bonds were also issued by the county clerks (until 1848). Vital registration in the counties existed from 1853 until 1892, with returns sent to the state, and resumed again in 1912, and the records are kept at the State Health Department in Richmond. Some cities also began registering vital records around the end of the nineteenth century. The earliest divorces were granted by the state legislature between 1803 and 1848. After 1827, the superior courts of chancery could also grant annulments and separations. After 1848, city and county courts with chancery jurisdiction handled divorce cases.

- Marriage registers for Virginia counties, 1853–1935 (film 2056971 ff.), at the Library of Virginia in Richmond. The commissioner of the revenue registered marriages for the county and then turned his books over to the clerk of the county court. The clerk made abstracts to send to the state auditor and preserved the books in his office.

Many county records have been filmed, such as:

- Albemarle County Clerk of the County Court marriage bonds, 1780–1853, 1898–1913 (film 0030271 ff.), marriage registers, 1806–67 (film 0030271), and marriage registers, 1854–1903 (film 0030271), at the Albemarle County Courthouse in Charlottesville. The county court was replaced by the circuit court in 1904.
- Northampton County Clerk marriage registers, 1702–1853 (film 0032735), 1853–1922 (film 0032801), at the Library of Virginia and at the Northampton County Courthouse in Eastville.

There are many published compilations, such as:

- Fisher, Therese. *Vital Records of Three Burned Counties: Births, Marriages, and Deaths of King and Queen, King William, and New Kent Counties, Virginia, 1680–1860* (Bowie, MD: Heritage Books, 1995).
- *Index to Marriage Notices in the Southern Churchman, 1835–1941* (1942. Reprint. Baltimore: Clearfield Co., 1996).
- *Some Marriages in the Burned Record Counties of Virginia* (Richmond: Virginia Genealogical Society, 1972).
- *Virginia Marriage Records: From The Virginia Magazine of History and Biography, the William and Mary College Quarterly, and Tyler's Quarterly* (Baltimore: Genealogical Publishing Co., 1982), also available on CD-ROM.
- Wardell, Patrick G. *Virginia & West Virginia Husbands and Wives*. 2 Vols. (Bowie, MD: Heritage Books, 1994, 1996).
- Wulfeck, Dorothy Ford. *Marriages of Some Virginia Residents, 1607–1800*. 2 Vols. (1961. Reprint. Baltimore: Genealogical Publishing Co., 1986).

PROPERTY AND INHERITANCE

1674 "An Act empowring *feme coverts* to make good acknowledgment of sales of lands," provides that in the conveyance of a joint deed, the wife must be "first privately examined by the court whether she acknowledges the same freely."

1705 in intestacy, a widow receives one-third of her husband's personal estate and one-third of his real estate for life.

1776 entail is abolished and property, real, personal, and in slaves, is to be held in fee simple.

1786 the practice of primogeniture is abolished, and the line of descent is changed to favor male and female children equally.

1792 "when a deed has been acknowledged by a *feme covert*, and no records made of her privy examination, such deed is not binding on the *feme* or her heirs (§ 7)." Also every estate in lands which shall hereafter be granted, conveyed, or devised . . . shall be in fee simple (§ 12)." Also, "every person aged twenty-one and upwards, being of sound mind, and not a married woman, shall have power . . . to devise all the estate, right, title, and interest . . . which he hath . . . at the time of his death (§ 1)." When "any widow shall not be satisfied with the provision made for her by the will of her husband, she may within one year . . . declare that she will not accept the provision . . . and renounce all benefit . . . and thereupon such widow shall be entitled to one-third part of the slaves whereof her husband died possessed, which she shall hold during her life . . . she shall moreover be entitled to such share of his other personal estate, as if he had died intestate, to hold as her as absolute property . . . (§ 25)." The widow of any person dying intestate, or otherwise, "shall be endowed of one full and equal third part of all the lands, tenements, and other real estate . . . to which she shall not have relinquished her right of dower . . . (Ch. 32 § 1)," also, "if any estate be conveyed by deed or will . . . for the jointure of the wife, in lieu of her dower . . . such conveyance shall bar her dower of the residue of the lands . . . but if the said conveyance were before the marriage . . . or if it were made after marriage, in either case, the widow may, at here election, waive such jointure, and demand her dower (Ch. 32 § 11)." A married woman may be "examined privily" by a judge to ascertain if she "willingly signed and sealed the said writing," and "acknowledged also by the husband . . . such commission and certificate, shall not only be sufficient to convey or release any right of dower thereby intended to be conveyed or released, but be as effectual for every other purpose as if she were an unmarried woman (§ 6)."

❧ *In Louisa County, between 1765 and 1812, half of the women who "consented" to land transfers did so seven days after the sale.*

Allan Kulikoff, *Tobacco and Slaves: The Development of Southern Cultures in the Chesapeake, 1680–1800* (Chapel Hill: University of North Carolina Press, 1986), 177.

1875 a wife's property is exempted from being used to settle the debts of her husband.

1877 a wife is "a separate and sole trader with her own estate," having the right to inherit, acquire, own, and dispose of her own property.

1879 a married woman's separate earnings are her separate property, if she is living separately from her husband.

1891 a married woman's separate earnings are her separate property.

1930 women have equal status with men in regard to guardianship of minor children; the property rights of women are expanded.

SUFFRAGE

1699 act stipulates that women are ineligible to vote.

1920 Virginia women receive complete suffrage by passage of the 19th Amendment to the Constitution.

CITIZENSHIP

One of the original Thirteen Colonies.

CENSUS INFORMATION

The 1790, 1800, and part of the 1810 federal censuses are missing.

1782–5 state enumerations were taken of the following counties: Albemarle, Amelia, Amherst, Charlotte, Chesterfield, Cumberland, Essex, Fairfax, Fluvanna, Frederick, Gloucester, Greenbrier, Greensville, Halifax, Hampshire, Hanover, Harrison, Isle of Wight, Lancaster, Mecklenburg, Middlesex, Monongalia, Nansemond, New Kent, Norfolk, Northumberland, Orange, Pittsylvania, Powhatan, Prince Edward, Princess Anne, the City of Richmond, Richmond, Rockingham, Shenandoah, Stafford, Surry, Sussex, Warwick, and the City of Williamsburg.

OTHER

1626 the first witch trial in English America is held in Surry County.

1646 local parishes must bear responsibility for the care of the poor. Originally, the parish vestry dealt with land processioning, care of the poor, apprenticeships and guardianships of orphans, levying of taxes, and other civil matters. About 1785 the counties set up civil agencies to take over many of these functions. Records are similar to those of Fredericksville Parish, Albemarle County, vestry book, 1742–87 (film 0031332), at the Library of Virginia.

1662 every county must maintain a dunking stool to punish gossipy women.

1781–1865 Virginia General Assembly public claims, slaves and free blacks (film 2027937 ff.), at the Library of Virginia, includes information on runaway slaves, slaves transported out of state, execution records, free Negroes willing to go to Liberia, etc.

1803 legislature grants a widow's pension to a woman whose husband is killed "performing his duty (Ch. 5 § 1)."

1807 the General Assembly grants a woman a pension for military service "who, in the Revolutionary War, in the garb, and with the courage of a soldier, performed extraordinary military services, and received a severe wound at the battle of Germantown . . . (Ch. 97 § 1)."

1888, 1900, 1902 acts for Confederate pension applications and card index of Confederate veterans' and widows' pension rolls, 1888–1934 (film 1439763 ff.), at the Library of Virginia. The index is not complete. The card index may be searched online at **<198.17.62.57/collections/CW.html>.**

1915–67 applications for the relief of needy Confederate women (film 2031631 ff.), at the Library of Virginia, are filed by the surname and given name of the woman and include the soldier's or sailor's name, company, and regiment; the physical condition of the applicant, income, means of support, birth date, and place of residence.

1950 women have the right to sit on juries, but not the obligation.

BIBLIOGRAPHY

Billings, Warren M. *The Old Dominion in the Seventeenth Century: A Documentary History of Virginia, 1606–1689* (Chapel Hill: University of North Carolina Press, 1975).

Bowler, Clara Ann. "Carted Whores and White Shrouded Apologies: Slander in the County Court of 17th Century Virginia." *Virginia Magazine of History and Biography* 85 (1977).

Brown, Kathleen M. *Good Wives, Nasty Wenches, and Anxious Patriarchs: Gender, Race, and Power in Colonial Virginia* (Chapel Hill: University of North Carolina Press, 1996).

Burks, Martin, Parks. *Notes on the Property Rights of Married Women in Virginia* (Lynchburg, VA, 1894).

Christian, George L. and Frank W. Christian. "The Virginia Married Women's Act." *Virginia Law Journal* I (1984): 63–75.

Virginia

Eure, John D. A *Guide to Legal Research in Virginia* (Richmond: Virginia Law Foundation, 1989).

First Flowerings: Early Virginia Quilts (Washington, DC: DAR Museum, 1987).

Gunderson, Joan R. and Gwen Victor Gampel. "Married Women's Legal Status in Eighteenth-Century New York and Virginia." *William and Mary College Quarterly* 38 (1982): 114–43.

Hamlin, Charles Hughes. *Virginia Ancestors and Adventurers*. 3 Vols. in 1 (1967. Reprint. Baltimore: Genealogical Publishing Co., 1975).

Hening, William Waller. *The Statutes at Large, Being a Collection of All the Laws of Virginia from the First Session of the Legislature in the Year 1619: Published Pursuant to an Act of the General Assembly of Virginia... [1619–1792]*. 13 Vols. (1819–23, film 0162029 ff.). For a name index to this and the three-volume supplement by Shepherd, see Casey, Joseph J. *Personal Names in Hening's Statutes at Large of Virginia, and Shepherd's Continuation* (1896. Reprint. Baltimore: Clearfield Co., 1994, fiche 6051115). Some of the original legislative petitions are on film, 1776–1833 (film 2048565 ff.), at the Library of Virginia. Legislative petitions were used as a way to remedy grievances of actions ranging from civil and religious matters, taxes, etc. brought before the General Assembly of Virginia. Kentucky was part of Virginia until 1792. West Virginia was part of Virginia until 1863.

Jones, Katherine. *Ladies of Richmond, the Confederate Capital* (Indianapolis: Bobbs-Merill, 1961).

Lebsock, Suzanne. *The Free Women of Petersburg: Status and Culture in a Southern Town, 1784–1860* (New York: W.W. Norton & Co., 1984).

—. *Virginia Women, 1660–1945: A Share of Honour* (Richmond: Virginia State Library, 1987).

Lewis, Jan. *The Pursuit of Happiness: Family Values in Jefferson's Virginia* (London: Cambridge University Press, 1983).

Lumpkin, William L. "The Role of Women in Eighteenth-Century Virginia Baptist Life." *Baptist Historical Heritage* 8 (1973): 158–67.

McIlwaine, H.R. *Minutes of the Council and General Court of Colonial Virginia [1622–1632, 1670–1676]*. 2nd ed. (Richmond: Virginia State Library, 1979).

Morgan, Edward S. *Virginians at Home: Family Life in the Eighteenth Century* (Williamsburg: Colonial Williamsburg Foundation, 1952).

Ransone, David R. "Wives for Virginia, 1621." *William and Mary College Quarterly* 48 (January 1991): 3–18.

Ray, Suzanne Smith. A *Preliminary Guide to Pre-1904 County Records in the Archives Branch, Virginia State Library and Archives* (Richmond: The Library and Archives, 1988).

Scott, Anne Firor and Suzanne Lebsock. *Virginia Women: The First Two Hundred Years* (Williamsburg: The Colonial Williamsburg Foundation, 1988).

Terry, Gail S. *Documenting Women's Lives: A User's Guide to Manuscripts at the Virginia Historical Society* (Richmond: The Society, 1996).

Treadway, Sandra G. "New Directions in Virginia Women's History." *Virginia Magazine of History and Biography* 100 (1992): 5–28.

Vogt, John and T. William Kethley, Jr. *Marriage Records in the Virginia State Library: A Researcher's Guide.* 2nd ed. (Athens, GA: Iberian Publishing Co., 1988).

—— . *Will and Estate Records in the Virginia State Library: A Researcher's Guide* (Athens, GA: Iberian Publishing Co., 1987).

Walmsley, James S. *Idols, Victims, and Pioneers: Virginia's Women from 1607* (Richmond: Virginia Chamber of Commerce, 1976).

SELECTED RESOURCES FOR WOMEN'S HISTORY

The Colonial Williamsburg Foundation
415 North Boundary Street
PO Box 1776
Williamsburg, VA 23187-1776

Fishburn Library
Hollins College
Hollins, VA 24020

Institute of Early American History and Culture
Earl Gregg Swem Library
College of William and Mary
PO Box 8781
Williamsburg, VA 23187-8781

Judy Mann DiStefano Women's History Collection
Annandale Campus Library
Northern Virginia Community College
8333 Little River Turnpike
Annandale, VA 22003

Ladies' Association of the Union Archives
Mount Vernon
Mount Vernon, VA 22121

Library of Virginia
11th Street at Capitol Square
Richmond, VA 23219-3491

Manuscripts Department
Alderman Library
University of Virginia
Charlottesville, VA 22901

United Daughters of the Confederacy
328 North Boulevard
Richmond, VA 23220-4057

Virginia Historical Society
428 North Boulevard
PO Box 7311
Richmond, VA 23211-0311

War Memorial Museum of Virginia
9285 Warwick Boulevard
Huntington Park
Newport News, VA 23607

Manuscript Sources for Women's History Research in the Special Collections Department of the Virginia Tech Libraries, available online at **<scholar2. lib.vt edu/spec/women/wmnunidx.htm>**

United Daughters of the Confederacy, available online at **<www.hsv.tis.net/~maxs/UDC/>**

WASHINGTON

IMPORTANT DATES IN STATE HISTORY

1818 Area occupied jointly by treaty by the U.S. and Great Britain.
1843 Laws of the Oregon Territory (not yet officially organized) adopted.
1846 Boundary between the U.S. and British North America established at the 49th Parallel.
1848 Part of the Oregon Territory.
1850 Port Townsend settled.
1851 Seattle founded.
1853 Created as a separate territory.
1855 Yakima War.
1856 Territorial Legislature repeals Oregon laws.
1872 Spokane founded.
1889 Statehood.

MARRIAGE AND DIVORCE

1854 dower is recognized.
1860 curtesy is recognized.
1864 dower and curtesy are recognized.
1869 the community property system of marital law is adopted.
1874 in divorce cases, a court may divide community and separate property "as shall appear just and equitable (§ 26.08.110)."
1881 premarital agreements are allowed. County auditors are required to issue and record marriage licenses. Marriage returns must be made to the judge of the probate court.

Where to Find Marriage and Divorce Records

Some records prior to 1853 are in the Oregon Provisional and Territorial Government records at the Oregon State Archives in Salem (see Oregon). Marriages were first recorded by county clerks in 1853. Records until 1968 are in the custody of the county auditor where the marriage took place. The two exceptions are the cities of Seattle and Tacoma. Seattle marriages, 1885 to the present, are at the Marriage License Bureau in Seattle. Tacoma marriages, 1860 to the present, are at the City-County Building in Tacoma. A few county records have been filmed by the FHL, such as:

- Columbia County marriage licenses, 1876–91 (film 0372500).

See also indexes and compiled publications, such as:

- Clark County marriages index and card file, 1862–1913 (film 1026366).
- Gage, Bertha S., Lewis County Clerk. *Lewis County, Washington Territorial Marriages, 1847–1889* (Chehalis, WA: Genealogical Committee of Lewis County Historical Society, 1978, film 1321477).
- *Index to Snohomish County, Washington Marriages [1867–1899]* (Edmonds, WA: Sno-Isle Genealogical Society, 1992, fiche 6125323)

There are also marriages and divorces recorded in the Bureau of Indian Affairs records, such as:

- Colville Agency vital statistics, births, marriages, divorces, and deaths, 1909–43 (film 1020973 ff.), at the NARA Pacific Alaska Region in Seattle.

The first divorces were recorded in the territorial district courts and are in the Washington Territory records at the Washington State Library in Olympia. The case files are mixed in with the other records of the court. There are two finding aids to help in the search:

- Washington Division of Archives and Record Management. *Frontier Justice: Abstracts and Indexes to the Records of the Territorial District Courts, 1853–1889* (Olympia: The Secretary of State, 1987).
- Frontier Justice Records Project. *Frontier Justice: Guide to the Court Records of Washington Territory, 1853–1889*. 2 Vols. (Olympia: National Historical Publications and Records Commission, 1987, film 1490089 ff.). Includes alphabetical name index to the case files, and abstract providing a brief summary of each case.

Divorces since 1889 have been under the jurisdiction of the county superior courts. Some records have been filmed, such as:

- Thurston County Superior Court divorce case files, 1889–1952 (film 1991582 ff.), at the Thurston County Courthouse in Olympia.

PROPERTY AND INHERITANCE

1869 first community property law (based on California law), referred to as "property held in common with the husband." A wife must file notice of her title to separate property.

1871 marital partnerships define common property and "partnership property" as being all property acquired during marriage, by either spouse, jointly or individually.

1873 the marital partnership act is repealed; an act is adopted which follows the 1869 act.

1879 amendment to the community property act provides that "the husband and wife are considered as constituting together a compound creation of the statute, called a community."

1889 a widow has access to her husband's personal estate; she may also devise her half of the community property.

1922 a married woman has the power to contract without restriction, except in the conveyance of real estate held as community property, where her husband must join in the deed.

SUFFRAGE

1910 Washington women receive complete suffrage.

CITIZENSHIP

1846 when Great Britain cedes its claims to the Oregon Territory, all residents who are not already citizens of the U.S. become citizens by treaty, except for Native Americans, whose tribes are considered a separate nation until 1924.

CENSUS INFORMATION

For pre-territorial federal censuses, see the Oregon Territory (1850).

1857–92 territorial and state censuses (film 1841781 ff.), at the Washington State Archives.

OTHER

1926 Seattle is the first large U.S. city to elect a woman mayor.

BIBLIOGRAPHY

Abbott, Newton Carl and Fred E. Carver. *The Evolution of Washington Counties* (Yakima: Yakima Valley Genealogical Society and Klickitat County Historical Society, 1978, fiche 6051194).

Andrews, Mildred T. *Woman's Place: A Guide to Seattle and King County History* (Seattle: Gemil Press, 1994).

—. *Washington Women as Pathbreakers* (Dubuque, IA: Kendall/Hunt Publishing, 1989).

Blair, Karen J. *Northwest Women: An Annotated Bibliography of Sources on the History of Oregon and Washington Women, 1787–1970* (Pullman: Washington State University Press, 1997).

Carlson, Laurie M. *On Sidesaddles to Heaven: The Women on the Rocky Mountain Mission* (Caldwell, ID: Caxton Printers, 1998).

Mumford, Esther Hale. *Seattle's Black Victorians, 1852–1901* (Seattle: Anase Press, 1980).

Petersen, Keith C. and Mary E Reed. *Discovering Washington: A Guide to State and Local History* (Pullman: Washington State University Press, 1989).

Told by the Pioneers: Tales of Frontier Life and Tales Told by Those Who Remember the Days of the Territory and Early Statehood of Washington (Olympia: Works Progress Administration, 1937–8).

Twelker, Nancyann J. *Women and Their Quilts: A Washington State Centennial Tribute* (Bothell, WA: That Patchwork Place, 1988).

SELECTED RESOURCES FOR WOMEN'S HISTORY

Coalition for Western Women's History
Washington State University
History Department
Pullman, WA 99164

Island County Historical Society
903 Alexander Street, Box 115
Coupeville, WA 98239

Seattle Public Library
1000 Fourth Avenue
Seattle, WA 98104

Washington State Archives
1120 Washington Street SE
Olympia, WA 98504-0238
(there are branches of the State Archives in Bellingham, Cheney, Ellensburg, and Seattle)

Washington State Historical Society Library
315 North Stadium Way
Tacoma, WA 98507-1422

Washington State Library
Washington Northeast Collection
PO Box 42460
Olympia, WA 98504-2460

Washington State University
Women's Resource and Research Center
Pullman, WA 99164-7204

APPLICATION TO TAKE OATH OF ALLEGIANCE TO THE UNITED STATES UNDER THE ACT OF JUNE 25, 1936, AS AMENDED, AND FORM OF SUCH OATH

To the Honorable, the Circuit Court of Sheboygan County, Wisconsin

This application, hereby made and filed, respectfully shows:

(1) My full, true, and correct name is Gertrude Sundell (My maiden name was Gertrude Newquist)
(Full, true name, without abbreviation, and any other name which has been used, must appear here)

(2) My present place of residence is 819 Georgia Avenue (Number and street) Sheboygan (City or town) Sheboygan (County) Wisconsin (State)

(3) My occupation is Housekeeper

(4) I am 49 years old. (5) I was born on March (Month) 11, (Day) 1892 (Year) in Stevens Point (City or town) Portage County Wisconsin (County, district, province, or state) U. S. A. (Country)

(6) My personal description is as follows: Sex Female; color White, complexion Fair, color of eyes Blue, color of hair Br-Gr., height 5 feet 1 inches, weight 124 pounds; visible distinctive marks None

(7) I am a widow; the name of my husband was Joseph Wilfred (Johnson) Sundell; we were married on June (Month) 10, (Day) 1915 (Year) at Eau Claire, Wisconsin (City or town) (State) (Country); he was born at (City or town) (County, district, province, or state) Sweden (Country) on August (Month) 16, (Day) 1892 (Year); and now resides at Deceased November 13, 1929 (Number and street) (City or town) (State) (Country)

(8) I lost, or believe that I lost, United States citizenship solely by reason of my marriage on June (Month) 10, (Day) 1915 (Year) to Joseph (Johnson) Sundell then an alien, a citizen or subject of Sweden, and my marital status with such person was terminated on November (Month) 13 (Day) 1929 (Year) by death (State by what means marital status terminated)

(9) I have resided continuously in the United States since the date of my marriage shown in paragraph 8 hereof, to wit, since birth (Month) (Day) (Year)

(10) I hereby apply to take the oath of renunciation and allegiance as prescribed in Section 335 (b) of the Nationality Act of 1940 (54 Stat. 1157) to become repatriated and obtain the rights of a citizen of the United States.

Subscribed and sworn to before me by the above-named applicant, in the office of the clerk of said court at Sheboygan Wisconsin this 4th day of August, Anno Domini 1941.

Gertrude Sundell

E. A. HICKEY, Clerk.
By *Raymond [illegible]*, Deputy Clerk.

STATE OF WISCONSIN
SHEBOYGAN COUNTY } ss:

In the Circuit Court of Sheboygan County, Wisconsin.

Upon consideration of the foregoing, it is hereby Ordered and Decreed that the above application be granted; that the applicant named therein be repatriated as a citizen of the United States, upon taking the oath of renunciation and allegiance to the United States; and that the clerk of this court enter these proceedings of record.

By the Court: *Henry A. Detling*, Judge.

OATH OF RENUNCIATION AND ALLEGIANCE

I hereby declare, on oath, that I absolutely and entirely renounce and abjure all allegiance and fidelity to any foreign prince, potentate, state or sovereignty of whom or which I have heretofore been a subject or citizen; that I will support and defend the Constitution and laws of the United States of America against all enemies, foreign and domestic; that I will bear true faith and allegiance to the same; and that I take this obligation freely without any mental reservation or purpose of evasion: SO HELP ME GOD. In acknowledgment whereof I have hereunto affixed my signature.

Gertrude Sundell
(Full, true, and correct signature of applicant, without abbreviation)

oath was administered to the petitioner in open court this 4th day of August, 1941.

E. A. HICKEY, Clerk.
By *Raymond [illegible]*

Repatriation of citizenship of Gertrude Newquist Sundell, Sheboygan County, Wisconsin Circuit Court, 4 August 1942 (State Historical Society of Wisconsin, film 2020596)

WEST VIRGINIA

IMPORTANT DATES IN STATE HISTORY

1735 First settlers arrive in the Berkeley County area.
1738 Frederick and Augusta counties created.
1782 Battle of Fort Henry.
1859 John Brown seizes Harper's Ferry Arsenal.
1861 Battle of Philippi.
1863 Secedes from the state of Virginia and gains independent statehood.

MARRIAGE AND DIVORCE

1867 grounds for absolute divorce are established (Ch. 207 §15).

1868 dower and curtesy are recognized (Ch. 65 § 1).

1882 the clerk of the county court in the bride's jurisdiction is required to issue a marriage license. Marriage returns must be filed with the clerk of the county court.

1931 curtesy is abolished.

Where to Find Marriage and Divorce Records

County clerks began recording marriages about 1754. Divorces have been granted by the county circuit courts since the creation of the county. A list of county records available on microfilm at the West Virginia State Archives in Charleston is available online at **<www.wvlc.wvnet.edu/history/bluenote. html>**. Many county records have been filmed, such as:

- Barbour County Clerk of the County Court marriage registers and license records, 1840–1969 (film 0808381 ff.), index, 1848–1969 (film 0808380), at the Barbour County Courthouse in Philippi.
- Barbour County Clerk of the Circuit Court chancery orders, 1843–1927 (film 1630467 ff.), and county and circuit clerks' orders, 1843–50 (film 0808883), at the Barbour County Courthouse. Divorce records may be included but are not indexed separately.

Pre-statehood records can be found in Virginia, such as a collection of vital statistics of West Virginia, 1853–60, by county (film 0034484 ff.), at the Library of Virginia in Richmond. See also published compilations on Virginia and West Virginia, such as:

- Scott, Carol A. *Marriage and Death Notices of Wheeling, West Virginia and the Tri-State Area [1818–1870]*. 3 Vols. (Apollo, PA: Closson Press, 1987).
- Wardell, Patrick. *Virginia and West Virginia Husbands and Wives*. 2 Vols. (Bowie, MD: Heritage Books, 1994, 1996).

PROPERTY AND INHERITANCE

1863 laws may be passed "as may be necessary to protect the property of married women from the debts, liabilities, and control of their husbands (Art. 6 § 49)."

1868 property conveyed to a married woman is "her sole and separate property, free from the debts of her husband, as if she were unmarried, and she can devise such property as if she were unmarried;" however, she may not convey her real estate without her husband joining "in the deed or other writing by which the same is sold or conveyed (Ch. 66 §1-3)." A married woman may "in her own name, carry on a trade or business" only if she is living separately from her husband.

1875 a wife must be "examined privily and apart from her husband" when conveying her real estate, the deed being signed by both the husband and the wife (Ch. 67 § 4).

1891 a married woman's wages are protected from "the control or disposal of her husband (Ch. 109 §

14)." A married woman may also convey her separate property, but her husband's signature is still required on the deed (Ch. 23 § 4).

1893 a married woman may not engage in business unless she is living apart from her husband (Ch. 13 § 14).

1931 a husband's consent to convey property is abolished, making "the wife on an equality with her husband in the ownership, control, and disposition of her own property (48-3-2)." It also provides a married woman with the right to sue as a single woman (48-3-19).

SUFFRAGE

1920 West Virginia women receive complete suffrage by passage of the 19th Amendment to the Constitution.

CITIZENSHIP

Within the jurisdiction of the original Thirteen Colonies.

CENSUS INFORMATION

For federal censuses prior to 1870, see Virginia. There are no state censuses for West Virginia.

OTHER

1871 a state board of charities is established. County courts kept separate records of welfare cases. Some of them have been filmed, such as Barbour County Court poor orders, 1881–1918 (film 1630845), at the Barbour County Courthouse in Philippi.

BIBLIOGRAPHY

Eagan, Shirley C. "Women's Work, Never Done: West Virginia Farm Women, 1880s–1920s." *West Virginia History* 49 (1990): 21–36.

Farr, Sidney S. *Appalachian Women: An Annotated Bibliography* (Lexington: University Press of Kentucky, 1981).

Forbes, Harold M. *West Virginia History: A Bibliography and Guide to Research* (Morgantown: West Virginia University Press, 1981).

Giesen, Carol A.B. *Coal Miner's Wives: Portraits of Endurance* (Lexington: University Press of Kentucky, 1995).

Greene, Janet W. "Strategy for Survival: Women's Work in the Southern Coal Camps." *West Virginia History* 49 (1990): 37–54.

Hensley, Frances S. *Missing Chapters II: West Virginia Women in History* (Charleston: West Virginia Women's Commission, 1986).

Johnston, Ross B. *West Virginia Estate Settlements: An Index to Wills, Inventories, Appraisements, Land Grants, and Surveys to 1850* (Baltimore: Genealogical Publishing Co., 1977).

McFarland, Kenneth T.H. *Early West Virginia Wills* (Apollo, PA: Closson Press, 1993).

McGinnis, Carol. *West Virginia Genealogy, Sources & Resources* (Baltimore: Genealogical Publishing Co, 1988).

Melosh, Barbara. "Recovery and Revision: Women's History and West Virginia." *West Virginia History* 49 (1990): 3-6.

Missing Chapters: West Virginia Women in History (Charleston: West Virginia Women's Commission, 1983).

Moore, Marat. *Women in the Mines: Stories of Life and Work* (New York: Twayne, 1996).

Pudup, Mary Beth. "Women's Work in the West Virginia Economy." *West Virginia History* 49 (1990): 7-20.

Siers, Jane J. *Traditions and Transitions: West Virginia Women in History* (Charleston: West Virginia Women's Commission, 1990).

Spindel, Donna J. "Women's Legal Rights in West Virginia, 1863-1984." *West Virginia History* 51 (1992): 29-54.

Vossler, Kathryn Babb. "Women and Education in West Virginia, 1810-1909." *West Virginia History* 36 4 (July 1975).

The West Virginia Heritage Encyclopedia. Vol. 25. *West Virginia Women* (Richwood, WV: Jim Comstock, 1974, fiche 6051350).

Worthy, Adrienne C. *West Virginia Women: In Perspective, 1870-1985* (Charleston: West Virginia Women's Commission, 1986).

SELECTED RESOURCES FOR WOMEN'S HISTORY

West Virginia Historical Society
West Virginia Division of Culture and History
Archives and History Section
The Cultural Center
Capitol Complex
1900 Kanawha Boulevard East
Charleston, WV 25305-0300

Women's History Museum
Box 209
108 Walnut Street
West Liberty, WV 26074

Women's Studies Program
West Virginia University
200 Clark Hall
Morgantown, WV 26506

History of Women in West Virginia, available online at **<www.wvlc.wvnet.edu/history/womhome.html>**

Women's Legal Rights in West Virginia, 1863-1984 (an article by Donna Spindel in Vol. 51 of *West Virginia History*), available online at **<www.wvlc.wvnet.edu/history/journal_wvh/wvh51-3.html>**

People's Home Journal, 1924

WISCONSIN

IMPORTANT DATES IN STATE HISTORY

1634 Sparsely settled by French fur traders and missionaries.
1760 Occupied by British colonial forces.
1763 Ceded by France to Great Britain.
1774 Part of Quebec.
1783 Ceded by Great Britain to the U.S.
1787 Part of the Northwest Territory.
1800 Part of the Indiana Territory.
1809 Part of the Illinois Territory.
1818 Part of the Michigan Territory.
1836 Created as a separate territory.
1848 Statehood; constitution is based on the common laws of New York, Ohio, and Massachusetts.

MARRIAGE AND DIVORCE

1823 Milwaukee County begins recording marriages.
1878 county registrars of deeds are required to keep marriage returns.
1887 the person solemnizing a marriage has thirty days to file a certificate with the city or county register of deeds.
1899 marriage licenses are required by law.

Where to Find Marriage and Divorce Records

Marriages have been recorded in the county registers of deeds since about 1823. Statewide registration began in 1907. County records prior to 1907 have been filmed and are also available at the Department of Vital Statistics in Madison. An index to registrations of marriages, Adams through Racine counties, 1852–1907 (fiche 6331479), includes marriage record page numbers, and marriage certificate numbers are stamped on each record. Because each county recorded and indexed their own records, access to original marriage records should be through the county in which they are located. Many county records have been filmed, such as:

- Chippewa County registration of marriages and index, 1869–1907 (film 1275669 ff.), at the Department of Vital Statistics.
- Milwaukee County Register of Deeds marriages and index, 1838–1911 (film 1013949 ff.), marriage certificates, 1836–76 (film 1032378 ff.), at the Milwaukee County Courthouse in Milwaukee.
- Milwaukee County marriages, 1837–1907, and index, 1852–1907 (film 1275674 ff.), at the Department of Vital Statistics.
- Racine County registration of marriages and index, 1837–1907 (film 1275708 ff.), at the Department of Vital Statistics.

Divorces are recorded in the records of the county circuit courts. Some have been filmed, such as:

- Chippewa County Court divorce records, 1907–50 (film 1994263 ff.), and 1921–43 (film 1993868 ff.), at the State Historical Society of Wisconsin in Madison.

See also compiled publications, such as:

- Erickson, Vernon. *Births, Deaths, Marriages, and Other Genealogical Gleanings from Newspapers for Crawford, Vernon, and Richland Counties, Wisconsin, 1873–1910* (Bowie, MD: Heritage Books, 1997).

PROPERTY AND INHERITANCE

1846 "all property, real and personal, of the wife, owned by her at the time of her marriage, and also that acquired after marriage by gift, devise, descent, or otherwise than by her husband shall be her separate property. Laws shall be passed for providing for the registry of the wife's property and more clearly defining the rights of the wife thereto . . . (Art. XIV § 1)."

1850 real and personal property owned by a woman at the time of her marriage "shall continue her sole and separate property free from the disposal or debts of her husband as if she were a single female."

1858 a married woman's separate property is her separate estate, but she may not enter into contracts, sue or be sued, engage in business, or have a right to her own earnings.

SUFFRAGE

1919 women are found eligible to vote in presidential elections.

1920 Wisconsin women receive complete suffrage by passage of the 19th Amendment to the Constitution.

CITIZENSHIP

1783 all residents of Wisconsin become U.S. citizens by treaty, except for Native Americans, whose tribes are considered a separate nation until 1924.

CENSUS INFORMATION

For pre-territorial federal censuses, see Michigan (Iowa County, 1820 and 1830).
1836 territorial census (film 1293919).
1838 territorial census (film 1293919).
1842 territorial census (film 1293919).
1846 territorial census (film 1293920).
1847 territorial census (film 1293921 ff.).
1855 state census (film 1032686 ff.).
1875 state census (film 1032689 ff.).
1885 state census (film 1032695 ff.).
1895 state census (film 1032705 ff.).
1905 state census (film 1020439 ff.).
All of the territorial and state censuses are at the State Historical Society of Wisconsin.

See also Bureau of Indian Affairs records, such as Green Bay census rolls, 1885–1908 (film 0576861 ff.), at the National Archives in Washington, DC.

OTHER

1660–1883 The Draper Manuscripts at the State Historical Society of Wisconsin cover the states of Illinois, Indiana, Kentucky, New York, Tennessee, Virginia, and Wisconsin. See Draper, Lyman Copeland. *Draper Manuscript Collections, 1600–1883* (Chicago: University of Chicago Library, n.d., film 0889897 ff.), and Harper, Josephine L. *Guide to the Draper Manuscripts* (Madison: State Historical Society of Wisconsin, 1983).

BIBLIOGRAPHY

Brown, Victoria. *The Uncommon Lives of Common Women: The Missing Half of Wisconsin History* (Madison: Wisconsin Feminist Project Fund, 1975).

Butler, Anna B., et al. *Centennial Records of the Women of Wisconsin* (Madison: Atwood & Culver, 1876).

Danky, James P. *Women's History Resources at the State Historical Society of Wisconsin.* 5th ed. (Madison: The Society, 1997).

Dexheimer, Florence Chambers. *Sketches of Wisconsin Pioneer Women* (Fort Atkinson, WI: W.D. Hoard & Sons, 1925).

Ernst, Kathleen. "Common Courage: Women on the Wisconsin Frontier." *Wisconsin Women* 3 (March 1990): 21–2.

Famon's Wisconsin Women. 12 Vols. (Madison: State Historical Society of Wisconsin, 1976).

Fiorenza, Mary and Michael Edmunds. *Women's History Resources at the State Historical Society of Wisconsin.* 5th ed. (Madison: The Society, 1997).

Hoke, Donald. *Dressing the Bed: Quilts and Coverlets from the Collection of the Milwaukee Public Museum* (Milwaukee: The Museum 1985).

Hurn, Ethel Alice. *Wisconsin Women in the War Between the States* (Madison: Wisconsin History Commission, 1911).

Krueger, Lillian. *Motherhood on the Wisconsin Frontier* (Madison: State Historical Society of Wisconsin, 1951).

McBride, Genevieve G. *On Wisconsin Women: Working for Their Rights from Settlement to Suffrage* (Madison: University of Wisconsin Press, 1994).

Patterson, Betty. *Some Pioneer Families of Wisconsin: An Index.* 2 Vols. (Madison: State Genealogical Society, 1977, 1987).

Ryan, Carol Ward. *Searching for Your Wisconsin Ancestors in the Wisconsin Libraries.* 2nd ed. (Green Bay: The Author, 1988).

State Historical Society of Wisconsin. *Genealogical Research: An Introduction to the Resources of the State Historical Society of Wisconsin* (Madison: The Society, 1986).

—. *Guide to Archives and Manuscripts in the University of Wisconsin-Whitewater Area Research Center* (Madison: The Society, 1990). There are also guides available for the other Area Research Centers.

❧ *There are Area Research Centers for Wisconsin counties at the State Historical Society, University of Wisconsin system, and the Superior Public Library. For a list of Area Research Centers and addresses, see* **<www.wisc.edu/shs~archives/arcnet/index.html>**

Uncapher, Wendy. *Wisconsin: Its Counties, Townships, and Villages* (Janesville, WI: Origins, 1994).

Waldvogel, Merikay. "Quilts in the WPA Milwaukee Handicraft Project, 1935–1943," in *Uncoverings 1984* (Mill Valley, CA: American Quilt Study Group, 1985).

Wilson, Victoria. *Genealogist's Guide to Northeastern Wisconsin* (Grawn, MI: Kinseeker Publications, 1987). Other regional guides are available by this author.

SELECTED RESOURCES FOR WOMEN'S HISTORY

State Historical Society of Wisconsin
186 State Street
Madison, WI 53706

University of Wisconsin
Women's Studies Research Center
209 North Brooks Street
Madison, WI 53715

Wisconsin Women's History: A Bibliography, available online at **<gopher://silo.adp.wisc.edu/11/.uwlibs/.womenstudies/.wwh>**

WYOMING

IMPORTANT DATES IN STATE HISTORY

1803 Part of the Louisiana Purchase.
1834 Fort Laramie established as a trading post on the Oregon Trail.
1851 Fort Laramie Treaty Council held with plains and mountain tribes.
1861 Part of the Dakota Territory.
1867 Gold discovered at South Pass: Fort Laramie Treaty made with the Lakota Indians.
1868 Created as a separate territory.
1890 Statehood.

MARRIAGE AND DIVORCE

1887 county clerks are required to issue and record marriage licenses.
1899 a wife may divorce her husband for conduct that "constitutes him a vagrant (§ 2988)."

Where to Find Marriage and Divorce Records

Marriages have been kept by the county clerks since about 1860. Statewide registration began in 1941 and is kept at the Vital Records Service in Cheyenne. Divorce records have been kept by the county clerk of the district court from the creation of the county. Some county records at the Wyoming State Archives in Cheyenne have been filmed, such as:

- Carbon County Clerk marriage records, 1840–1930 (film 0968106 ff.).
- Sheridan County Clerk marriages, 1888–1925 (film 0973846 ff.).

See also indexes and compiled publications, such as:

- Marriage License Card Index (film 0820155 ff.), compiled by members of the Church of Jesus Christ of Latter-day Saints from marriage license records in the Lincoln County Courthouse in Kemmerer.
- CD-ROM: *Territorial Vital Records: Births, Divorces, Guardianships, Marriages, Naturalizations, Wills; 1800s Thru 1906, Utah Territory, Arizona, Colorado, Idaho, Nevada, Wyoming, Indian Territory; LDS Branches, Wards; Deseret News Vital Records; J.P. Marriages; Methodist Marriages* (Saint George, UT: Genealogical CD Publishing, 1994).

PROPERTY AND INHERITANCE

1869 a married woman's earnings are her separate property.
1876 a married woman's separate property is her separate estate, which she may devise by will.
1882 a married woman is granted *feme sole* status to administer her separate estate.

SUFFRAGE

1869 Suffrage Act gives women in the Wyoming Territory complete suffrage.

CITIZENSHIP

1803 all residents of Wyoming become U.S. citizens by legislation, except for Native Americans, whose tribes are considered a separate nation until 1924.

CENSUS INFORMATION

For pre-territorial federal censuses, see Utah (1850 and 1860, Salt Lake County), and Nebraska (1860, unorganized land).
1905 state census, at the Wyoming State Archives.

OTHER

1869 women are eligible to hold political office.
1870 women may serve on juries in territorial courts.
1910 Wyoming becomes the first state to elect a woman to the state legislature.
1925 Wyoming becomes the first state to elect a female governor.

BIBLIOGRAPHY

Bauman, Paula M. "Single Women Homesteaders in Wyoming, 1880–1930." *Annals of Wyoming* 58 (Spring 1986): 39–49.

Beach, Cora M. *Women of Wyoming: Including a Short History of Some of the Early Activities of Women of Our State, Together with Biographies of Those Women Who Were Our Early Pioneers as Well as of Women of Our State, Together with Biographies of Women Who Have been Prominent in Public Affairs and in Civil Organizations and Service Work.* 2 Vols. (Casper: S.E. Boyer, 1927).

Beard, Frances B. *Wyoming from Territorial Days to the Present.* 3 Vols. (Chicago: American History Society, 1933, film 1000827).

Brown, Dee. "The Wyoming Tea Party," in *The Gentle Tamers: Women of the Old West* (New York: G.P. Putnam's Sons, 1958), 238–51.

Garceau, Dee. *The Important Things of Life: Women, Work, and Family in Sweetwater County, Wyoming, 1880–1929* (Lincoln: University of Nebraska Press, 1997).

King, Jennifer. *Guide to Women's History Resources at the American Heritage Center.* 2nd ed. (Laramie: American Heritage Center, University of Wyoming, 1995).

Sackett, Margaret W. "Pioneer Ranch Life in Wyoming." *Annals of Wyoming* 14 (1942): 172.

Schily, Thomas and Jodye L.D. Schily. "Amazons, Witches, and Country Wives: Plains Indian Women in Historical Perspective." *Annals of Wyoming* 59 (Spring 1987): 48–56.

Shields, Alice M. "Army Life on the Wyoming Frontier." *Annals of Wyoming* 13 (1941): 331–45.

Spiros, Joyce V. Hawley. *Genealogical Guide to Wyoming* (Gallup, NM: Verlene Publishing, 1982, fiche 6051442).

Walker, Tacetta B. *Stories of Early Days in Wyoming: Big Horn Basin* (Laramie City: Daily Sentinel Print, 1875).

Wheeler, Denice. *The Feminine Frontier: Wyoming Women, 1850–1900* (n.p.: The Author, 1987).

SELECTED RESOURCES FOR WOMEN'S HISTORY

Women's History Research Center
American Heritage Center
University of Wyoming
Box 3924
Laramie, WY 82071-3924

Wyoming State Archives and Historical Department
Barrett State Office Building
6101 Yellowstone Road
Cheyenne, WY 82002

Wyoming

Wyoming State Library
Supreme Court Building
2301 Capitol Avenue
Cheyenne, WY 82002

Brilliant Women of all Times Suggesting to Modern Woman that Feminism is as old as History. On the left: Sappho, Susan B. Anthony, Mme. Curie, Catherine the Great, Marie de Medici, Delphic Oracle, Semiramus. On the right: George Eliot, Jeanne d'Arc, Mary-Queen of Scots, Rebecca, Rosa Bonheur, Cleopatra, Queen Elizabeth, Marie Louise

The Woman's Home Companion, 1912

GLOSSARY

act. To do or perform judicially; to enter at record.

affinity. A relationship through marriage rather than by blood.

allotment. Surveyed reservation land distributed by the government to individual Indians.

antenuptial agreement. A contract between a man and a woman who are planning to be married, usually establishing a woman's right to property held prior to marriage, often from a previous marriage.

bequest. A gift by will of personal property.

chancery. Equitable jurisdiction, a court of equity.

chattels. An article of personal property; moveables.

civil law. Based on ancient Roman law, codified by Justinian in AD 533.

clan mother. Eldest female member of a clan; serves as a clan leader in a matrilineal society.

code. A collection or compendium of laws.

Code Napoleon. The code which embodies the civil law of France.

cohabitation. The act of living together.

common law. As distinguished from Roman law, that system of jurisprudence originating in England.

common-law marriage. Also called consensual marriage and a contract *per verba de praesenti*; a verbal contract between a man and a woman to consider themselves as husband and wife, ratified by cohabitation.

community property. Property acquired by a husband or a wife, during marriage, when not acquired as the separate property of either party.

consanguinity. The connection or relation of persons who are descended from the same ancestor.

consort. A husband or wife.

contubernial relation. Cohabitation or "marriage" between slaves.

conveyance. The transfer of the title of land from one person or persons to another.

coverture. State of a married woman, a *feme covert*.

curtesy. A husband's interest in the property of his deceased wife.

Custom of Paris. Particular customs within the city of Paris with regard to trade, widows, orphans, and other matters.

degree of blood. Measure of Indian blood of a tribal member.

degree of relationship. The number of generations a relative is removed from the closest common ancestor.

de jure. By right of law.

devise. Gift of realty by will.

devisee. A person who takes a gift of realty under a will.

dower. A widow's estate in her husband's property.

dower right. The right of every widow to a life estate in one-third of all her husband's real estate owned by him at death.

emancipation. Act by which one who is enslaved or unfree is set at liberty.

endowment. Bestowment of dower.

enrollment rolls or lists. Official records of the recognized members of an Indian tribe.

entail, or fee-tail. To settle or limit the succession to real property.

entrywoman. A woman who is the original patentee of a federal or state land grant.

equity. Term denoting the habit of fairness, justness, and right dealing; courts established to do justice where common law does not provide adequate redress, also called courts of chancery.

escheat. Claim of the state to property of a decedent dying without heirs.

fee simple. A freehold estate of inheritance, absolute and unqualified.

feme covert. A married woman.

feme sole. A single woman.

goodwife. Colonial term for Mrs.

head of a family/household. A person who maintains a family, not necessarily a husband or father.

heir. One who succeeds by right of blood.

inchoate. Begun but not completed, as a contract not executed by all parties.

indenture. A deed between two or more parties entering into reciprocal grants or obligations toward each other.

Glossary

intemperance. Habitual drunkenness.

jointure. A marriage settlement by which the family of the bride contributes money or personal property as dower, followed by an equal amount being set aside by the family of the groom, in the name of the bride.

jurisdiction. The power and authority conferred upon a judge.

laws of descent. Hereditary succession.

legacy. A bequest or gift of personal property by last will and testament.

legislative divorce. A divorce decree, by petition, granted by a majority of a state legislature.

lucrative title. Under Spanish law, property received by donation or gift.

manumission. The act of liberating a slave from bondage.

marriage settlement or contract. See antenuptial agreement.

matrilineal descent. Rules to determine family or clan membership by tracing kinship through female ancestors.

mensa et thoro. "From bed and board," a legal marital separation.

mensa et vinculo A decree of absolute divorce.

miscegenation. Marriage between persons of different races.

moveables. See chattels.

naturalization. Process by which an alien is granted citizenship in a new country.

onerous title. Under Spanish law, property received in exchange for time, labor, or skill, or in exchange for money or other property.

ordinance. A measure passed by a municipal body to regulate local matters.

Ordinary. A judge (found in the Southern and Middle colonies) with power over wills, marriages, etc.

paraphernalia. Personal effects brought by the wife to the husband's house and which remain her separate property and under her control.

partible inheritance. The division of an estate among all heirs in the same degree.

picture bride. A practice of arranged marriage whereby a wife is selected for matrimony from her photograph.

pin money. A husband's allowance to his wife for her dress and personal expenses, sometimes created by settlement; it can be specific in amount or purpose, or a gift.

polygamy. Where either party has a present husband or wife at the time of a second marriage.

primogeniture. The right of the eldest son or his immediate male heir to inherit the real estate of an intestate parent, to the exclusion of the younger sons and daughters.

putative marriage. In civil law, a lawful marriage found to be invalid or voidable by a legal infirmity.

relict. The survivor of a pair of married people, whether husband or wife.

removal records. Muster rolls of the voluntary and forced relocations of Native Americans from their hereditary tribal lands to Indian territory and reservations.

repatriation. The regaining of nationality to the country of birth or citizenship.

seise. To take possession of.

separate estate. The individual property of one of two persons who stand in a social or business relationship, as distinguished from that which is held jointly.

separate property. Property owned by a married person in his or her own right during marriage.

statute. An act of legislature.

tenancy by the entirety. One who holds or possesses lands or tenements by any kind of right or title without division, separation, or diminution.

tenure. The mode by which one holds an estate in land.

BIBLIOGRAPHY

General U.S. Genealogy Reference

Arends, Marthe. *Genealogy Software Guide* (Baltimore: Genealogical Publishing Co., 1998).

Barsi, James C. *The Basic Researcher's Guide to Homesteads & Other Federal Land Records* (Colorado Springs: Nuthatch Grove Press, 1994).

Bentley, Elizabeth P. *The County Courthouse Book.* 2nd ed. (Baltimore: Genealogical Publishing Co., 1995).

—. *The Genealogist's Address Book.* 4th ed. (Baltimore: Genealogical Publishing Co., 1998).

Carmack, Sharon DeBartolo. *Genealogist's Guide to Discovering Your Female Ancestors* (Cincinnati: Betterway Books, 1998).

—. *The Genealogy Sourcebook* (Los Angeles: Lowell House, 1997).

Evans, Barbara Jean. A *to Zax: A Comprehensive Genealogical Dictionary for Genealogists and Historians.* 3rd ed. (Alexandria, VA: Hearthside Press, 1995).

Filby, P. William. *A Bibliography of American County Histories* (Baltimore: Genealogical Publishing Co., 1987).

—. *American & British Genealogy & Heraldry.* 3rd ed. (Boston: New England Historic Genealogical Society, 1982, supp., 1985).

Greenwood, Val D. *The Researcher's Guide to American Genealogy.* 2nd ed. (Baltimore: Genealogical Publishing Co., 1990).

Guide to Genealogical Research in the National Archives (Washington, DC: The National Archives and Records Administration, 1985).

Hoffman, Marian. *Genealogical and Local History Books in Print.* 4 Vols. 5th ed. (Baltimore: Genealogical Publishing Co., 1997).

Hone, Wade. *Land and Property Research in the United States* (Salt Lake City: Ancestry, Inc., 1997).

Howells, Cyndi. *Netting Your Ancestors: Genealogical Research on the Internet* (Baltimore: Genealogical Publishing Co., 1997).

Kemp, Thomas Jay. *International Vital Records Handbook.* 3rd ed. (Baltimore: Genealogical Publishing Co., 1994).

Lainhart, Ann S. *State Census Records* (Baltimore: Genealogical Publishing Co., 1992).

Matchette, Robert B., et al. *Guide to the Federal Records in the National Archives of the United States.* 3 Vols. (Washington DC: National Archives and Records Administration, 1995).

Mills, Elizabeth Shown. *Evidence! Citation & Analysis for the Family Historian* (Baltimore: Genealogical Publishing Co., 1997).

Neagles, James C. *The Library of Congress: A Guide to Genealogical and Historical Research* (Salt Lake City: Ancestry, Inc., 1990).

—. *U.S. Military Records: A Guide to Federal and State Sources, Colonial America to the Present* (Salt Lake City: Ancestry, Inc., 1994).

Rubincam, Milton. *Genealogical Research: Methods and Sources*. Vol. 1 (Washington, DC: The American Society of Genealogists, 1960).

Schaefer, Christina K. *Genealogical Encyclopedia of the Colonial Americas: A Complete Digest of the Records of All the Countries of the Western Hemisphere* (Baltimore: Genealogical Publishing Co., 1998).

—. *Guide to Naturalization Records of the United States* (Baltimore: Genealogical Publishing Co., 1997).

Sperry, Kip. *Reading Early American Handwriting* (Baltimore: Genealogical Publishing Co., 1998).

Stryker-Rodda, Kenn. *Genealogical Research: Methods and Sources*. Vol. 2 (Washington, DC: The American Society of Genealogists, 1971).

Szucs, Loretto Dennis and Sandra Hargreaves Luebking. *The Source: A Guidebook of American Genealogy*. Rev. ed. (Salt Lake City: Ancestry, Inc., 1997).

Tepper, Michael. *American Passenger Arrival Records*. Updated and enlarged ed. (Baltimore: Genealogical Publishing Co., 1993).

Vandagriff, G.G. *Voices in Your Blood: Discovering Identity Through Family History* (Kansas City: Andrews & McMeel, 1993).

General U.S. Law Reference

Bishop, Joel. *Commentary on the Laws of Marriage and Divorce* (Boston: Little, Brown & Co., 1852).

—. *New Commentaries on the Laws of Marriage, Divorce, and Separation as to the Law, Evidence, Pleading, Practice, Forms, and the Evidence of Marriage in All Issues on a New System of Legal Exposition*. 2 Vols. (Chicago: T.H. Flood & Co., 1891).

Blake, Nelson M. *The Road to Reno: A History of Divorce in the United States* (New York: Macmillan & Co., 1962).

Cohen, Morris L. *How to Find the Law*. 9th ed. (Saint Paul: West Publishing Co., 1989).

Cord, William H. *Treatise of Legal and Equitable Rights of a Married Woman, as Well as in Respect to Their Property and Persons as to Their Children*. 2 Vols. 2nd ed. (Philadelphia: Kay and Brother, 1885).

Dow, Susan L. *State Document Checklists: An Historical Bibliography* (Buffalo: William S. Hein, 1990).

Doyle, Francis R. *Searching the Law, the States: A Selective Bibliography of State Practice Materials in the Fifty States* (Dobbs Ferry, NY: Transnational, 1989).

Finkelman, Paul and Stephen E. Gottlieb. *Toward a Usable Past: Liberty Under State Constitutions* (Athens: University of Georgia Press, 1991).

Flaherty, David H. "A Select Guide to the Manuscript Court Records of Colonial New England." *American Journal of Legal History* 11 (1967): 107–26.

—. *Essays in the History of Early American Law* (Chapel Hill: University of North Carolina Press, 1969).

Bibliography

Friedman, Lawrence M. *History of American Law.* 2nd ed. (New York: Simon & Schuster, 1985).

—. "Rights of Passage: Divorce Law in Historical Perspective." *Oregon Law Review* 63 4 (1984): 649–78.

Grossberg, Michael. *Governing the Hearth: Law and Family in Nineteenth-Century America* (Chapel Hill: University of North Carolina Press, 1985).

Hall, Kermit L., William M. Wiecek, and Paul Finkelman. *American Legal History: Cases and Materials.* 2nd ed. (New York: Oxford University Press, 1996).

Hoffer, Peter Charles. *Law and People in Colonial America.* Rev. ed. (Baltimore: Johns Hopkins University Press, 1998).

Hood, John. *Index of Colonial and State Laws Between the Years of 1663 and 1877 Inclusive* (Trenton: John L. Murphy, 1877).

Hurst, Willard. *Law and the Conditions of Freedom in the Nineteenth-Century United States* (Madison: University of Wisconsin Press, 1956).

Keezer, Frank. *The Law of Marriage and Divorce: Giving the Law in All the States and Territories* (1906. Reprint. Littleton, CO: F.B. Rothman, 1991).

Keitt, Lawrence. *An Annotated Bibliography of Bibliographies of Statutory Materials in the United States* (Cambridge: Harvard University Press, 1934).

Kelly, John F. *The Law of Contracts of Married Women* (Jersey City: F.D. Linn, 1882).

The Legal Researcher's Desk Reference (Teaneck, NJ: Infosources, 1995).

McClanahan, W.S. *Community Property Law in the United States* (Rochester, NY: The Lawyers' Cooperative Publishing Co., 1982).

Merryman, John Henry. *The Civil Law Tradition.* 2nd ed. (Stanford: Stanford University Press, 1985).

Morris, Richard B. *Studies in the History of Early American Law: With Special Reference to the Seventeenth and Eighteenth Centuries.* 2nd ed. (Philadelphia: Mitchell, 1959).

North, S. *Marriage Laws in the United States, 1887–1906* (1908. Reprint. Conway: Arkansas Research, 1994).

Parish, David W. *State Government Reference Publications: An Annotated Bibliography* (Littleton, CO: Libraries Unlimited, 1981).

Pencak, William. *The Law in America, 1607–1861* (New York: New-York Historical Society, 1989).

Ryskamp, George R. "Fundamental Common-Law Concepts for the Genealogist: Marriage, Divorce, and Coverture." *National Genealogical Society Quarterly* 83 3 (September 1995): 165–79.

Subject Compilations of State Laws (Westport, CT: Greenwood Press, 1981-91).

Vernier, Chester O. *American Family Laws: A Comparative Study of the Family Laws of Forty-eight American States, Alaska, the District of Columbia, and Hawaii.* 5 Vols. (1932. Reprint. Westport, CT: Greenwood Press, 1971).

Wypyski, Eugene M. *The Law of Inheritance in All Fifty States* (New York: Oceana, 1984).

Zainaldin, Jamil. *Law in Antebellum Society* (New York: Alfred A. Knopf, 1983).

General U.S. History Reference

Brownstone, Douglass L. *A Field Guide to America's History* (New York: Facts on File, 1984).

Davidson, James West and Mark Hamilton Lytle. *After the Fact: The Art of Historical Detection.* 2nd ed. (New York: Alfred A. Knopf, 1986).

Deetz, James. *In Small Things Forgotten: The Archaeology of Early American Life* (Garden City, NY: Anchor Press, 1976).

Editors of American Heritage. *The American Heritage Cookbook and Illustrated History of American Eating and Drinking* (New York: Simon and Schuster, 1964).

Fischer, David Hackett. *Albion's Seed: Four British Folkways in America* (New York: Oxford University Press, 1989).

Gard, Wayne. *Frontier Justice* (Norman: University of Oklahoma Press, 1949).

Green, Harvey. *The Uncertainty of Everyday Life, 1915–1945* (New York: Harper & Row, 1993).

Hawke, David Freeman. *Everyday Life in Early America* (New York: Harper & Row, 1988).

Hume, Ivor Noël. *A Guide to Artifacts of Colonial America* (New York: Alfred A. Knopf, 1970).

Larkin, Jack. *The Reshaping of Everyday Life, 1790–1840* (New York: Harper & Row, 1988).

Leone, Mark P. and Neil Asher Selberman. *Invisible America: Unearthing Our Hidden History* (New York: Henry Holt & Co., 1995).

Library of Congress, Manuscript Division. *Index to Personal Names in the National Union Catalog of Manuscript Collections 1959–1984.* 2 Vols. (Alexandria, VA: Chadwyck-Healey, 1987). Based on the card index to the personal and family names in the National Union Catalog of Manuscript Collections housed in the Library of Congress.

McCutcheon, Marc. *The Writers' Guide to Everyday Life from Prohibition Through World War II* (Cincinnati: Writer's Digest Books, 1995).

—. *The Writers' Guide to Everyday Life in the 1800s* (Cincinnati: Writer's Digest Books, 1993).

Prucha, Francis Paul. *Handbook for Research in American History: A Guide to Bibliographies and Other Reference Works* (Lincoln: University of Nebraska Press, 1994).

Rothman, Ellen K. *Hands and Hearts: A History of Courtship in America* (New York: Basic Books, 1984).

Schlereth, Thomas J. *Victorian America: Transformations in Everyday Life, 1876–1915* (New York: Harper & Row, 1992).

Shammas, Carole, Marylynn Salmon, and Michael Dahlin. *Inheritance in America: From Colonial Times to the Present* (Galveston, TX: Frontier Press, 1987).

Sutherland, Daniel E. *The Expansion of Everyday Life, 1860–1876* (New York: Harper & Row, 1990).

Taylor, Dale. *The Writers' Guide to Everyday Life in Colonial America* (Cincinnati: Writer's Digest Books, 1997).

Trattner, Walter I. *From Poor Law to Welfare State: A History of Social Welfare in America.* 4th ed. (New York: Free Press, 1989).

Upton, Dell. *America's Architectural Roots: Ethnic Groups That Built America* (New York: Preservation Press / National Trust for Historic Preservation, 1986).

Wall, Helena M. *Fierce Communion: Family and Community in Early America* (Cambridge: Harvard University Press, 1990).

Weitzman, Davis. *Underfoot: An Everyday Guide to Exploring the American Past* (New York: Charles Scribner's Sons, 1976).

Wolf, Stephanie Gruman. *As Various as Their Land: The Everyday Lives of Eighteenth-Century Americans* (New York: Harper & Row, 1993).

Women's Studies, General

Arnold, Eleanor. *Voices of American Homemakers* (Bloomington: Indiana University Press, 1985).

Ballou, Patricia K. *Women: A Bibliography of Bibliographies* (Boston: G.K. Hall, 1980).

Bannon, Lois W. *Women in Modern America: A Brief History.* 2nd ed. (New York: Harcourt, Brace, Jovanovich, 1984).

Basch, Norma. "The Emerging Legal History of Women in the United States: Property, Divorce, and the Constitution." *Signs* 12 1 (Autumn 1986): 97–117.

Baxandall, Rosalyn and Linda Gordon. *America's Working Women: A Documentary History, 1600 to the Present.* Rev. and updated (New York: W.W. Norton & Co., 1995).

Beard, Mary. *Women As a Force in History* (1946. Reprint. New York: Octagon Books, 1985).

Benson, Mary Sumner. *Women in Eighteenth-Century America: A Study of Opinion and Social Usage* (1935. Reprint. New York: AMS Press, 1976).

Berkin, Carol. *First Generations: Women in Colonial America* (New York: Hill & Wang, 1996).

— and Mary Beth Norton. *Women of America: A History* (Boston: Houghton Mifflin, 1979).

Blair, Karen J. *The Clubwoman as Feminist: True Womanhood Redefined, 1868–1914* (New York: Holmes & Meier, 1980).

—. *The History of American Women's Voluntary Organizations, 1810–1960: A Guide to Sources* (Boston: G.K. Hall, 1989).

Bluementhal, Walter Hart. *Brides from Bridewell: Female Felons Sent to Colonial America* (Westport, CT: Greenwood Press, 1962).

Brackman, Barbara. *Clues in the Calico: A Guide to Identifying and Dating Antique Quilts* (McClean, VA: EPM Publishers, 1989).

Brockett, L.P. and Mary C. Vaughan. *Woman's Work in the Civil War* (Philadelphia: Zeigler, McCurdy & Co., 1867).

Brown, Dorothy M. *American Women in the 1920s: Setting a Course* (Boston: Twayne Publishers, 1987).

Brownlee, W. Elliot and Mary M. Brownlee. *Women in the American Economy: A Documentary History, 1625–1929* (New Haven: Yale University Press, 1976).

Carter, Sarah. *Women's Studies: A Guide to Information Sources* (Jefferson, NC: McFarland, 1990).

Case, Barbara Silver and Ann E. Wiederrecht. *The Women's Rights Movement in the United States, 1848– 1970: A Bibliography and Sourcebook* (Metuchen, NJ: Scarecrow Press, 1972).

Chafe, William H. *The American Woman: Her Changing Social, Economic, and Political Roles, 1920–1970* (New York: Oxford University Press, 1972).

Chapman, Anne. *Approaches to Women's History: A Resource Book and Teaching Guide* (Washington, DC: American Historical Association, 1979).

Chused, Richard H. "Married Women's Property Law: 1800–1850." *Georgetown Law Journal* 71 (1983): 1359–1461.

—. "The Oregon Donation Act of 1850 and Nineteenth-Century Federal Married Women's Property Law." *Law and History Review* 2 (Spring 1984): 44–78.

Claghorn, Charles E. *Women Patriots of the American Revolution: A Biographical Dictionary* (Metuchen, NJ: Scarecrow Press, 1991). Compiled from official state records; covers the Thirteen Colonies, Maine, Vermont, Kentucky, Tennessee, and West Virginia.

Clark, Alice. *The Working Life of Women in the Seventeenth Century: Laboring and Dependent Classes in Colonial America, 1607–1783* (Chicago: University of Chicago Press, 1931).

Cline, Cheryl. *Women's Diaries, Journals, and Letters: An Annotated Bibliography* (New York: Garland Publishing, 1989).

Conway, Jill Kerr. *The Female Experience in Eighteenth- and Nineteenth-Century America: A Guide to the History of American Women* (Princeton: Princeton University Press, 1985).

Cook, Margaret. *America's Charitable Cooks: A Bibliography of Fund-Raising Cookbooks Published in the United States (1861–1915)* (Kent, OH: Cookery Bibliography, 1971).

Cooper, Patricia and Norma B. Buford. *The Quilters: Women and Domestic Art* (New York: Doubleday, 1977).

Culley, Margo. *A Day at a Time: The Diary Literature of American Women from 1764 to the Present Day* (New York: Feminist Press, 1985).

Davison, Jane and Lesley Davison. *To Make a House a Home: Four Generations of American Women and the Houses They Lived In* (New York: Random House, 1994).

Depauw, Linda G. *Founding Mothers: Women in America in the Revolutionary Era* (Boston: Houghton Mifflin, 1975).

Dexter, Elizabeth W. *Colonial Women of Affairs: A Study of Women in Business and the Professions in America Before 1776* (Fairfield, NJ: Augustus Kelley, 1972).

—. *Career Women of America, 1776–1840* (Francestown, NY: Marshall Jones, 1950).

Bibliography

Dewhurst, Kurt C., Betty MacDowell, and Marsha MacDowell. *Artists in Aprons: Folk Art by American Women* (New York: E.P. Dutton & Co., 1979).

Dublin, Thomas. *Farm to Factory: Women's Letters, 1830–1860.* 2nd ed. (New York: Columbia University Press, 1993).

Dudden, Faye. *Serving Women: Household Service in Nineteenth-Century America* (Middletown, CT: Wesleyan University Press, 1983).

Earle, Alice Morse. *Home Life in Colonial Days* (New York: Macmillan & Co., 1898).

Edmunds, Mary Jaene. *Samples and Samplemakers: An American Schoolgirl Art, 1700–1850* (London: Charles Letts & Co., Ltd., 1991).

Evans, Elizabeth. *Weathering the Storm: Women of the American Revolution* (New York: Charles Scribner's Sons, 1975).

Ferreo, Pat and Elaine Hedges. *Hearts and Hands: The Influence of Women and Quilts on American Society* (San Francisco: Quilt Digest Press, 1987).

Fischer, Gayle. *Journal of Women's History: Guide to Periodical Literature* (Bloomington: Indiana University Press, 1992).

Fleming, E. McCluny. "Early American Decorative Arts as Social Documents." *Mississippi Valley Historical Review* 45 2 (September 1958): 276–84.

Fox, Sandi. *Wrapped in Glory: Figurative Quilts & Bedcovers, 1700–1900* (New York: Thames and Hudson, Los Angeles County Museum of Art, 1990).

Gabbaccia, Donna. *Immigrant Women in the United States: A Selectively Annotated Multi-Disciplinary Autobiography* (Westport, CT: Greenwood Press, 1989).

—— . *From the Other Side: Women, Gender, and Immigrant Life in the U.S., 1820–1920* (Bloomington: Indiana University Press, 1994).

Glazer, Pemna M. and Miriam Slater. *Unequal Colleagues: The Entrance of Women into the Professions, 1890–1940* (New Brunswick: Rutgers University Press, 1986).

Green, Harvey. *The Light of the Home: An Intimate View of the Lives of Women in Victorian America* (New York: Random House, 1983).

Greenwald, Maurice M. *Women, War, and Work: The Impact of World War I on Women Workers in the United States* (Westport, CT: Greenwood Press, 1980).

Grigg, Susan. "Women and Family Property: A Review of U.S. Inheritance Studies." *Historical Methods* 22 (Summer 1989): 116–22.

Haber, Barbara. *Women in America: A Guide to Books, 1963–1975* (Urbana: University of Illinois Press, 1981).

Hall, Kermit L. *Women, the Law, and the Constitution: Major Historical Interpretations* (New York: Garland Publishing, 1987).

Harrison, Cynthia E. *Women in American History: A Bibliography.* 2 Vols. (Santa Barbara, CA: CLIO, 1979).

Hartman, Susan M. *American Women in the 1940s: The Home Front and Beyond* (Boston: Twyane Publishers, 1982).

Hinding, Andrea. *Women's History Sources: A Guide to Archives and Manuscript Collections in the United States* (New York: R.R. Bowker, 1979).

History of Women: Guide to the Microfilm Collection (Woodbridge, CT: Research Publications, 1983).

Hoff, Joan. *Law, Gender, and Injustice: A Legal History of U.S. Women* (New York: New York University Press, 1991).

—. "Hidden Riches: Legal Records and Women, 1750–1825," in Kelley, Mary, *Woman's Being, Woman's Place: Female Identity and Vocation in American History* (Boston: G.K. Hall, 1979), 7–25.

Huls, Mary Ellen. *United States Government Documents on Women, 1800–1990: A Comprehensive Bibliography*. 2 Vols. (Westport, CT: Greenwood Press, 1993).

Jeffrey, Julie Roy. *Frontier Women: The Trans-Mississippi West, 1840–1880* (New York: Hill & Wang, 1979).

Juster, Norton. *A Woman's Place: Yesterday's Rural Women in America* (Golden, CO: Fulcrum Publishing, 1996).

Kennedy, Susan E. *America's White Working Class Women: A Historical Bibliography* (New York: Garland Publishing, 1981).

Kerber, Linda L. *Women of the Republic: Intellect and Ideology in Revolutionary America* (Chapel Hill: University of North Carolina Press, 1980).

— and Jane S. DeHart. *Women's America: Refocusing the Past* (New York: Oxford University Press, 1995).

Kessler-Harris, Alice and Kathryn Kish Sklar. *U.S. History as Women's History* (Chapel Hill: University of North Carolina Press, 1995).

Kiracofe, Roderick. *The American Quilt: A History of Cloth and Comfort, 1750–1950* (New York: Clarkson N. Potter, 1993).

Leach, Kristine. *In Search of a Common Ground: 19th and 20th Century Immigrant Women in America* (Bethesda, MD: Austin & Winfield Publishers, 1995).

Lerner, Gilda. *The Female Experience: An American Documentary* (New York: Oxford University Press, 1977).

Loeb, Catherine R. *Women's Studies: A Recommended Core Bibliography, 1980–1985* (Littleton, CO: Libraries Unlimited, 1986).

MacArthur, Burke. *United Littles: The Story of the Needlework Guild of America* (New York: Coward-McCann, 1955). Includes a list of towns having organizational branches.

Macdonald, Anne L. *No Idle Hands: The Social History of American Knitting* (New York: Ballantine Books, 1988).

Mankiller, Wilma, et al. *The Reader's Companion to U.S. Women's History* (New York: Houghton Mifflin, 1998).

Manning, Caroline. *The Immigrant Woman and Her Job* (1936. Reprint. New York: Arno Press, 1970).

Matthaei, Julie A. "Husbandless Women in the Colonial Economy: Women Working for Income," in *An Economic History of Women in America* (New York: Schocken Books, 1982).

Bibliography

May, Elaine Tyler. *Great Expectations: Marriage and Divorce in Post-Victorian America* (Chicago: University Press, 1980).

McFeely, Mary Drake. *Women's Work in Britain and America from the Nineties to World War I: An Annotated Bibliography* (Boston: G.K. Hall, 1986).

Mehaffey, Karen Rae. *Victorian American Women, 1840–1880: An Annotated Bibliography* (New York: Garland Publishing, 1992).

Melder, Keith. *The Beginnings of Sisterhood: The Women's Rights Movement in the United States, 1800–1840* (New York: Schocken Books, 1977).

Morris, Richard B. "Women's Rights in Early American Law," in *Studies in the History of American Law with Special Reference to the Seventeenth and Eighteenth Centuries* (New York: Columbia University Press, 1964): 126–200.

Narbasse, Elizabeth Bowles. *The Changing Legal Rights of Married Women, 1800–1861* (New York: Garland Publishing, 1986).

Neidle, Cecyle. *America's Immigrant Women: Their Contribution to the Development of a Nation from 1609 to the Present* (New York: Hippocrene Books, 1975).

Norton, Mary Beth. "Eighteenth-Century American Women in Peace and War: The Case of the Loyalists." *William and Mary College Quarterly* 33 (1976): 386–98.

Palmer, Phyllis. *Domesticity and Dirt: Housewives and Domestic Servants in the United States, 1920 to 1945* (Philadelphia: Temple University Press, 1990).

Penny, Virginia. *The Employments of Women: A Cyclopedia of Woman's Work* (Boston: Walker, Wise & Co., 1863).

Plante, Ellen M. *Women at Home in Victorian America: A Social History* (New York: Facts on File, 1997).

Riley, Glenda. *Divorce: An American Tradition* (New York: Oxford University Press, 1991).

Rogers, Madeline. "Jacquard Coverlets: Where Genealogy and Textiles Meet." *American Art and Antiques* (January/February 1979).

Rowbotham, Sheila. *Hidden from History: Rediscovering Women in History from the Seventeenth Century to the Present* (1976. Reprint. New York: Pluto Press, 1997).

Ryan, Mary P. *Womanhood in America from Colonial Times to the Present* (New York: New Viewpoints Press, 1975).

Sacareno, Chiara. "Women, Family, and the Law, 1750–1942." *Journal of Family History* 15 4 (October 1990): 427–42.

Salmon, Marylynn. *Women and the Law of Property in Early America* (Chapel Hill: University of North Carolina Press, 1986).

Samuelson, Nancy B. "The Fate Worse than Death: Women Captives of the Indian Wars." *Minerva: Quarterly Report on Women and the Military* 3 (Winter 1985): 117–37.

Schneider, Dorothy and Carl J. Schneider. *American Women of the Progressive Era, 1900–1920* (New York: Anchor Books, 1993).

Scott, Anne Firor. *Making the Invisible Woman Visible* (Urbana: University of Illinois Press, 1984).

Seeley, Charlotte Palmer. *American Women and the U.S. Armed Forces: A Guide to the Records of Military Agencies in the National Archives Relating to American Women* (Washington, DC: National Archives and Records Administration, 1992).

Smith, Page. *Daughters of the Promised Land: Women in American History* (Boston: Little, Brown & Co., 1970).

Sochen, June. *Herstory: A Woman's View of American History* (New York: Alfred Publishing, 1974).

Solomon, Barbara Miller. *In the Company of Educated Women: A History of Women and Higher Education* (New Haven: Yale University Press, 1986).

Stanek, Edward. *Legal Status and Rights of Women: A Selected Bibliography* (Monticello, IL: Vance, 1987).

Stineman, Esther. *Women's Studies: A Recommended Core Bibliography* (Littleton, CO: Libraries Unlimited, 1979).

Thompson, Roger. *Women in Stuart England and America* (London: Routledge, 1974).

Ulrich, Laura Thatcher. "Of Pens and Needles: Sources in Early American Women's History." *Journal of American History* 77 1 (June 1990): 200–7.

Waldvogel, Merikay and Barbara Brockman. *Patchwork Souvenirs of the 1933 World's Fair* (Nashville: Rutledge Hill Press, 1993).

Wandersee, Winifred D. *Women's Work and Family Values, 1920–1940* (Cambridge: Harvard University Press, 1981).

Ware, Susan. *American Women in the 1930s: Holding Their Own* (Boston: Twayne Publications, 1982).

Weathersford, Doris. *Foreign and Female: Immigrant Women in America, 1840–1930* (New York: Schocken Books, 1986).

—. *American Women and World War II* (New York: Facts on File, 1990).

Wedborn, Helena. *Women in the First and Second World Wars: A Checklist of Holdings of the Hoover Institution on War, Revolution, and Peace* (Stanford: Hoover Institution Press, 1988).

Weisberg, D. Kelly. *Women and the Law: The Social Historical Perspective*. 2 Vols. (Cambridge, MA: Schenkman Publishing Co., 1982).

Weisman, Judith Reiter and Wendy Lavitt. *Labors of Love: America's Textiles and Needlework, 1650–1930* (New York: Wings Books, 1987).

Wilson, Jennie L. *The Legal and Political Status of Women in the United States* (Cedar Rapids, IA: Torch, 1912).

Woloch, Nancy. *Women and the American Experience*. 2nd ed. (New York: McGraw-Hill, 1994).

Women, the Law, and the Constitution: Major Historical Interpretations (New York: Garland Publishing, 1987).

Wortman, Marlene Stein. *Women in American Law*. Vol. 1 *From Colonial Times to the New Deal* (New York: Holmes & Meier, 1985).

Women's Studies, References for Ethnic Research (see also sections for regional research, following, and chapters for individual states)

Abajian, James T. *Blacks in Selected Newspapers, Censuses, and Other Sources: An Index to Names and Subjects*. 3 Vols. (Boston: G.K. Hall, 1977).

Albers, Patricia and Beatrice Medicine. *The Hidden Half: Studies of Plains Indian Women* (Washington, DC: University Press of America, 1983).

Barton, Arnold H. "Scandinavian Immigrant Women's Encounter with America." *Swedish Pioneer Historical Quarterly* XXV (1974): 37–42.

Bataille, Gretchen M. and Kathleen Mullen Sands. *American Indian Women, Telling Their Lives* (Lincoln: University of Nebraska Press, 1984).

—. *American Indian Women: A Guide to Research* (New York: Garland Publishing, 1991).

Benberry, Cuestra. *Always There: The African-American Presence in American Quilts* (Louisville: Kentucky Quilt Project, 1992).

Boyer, Ruth McDonald and Narcissus Duffy Gayton. *Apache Mothers and Daughters* (Norman: University of Oklahoma Press, 1992).

Brown, Elsa Barkley. "Afro-American Women's Quilting: A Framework for Conceptualizing and Teaching African American Women's History." *Signs* 14 (Summer 1989): 921–9.

Brown, Hallie Q. *Homespun Heroines and Other Women of Distinction* (1926. Reprint. New York: Oxford University Press, 1988).

Buchanan, Kimberly Moore. *Apache Women Warriors* (El Paso: Texas Western Press, 1973).

Caroli, Betty B., et al. *The Italian Immigrant Woman in North America* (Toronto: The Multi-Cultural History Society of Ontario, 1978).

Cotera, Martha. *Latina Sourcebook: Bibliography of Mexican American, Cuba, Puerto Rican, and Other Hispanic Women* (Austin: Information Systems Development, 1982).

Diner, Hasia R. *Erin's Daughters in America: Irish Immigrant Women in Nineteenth-Century America* (Baltimore: Johns Hopkins University Press, 1983).

Epstein, Helen. *Where She Came From: A Daughter's Search for Her Mother's History* (Boston: Little, Brown & Co., 1997). A Czech-Jewish family history from the 1800s through the Holocaust.

Foreman, Carolyn Thomas. *Indian Women Chiefs* (Washington, DC: Zenger Publishing, 1976).

Frankel, Noralee. "From Slave Women to Free Women: The National Archives and Black Women's History in the Civil War Era." *Prologue* 29 (Summer 1997): 100–31.

Frazier, Patrick. *Many Nations: A Library of Congress Resource Guide for the Study of Indian and Alaska Native Peoples of the United States* (Washington, DC: USGPO, 1996).

Freeman, Ronald L. *A Communion of the Spirits: African American Quilters, Preservers & Their Stories* (Nashville: Rutledge Hill Press, 1996).

Frisbie, Charlotte J. "Traditional Navajo Women: Ethnographic and Life History Portrayals." *American Indian Quarterly* 6 (1982): 11–33.

Fry, Gladys-Marie. *Stitched from the Soul: Slave Quilts from the Ante-Bellum South* (New York: Dutton, Museum of American Folk Art, 1990).

Glenn, Evelyn Nakano. *Issei, Nissei, War Bride: Three Generations of Japanese American Women in Domestic Service* (Philadelphia: Temple University Press, 1986).

Green, Rayna. *Native American Women: A Contextual Bibliography* (Bloomington: Indiana University Press, 1984).

—. *Women in American Indian Society* (New York: Chelsea House Publishers, 1992).

Gridley, Marion E. *American Indian Women* (New York: Hawthorn, 1974).

Hine, Darlene Clark, et al. *Black Women in America: An Historical Encyclopedia.* 2 Vols. (Brooklyn: Carlson Publishing, 1993).

— and Kathleen Thompson. *A Shining Thread of Hope: The History of Black Women in America* (New York: Broadway Books, 1998).

—, Wilma King, and Linda Reed. *We Specialize in the Wholly Impossible: A Reader in Black Women's History* (Brooklyn: Carlson Publishing, 1995).

Holt, Constance Wall. *Welsh Women: An Annotated Bibliography of Women in Wales and Women of Welsh Descent in America* (Metuchen, NJ: Scarecrow Press, 1993).

Hunter, Tera W. *To 'Joy My Freedom: Southern Black Women's Lives and Labors After the Civil War* (Cambridge: Harvard University Press, 1997).

Hyman, Paula and Deborah Dash Moore. *Jewish Women in America: An Historical Encyclopedia.* 2 Vols. (London: Routledge, 1997).

Jones, Jacqueline. *Labor of Love, Labor of Sorrow: Black Women, Work, and the Family From Slavery to the Present* (New York: Vintage Books, 1986).

Lerner, Gerda. *Women Are History: A Bibliography on the History of American Women* (Madison: University of Wisconsin Press, 1972).

—. *Black Women in White America: A Documentary History* (New York: Vintage Books, 1973).

Libo, Kenneth and Irving Howe. *We Lived There Too: In Their Own Words and Pictures, Pioneer Jews and the Westward Movement of America, 1630–1930* (New York: Schocken Books, 1984).

Lowenberg, Bert and Ruth Bogen. *Black Women in Nineteenth-Century Life: Their Thoughts, Their Words, Their Feelings* (University Park: Pennsylvania State University Press, 1976).

Lucas, Henry S. *Dutch Immigrant Memoirs and Related Writings* (Assen, The Netherlands: Van Gorcum, 1955).

Marcus, Jacob Rader. *The American Jewish Woman, 1654–1980* (New York: KTAV Publishing House, 1981).

Bibliography

Martin, Patricia P. *Songs My Mother Sang to Me: An Oral History of Mexican American Women* (Tucson: University of Arizona Press, 1992).

Mirande, Alfredo and Evangelina Enriquez. *La Chicana, The Mexican American Woman* (Chicago: University of Chicago Press, 1979).

Ichioka, Yuji. "Amerika-Nadeshiko: Japanese Immigrant Women in the United States, 1900–1924." *Pacific Historical Review* LXIX (May 1980): 339–57.

Newman, Debra L. *Selected Documents Pertaining to Black Workers Among the Records of the Department of Labor and Its Component Bureaus, 1902–1969.* SL 40 (Washington, DC: National Archives and Records Administration, 1977).

Nolan, Janet A. *Ourselves Alone: Women Immigrants from Ireland* (Lexington: University of Kentucky Press, 1989).

Palmer, Phyllis. "Black Domestics During the Depression." *Prologue* (Summer 1997): 127–31.

Pehotsky, Bessie O. *The Slavic Immigrant Woman* (Cincinnati: Powell & White, 1925).

Roessel, Ruth. *Women in Navajo Society* (Rough Rock, AZ: Navajo Resource Center, 1981).

Ross, Carl and K. Marianne Wargelin Brown. *Women Who Dared: The History of Finnish American Women* (Saint Paul: Immigration History Research Center, 1986).

Ruiz, Vicki and Ellen Carol DuBois. *Unequal Sisters: A Multi-Cultural Reader in U.S. Women's History*. 2nd ed. (London: Routledge, 1994).

Shukert, Elfrieda B. *War Brides of World War II* (Novato, CA: Presidio Press, 1988).

Sonneborn, Liz. *Encyclopedia of Women: A to Z of Native American Women* (New York: Facts on File, 1998).

Sterling, Dorothy and Mary Helen Washington. *We Are Your Sisters: Black Women in the Nineteenth Century* (New York: W.W. Norton & Co., 1997).

Stoner, K. Lynn. *Latinas of the Americas: A Source Book* (New York: Garland Publishing, 1989).

Telford, Ted A. *Women and Traditional Sources: Chinese Clan Genealogies: Tracing the Female Line* (Salt Lake City: Corporation of the President, 1980).

Terrell, John Upton and Donna M. Upton. *Indian Women of the Western Morning: Their Life in Early America* (Garden City, NY: Anchor Books, 1976).

Van Kirk, Sylvia. *Many Tender Ties: Women in Fur Trade Society, 1670–1870* (Norman: University of Oklahoma Press, 1980).

Weinberg, Sydney Stahl. *The World of Our Mothers: The Lives of Jewish Immigrant Women* (New York: Schocken Books, 1988).

Wilson, Terry P. "Osage Indian Women During a Century of Change, 1870–1980." *Prologue* 14 (Winter 1982): 185–20.

Yu, Eui-Young and Earl H. Phillips. *Korean Women in Transition: At Home and Abroad* (Los Angeles: Center for Korean-American and Korean Studies, California State University, 1987).

Yung, Judy. *Chinese Women of America: A Pictorial History* (Seattle: University of Washington Press, 1986).

Women's Studies and General Reference, New England

Bassett, Lynne Z. *Northern Comfort: New England's Early Quilts, 1780–1850* (Nashville: Rutledge Hill Press, 1998).

Bogdonoff, Nancy D. *Handwoven Textiles of New England: The Legacy of a Rural People, 1640–1880* (Harrisburg: Stackpole Books, 1975).

Cobbledick, M.R. "The Property Rights of Women in Puritan New England." *Studies in the Science of Society* (New Haven: Yale University Press, 1937): 107–16.

Cott, Nancy F. *The Bonds of Womanhood: Women's Sphere in New England, 1870–1835* (New Haven: Yale University Press, 1977).

Dow, George Francis. *The Arts and Crafts in New England, 1704–1775: Gleanings from Boston Newspapers* (Topsfield, MA: The Wayside Press, 1927).

Jeffrey, William. *Early New England Court Records: A Bibliography of Published Materials* (Boston: Boston Public Library Quarterly, 1954, film 0234519).

Karlsen, Carol F. *The Devil in the Shape of a Woman: Witchcraft in Colonial New England* (New York: W.W. Norton & Co., 1987).

Lindberg, Marcia W. *Genealogist's Handbook for New England Research.* Rev. ed. (Boston: New England Historic Genealogical Society, 1993).

Rogers, Kim Lacy. "Relicts in the New World: Conditions of Widowhood in Seventeenth-Century New England," in Kelley, Mary, *Woman's Being, Woman's Place: Female Identity and Vocation in American History* (Boston: G.K. Hall, 1979), 26–52.

Rothman, Ellen K. *New England Women and Their Families in the 18th and 19th Centuries: Personal Papers, Letters, and Diaries* (Bethesda, MD: University Publications of America, 1997–). Themes of the papers in this microform series include various aspects of home life: courtship, slavery, education, child rearing, marriage, and religion. Series A is from the holdings of the American Antiquarian Society in Worcester, Massachusetts. More series are planned (a reel guide is available online at **<www.upapubs. com/guides/>**).

Savage, James. *A Genealogical Dictionary of the First Settlers of New England.* 4 Vols. (1860–2. Reprint. Baltimore: Genealogical Publishing Co., 1998).

Torrey, Clarence A. *New England Marriages Prior to 1700.* (Baltimore: Genealogical Publishing Co., 1985). See also the first and second supps., by Melinde L. Sanborn (Baltimore: Genealogical Publishing Co., 1991, 1995).

Ulrich, Laurel Thatcher. *Goodwives: Images and Reality in the Lives of Women in Northern New England, 1650–1750* (New York: Vintage Books, 1980). Focuses on women in Maine, Massachusetts, and New Hampshire.

Women's Studies and General Reference, Mid-Atlantic

Berkin, Carol. "In a Babel of Confusion: Women in the Middle Colonies," in *First Generations: Women in Colonial America* (New York: Hill & Wang, 1996), 79–102.

Fabend, Firth Haring. *A Dutch Family in the Middle Colonies, 1660–1880* (New Brunswick: Rutgers University Press, 1991).

Grumet, Robert S. "Sunksquaws, Shamans, and Tradeswomen: Middle Atlantic Coast Algonkian Women During the 17th and 18th Centuries," in Etienne, Mona and Eleanor Leacock, *Women and Colonization: Anthropological Perspectives* (New York: Praeger, 1980), 43–62.

Jensen, Joan M. *Loosening the Bonds: Mid-Atlantic Farm Women, 1750–1850* (New Haven: Yale University Press, 1986).

Levy, Barry. *Quakers and the American Family: British Settlement in the Delaware Valley* (New York: Oxford University Press, 1988).

Vaux, Trina. *Guide to Women's History in the Delaware Valley* (Philadelphia: University of Pennsylvania Press, 1984).

Women's Studies and General Reference, the South

Andrews, Matthew Page. *The Woman of the South in War Times* (Baltimore: Norman Remington Co., 1920).

Bernhard, Virginia, et al. *Hidden Histories of Women in the New South* (Columbia: University of Missouri Press, 1994).

Blee, Kathleen M. *Women of the Klan: Racism and Gender in the 1920s* (Berkeley: University of California Press, 1991).

Blesser, Carol. *In Joy and Sorrow: Women, Family, and Marriage in the Victorian South* (New York: Oxford University Press, 1991).

Bynum, Victoria E. *Unruly Women: The Politics of Sexual Control in the Old South* (Chapel Hill: University of North Carolina Press, 1992).

Cashin, Joan E. *A Family Venture: Men and Women on the Southern Frontier* (Baltimore: Johns Hopkins University Press, 1994).

Clinton, Catherine. *Half-Sisters of History: Southern Women and the American Past* (Durham, NC: Duke University Press, 1994).

Fox-Genovose, Elizabeth. *Within the Plantation Household: Black and White Women of the Old South* (Chapel Hill: University of North Carolina Press, 1988).

Gray, Deborah. *A'n't I A Woman? Female Slaves in the Plantation South* (New York: W.W. Norton & Co., 1985).

Hagood, Margaret Jarman. *Mothers of the South: Portraiture of White Tenant Farm Women* (Chapel Hill: University of North Carolina Press, 1991).

Hardy, Steal P. *Colonial Families of the Southern States of America* (1958. Reprint. Baltimore: Genealogical Publishing Co., 1991).

Lebsock, Suzanne D. "Radical Reconstruction and the Property Rights of Southern Women." *Journal of Southern History* 43 (May 1977): 195–216.

McWhiney, Grady. *Cracker Culture: Celtic Ways in the Old South* (Tuscaloosa: University of Alabama Press, 1988).

Ramsey, Bets and Merikay Waldvogel. *Southern Quilts: Surviving Relics of the Civil War* (Nashville: Rutledge Hill Press, 1998).

Scott, Anne Firor. *The Southern Lady: From Pedestal to Politics, 1830–1930* (Chicago: University of Chicago Press, 1970).

—. *Southern Women and Their Families in the 19th Century: Papers and Diaries* (Bethesda, MD: University Publications of America, 1998). Themes of the papers in this microform series include various aspects of home life: courtship, slavery, education, child rearing, marriage, and religion. The series are from the holdings of the following institutions (a detailed reel guide is available on line at **<www.upapubs.com/guides/>**):

- Series A: Southern Historical Collection, University of North Carolina, Chapel Hill
- Series B: The Colonial Williamsburg Foundation Library, Carter Family Papers
- Series B: Earl Gregg Swem Library, The College of William and Mary, Williamsburg
- Series D: The Virginia Historical Society, Richmond
- Series E: Louisiana and Lower Mississippi Valley Collections, Louisiana State University Libraries, Baton Rouge
- Series F: Center for American History, University of Texas at Austin

Schweninger, Loren. "Property-Owning Free African American Women in the South, 1800–1870." *Journal of Women's History* 1 (Winter 1990): 13–44.

Simkins, Francis B. and James Welch Patton. *The Women of the Confederacy* (Richmond: Garret & Massie, 1936).

Special Aids to Genealogical Research on Southern Families (Washington, DC: National Genealogical Society, 1962).

Spruill, Julia Cherry. *Women's Life and Work in the Southern Colonies* (1938. Reprint. New York: W.W. Norton & Co., 1972).

Stevenson, Brenda E. *Life in Black and White: Family and Community in the Slave South* (New York: Oxford University Press, 1996).

Wiley, Bell Irvin. *Confederate Women* (Westport, CT: Greenwood Press, 1975).

A Woman's War: Southern Women, Civil War, and the Confederate Legacy (Charlottesville: University Press of Virginia, 1996).

Women's Studies and General Reference, the Midwest

Cordier, Mary Hurlbut. *Schoolwomen of the Prairies and Plains: Personal Narratives from Iowa, Kansas, and Nebraska, 1860s to 1920s* (Albuquerque: University of New Mexico Press, 1990).

Cox-Paul, Lori A. and James W. Wengert. *A Frontier Army Christmas* (Lincoln: Nebraska State Historical Society, 1996).

Eales, Anne Bruner. *Army Wives on the American Frontier: Living by the Bugles* (Boulder: Johnson Books, 1996).

Fairbanks, Carol and Sara Brooks Sundberg. *Farm Women on the Prairie Frontier: A Sourcebook for Canada and the United States* (Metuchen, NJ: Scarecrow Press, 1983).

Gutman, Herbert G. *The Black Women in the Middle West Project: A Comprehensive Resource Guide* (Indianapolis: Indiana Historical Bureau, 1986).

Hampsten, Elizabeth. *Read This Only to Yourself: The Private Writings of Midwestern Women, 1880–1910* (Bloomington: Indiana University Press, 1982).

Hargreaves, Mary W.M. "Homesteaders and Homemaking on the Plains: A Review." *Agricultural History* 47 (April 1973): 156–63.

—— . "Women in the Agricultural Settlement of the Northern Plains." *Agricultural History* 50 (January 1976): 179–89.

Holt, Marilyn I. *Linoleum, Better Babies & the Modern Farm Woman, 1890–1930* (Albuquerque: University of New Mexico Press, 1995).

Jeffrey, Julie Roy. *Frontier Women: The Trans-Mississippi West, 1840–1880* (New York: Hill & Wang, 1979).

Lareau, Paul J. and Elmer Courteau. *French-Canadian Families of the North Central States: A Genealogical Dictionary* (Saint Paul: Northwest Territory French and Canadian Heritage Institute, 1981, fiche 6010503 ff.).

Meredith, Howard. *Dancing on Common Ground: Tribal Cultures & Alliances on the Southern Plains* (Lawrence: University Press of Kansas, 1995).

Murphy, Lucy E. "Business Ladies: Midwestern Women and Enterprise, 1850–1880." *Journal of Women's History* 3 (Spring 1991): 65–89.

Neth, Mary. *Preserving the Family Farm: Women, Community, and the Foundations of Agribusiness in the Midwest, 1900–1940* (Baltimore: Johns Hopkins University Press, 1998).

O'Meara, Walter. *Daughters of the Country: The Women of the Fur Traders and the Mountain Men* (New York: Harcourt, Brace & World, 1968).

Pickle, Linda S. *Contented Among Strangers: Rural German-Speaking Women and Their Families in the Nineteenth-Century Midwest* (Champaign: University of Illinois Press, 1996).

Riley, Glenda. "Women on the Great Plains: Recent Developments in Research." *Great Plains Quarterly* 5 (Spring 1985): 81–92.

Schloff, Linda Mack. *"And Prairie Dogs Weren't Kosher:" Jewish Women in the Upper Midwest Since 1855* (Saint Paul: Minnesota Historical Society Press, 1996).

Stansell, Christine. "Women on the Great Plains, 1865–1890." *Women's Studies* 4 (1976): 87–9.

Walden, Blanche Lea. *Pioneer Families of the Midwest* (1939. Reprint. Baltimore: Clearfield Co., 1998).

Women's Studies and General Reference, the West

Allen, Marsha. *Traveling West: Nineteenth-Century Women on the Overland Routes* (El Paso: Texas Western University Press, 1987).

Armitage, Susan. *Women and Western American History* (Wellesley: Wellesley College Center for Research on Women, 1984).

——, et al. *Women in the West: A Guide to Manuscript Sources* (New York: Garland Publishing, 1991). Covers Alaska, Arizona, California, Colorado, Hawaii, Idaho, Kansas, Montana, Nebraska, Nevada, New Mexico, North Dakota, Oklahoma, South Dakota, Texas, Utah, Washington, and Wyoming.

Beers, Henry. *Spanish and Mexican Records of the American Southwest* (Tucson: University of Arizona Press, 1979).

Brown, Dee. *The Gentle Tamers: Women of the Old West* (New York: G.P. Putnam's Sons, 1958).

Butler, Anne M. and Mary Siporan. *Uncommon Common Women: Ordinary Lives of the West* (Salt Lake City: Utah State University Press, 1996).

Conran, Teri. *Women in the West: A Bibliography, 1984–1987* (Pullman, WA: Coalition for Western Women's History, 1988).

Dary, David. *Seeking Pleasure in the Old West* (New York: Alfred A. Knopf, 1995).

DeGraff, Lawrence B. "Race, Sex, and Regions: Black Women in the American West." *Pacific Historical Review* (Mary 1980): 285–313.

Deutsch, Sarah. *No Separate Refuge: Culture, Class, and Gender on the Anglo-American Frontier in the American Southwest, 1880–1940* (New York: Oxford University Press, 1987).

Ellet, Elizabeth F. *The Pioneer Women of the West* (Philadelphia: Porter & Coats, 1873).

Faragher, John Mack. *Women and Men on the Overland Trail* (New Haven: Yale University Press, 1979).

Fischer, Christiane. *Let Them Speak for Themselves: Women in the American West, 1849–1900* (Hamden, CT: Archon Books, 1977).

Holmes, Kenneth L. *Covered Wagon Women: Diaries and Letters from the Western Trails, 1840–1890.* 11 Vols. (Glendale, CA: Arthur H. Clark Co., 1983–91). Contains transcripts of diaries, letters, journal entries, etc. written by pioneer women who traveled the various trails west to Utah, Nevada, Oregon, California, and elsewhere.

Jameson, Elizabeth and Susan Armitage. *Writing on the Range: Race, Class, and Culture in the Women's West* (Norman: University of Oklahoma Press, 1998).

Jordan, Teresa. *Cowgirls: Women of the American West* (Garden City, NY: Anchor Press, 1982).

Lawless, Chuck. *The Old West Sourcebook: A Travelers' Guide* (New York: Crown Trade Paperbacks, 1994).

Lind, Anna M. "Women in Early Logging Camps: A Personal Reminiscence." *Journal of Forest History* 19 3 (1975): 128–35.

Luchetti, Cathy. *I Do! Courtship, Love, and Marriage on the American Frontier* (New York: Crown Publishing, 1996).

— and Carol Olwell. *Women of the West* (Saint George, UT: Antelope Island Press, 1982).

Moynihan, Ruth B., Susan Armitage, and Christiane Fischer Duchamp. *So Much to Be Done: Women Settlers on the Mining and Ranching Frontier* (Lincoln: University of Nebraska Press, 1990).

Myres, Sandra L. *Westering Women and the Frontier Experience, 1800–1915* (Albuquerque: University of New Mexico Press, 1982).

— . "Army Women's Narratives as Documents of Social History: Some Examples from the Western Frontier, 1840–1900." *New Mexico Historical Review* 65 (April 1990): 175–98.

Neiderman, Sharon. *A Quilt of Words: Women's Diaries, Letters, and Original Accounts of Life in the Southwest, 1860–1960* (Boulder: Johnson Books, 1988).

Bibliography

Peavy, Linda and Ursula Smith. *Pioneer Women: The Lives of Women on the Frontier* (Norman: University of Oklahoma Press, 1998).

—. *Women in Waiting in the Westward Movement* (Norman: University of Oklahoma Press, 1994).

Peffer, George Anthony. "Forbidden Families: Emigration Experiences of Chinese Women under the Page Law, 1875–1882." *Journal of American Ethnic History* 6 (Fall 1986): 28–46.

Read, Georgia W. "Women and Children on the Oregon-California Trail in the Gold Rush Years." *Missouri Historical Review* 39 (1944): 6.

Riley, Glenda. "American Daughters: Black Women in the West." *Montana* 38 (Spring 1988): 14–27.

Scadron, Arlene. *On Their Own: Widows and Widowhood in the American Southwest, 1848–1939* (Urbana: University of Illinois Press, 1988).

Schlissel, Lillian. *Western Women: Their Land, Their Lives* (Albuquerque: University of New Mexico Press, 1988).

—. *Women's Diaries of the Westward Journey* (New York: Schocken Books, 1992).

Sibbald, John R. "Camp Followers All: Army Women of the West." *American West* III (Spring 1966): 56–7.

Sunoo, Sonia S. "Korean Women Pioneers of the Pacific Northwest." *Oregon Historical Quarterly* 79 (March 1978): 50–63.

Williams, Jacqueline. *Wagon Wheel Kitchens: Food on the Oregon Trail* (Lawrence: University Press of Kansas, 1993).

Woyski, Margaret. "Women and Mining in the Old West." *Journal of the West* 20 2 (1981): 38–47.

Zani, Sally. *A Mine of Her Own: Woman Prospectors in the American West, 1850–1950* (Lincoln: University of Nebraska Press, 1997).

Index